S0-EDK-751

An Introduction to Business Cycles and Forecasting

David A. Bowers

Case Western Reserve University

ADDISON-WESLEY PUBLISHING COMPANY

Reading, Massachusetts ■ Menlo Park, California ■ Don Mills, Ontario
Wokingham, England ■ Amsterdam ■ Sydney ■ Singapore ■ Tokyo
Mexico City ■ Bogotá ■ Santiago ■ San Juan

Library of Congress Cataloging in Publication Data

Bowers, David A., 1934–
    An introduction to business cycles and forecasting.

    1. Business cycles — Mathematical models. 2. Economic
forecasting—Mathematical models. I. Title.
HB3711.B637   1985   338.5′42   84-16786
ISBN 0-201-10163-7

Copyright © 1985 by Addison-Wesley Publishing Company, Inc. All rights reserved. No part
of this publication may be reproduced, stored in a retrieval system, or transmitted, in any
form or by any means, electronic, mechanical, photocopying, recording, or otherwise, without
the prior written permission of the publisher. Printed in the United States of America. Published
simultaneously in Canada.

ABCDEFGHIJ-MA-898765

PREFACE

Since it has been my observation that professors usually read the preface and students rarely do, I will address my remarks to the instructor. Students may eavesdrop if they like.

While this text is designed for a course with a title similar to "Business Cycles and Forecasting," the overall purpose of the book is to integrate by application the student's knowledge of economics, money and banking, and elementary statistical procedures. The application is to the changing economic environment within which all economic entities must operate. We seek to enhance the student's understanding of why the economic climate is what it is and how it is likely to change.

This book is designed to be used with students having heterogeneous backgrounds. While students studying this subject usually have some background in macroeconomics and microeconomics, banking and finance, and elementary statistics, I have learned not to rely too heavily on prerequisites. I have found that advanced undergraduate and especially MBA students need at least a brief reiteration of several fundamental topics. Hence, most chapters start at a very elementary level but move fairly rapidly to more advanced material. To ensure that the student has ready access to the necessary fundamentals, we touch on more topics than anyone would want to cover in a single course. Thus you may select what you want to emphasize.

In the first chapter we try to define the business cycle and our reasons for studying it. We argue that although there is no statistically observable periodicity, the recurrent pattern of business fluctuations is worthy of study. We try to place the study of business fluctuations in historical context. We also seek to establish the relevance of theory for the student by showing its practical application to understanding the contemporary economic environment.

Chapters 2 through 6 (approximately 100 pages) present economic theory, both fundamental and advanced. Of course, the advanced material is selected on the basis of what is most relevant to the study of fluctuations in the overall level of economic activity.

Chapters 7 through 10 (also about 100 pages) are real-world applications, iv ı / Preface

or corruptions, of the economic theory discussed in the previous chapters. We begin with time series analysis and end with a discussion of the cyclical behavior of the components of aggregate demand.

Chapters 11 through 14 (another 80 pages) are concerned with national economic policy. We first consider the problems inherent in simultaneously seeking price stability and full employment. We then describe in some detail the making and measurement of monetary and fiscal policy.

Chapters 15 and 16 (about 50 pages) include a business cycle history of the U.S. economy with the degree of detail increasing as we become closer to the present.

Chapter 17 discusses contemporary macroeconomic forecasting. A generalized forecasting sequence is presented for the uncertain student doing an economic forecast as a term paper. In addition, the student is also led by the hand through the construction and use of a simple (three equations and one identity) econometric model. There is also a discussion and an evaluation of the large econometric models and forecasting services.

The last chapter discusses the business cycle in the context of international trade and finance. In particular, we discuss the impact of differing exchange rate arrangements on the transmission of cyclical fluctuations from one economy to another. Of course, while the rest of the text is necessary for understanding the international chapter, this last chapter can be deleted by those of us who run out of calendar before we run out of material.

The following reviewers have made valuable contributions during the process of development of this book: Edgar S. Bagley, Kansas State University; Wen-Yu Cheng, Marietta College; Hae-Shin Hwang, Texas A & M University; R. D. Peterson, Colorado State University; and Theodore W. Roesler, University of Nebraska.

Cleveland, Ohio   **D.A.B.**
December 1984

CONTENTS

CHAPTER 4: MONETARY THEORY

CHAPTER 5: THEORY OF MONETARY AND FISCAL POLICY

CHAPTER 6: SOME THEORIES OF THE BUSINESS CYCLE

CHAPTER 7: TIME SERIES ANALYSIS

CHAPTER 17:   MACROECONOMIC FORECASTING

CHAPTER 18:   INTERNATIONAL ASPECTS OF THE BUSINESS CYCLE

Introduction

On the Necessity of Forecasting

The purpose of our study of the business cycle is to better understand the economic environment. We will look at what economists know about the business cycle and, equally important, what we don't know. The subject of business cycle forecasting is the butt of numerous jokes. Some are fairly clever and amusing, but all are fairly irrelevant since to live is to forecast. No business decision is made without an explicit or implicit economic forecast. No factories are built or inventories acquired without the assumption that the Great Depression is not starting next week.

The number of more or less accurate forecasts people make every day is truly amazing. One arranges to be at a particular geographical location a thousand miles away, days, weeks, or months ahead of time. Often, as in business, such commitments cannot be changed without substantial penalty. A professor commits to long-term mortgage payments. A student makes a deposit on a ski holiday weeks in advance. The professor forecasts that a solvent university will renew his or her contract, and the student forecasts that it will snow.

Economic forecasting is not as much a proud science as it is a necessary evil. The external environment can make or break almost any economic endeavor. An understanding of the economic environment cannot work miracles, but it can be very useful. The goal of this study is modest. Knowing most of the time where in the business cycle the economy stands *today* would probably provide a substantial jump on the competition. Most economists discover that a turning point has been reached three to six months or more after the fact.

Is There Any Such Thing as the Business Cycle?

Is there a functioning mechanism that can be studied as the "business cycle"? Certainly no one has ever discovered a set of equations that generate a nice, neat, periodic movement describing the movements in the general level of economic activity. Part of the problem is that the economy simply fails to show any periodicity. A popular government publication to be referenced throughout this book was originally entitled *Business Cycle Developments*. Today that publication is called *Business Conditions Digest*. Some years ago, "cycles" fell out of favor because of its connotation of periodicity ("fluctuations" was in). The change caused no great problems since everyone refers to the publication by its initials *BCD* anyway.

Not only is the cycle devoid of mathematical periodicity, but no two cycles are even alike with respect to the magnitude and timing of the movement of particular sectors of the economy. Later in this book we will discuss the "typical" business cycle. We will note such things as the fact that in the typical cycle industrial production reaches a peak before interest rates do. But there have been downturns when this relationship was reversed. During a particular recession there will be sectors of the economy that are doing better than ever, and in a boom it is not difficult to find some sector of the economy that has fallen on hard times.

Given that the general level of economic activity does rise and fall, doesn't that indicate that the business cycle exists? Not necessarily. If each sector of the economy is following its own independent ups and downs, a recession might be only a coincidence of timing. A large number of sectors of the economy might have just happened to hit a downturn at the same time. A boom might simply be the coincidental juxtaposition of an upward blip in a large number of sectors at the same time. Of course, if this is what the business cycle really were, life would be somewhat less complicated. Any economic forecast would be as good as any other since all forecasters would just be trying to guess the next move in a series of random numbers.

Fortunately for the unemployment rate among economists, there is more to the business cycle than mere coincidence of movements. The first lecture in an introductory macroeconomics course usually makes the point that the expenditures of one economic unit are the incomes of other economic units. The old "circular flow diagram" (which is reviewed in Chapter 3) should certainly destroy any illusion that particular sectors of the economy can expand or contract their operations without influencing other sectors. It is these interrelationships we shall seek to understand in our study of the business cycle.

The application of macroeconomic theory, including the monetary mechanisms, provides a fairly firm basis for expecting sympathetic movements in many sectors of the economy. A good theoretical basis and substantial empirical support exist for cumulative upward and downward movement in the economy. One sector's expansion is the basis for another sector's expansion, general prosperity lowers risks and makes credit more readily available, and so on; but the weakest part of business cycle theory and the toughest problem of forecasting is turning points. Why does the general upward or downward movement end? This is the area of cyclical behavior in which the "typical" behavior shows even more diversity than the cumulative upward or downward movement. Although all the expansions and contractions have a number of characteristics in common, peaks and troughs do not. When a war begins or ends, with a commensurate and dramatic change in military expenditures, the cause of the beginning or end of a boom is fairly unambiguous. Historically, however, only a small minority of the turning points are the result of specific, identifiable governmental actions. We will return to this problem of explaining turning points in Chapter 6, "Some Theories of the Business Cycle."

Even with the dramatic impacts of war and peace the economy rarely turns up or down precipitously. In particular, the U.S. economy today is a large, complex juggernaut of a machine with a tremendous amount of inertia. As will be seen in Chapter 16 when recent business cycle history is reviewed, economists and business are always forecasting a recession six months to a year before it actually arrives. Similarly, after the economy has stopped dropping and the recession is supposed to be over, everybody concerned is always disappointed in the strength of the recovery for the first eight to twelve months. When the U.S. economy is booming it takes a long time to slow it down, and when it is slowed down it takes a substantial amount of time for any recovery to be noticeable.

Although something worthy of being called the business cycle does exist, attempts at finer classifications or subcategories of business cycles seem not to have been particularly fruitful. Some economists have simply used a broad dichotomy between "major" and "minor" cycles.[1] Descriptively this can be meaningful. The depression of the 1930s was quantitatively different from the 1970 recession. Real output fell by almost 50% in the former and by less than 1% in the latter.

It is also useful, at least descriptively if not analytically, to speak of the cycles of specific time series; i.e., the interest rate cycle, the inventory cycle, the construction cycle, etc. Given the diversity of general economic cycles, one can find turns in the general level of economic activity in which individual time series do, at least for a time, appear to be independent of the rest of the economy. The most frequently mentioned individual time series cycles are as follows: the inventory cycle, the building or construction cycle, and the agricultural cycle. The standard business cycle is sometimes referred to as the inventory cycle, and some business cycle theorists popularly explain the severity of turns in the economy by the coincidence of turns in the individual cycles. Again, this is useful in describing the past, but not much help in forecasting the future since these individual cycles have no more periodicity than the overall business cycle.

One particular theory implying a degree of periodicity that has continuing popular appeal is the so-called Kondratieff, or 50-year cycle. These "long cycles" of course face an inherent statistical problem. Even if one is willing to accept the recorded economic time series data as having some degree of validity for the last 100 to 150 years, there are only two or three complete cycles to observe. Statistically speaking, two or three data points do not establish a pattern. Of course, with so little meaningful data it is impossible to refute those who insist that 50-year periodicity is observable.

This author feels that proponents of the "Kondratieff Wave" are bordering on the "crackpot fringe" since the theory implies that the two world wars (and perhaps the Civil War) were foreordained by the periodicity of the 50-year cycle. It is, however, easy to understand the current appeal of such a theory. World-wide economic progress has been slow for the past decade or two, and the long-cycle theorist can proclaim the good news that we are standing on the eve of a long period of growth and renewal.[2]

In this text we will be content merely to accept the fact that the general level of economic activity has fluctuated since the beginning of recorded time, although, as noted above, the fluctuations are recurrent, but not periodic.

On Theory

The next five chapters are devoted to economic theory. Since the study of business cycles consists of applied economic theory, it is worth our time to review and extend our theoretical knowledge. A recently discovered manuscript in the Harvard University Archives, written by that giant of business cycle theory, Joseph Schumpeter, put the necessity of theory rather well. Although the manuscript was probably written in 1931, it is equally timely today:

> There is . . . a general impression among educated men and even among professed economists themselves that our science has no methods or results which are universally accepted . . . that it consists of an indefinite number of conflicting systems between which there is little to choose . . . in short that its state is simply chaotic. . . . Many of these endless and inconclusive discussions, which are, and have been, the curse of our science, are simply due to the lack of scientific equipment on one or both sides . . . they are all duels between combatants who have not learned the art of fencing. No wonder the result looks like chaos to the public.[3]

The same work by Schumpeter elaborates on the practical use of theory. A theory helps us to avoid having to solve the same problem over and over again. Or, as Schumpeter explains:

> When the discussion of a group of questions referring to interrelated phenomena has gone on for some time, people discover that certain arguments and some chains of reasoning tend to repeat themselves. . . . The human mind . . . makes use of this discovery. . . . It

refines them so as to make them better and better tools for future discussions as they may turn up, in order to do once and for all what otherwise would have to be repeated in every particular case. As soon as this is being done . . ."theory" in the true sense of the word emerges.[4]

In these chapters we will first review introductory micro- and macro-economic theory, emphasizing those things most relevant to the study of the business cycle and adding some elements you might not have received in an introductory course. We conclude our tour through pure theory in Chapter 6 with some selected theories of the business cycle.

On Applications

The larger part of this book is devoted to attempts to apply theory to real world problems and runs from "Time Series Analysis" to "Macroeconomic Forecasting." There are two important elements not given much explicit treatment in those chapters. Both are somewhat outside the scope of this introductory text, but both are important in understanding the functioning of the economy and applying that understanding to the fine art of forecasting. The first element we need to consider here and keep in mind thereafter is the recognition that we live in a stochastic world — all you can do is play the odds. In evaluating your own and others' forecasting performance it must be remembered that the player who takes a hit at 19 in blackjack and wins is not a genius. He is lucky. Unless you believe him to be guided by some deity, you don't hire him to handle your investments. It is true that "it's better to be lucky than smart," but there are no known books that can make you lucky. Some study may make a contribution to your performance using the other desirable characteristic.

It is all right to play the long shots at the racetrack for fun, but a serious attempt to plan and forecast (and one implies the other) for economic endeavor requires going for what is "most likely" even though history is filled with multitudes of highly unlikely, and thereby unpredictable, occurrences. In other words, one must make such decisions on the basis of all the information obtainable and hope that during one's career and life, totally unpredictable events will serve for your gain as much as for your loss.

The second item, which is mentioned only briefly in Chapter 7, is the importance of what the user of a forecast plans to do with it. As noted in that chapter, the one sure thing about an exact point forecast (whether it is for the GNP or a company's sales) is that it will be wrong. The question is only by how much and in what direction it will be wrong. It often makes a great deal of difference to the user whether the error is positive or negative. If a user bases his or her action on your forecast and the actual outcome is higher than the forecast, he or she may be richer than he or she expected to be. If, however, the result is low by more than the company's net worth, you may all be in bankruptcy court. A particular example of this is the case in which competent economic advice is deliberately rejected each business cycle. When interest rates break during a recession, most corporate treasurers quickly go into the long-term bond market to raise funds to pay off short-term bank debt. They do this despite the fact that their economist is telling them that since interest rates lag the rest of the economy, they could most likely borrow at lower rates if they would wait a year or so. But as one corporate treasurer explained, "I have 90% confidence in your forecast. I would give 10 to 1 odds you are correct, but if the 1 chance in 10 comes up and this corporation has not refinanced, we are in *big* trouble — and I am probably out of a job. The potential interest rate savings are simply not worth the risk."

The formal mathematical terminology for considering such factors in a forecast is minimizing a "loss function." There is a limited technical vocabulary and few procedures for doing this,[5] but the mathematics get rather complex and the practical applications have been nil. In any case, such formal procedures lie beyond the scope of this book. Nevertheless, I would urge any practitioner of forecasting as either originator or user to have one or more "loss functions" in his head. You should recognize what it costs you and your organization for forecasts that turn out too high or too low. You should also recognize the loss functions of those preparing forecasts for you. If the company gives a bonus based on sales in excess of forecast, don't expect an upward bias.

● Questions for Discussion

1. Is there any such thing as the business cycle?
2. Evaluate the comment: "I know a guy who made a fortune buying stocks on the basis of their location on the financial page. Boy was he smart!"
3. Would you bet on a single flip of a coin from which you could receive $2 for each $1 you bet if the minimum bet were as follows: $5? $50? $100? $500? $5000? When you say "no," explain why.

● Source Notes

[1]See, for example, Robert A. Gordon, *Business Fluctuations*. (2nd ed.) New York: Harper & Row, 1961, Chapter 11.

[2]See, for example, Paul Lewis. The Kondratieff wave, boom and bust theory shines like new. *The New York Times,* October 17, 1982, p. 2E; and Mensch, Gerhard. *Stalemate in Technology*. Cambridge, Mass.: Ballinger, 1979, Chapter 2.

[3]The 'crisis' in economics — fifty years ago. *Journal of Economic Literature,* Vol. 20, No. 3, September 1982, p. 1052.

[4]*Ibid.*, p. 1056.

[5]See, for example, Carl F. Christ. *Econometric Models and Methods.* New York: John Wiley, 1966, pp. 256–283.

Relevant Microeconomic Theory

2

Although we assume that the readers of this book have had an introductory course in economics, a review of basic concepts is always useful. Furthermore, certain elements of microeconomic theory, which have special importance for the study of business cycles, must be emphasized.

Supply and Demand

First, let us review the basic concepts of supply and demand. These are the terms used to describe the functioning of a market. The demand curve describes graphically how buyers would react quantitatively to different market prices. Similarly, the supply relationship depicts the quantity that would be forthcoming from the suppliers at different prices, shown in Fig. 2.1.

Figure 2.1 indicates the equilibrium price and quantity as P_e and Q_e, respectively. At any price higher than P_e (for example, P_1), there would be a surplus that would tend to lower the price toward the equilibrium level, P_e. At any price lower than P_e (for example, P_2), there would be a shortage that would tend to raise the price toward P_e.

Supply-demand relationships can be depicted graphically, as in Fig. 2.1; in the form of a table, as below; or algebraically:

$$Q_s = .2P \text{ and } Q_d = 10 - .3P,$$

where Q_s = quantity supplied, and Q_d = quantity demanded.

P	Q_s	Q_d
$0	0	10
5	1	8.5
10	2	7
15	3	5.5
20	4	4
25	5	2.5
30	6	1
35	7	0

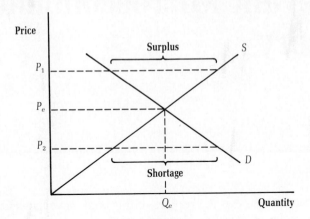

FIGURE 2.1 Supply, Demand, and Static Equilibrium.

We find the equilibrium price in all three cases by merely determining that price at which the quantity supplied equals the quantity demanded. In the table it is obvious that the equilibrium price is $20, and the equilibrium quantity is 4 units per time period. Algebraically:

If $Q_s = Q_d$, then $.2P = 10 - .3P$, and $.5P = 10$.

$P_e = (10)/(.5) = 20$.

The equilibrium quantity of 4 units can then be determined by substituting a $20 price into either the supply or demand equation.

Simply determining the equilibrium value for one or more variables is known as a problem of *statics* in economic analysis. More frequently we are concerned with a problem in *comparative statics*. Suppose, for example, that there were some technological improvement in the production of this item. This improvement dramatically lowers the cost of production, making the suppliers willing to supply a larger quantity at each price. Graphically we could show this as a shift in the supply curve as shown in Fig. 2.2.

In tabular form we would have a new supply schedule with, for example, 5 units more offered at each price.

P	Q_s	Q_d
$0	5	10
5	6	8.5
10	7	7
15	8	5.5
20	9	4
25	10	2.5
30	11	1
35	12	0

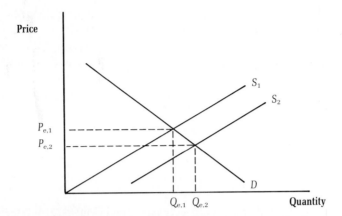

FIGURE 2.2 Supply, Demand, and Comparative Statics.

Obviously, the new equilibrium price is $10 and the new equilibrium quantity is 7 units per time period. With the improved technology of production our comparative statics analysis indicates that the price falls from $20 to $10 and the quantity purchased rises from 4 to 7 units. Using the revised supply function, $Q_s = .2P + 5$, identical results can be obtained algebraically.

We have defined what we mean by statics and comparative statics in economic analysis. In the study of business cycles, however, we will more often be interested in the study of *dynamics*. Statics is the determination of the equilibrium level of an economic variable, and comparative statics is the determination of a change in an equilibrium level. Dynamics is concerned with the path from the old to the new equilibrium level. In comparative statics, we *assume* the market price moves from $20 to $10. In dynamics, we ask how.

To consider the step-by-step adjustment of a market to changed conditions, we must make some very specific assumptions regarding the behavior of the market participants in a nonequilibrium situation and give explicit recognition to the time dimension. Let us assume our producers must make commitments for labor and material at least one period in advance; thus they base their production of goods to be ready for market in period t on the price prevailing in period $t - 1$. Our original supply equation would then be $Q_{s,t} = .2P_{t-1}$. We will have our buyers base their purchases on the current period's price, $Q_{d,t} = 10 - .3P_t$. At this point, if we define equilibrium as the price at which $Q_{s,t} = Q_{d,t}$ we obtain

$$.2P_{t-1} = 10 - .3P_t,$$
$$.3P_t = 10 - .2P_{t-1},$$
$$P_t = 33\ 1/3 - (2/3)P_{t-1},$$

which does not give us a unique equilibrium price level. Since we have now allowed for the possibility of disequilibrium values, we must be more specific about what we mean by equilibrium in this dynamic context. What we mean by equilibrium is that price and quantity cease their adjustments and hold constant. Equilibrium in this case would be when $P_t = P_{t-1}$; the price does not change from one period to the next. In this case if $P_t = P_{t-1}$, then

$$P_t = 33\ 1/3 - (2/3)P_{t-1},$$

would be $\qquad$ $P_e = 33\ 1/3 - (2/3)P_e,$

$$(5/3)P_e = 33\ 1/3 \text{ and } P_e = 20.$$

The equilibrium price, at \$20, is the same as before. Similarly, the equilibrium quantity will be 4 units per time period.

Let us now examine the behavior of this market if for some reason it were not in equilibrium. Assume that some disaster befell the producers (for example, a bad crop year) so that only one unit of output could be produced for that particular time period. With a demand schedule of $Q_{d,t} = 10 - .3P_t$ the price would have to rise to \$30 for the demand to be satisfied. The price of \$30 would encourage a substantial increase in production in the next time period; specifically an increase to a level of 6 units, which would drive the price down to \$13.33. The time sequence of quantity and price would be as follows:

t	Q	P
0	1	\$30
1	6	13.33
2	2.67	24.44
3	4.89	17
4	3.40	22
.	.	.
.	.	.
.	.	.
∞	4	20

If nothing changes to disturb the system, this converging cyclical sequence would asymptotically approach the equilibrium quantity of 4 units and a price of \$20. Figure 2.3 depicts the sequential movement of price and quantities. We have just described one of the oldest and simplest theories of the business cycle. It has historically been applied most frequently to agricultural commodities, but it is equally appropriate for any product with a substantial time lag between commitment to production and delivery to the market. This model is called the *cobweb theorem* due to the spidery appearance of the graphic presentation, as shown in Fig. 2.3.

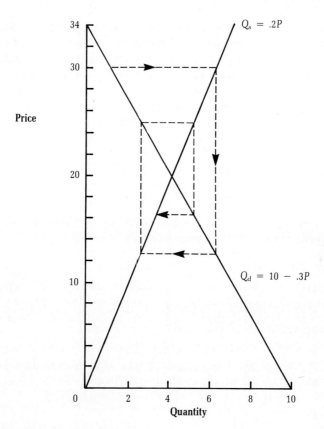

FIGURE 2.3 Supply, Demand, and Dynamics.

Difference Equations

The cobweb theorem can result in a cycle that repeats the same sets of values indefinitely, a cycle of increasing amplitudes that eventually explodes to plus and minus infinity, or a cycle that will converge to equilibrium. We will be considering such models in a number of different contexts. To appreciate such cyclical mechanisms, we must closely examine their algebraic formulations, known as *nonhomogeneous, first-order difference equations*. The general form of a nonhomogeneous, first-order difference equation is $Y_t = a + bY_{t-1}$.* We will find that there are many economic behavioral assumptions which imply cyclical behavior resulting from the value of some

---

*In mathematical terminology the equation is nonhomogeneous because it has a nonzero intercept, a, and it is first-order because it has only Y_{t-1}, not Y_{t-2} or other higher-order lagged terms.

particular economic variable in the present time period being a linear function of its value in the immediately preceding time period. In the previously discussed supply-demand model, for example, the quantity supplied in the present period is a function of the price prevailing in the previous period. By requiring the quantity supplied to equal the quantity demanded in each period, we derived the formula for price; $P_t = 33 \ 1/3 - 2/3(P_{t-1})$ where the price in the period t depends only on the price in $t - 1$, as long as the parameters of the supply and demand functions remain unchanged. Through similar algebraic manipulations we could have derived the following equation for the quantity traded in any particular time period: $Q_t = 6 \ 2/3 - 2/3 (Q_{t-1})$. Both of these equations are obviously nonhomogeneous, first-order difference equations. From the calculated values given in the table, we can see that both generate a fluctuating time series in which the cycles become smaller and smaller as the price and quantity approach their equilibrium values of \$20 and 4 units of output.

The cyclical behavior of a variable that is a linear function of itself lagged one period depends on the answers to the following three questions:

1. Is it at its equilibrium value? If so, it will stay there indefinitely.

2. Is the coefficient of the lagged term, b, positive or negative? If it is negative there will be cycles; if positive it will move smoothly.

3. Is the coefficient of the lagged term, b, greater or less than 1.00 in absolute value? If it is greater, it will diverge farther and farther from equilibrium; if less, it will move toward equilibrium.

The third question is known as the *stability condition*. If the coefficient of the lagged term is less than 1.00, the system is stable. If a random shock knocks it away from its equilibrium value, it will tend to return to equilibrium, as when one kicks a rocking chair (cyclical convergence) or pulls back the spring on a mousetrap (convergence without cycling). If the coefficient is greater than 1.00, the system is unstable. If it is forced off its equilibrium value, it will depart even further from its original equilibrium, like a marble at the top of a pyramid.

The general form of the equilibrium value can be found by setting $Y_t = Y_{t-1}$, then $Y_e = a + bY_e$ and $Y_e = (a)/(1 - b)$. In the price equation of the cobweb theorem example, $a = 33 \ 1/3$ and $b = -2/3$. Therefore $Y_e = (33 \ 1/3)/(1 \ 2/3) = 20$. Since b is negative, we know that if the price is not equal to its equilibrium level it will cycle, but the cycles will be of decreasing magnitude since 2/3 is less than 1.00. Similar observations can be made regarding the quantity traded in this market. Solving the equation for the equilibrium quantity with the values of $a = 6 \ 2/3$ and $b = -2/3$ will give us the previously used value of $Y_e = 4$. Table 2.1 illustrates the six time patterns that are possible with this simple cyclical model.

TABLE 2.1   Behavior of Time Series Based on a Nonhomogeneous First-Order Difference Equation*

$$Yt = a + bYt - 1$$
$$a = 10$$

If b =	Then the Equation Is:	And the Equilibrium Is $Ye = a/(1\text{-}b)$	Pattern of Time Series Resulting from Disequilibrium, i.e., if Yt ≠ Ye:
.8	Yt = 10 + .8Yt − 1	10/.2 = 50	Converges toward Ye monotonically
− .25	Yt = 10 − .25Yt − 1	10/1.25 = 8	Damped cycles
1.0	Yt = 10 + Yt − 1	10/0 = ?	Increases by 10 units per time period forever
1.5	Yt = 10 + 1.5Yt − 1	10/(−.5) = − 20	Increases or decreases monotonically away from Ye
− 1.5	Yt = 10 − 1.5Yt − 1	10/2.5 = 4	Cycles of ever increasing amplitude
− 1.0	Yt = 10 − Yt − 1	10/2 = 5	Cycle of contant amplitude; fluctuates between the same two values forever

If $Y_e = 10$ and $b =$

t	.8	− .25	1.0	1.5	− 1.5	− 1.0
0	10	10	10	10	10	10
1	18	7.50	20	25	− 5	0
2	24.4	8.13	30	47.5	17.5	10
3	29.5	7.97	40	81.3	− 16.3	0
4	33.6	8.01	50	131.9	34.4	10
.	.	.	.	.	.	.
.	.	.	.	.	.	.
.	.	.	.	.	.	.
∞	50	8	+ ∞	+ ∞	+ or −	10 or 0

*For the mathematically inclined, the general solution to this equation is

$$Y_t = Y_e + (b)^t(Y_o - Y_e) \text{ where } Y_e = (a)/(1-b).$$

Ex Post, Ex Ante, and Equilibrium

Let us examine this concept of "equilibrium" somewhat more closely. When economists refer to the equilibrium price of, for example, a common stock traded on the New York Stock Exchange, they mean that there is no tendency for the price to change — there are just as many shares for sale at that price as there are bids to buy the stock, so the specialist merely matches them up. Economists extend this concept of equilibrium to cover all economic variables with which they are concerned, such as the equilibrium level of interest rates and employment. Individual markets are never in equilibrium for very long, and the entire economy is never in equilibrium because it is always changing. What then is the value of the concept? If we know the equilibrium value relative to the current value, we can at least predict something about the way markets might move. In the case of the common stock, for example, if the announcement is made that the company just discovered gold on its property, most economists would make the obvious statement in the technical terms that the equilibrium price for the stock has risen. In short, equilibrium means the level toward which the combination of market forces is pushing an economic variable; i.e., the level at which there will be no tendency for further movement.

We can further explore this concept of equilibrium, however, by introducing two other technical terms: *ex ante* and *ex post*. Ex ante refers to the value of economic variables that are planned, desired, or expected *before* the market participants act. Ex post refers to the bookkeeping values observable *after* the market participants have acted. These two concepts, without the erudite names, are used by all of us in everyday business life. Consider, for example, the stockbroker's report on the evening news that "a wave of *selling* hit the market today." Now we all know that for the market as a whole and for each individual stock, the number of shares sold was exactly equal to the number of shares bought! How does the broker know that it was not a wave of *buying* that hit the market? The broker must have had a reason for saying that prices fell because there were more sellers than buyers. The answer is that ex post (after the fact) sales equal purchases both in number of shares and dollars. Ex ante (before the day's transaction took place), however, there were more shares offered for sale than there were bids to buy *at that price*. The beginning price was not an equilibrium price because the quantity supplied was greater than the quantity demanded ex ante. Ex post, the quantity supplied must always equal the quantity demanded.

Let us consider the process of moving from one equilibrium price to another in terms of ex ante and ex post values. Let us assume that at the close of the market on Friday, a particular stock was selling at 100. Over the weekend, investors read the financial section of the paper and some decided that at that price they would like to sell, while others decided that they would like to buy. These plans are, of course, the ex ante supply and demand for the stock when the bell rings and the market opens on Monday morning. Suppose the offers to sell exceed the offers to buy; ex ante supply is greater than ex ante demand. The specialist on the floor of the New York Stock Exchange would observe that the current price is not an equilibrium price, make the trades that do match up, knock the price down by a quarter of a point, and, if offers to sell still exceeded offers to buy, lower the price still further. As the price falls, some of those who thought 100 was a great price at which to sell would decide that at a price of 98 they would wait. On the other side of the market, some investors who thought that a price of 100 was too high might decide that at 98 they were interested in buying.

Note that although ex ante the quantity supplied is greater than the quantity demanded if the price is falling, and that ex ante the quantity demanded must be greater than the quantity supplied if the price is rising, if we stop this process and add up the figures for any particular time period, the quantity supplied will exactly equal the quantity demanded, because purchases will equal sales both in terms of number of shares and dollars paid and received. The important thing for matters we will discuss later is that in this market example, we have two groups (buyers and sellers) whose decisions must balance out in the market place (purchases must equal sales), and the price will change until the ex ante values equal the ex post sales. The technical definition of the equilibrium price of this stock is for the ex ante values for quantities supplied and demanded to be equal along with the ex post values.

The field of economics contains many values being decided by different groups of people that must be equal ex post. Total borrowing must equal total lending, total expenditures must equal total income, total cash holdings must equal the money supply, and so on. Some of these concepts are more complicated than our stock market example, but the principle is the same. Changes in interest rates, employment, prices, and all other economic variables can be viewed as movements toward an equilibrium level from which there would be no tendency to move.

Diminishing Returns, Profit Maximization, and the Theory of the Firm

We considered a simple microeconomic market in our previous discussion of supply and demand. Economists agree that almost all supply curves are positively sloped and that almost all demand curves are negatively sloped. In most cases, economic decision makers are faced with a relationship between price and quantity that is negative if they are sellers considering the potential demand for their product. More can be sold only at a lower price. On the other hand, we expect the relationship between price and quantity faced by buyers to be positive. To obtain a substantially increased supply of something, a higher price must be paid.

The expectation of positively sloped supply curves and negatively sloped demand curves is based on a very general concept described by various names, such as *diminishing returns, diminishing marginal productivity, diminishing marginal utility,* and *the law of variable proportions.* In its simplest form, this concept means that the first cup of water given to a thirsty person has a very high value, the next cup slightly less, and so on. Water to bathe in is less valuable per unit than water to drink. In the extreme case (flood), the utility of water actually becomes negative, with very large amounts available for both swimmers and nonswimmers. We would expect a negative relationship to exist between the quantity demanded per unit of time for food and drink and the price consumers would be willing to pay. In other words, the demand curve for these products probably has a negative slope because of their diminishing marginal utility.

Similarly, with producer goods we assume buyers will be willing to buy more if the price is lowered. In this case, the relationship is based on diminishing marginal *productivity*, instead of diminishing marginal *utility*. The demand for producer goods (including labor) is based on the ability of the buyer to use that good as an input to the production of the goods being sold. Suppose a ton of chemical fertilizer will increase the yield of a farmer's field by 100 bushels per year. If he expects to sell his crop for $3 per bushel, he certainly will not pay more than $300 per ton for the fertilizer. With a fixed amount of land, it is probable that if the first ton of fertilizer increased output by 100 bushels, an additional ton would result in an additional increase of something less than 100 bushels. Therefore the maximum amount the farmer would be willing to pay for the second ton of fertilizer would be correspondingly below $300. If a second ton of fertilizer applied each year would only increase output by another 75 bushels, the farmer would not be interested in purchasing it unless it were obtainable for something less than $225. (Of course, the calculation that an additional 75 bushels is worth $225 is based on the assumption that the farmer is not faced with a negatively sloped demand curve and his selling price holds firm at $3 per bushel.) It seems intuitively obvious that the productivity of this resource, chemical fertilizer, would at some point become negative as the crop was buried in nitrates or some other chemical. Hence, the negatively sloped demand curve is based on *diminishing marginal productivity*.

Law of variable proportions is a term preferred by some economists who emphasize that the diminishing productivity we decribed depends on the amount of land remaining fixed. If the farmer could expand his use of fertilizer and land in the ideal proportion, he could expand production without confronting diminishing productivity of fertilizer. For the economy as a whole, of course, an unlimited supply of high-quality arable land does not exist. As the production of some crop is expanded, we confront diminishing productivity of labor and chemicals because less land suited to raising that particular crop is available.

We have illustrated the basis for negatively sloped demand curves for consumers' and producers' goods via diminishing marginal utility and productivity. A belief in positively sloped supply curves can be justified in a similar fashion. Our hypothetical farmer, for example, must decide whether to increase production by adding more fertilizer on the basis of both the price of fertilizer and the price of his crop. With diminishing marginal productivity of fertilizer, the farmer must require ever higher prices to make it profitable to increase production. In our example, we assumed that the first ton of fertilizer increased output by 100 bushels, each of which could be sold for $3. As noted previously, the farmer would undertake that production only if fertilizer were obtainable for something less than $300 per ton. If the price of fertilizer held constant at or just below $300 per ton, its diminishing productivity would require a higher crop price for output to be increased. If the second ton of fertilizer increased output by only 75 bushels, the cost of fertilizer per bushel would be $4, or $300/75. The farmer would use the second ton of fertilizer to raise the additional 75 bushels only if the crop price rose to more than $4 per bushel. The manufacture or mining of fertilizer is probably also subject to a positively sloped cost curve, giving the supply curve of the agricultural commodity an even greater positive slope. Diminishing returns can produce increasing costs that result in positively sloped supply curves.

The phenomenon of diminishing returns is an important factor in the cyclical behavior of the economy. As the economy expands in the early stage of recovery from recession, all sectors expand in a more or less coordinated fashion so that no particularly steep supply curves are encountered. There are certain factors of production, however, that cannot be increased without limit. Such factors include land, highly skilled labor, and mineral and agricultural commodities. Furthermore, basic manufactured goods that require long lead times for an increase in capacity, such as chemicals and steel, produce very steep cost curves at higher levels of output. As the boom matures, some of these products become scarce and their costs rise dramatically. Producers using them face a profit squeeze, cease increasing production, and may even reduce output.

The behavior of the economy as a whole is certainly the sum of the behavior of the individual firms and other economic units. Many diverse factors influence the behavior of each of the producers and consumers in the economy. As economists, however, we believe a major motivating force is business firms seeking to maximize net income — the difference between income and expense that we call profit. This phenomenon directly relates to our study of the business cycle since a firm will expand production only when increased production is expected to lead to an increase in profits. Similarly, a firm will reduce production if this will either increase profits or, what amounts to the same thing, reduce losses.

If the price at which a product can be sold declines as output is increased due to the laws of diminishing marginal utility and diminishing marginal productivity, then the incremental revenue will be a negative function of sales level. If the cost of additional inputs including labor rises with the purchase of additional amounts, then costs per unit will also rise with additional output. This phenomenon reflects the familiar theorem that the optimum level of output for the firm is that point at which marginal costs equal or rise above marginal revenues. If we are describing discrete units of output, the marginal revenue received for the last unit produced should be minimally above the marginal cost for producing the unit. Moreover, the next unit is not produced since its marginal cost of production would be greater than the marginal revenue to be received for it.

Let us consider a specific numerical example. Suppose a firm's costs and revenues are as given in Table 2.2 and Fig. 2.4.

The firm whose costs and revenues are given in Table 2.2 will maximize its profits at a level of output between 6 and 7 units per time period if fractional adjustments are permitted; otherwise, it will stop at 6 units of output. At an output level of 6 units, total profit is $78, but at an output level of 7 units, profit falls to $77. Expansion from 6 to 7 units results in an increase in total cost, marginal cost, of $15 while generating an increase in total revenue, marginal revenue, of only $14. With costs rising by $15 and revenues by only $14, profit falls by $1.

Figure 2.4 illustrates profit maximization from a different viewpoint. In the first panel (upper left) depicting the absolute dollar level of profits, it is obvious that 6 units is the optimum level of production. On the second panel (upper right) showing the changes in total cost (marginal cost) and changes in total income (marginal revenue) for each unit of production, we can see that the production of the sixth unit is profitable since it increases revenues more than costs. The seventh unit obviously should not be produced since it increases costs more than revenues.

The two lower panels, showing the total and average levels of costs and revenues, are somewhat less informative. It is possible to determine the profit maximizing level of output from the lower left-hand panel showing total cost and revenue by measuring the distance between the two. The figure showing average cost and revenue, however, is quite uninformative regarding the optimum level of production. Profit is *not* maximized at the point where average cost is lowest (4 and 5 units). Profit is *not* maximized where the spread between average cost and average revenue is greatest. At 4 units, the average cost is $7 and the average revenue is $23, for an average profit of $16 per unit; but total profits will be increased by producing the fifth and sixth units even though average profit per unit falls to $13 at an output level of 6 units.

In the real world of business the locations of cost and revenue curves are not known with any degree of certainty. In addition, to the extent they are known, they are not stationary. The problem of the optimum level of

TABLE 2.2 Illustrative Costs, Revenues, and Profits

Quantity	Average Cost	Total Cost	Marginal Cost	Average Revenue	Total Revenue	Marginal Revenue	Total Profit	Marginal Profit
0	–	0	–	–	0	–	0	–
1	$10	$10	$10	$26	$26	$26	$16	$16
2	9	18	8	25	50	24	32	16
3	8	24	6	24	72	22	48	16
4	7	28	4	23	92	20	64	16
5	7	35	7	22	110	18	75	11
6	8	48	13	21	126	16	78	3
				Maximum Profit				
7	9	63	15	20	140	14	77	–1
8	10	80	17	18	144	4	64	–13
9	11	99	19	16	144	0	45	–19
10	12	120	21	14	140	–4	20	–25

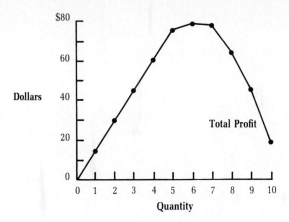

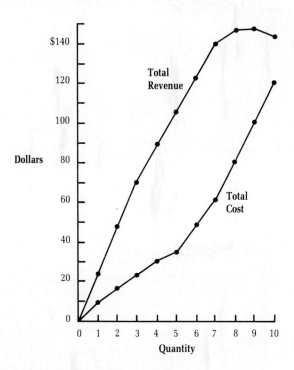

FIGURE 2.4   Illustrative Costs, Revenues, and Profit.

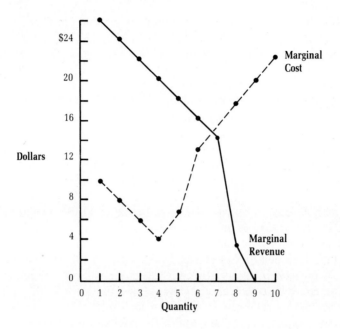

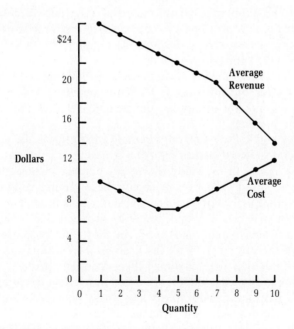

FIGURE 2.4 (Continued)

economic activity for any economic unit is a dynamic problem. The planner is always shooting at a moving target. Technological innovations shift cost curves both up and down. Demand for consumer goods is a psychological problem. Demand for producer goods is based on the buyers' ex ante expectations of the market for *this* product.

We would expect that any equilibrium level of output for any individual firm, and certainly for the economy as a whole, would not stay fixed for very long. Output decisions are made on an ex ante basis. The data exist in the mind of the beholder. This is not to say that accounting data are not relevant to the decision-making process. The whole approach of ex post accounting, however, is quite different from the idea of maximizing economic profit.

A major difference between accounting data and the economic concept of profit maximization is in the definition of costs. All accounting costs represent present or past cash outlays. Wages are paid for labor, a present cash outlay. Depreciation is charged off based on the original cost of the building, a past cash outlay. In contrast, the basis for economic costs is strictly *alternative cost*. Conceptually, alternative cost is the opportunity cost of not using a resource in an alternative activity. It is what is lost by the foregone opportunity. The owner of a small store may pay herself only $18,000 per year. If she could work for a chain store and earn $25,000 as a store manager, the economist would record an (alternative) cost for her services of $25,000. (She presumably receives $7,000 a year worth of satisfaction by being her own boss.) Because the building she owns and uses for her store may have been completely depreciated, her accountant records no capital costs. The economist would ask what the building could be rented for if the store owner did not occupy it. If the owner is losing $2,000 a month in rental income by occupying the building, that is the economic cost for using the building.

We can only imagine the numerous alternative uses for all the productive resources in a giant national corporation and what they might earn in other employments. Business firms establish large, complex "management information systems" in an effort to determine the optimum deployment of their assets. Nevertheless, we have substantial shifts in management's opinion regarding the optimum levels of output, inventory accumulation or liquidation, the construction of new plants, and so on. In short, the business cycle is the summation of the attempts by all the firms in the economy to produce at the level of output that will maximize their economic profit.

As we discuss the various factors involved in cyclical fluctuations, try to imagine how each factor might affect a business manager's perceptions of the optimum level of production. Changes in taxes, interest rates, technological innovations, for example, all tend to result in expansion or contraction of the level of economic activity perceived to be optimum for various economic entities. The actual recorded behavior of the economy is the result of these decisions both when the business manager's decisions are correct and when they are substantially in error.

● Questions for Discussion

1. Since purchases always equal sales, doesn't supply always equal demand?
2. What is meant by the statement "Inflation is not *high* prices, it is rising prices." Explain in terms of statics, comparative statics, and dynamics.
3. Define: diminishing marginal productivity, alternative cost, and accounting cost.

● Exercises

1. Assume the following microeconomic market:

Price	Quantity Supplied Per Time Period	Quantity Demanded Per Time Period
$1	2 units	22 units
2	4	20
3	6	18
4	8	16
5	10	14
6	12	12
7	14	10
8	16	8
9	18	6
10	20	4

Assume that the suppliers base their action on the market clearing price of *the previous time period*.

a. If the initial market clearing price is $3, what will be the time series of prices in subsequent periods?
b. If the initial market clearing price is $6, what will be the time series of prices in subsequent periods?

2. Assume the quantities supplied and demanded in each time period t can be described by the following equations:

$$Q_{s,t} = 2 P_{t-1} \quad \text{and} \quad Q_{d,t} = 15 - P_t.$$

a. What are the equilibrium levels of price and quantity?
b. Suppose there is a new government regulation that lowers productivity in this industry to such an extent that the supply curve is shifted to $Q_{s,t} = P_{t-1}$. What are the new equilibrium price and quantity?
c. Assume the market was in the original equilibrium position at the outset ($t = 0$) when the shift in the supply function described in b. took place. What would be the market clearing price in periods 1, 2, 3, and 4? In periods 436 and 437?

3. Given the following supply and demand schedules:

Price	Quantity Supplied	Quantity Demanded
$100	1,700	0
90	1,500	0
80	1,300	100
70	1,100	200
60	900	300
50	700	400
40	500	500
30	300	600
20	100	700
10	0	800
0	0	900

a. What is the equilibrium price? What is the magnitude of the shortage at a price ceiling of $20? What is the magnitude of the surplus if a price floor is set at $30?

b. If there is no price ceiling or floor (a free market), but the government places a sales tax of $30 per unit on this item, then what is the new equilibrium total price (including tax) the buyer must pay? What is the net price (excluding tax) to the seller?

4. Assume the market for wheat produced in the United States can be represented by the following supply and demand schedules:

Price per Bushel	Quantity Supplied	Quantity Demanded
$ .50	0	100
1.00	10	90
1.50	20	80
2.00	30	70
2.50	40	60
3.00	50	50
3.50	60	40
4.00	70	30
4.50	80	20
5.00	90	10
5.50	100	0

a. In the absence of government intervention, what would the price be?

b. Assume the farmers convince the government to guarantee a price no lower than $4 per bushel. If the government does this by buying up the surplus wheat, by how much will the government's stock of surplus wheat grow per time period?

c. Now assume the unhappy buyers of wheat (Bakers' Monopoly, Inc.) combine lobbying forces with the farmers to have the minimum price raised to $5 per bushel, but this price to the farmers must be maintained by a subsidy to the buyers. How much wheat will be produced? How many dollars per bushel must the government pay the buyers to clear the market?

5. Consider the following supply and demand schedules:

Price	Quantity Supplied	Quantity Demanded
$11	11	5
10	10	6
9	9	7
8	8	8
7	7	9
6	6	10
5	5	11
4	4	12
3	3	13
2	2	14
1	1	15

As any aspiring economist can see, the equilibrium price in this market is $8, with the supply and demand equal at 8 units each.

a. Suppose the government imposes a sales tax of $4 per unit. What will the new equilibrium price (including the tax) be, and how many units will be produced?

b. Using the supply and demand schedules as given (no tax), assume the government wants to guarantee that the sellers receive a price of $9 per unit but does not want to buy a surplus; thus the government decides to subsidize the buyers. How big must the rebate to the buyers be to clear the market at $9?

● Selected Additional Readings

Allen, R. G. D. *Mathematical Economics*. New York: St. Martins Press, 1956. Chapter 6.

Baumol, William J. *Economic Theory and Operations Analysis*. (4th ed.) Englewood Cliffs, N.J.: Prentice-Hall, 1977.

Ezekiel, Mordecai. The cobweb theorem. *Quarterly Journal of Economics*. February 1938.

Mohanty, Aroop K. *Intermediate Microeconomics with Applications*. New York: Academic Press, 1980.

Fundamental
Macroeconomic
Relationships

3

The Circular Flow of Expenditure and Income

The first thing to consider in a simplified model of the entire economy is an ex post equality mentioned in the previous chapter. Total income must equal total expenditures. What is an expenditure to one person is income to another person or business firm. Let us assume that our economy consists of only two economic groups, households and business firms. In this economy the households provide the business firms with labor, land, and other productive resources for which they are paid all types of money income — wages, rents, profits, interest, and so on. (See Fig. 3.1.) If the firms buy these inputs they must produce something. Let us say for the moment that the total production of this economy consists of consumer goods and services. If we assume initially that this economy is in equilibrium (all the ex ante values match up), then the firms would be producing exactly those goods that the households want to buy. If the firms produce consumption goods valued at $100 billion at retail, they would have generated exactly $100 billion in income (including the firms' profits). The very production of the goods generates the income with which to buy the goods.

If we should insist that every cent received in income be immediately spent on consumption goods (as some early economists assumed) this system would have to be in equilibrium. If the firms suddenly decided to expand production to $110 billion worth of consumption goods, the households would suddenly find themselves with $110 billion of income and would buy the extra $10 billion worth of goods. However, if consumers were to put the extra $10 billion into their local savings banks, the business firms would find themselves with an "investment" of $10 billion worth of inventory. Ex post savings would equal investment but ex ante savings would be greater than investment. Had the business firms desired a $10 billion increase in inventories, ex ante savings would equal ex ante investment and there would be no tendency for the level of income and output to change. If the business firms merely got "stuck" with this inventory, however, in the next time period they would undoubtedly reduce output (and income) to some lower level. In general, if consumers in this economy want to save

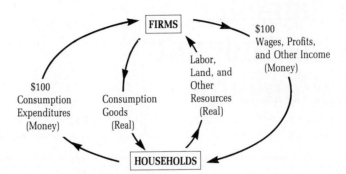

Firms sell all consumption goods produced.

FIGURE 3.1 Simple Macroeconomic Equilibrium.

more than business people want to invest, the equilibrium level of income is below the present level. (See Fig. 3.2.)

Let us consider the opposite case. Suppose that we were rolling along in equilibrium with $100 billion of income and output through the production and sale of $100 billion of consumer goods, when suddenly the business firms decided to spend an extra $10 billion on investment goods to construct a new factory (or to accumulate inventory, for that matter). The expenditure of $10 billion on the new plant would give $10 billion in extra income to the households. If the households chose to save it, savings would equal investment ex ante and we would remain in equilibrium. But if the receipt of the extra income induced an equal amount of expenditures for consumption goods, the economy would not be in equilibrium. We can visualize any number of adjustments that might take place. The most obvious one is that

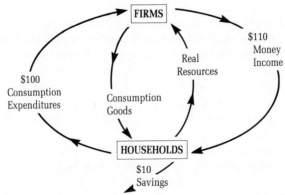

Firms cannot sell all the consumption goods produced. Production will be cut back.

FIGURE 3.2 Ex Ante Savings Greater than Investment.

the households would surprise the firms with an extra $10 billion worth of demand for consumption goods, which would have to be drawn out of existing inventory. The business firms would then have a + $10 billion of investment in plant and equipment and a − $10 billion in inventory investment for a net investment of zero. Ex post, investment would equal savings with both at zero, but ex ante investment is greater than savings by $10 billion. Which way are income and output likely to move when investment is greater than savings ex ante? Up, of course, as the business firms try to rebuild their inventories. (See Fig. 3.3.)

Ex post savings and investment must be equal in this simplified model of the economy because output consists only of consumption goods and investment goods, and all income is either spent for consumption goods or saved. Income must equal output; 100% of the output must be purchased by someone, and no more than 100% of the output is available for purchase. When ex ante savings is greater than ex ante investment the households' demand for consumption goods plus the business firms' demand for investment goods add up to less than the current level of output. Ex post, savings will equal investment, but someone is going to be dissatisfied with this state of affairs. Either the firms will accumulate excess inventories or the price of consumer goods will fall so that households can engage in the desired level of savings and still have enough money left to buy the entire output of consumption goods. In either case, when the desired level of purchases is less than the current level of output, income and output will tend to fall. Conversely, when ex ante investment is greater than ex ante savings, the households and firms taken together are trying to purchase more than 100% of the output at current prices. On an ex ante basis, the productive capacity that the households are giving up by their savings is more than offset by the desired level of investment by business. Of course, ex post savings and

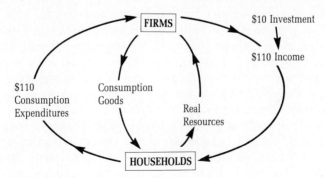

Consumers want to buy more consumption goods than are being produced.
Production will be increased.

FIGURE 3.3 Ex Ante Investment Greater than Savings.

investment have to be equal so that the actual level of investment must be lower than the planned level (due to reductions in inventory) or ex post savings must be greater than planned savings (due to the forced reduction in consumption brought about by an increase in the price of consumption goods).

Economists refer to the forces at work to increase output and prices as *inflationary* pressures and to the forces at work to decrease income and prices as *deflationary* pressures. Such pressures change the equilibrium level of output, income, and prices. From the foregoing discussion you should now be able to see that a large jump in business investment plans would result in inflationary pressures. On the other hand, a mad desire on the part of consumers to cut back consumption severely to engage in savings would result in deflationary pressures as the business firms are caught with stocks of unsold consumption goods (involuntary investment).

Although this is the essence of "Keynesian revolution" it is not all that new. A monk living in a much earlier time reportedly observed that if the entire population became so frugal as to desire only sackcloth and the simplest of food, the economy's production would likely consist only of sackcloth and the simplest of food.

Savings and Investment

From even the very simple model just presented we can derive some important economic conclusions regarding savings. First, we must make the definition of *saving* very precise. By saving, the economist means earning income and not spending it for consumption goods. The amount of saving is the increase in an individual's net worth in any particular time period. Saving (not consuming all of one's income) does *not* mean making a deposit in a savings account. Exactly the form in which the accumulated assets are held is a separate decision — one which the economist refers to as the *portfolio decision*. The portfolio decision involves whether to hold accumulated assets in the form of cash, a savings account, a common stock, or real estate. It is possible for an individual or the economy as a whole to have no savings in a particular period (100% of income spent for consumption goods) but for "savings accounts" to grow substantially, as people make the portfolio decision to move from, say, cash or common stocks to savings accounts. Similarly, it is possible for people to have a large amount of savings in the sense the term is used here (a large excess of income over current consumption expenditures), but not add anything to their savings accounts. Instead they might use this increase in their net worth to buy common stocks or pay off a mortgage debt.

We have given an exact definition of the term saving in the peculiar way that economists use it. Let us now do the same for the term *investment*.

Investment, in macroeconomics, means (on the production side) the production of goods that are not immediately available for consumption. It is the opposite of saving, in that saving is the earning of income while making no claim on the economy's output of consumption goods. Investment is producing goods and thereby generating income while not making any consumption goods available on which the income can be spent. Saving is a voluntary withdrawal of dollars from the spending stream. Investment in newly produced capital goods is a net injection into the spending stream.

We can now conclude that there must be savings to be investment. If businesses are going to put people to work and generate income without generating any consumption goods on which that income can be spent, someone in the economy has to receive income and not spend it for consumption goods. That is, if there is to be investment, there must be savings. When a business hires someone to put together bricks and mortar for a new plant, the person so employed does not wish to spend the income received from that activity for a part of the plant; but rather wants shoes for the kids and groceries for the table. Hence, investment activity requires that some people relinquish their claims to output of the economy (save) to allow other people to produce goods that are not immediately available for consumption (invest). All the adjustments required to make ex post savings equal to investment are just a reconciliation by producers and buyers to the basic truth that only 100% of the output of the economy is available for purchase and that 100% of the output must be purchased by someone.

The prime virtue of savings is that it allows investment. However, if the desired level of savings exceeds the desire of business to invest, savings can be a vice instead of a virtue. As we have noted, if the combined demand of both business firms and households is less than the current level of output, the level of output will tend to fall. In times of depression, saving just means that fewer consumption goods will be produced. In boom times saving means that more investment can be undertaken and inflationary pressures will be lessened. So how do you answer the question, "Is savings a virtue or a vice?" You have to give the typical professorial dodge, "It all depends." If the economy is suffering from too much inflationary pressure, saving is a virtue. It helps to stabilize the national economy. (It is always a virtue on a personal level.) If the economy is suffering from the deflationary problems of depression, unemployment, and unutilized plant capacity, then saving by consumers only makes things worse.

Government Expenditures and Taxes

Let us now make our model of the economy just slightly more complicated by introducing government taxes on individuals and government purchases of goods and services — fiscal policy. This changes our basic equality of

$$\text{output} = \text{income},$$

from: consumption goods + investment goods = consumption expenditures + savings,

to: consumption goods + investment goods + government expenditures for goods and services = consumption expenditures + savings + taxes.

We are now classifying all output of the economy into one of three categories: consumption goods, investment goods, and those goods purchased by the government. On the income side, we previously assumed that the only things households could do with their income were spend it for consumption goods or save it. They now have the third alternative of paying taxes with it.

Government payments to individuals are analogous to investment in that income is generated by such payments but there are no consumption goods on which this income can be spent. Conversely, taxes are analogous to savings in that they are income earned but not spent for consumption goods.

A brief algebraic review of our two simplified models of the economy would perhaps be helpful at this point. Without government expenditures and taxes we had

$$\text{income} = \text{output},$$

consumption expenditures (C) + savings (S) = consumption goods (C) + investment goods (I).

Since expenditures for consumption goods is by definition equal to the production of consumption goods $(C = C$; additions to inventories of consumption goods are classed as investment), the foregoing implies savings equal to investment.

$$C + S = C + I,$$
$$S = I.$$

As we discussed, $S = I$ is always true ex post, but it is only true ex ante when total output and expenditures (Y) are in equilibrium with no tendency to increase or decrease.

Introducing government expenditures (G) and taxes (T) merely expands our model:

$$\text{income} = \text{output},$$
$$C + S + T = C + I + G,$$
$$S + T = I + G.$$

For the economy to be in equilibrium (no inflationary or deflationary pressures), planned savings plus taxes must equal planned investment plus government expenditures for goods and services. The income earned but not spent for consumption goods must equal the expenditures for nonconsumption goods, investment, and government expenditures. That $S + T = I + G$ is always true ex post. When it is not true ex ante there are pressures for total income and output to decrease or increase. In the first instance, if the plans of consumers, business, and government are such that income earned but not spent on consumption goods (because it is saved or taxed away) is greater than the expenditures by business and government on nonconsumption goods, then income and output will tend to fall. Taxes and savings are taking more out of the current level of income than government expenditures and business investment are injecting into it. Business, households, and government simply do not want to buy all the current output of the economy at current prices.

In the opposite case, total expenditures (Y) will tend to rise if the planned nonconsumption expenditures by business and government exceed the planned saving and tax payments. Households, business firms, and government together are attempting to buy more than 100% of current output at current prices.

To put fiscal policy in proper perspective, we can rewrite the equilibrium condition of the second model as

$T - G = I - S$,

which in disequilibrium implies that

if $T - G > I - S$, we have deflationary pressure,
and if $T - G < I - S$, we have inflationary pressure.

Note that we can have savings exceeding investment ($S>I$) in this model and no tendency for income to fall if the government runs a large enough deficit ($G>T$). In other words, government expenditures can take up the "slack" left in the economy when private demand for output is insufficient to maintain total expenditures at the desired level. Either an increase in government expenditures or a decrease in taxes can be used to support total expenditures if the economy is suffering from deflationary pressures in the private sector.

Conversely, total expenditures need not rise merely because desired saving is less than planned investment ($S<I$). The inflationary forces thus generated can be offset by a government surplus ($T>G$). The excess of taxes over government expenditures can be thought of as "forced savings" used to finance the excess of planned investment over voluntary savings. If the economy is at the full employment level of total expenditures and a further increase in total expenditures would only cause inflationary price increases, the government can offset a rise in planned investment above planned savings by either an increase in taxes or a decrease in government expenditures. The increased taxes would be forced saving to match the investment. The decrease in government expenditures would be the substitution of private expenditures for government expenditures.

Monetary Effects of Government Deficits

Thus far we have mentioned only the effect of a government surplus or deficit on incomes and expenditures in the circular flow model. In addition, a government surplus or deficit always has some purely monetary implications. The monetary implications of, say, a federal government deficit will depend on whether the deficit is covered by printing new money or selling securities to the public to borrow the money. Strictly speaking, when the government covers a deficit by "printing money" it increases the size of what is called the *monetary base*. The monetary base is currency in the hands of the public (truly printing press money) plus bank reserves. The bank reserves serve as the base for further monetary expansion, which we will consider later. At present we need only note that bank reserves are printing press money that the public has chosen to deposit in the banking system instead of holding in the form of currency.

If the government runs a deficit and does not want to increase the monetary base it must borrow the money from the public. There are only two ways to finance a deficit: borrow the money, or "print" it and expand the monetary base. A useful bookkeeping identity is

$$G - T = \Delta D + \Delta MB,$$

where

G = total federal government expenditures for goods and services,
T = total federal government tax revenues minus any transfer payments (net government revenues),
ΔD = change in the publicly held government debt, and
ΔMB = change in the monetary base.

This equation can be rearranged as follows:

$$G = T + \Delta D + \Delta MB.$$

In this form it states that there are only three possible sources of money for the federal government: collect taxes (T), borrow money (ΔD), or print it (ΔMB).

Of course, the money creation power is unique to the federal government. State and local governments have no such power (as New York City and Cleveland demonstrated rather conclusively in the 1970s). The impact on aggregate demand of expenditures and taxes via the circular flow of income and expenditures is the same whether we are discussing the federal government or state and local governmental units. Indeed, one can cancel out the other. The inflationary impact of a large federal government deficit can be mitigated by a surplus (a form of savings) by state and local governments. Business cycle analysts always consider the net position of all governmental units combined. State and local debt financing does have an impact on the money and capital markets, but it is virtually identical to deficit financing by the private sector. Only the federal government has the option to print and spend money.

Real Versus Nominal GNP — Aggregate Demand and Supply

Governmental policies concerning expenditures, taxes, debt, and the monetary base can always generate an increase in the level of total dollar expenditures in the economy. The important question is, are we better off as a result? In strictly economic terms, are more goods and services being produced or are we just increasing prices while real output stays the same? In supply and demand terms, we can give the people more money to spend and increase aggregate (total) demand, but will the supply mechanisms in the economy respond to the increased demand with additional output?

To consider this problem we have to have some measure of "real" or price-deflated output, say Q. If Y is a measure of output in current dollars and P is some aggregate index of the price level, then $Q = (Y)/(P)$. Real output equals the current dollar measure of the output of the economy divided by the price index. (See Table 3.1.) Although we will have a great deal more to say about price indexes in Chapter 9, we must note here the strange convention of multiplying the mathematical value of an index by 100. For example, $105 must be divided by 1.03, not by 103, to find the level of real output. Since that is the way all government indexes are published we will follow the same convention in this text.

In Table 3.1, current dollar output grew by 5%, but since prices rose by 3%, real output was up by only 2%. In supply and demand terms, our aggregate expenditures of $100 could represent an infinite number of combinations of price and quantity. For example,

if $P =$ 1   2   3   ...   33 1/3   50   100,
then $Q =$ 100   50   33 1/3   ...   3   2   1.

Graphically, we would have something like the demand curves shown

TABLE 3.1

Year	Output Measured in Current Dollars, Y	Price Index, P	Real Output, Q
1	$100	100	$100
2	$105	103	$102
% Change	+5%	+3%	+2%

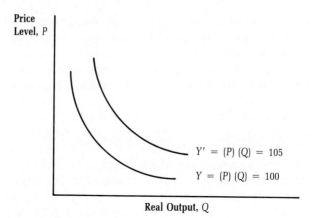

FIGURE 3.4 Aggregate Demand Curves.

in Fig. 3.4. An increase in total expenditures from Y (at \$100) to Y' (at \$105) is a shift in the aggregate demand curve to the right. The very important policy question is: What does the aggregate supply curve look like? The early "classical" economists thought it looked like the one shown in Fig. 3.5. An aggregate supply curve such as shown in Fig. 3.5 would indeed simplify macroeconomic policy. The quantity of real output Q_2 is obviously the limit of the capacity of this economy to produce output. It has to be "full employment" of people and machines in every sense of the term. If aggregate demand is equal to Y and real output is at Q_1, all policy makers have to do is cut taxes or increase government expenditures enough to increase aggregate demand to Y'. Output will rise to Q_2 with no increase in the price level. Policy makers will know when they have arrived at full employment, because if they overshoot it and go on to Y'', prices will rise as output holds constant. In other words, policy makers should increase

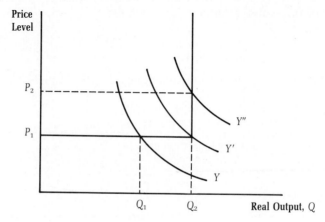

FIGURE 3.5 Aggregate Demand and Fixed Supply.

aggregate demand as long as more expenditure results in more output. When full employment is reached, increases in output will be replaced by increases in the price level.

Unfortunately, the economy does not have a nice, neat right-angle supply curve. The real world appears to behave more like Fig. 3.6. An increase in aggregate demand will increase *both* prices and output. In terms of comparative statics, we do believe in diminishing returns. The ratio of the increase in real output to the increase in prices falls as we go farther out on the aggregate supply curve. In the move from Y to Y' the price level moves by a relatively small amount from P_1 to P_2. The move from P_2 to P_3 is relatively large even though the increase in the output is approximately the same.

In algebraic terms, we can say that since

$$Y = (P)(Q), \text{ then } \%\Delta Y = \%\Delta P + \%\Delta Q.$$

The percentage change in total expenditures is approximately equal to the percentage change in the price index plus the percentage change in real output.* The change in total expenditures can be divided into the inflation rate and the rate of growth in output. In our numerical example, $\%\Delta Y = 5\%$, $\%\Delta P = 3\%$, and $\%\Delta Q = 2\%$. In the case of the nice, convenient right-angle aggregate supply curve shown in Fig. 3.5, as long as we are operating below capacity ($Q < Q_2$) all the increase in aggregate demand would be reflected in increases in real output, $\%\Delta Y = \%\Delta Q$, $\%\Delta P = 0$. When we push aggregate demand from Y' to Y'', however, all increases in total expenditures would be reflected in prices, $\%\Delta Y = \%\Delta P$, $\%\Delta Q = 0$. In the more realistic example shown in Fig. 3.6, we get a little of both.

*For an elaboration of this relationship explaining why the equation is only "approximately" true, see Chapter 9.

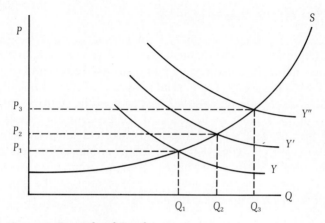

FIGURE 3.6 Aggregate Demand and Supply.

Some Useful Elasticities

In terms of the ratios of percentage changes, known as elasticities, we can start with

$\%\Delta Y = \%\Delta P + \%\Delta Q$ and divide by $\%\Delta Y$ to obtain

$(\%\Delta P)/(\%\Delta Y) + (\%\Delta Q)/(\%\Delta Y) = 1.00$.

The elasticity of prices with respect to total expenditures plus the elasticity of real output with respect to total expenditures add up to one. Simply, the proportion of the change in aggregate demand reflected in prices plus the proportion reflected in real output must add up to 100% of the change in aggregate demand. In the case of the supply curve in Fig. 3.5 we had

$E_{p/y} = (\%\Delta P)/(\%\Delta Y) = 0;\ E_{q/y} = (\%\Delta Q)/(\%\Delta Y) = 1.00$,

as long as $Q < Q_2$.

If $Q > Q_2$, then $E_{q/y} = 0$, and $E_{p/y} = 1.00$.

Although we will take a closer look at the impact of the money supply later, this is an appropriate point at which to introduce the concept of *income velocity*. Income velocity, V, is simply the ratio of total income or output in current dollar terms to the money supply, M; that is,

$V = (Y)/(M)$ and $Y = (M)(V)$.

Just as with $Y = (P)\ (Q)$, it is true that

$\%\Delta Y = \%\Delta M + \%\Delta V$ and $E_{m/y} + E_{v/y} = 1.00$.

If the current dollar GNP goes up by 10% and money supply goes up by only 7%, then the velocity of the money supply has to have risen by approximately 3%.

Aggregate Sources and Uses of Funds

The velocity of the money supply is a subject that we will discuss in some detail in Chapter 4. For the moment, we need to use the concept of total expenditures made in a money economy to establish another important identity. If we consider all the possible sources of funds for individuals, a business firm, or a government, we have as possible sources: total income (Y), borrowings (B), and in the case of the government, printing money (ΔM). All the possible uses of the funds are: consumption expenditures (C), investment in real goods (I), investment in financial assets or lending (L), and the hoarding of cash balances (H). An algebraic statement that the sum of the sources of funds must equal the sum of the uses of funds (including the building up of cash balances) is

$Y + B + \Delta M = C + I + L + H$.

Isolating the terms that represent factors in the aggregate demand for goods and services as depicted in our circular flow diagrams discussed earlier, we have: Y, C, and I. Collecting Y and C on the left-hand side of the equation gives us

$$(Y - C) + B + \Delta M = I + L + H \text{ or } S + B + \Delta M = I + L + H,$$

where S = savings as previously defined, $Y - C$. This equation can usefully be rearranged further to read

$$(I - S) + (L - B) + (H - \Delta M) = 0.$$

The first parenthetical expression refers to the demand and supply of goods and services as depicted in our circular flow diagram. We know that ex post $S = I$ and the expression would be equal to zero. We also know that if $I > S$ ex ante there is an excess demand for goods and if $S > I$ there is an excess supply of goods.

The second parenthetical expression $(L - B)$ really has to do with the demand and supply of financial (paper) assets. Borrowing, B, is actually accomplished by supplying an I.O.U. of some variety, a paper asset, to the lender. A willing lender has a demand for a financial asset. Ex post, of course, borrowing must equal lending. The supply of financial assets must equal the demand for them just as saving must equal investment in the goods market. Ex ante, some people can be trying to borrow more than others want to lend and that is what drives interest rates up. If on an ex ante basis borrowing is greater than lending, the supply of financial assets will be greater than the demand for financial assets and one would expect downward pressure on the price of bonds and other financial assets. A fall in bond prices is, of course, a rise in interest rates.

The third parenthetical expression represents the supply and demand for cash balances. If there is more money created (ΔM) than people want to hold (H), the supply exceeds the demand for money. Of course, this can only be true ex ante because ex post all the money must be held by someone.

In summary, if $(I - S)$ is positive there is an excess demand for goods, if $(L - B)$ is positive there is an excess demand for financial assets, and if $(H - M)$ is positive there is an excess demand for cash balances. These markets, however, are not independent. The entire equation is trivially true ex post, since each market will have zero excess demand and each parenthetical expression will be equal to zero. It is important to note, however, that the entire equation is always true ex ante both for an individual and for the entire economy. Consider our previous discussion of a deflationary situation in which the consumers are trying to save more than business wants to invest ($S > I$, ex ante). What do the consumers plan to do with this savings? Their only alternatives are to hold the excess of their income over their consumption in the form of increased cash balances or to lend it to someone, thereby demanding a financial asset. If consumers sought to acquire real assets with this saving, they would be investing and we would not have an ex ante excess of savings over investment. In terms of the entire equation, savings greater than investment ($S > I$) gives us a negative component. Since this excess of savings must either be lent out and create a demand for a financial asset ($L > B$) or held in the form of cash ($H > \Delta M$), the entire equation will always be true both ex ante and ex post by one of the other parenthetical expressions being positive. In other words, the excess supply in the goods market implies an excess demand in one of the other markets.

The truth of this *general equilibrium* equation is perhaps easiest to see in the contention of some economists that in discussing demand *and* supply we have twice as many variables as we need. Effective economic demand implies a supply of something or it is not demand. Wishing for a luxury car is not economic demand. An ability and willingness to supply cash in exchange for the car makes it a demand in the economic sense of that term. One can contend that there is no such thing as independent supply, only demand, since demand requires a supply. General Motors has a demand for money, which it makes effective in the marketplace by its willingness to supply automobiles.

In terms of the algebra of our equation, any excess demand in one market must be exactly matched by an equal excess supply in another market, and vice-versa. If the money supply is excessive ($\Delta M > H$) with respect to the public's desire to hold cash, they must want to exchange it for real goods ($I > S$) or lend it in exchange for financial assets ($L > B$). The first inequality, ($I > S$), would tend to drive up the price of goods while the latter, ($L > B$), would drive up the price of bonds (thereby driving down interest rates).

In these relationships we must distinguish between what must be true for the economy as a whole but need not be true for any individual economic unit. Specifically, ex post, each parenthetical expression must be equal to zero for the economy as a whole. Total supply must equal total demand ex post whether one is talking about goods, bonds, or cash balances. However, any individual economic unit can have a net supply or demand for goods, bonds, or money as long as it is offset in another market. People can save (thereby creating a net supply of goods) by holding some of their income in cash (thereby creating a net demand for cash balances). For any individual economic unit each parenthetical expression need not be zero ex post or ex ante, but the entire equation must be true both ex post and ex ante. For the entire economy each parenthetical expression must be equal to zero ex post but need not equal zero ex ante. The entire equation is true for the entire economy both ex post and ex ante.

The Determination of Aggregate Demand

In our circular flow model in which we discussed whether there would be an excess of demand for goods and services ($I > S$) or an excess supply ($S > I$), we took the level of S and I as given. Although the behavior of consumers and investors is still something of a mystery to economists, some assumptions are standard; these will be discussed in this chapter. In a later chapter of this book, when we look at real world data, we will take up the question again.

It is generally assumed (and to some extent supported by empirical evidence) that the primary determinant of the amount of savings is the amount of income, if they are both measured in either current or price deflated dollars. This behavioral assumption, when combined with the equilibrium condition of $S = I$, gives us the famous macroeconomic multiplier. If the public insists on saving 20¢ out of every dollar, and business wants to invest $100 per time period, it is obvious that for savings to equal investment, total income must be $500. With $500 in total income and expenditure everybody's ex ante plans can be met. Business produces $100 worth of investment goods and $400 worth of consumer goods. The households receive $500 for producing these goods, spend $400 for consumption goods, and acquire cash or financial assets with the other $100, which finances $100 worth of investment.

Should businesses happen to turn optimistic and decide that beginning with the current time period they want to invest $110 instead of $100, then income will have to rise to $550 to generate the additional $10 in savings. The multiplier is 5, the reciprocal of the *marginal propensity to save* which is .20 or 20¢ on the dollar. The definition of the marginal propensity to save is, of course, the percentage of an additional dollar that consumers will save. Conversely, the *marginal propensity to consume* in this case is .80 or 80¢ on the dollar.

Algebraically, the statics and comparative statics of the example we just described can be formulated as follows:

Total income and output $Y = C + I = C + S$,
Equilibrium condition $\quad I = S$,
Consumption function $\quad C = .8Y$,
Investment given $\quad I_1 = \$100$.

Solving for the equilibrium level of income and expenditures,

$Y_1 = .8Y_1 + 100$,

$Y_1 = (100)/(.2) = (5)(100) = \$500$.

The comparative statics problem of an increase in investment to $110 is as follows:

$$I_2 = 110,$$
$$Y_2 = .8Y_2 + 110,$$
$$Y_2 = (110)/(.2) = (5)(110) = \$550.$$

The increase in income ($50) is 5 times the increase in investment ($10) so the multiplier is 5 (50/10).

To consider the dynamics of this problem, let us assume that consumers base their savings-consumption decision for this time period on the income they received in the immediately previous time period: $C_t = .8Y_{t-1}$.

Then if

$$Y_t = C_t + I_t; \ Y_t = I_t + .8Y_{t-1}.$$

This is, of course, a nonhomogeneous, first-order difference equation of the type we examined in some detail in Chapter 2. From our previous discussion of this example we know that the equilibrium value is $Y_e = (I)/(1 - .8) = (5)(I)$, or 500 when $I = 100$, and 550 when $I = 110$. We also know from our previous discussion of difference equations that since the coefficient of Y_{t-1} is positive and less than 1.00 with a value of .8, the dynamic behavior of this model will be stable and noncyclical. It will converge toward the new equilibrium smoothly. Specifically,

t	I	+	C	=	Y
0	100		400		500
1	100		400		500
2	110		400		510
3	110		408		518
4	110		414		524
5	110		420		530
6	110		424		534
7	110		427		537
8	110		430		540
9	110		432		542
10	110		433		543
.	.		.		.
.	.		.		.
.	.		.		.
∞	110		440		550

At this point we have established the level of aggregate demand by making consumption a function of income but leaving investment demand exogenous, determined outside the system. Although investment expenditures by business do seem to be pretty nearly an independent variable and undoubtedly are the source of much instability in the system, it is generally felt that investment decisions are based on the prospective profitability of the investment. Remember that in terms of aggregate demand, the acquisition of cash or a financial asset is not investment. These are alternatives to real investment for the individual saver. Conversely, potential investors may have no financial assets at all and have to borrow to finance their investments. In equilibrium the owners of wealth would have equalized the expected rates of return on all types of assets. If one expected inflation (rising prices of goods), one would want to hold goods and not money or bonds. Conversely, if one expected the price of goods to fall, one would want to hold money or bonds. More specifically, business firms consider a real investment to be attractive if the expected rate of return on this investment exceeds the rate of interest at which it must be financed. If you can borrow money at 10% and expect to earn 20% on your investment, you borrow and invest. If borrowing costs were 22% or the prospective returns on the investment were 8% you would not be interested.

Keynes referred to investors' expected return on an incremental investment project as the *marginal efficiency of capital*, or the MEC. Investment will be undertaken up to the point at which the rate of interest equals the MEC. In Fig. 3.7 we have a negatively sloped marginal efficiency of capital schedule labeled MEC. This schedule depicts the rate of return that firms feel is available on each additional investment undertaken. It is negatively sloped because of economists' long-standing faith in the law of diminishing returns and on the reasonable assumption that investors will undertake the highest yielding investments first and move down the schedule to progressively lower yields. If interest rates are relatively high at r_1, the level of investment will be relatively low at I_1. If the interest rate falls to r_2, investment will increase to I_2. If the MEC schedule were stable, we could go a long way

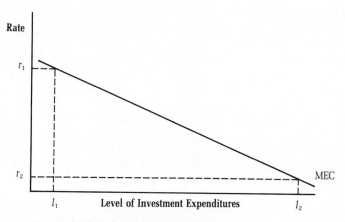

FIGURE 3.7 A "Marginal Efficiency of Capital" Schedule.

toward influencing the level of aggregate demand via the multiplier by the manipulation of interest rates. Unfortunately this is not the case, although interest rates are certainly one factor in the determination of the level of investment.

Investment in real goods in the hope of a positive return is, of course, trading present goods for future goods. Similarly, investment in financial assets such as bonds is trading present money for future money at the rate indicated by the rate of interest. With both alternatives open to savers, if interest rates on financial assets are high, investment is discouraged; if rates are low, investment is encouraged. In Chapter 4 on monetary theory we will discuss the determination of the level of interest rates. But first we will conclude this chapter with a very important attribute of investment — its impact on aggregate supply by increasing the ability of the economy to produce additional goods and services.

A Simple Growth Model

Investment has an immediate and significant impact on the level of aggregate demand via the multiplier mechanism just illustrated. However, investment not only affects the level of aggregate demand, but it also has a direct effect on the level of aggregate supply as well. We discussed earlier the concept of *capacity* in the economy — full employment of people and machines. Presumably investment is undertaken for the purpose of increasing the capacity of the economy to produce additional goods and services — that is, economic growth. Economic growth is a shift in the aggregate supply curve to the right (as illustrated in Fig. 3.8) from S to S'.

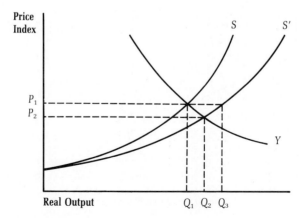

FIGURE 3.8 Economic Growth with a Falling Price Level.

Note that if aggregate demand (the level of total expenditures) were held constant at Y, the price level would have to fall from P_1 to P_2 for ex ante supply to equal ex ante demand. Alternatively, if prices were inflexible downward, fixed at P_1, the suppliers would be willing and able to supply Q_3 but the buyers would only want Q_1. The difference would presumably represent unemployed resources creating some deflationary pressure on the price level.

For economic growth without deflationary or inflationary pressures, one needs to increase aggregate demand and supply at identical rates (as illustrated in Fig. 3.9). As the capacity of the economy grows from S to S', aggregate demand increases from Y to Y' thereby creating a demand for all the goods offered at P_1 with no deflationary or inflationary pressure.

We can illustrate this problem and one particular solution by assuming a fixed *capital-output ratio* on the supply side. Let us assume that in the range of current levels of output an investment of $\$\alpha$ of capital, K, is required for each $1 of additional output.

$$(K)/(Q_s) = \alpha = \text{the capital-output ratio,}$$

and thereby $K = (\alpha)(Q_s)$.

Investment, I, is of course the change in the capital stock so

$$\Delta K = I = (\alpha)(\Delta Q_s), \text{ or } \Delta Q_s = (I)/(\alpha)$$

If we are in complete equilibrium with everything fixed (no growth), then $\Delta Q_s = 0$ and $I = 0$ — not a very interesting state of affairs. Let us consider the problem of having the effects of investment on aggregate demand via the multiplier just exactly match up with the resulting increase in aggregate

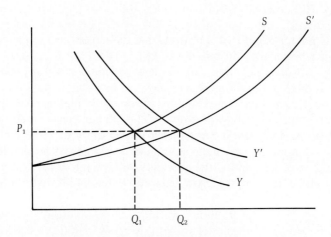

FIGURE 3.9 **Economic Growth with a Constant Price Level.**

supply. This will ensure no inflationary or deflationary pressure in the economy. We have just derived the relationship between the increase in potential output (ΔQ_s) and the level of investment (I). Earlier in our discussion of the multiplier, we found the relationship between aggregate demand (Y) and investment (I) to be the reciprocal of the marginal propensity to save (MPS) as

$$(\Delta Y)/(\Delta I) = 1/(\text{MPS}) \text{ or } \Delta Y = (\Delta I)/(\text{MPS}).$$

For a zero inflation rate, the rate of growth in total expenditures must exactly equal the rate of growth in aggregate supply; that is,

$$\Delta Y = \Delta Q_s, \text{ which requires } (\Delta I)/(\text{MPS}) = (I)/(\alpha).$$

Increase in aggregate demand = increase in aggregate supply. The terms in the last equation can be rearranged so that we have

$$(\Delta I)/(I) = (\text{MPS})/(\alpha),$$

which says that for noninflationary growth we must have the percentage rate of growth in investment equal to the marginal propensity to save divided by the capital-output ratio.

In the jargon of the economist this rate of growth is known as the *warranted* rate of growth. For example, if the marginal propensity to save were .20 and the capital-output ratio were 10, the warranted rate of growth in investment would be .02 or 2%. If the actual rate of growth in investment is greater than the warranted rate, there will be a larger increase in aggregate demand than the increase in the capacity of the economy to supply the goods; inflationary pressures will result. Conversely, if the rate of growth in the level of investment is less than the warranted rate, aggregate supply will grow more rapidly than aggregate demand and there will be deflationary problems. Either prices must fall or the additional capacity to produce will not be utilized.

From this formulation it is obvious that the larger the marginal propensity to save, the larger the warranted rate of growth. This dramatizes the virtue of saving. An economy that saves a large proportion of any increment in output can have a rapidly increasing level of investment (and a high growth rate) without inflationary pressures. Conversely, a high capital-output ratio reduces the warranted rate of growth. This makes sense since the capital-output ratio is really the inverse of the productivity of investment. If, in a particular economy, a very large amount of investment is needed to generate a small increase in capacity, the economy will run into inflationary problems very quickly if it seeks to grow rapidly. It has a low warranted rate of growth.

Although these observations are more or less intuitively obvious, one lesson from this growth model seems downright paradoxical. Consider the policy advice regarding stimulating or discouraging investment one must give when the lessons of this model are considered. If you are faced with a general lack of aggregate demand, such as the U.S. economy in 1934, then there is virtually no investment being undertaken and massive amounts of unused capacity stand idle. What policy do you recommend? One must recommend that the construction of additional productive capacity be encouraged. What this economy needs is more investment! If aggregate demand is less than aggregate supply, it has to mean that $(\Delta I)/(I)$ is less than $(MPS)/(\alpha)$. One can urge people to save less so that the required level of investment will be lower, but with respect to the construction of additional capacity one must say "more!" in the face of all that excess capacity. Of course, if investors can be persuaded to start building capacity at a very rapid rate, it will not be long before the excess capacity will all have disappeared. The problem then will be that demand is growing faster than supply and the economy has inflationary pressure and a "shortage" of capacity. In the case mentioned above where the MPS is 20% and the capital-output ratio is 10, each $1 of investment will increase aggregate demand by $5 and potential supply by only 10¢. Of course the demand will begin to run down as soon as the investment stops, while the increase in aggregate supply is presumably permanent.

It is possible to make a case from this sort of model that economies are inherently unstable, if one assumes some relationship that makes the inequality of changes in aggregate demand and aggregate supply cumulative. For example, suppose that when business firms see the demand for output exceeding the supply, they are induced to invest more in an effort to relieve the "shortage" of capacity. Similarly, suppose that investment is discouraged as "excess" capacity appears, because aggregate demand falls short of the economy's ability to supply goods and services. These are not unreasonable assumptions regarding the determination of investment.

These assumptions imply that if the actual rate of growth in investment exceeds the warranted rate, and thereby the growth in aggregate demand is greater than aggregate supply, investment will be increased by even more in an ever-upward inflationary spiral. On the other hand, if the actual rate of growth is less than the warranted rate of growth, aggregate demand will fall short of the capacity of the economy and business will cut back investment. Demand will fall (or grow less than supply) and a downward deflationary spiral will ensue.

Such a model is essentially the same as a first-order difference equation with the coefficient of the lagged term positive and greater than one. For example,

$$Y_t = 1.05 Y_{t-1} - 10.$$

If $Y_t = Y_e = 200$, then the value of Y will hold constant at this equilibrium level, but the system is unstable. If pushed off equilibrium it will move monotonically toward plus or minus infinity. This leaves the economy balanced on a razor's edge at the warranted rate. Either the economy grows at the warranted rate, or it explodes into hyperinflation or collapses into deep depression. Casual observation indicates, fortunately, that this sort of model is not close to being a complete description of how the economy operates. However, there is certainly an element of truth and some explanation of some cyclical movements in the "Harrod-Domar" growth models.[1]

APPENDIX: Summary of Important Macroeconomic Relationships

1. Federal government's budget constraint

$$G = \text{Rev} + \Delta D + \Delta MB =$$

where

G = total federal government expenditures for goods and
   services =
Rev = total federal government revenues net of
   transfer payments =
ΔD = change in the publicly held government debt =
ΔMB = change in the monetary base (bank reserves plus currency in
   the hands of the public).

This equation states that there are only three sources of money for the federal government: taxes and other revenue (Rev), borrowings (ΔD), and the printing press (ΔMB).

An alternative formulation is

$$G - \text{Rev} = \Delta D + \Delta MB.$$

This places the fiscal policy variables together on the left-hand side and the monetary policy variables together on the right-hand side. In this form the equation states that the federal government's cash deficit must be covered either by increased debt, increases in printing press money, or some combination of the two.

2. GNP, the price level and real output, the money supply and velocity
   a. $\text{GNP} = C + I + G + Nx$,

where

GNP = total output of the economy,
   C = total output of consumer goods purchased by consumers,
   I = output of investment goods purchased by the private sector,
   G = output of goods and services claimed by all levels of government,
   Nx = net exports of goods and services (exports minus imports).

   b. We define a price deflated or "real" GNP, Q, as

$$Q = \frac{\text{GNP}}{P} \text{ or GNP} = P\,Q,$$

where P = a general price index.

c. We define the "velocity" of the money supply as

$$V = \frac{\text{GNP}}{M} \text{ or GNP} = M\,V,$$

where M = whatever definition of the money supply we happen to be using.

d. In summary, all of this implies:

GNP $= C + I + G + Nx = P\,Q = M\,V.$

e. In terms of percentage changes it is *approximately* true that:

$\%\Delta\text{GNP} = \%\Delta P + \%\Delta Q = \%\Delta M + \%\Delta V.$

3. General equilibrium
   a. As sources and uses of funds

	sources		uses
where	S + B + ΔM	=	I + L + H
	S = savings		I = investment
	B = borrowing		L = lending
	ΔM = money creation		H = increase in the holdings of cash balances.

   b. As the supply and demand for goods, bonds, and cash

$(S - I) + (B - L) + (\Delta M - H) = 0,$

where

$(S - I)$ = net supply in the goods market,
$(B - L)$ = net supply in the bond and other financial assets market,
$(\Delta M - H)$ = net supply of cash balances.

   c. Each of the parenthetical expressions is equal to zero *ex post* for the economy as a whole but not for the individual economic unit.
   d. The entire equation is always true both *ex ante* and *ex post* for the entire economy and for each individual economic unit in it. (You cannot *demand* goods unless you *supply* money or another financial asset.)

● Questions for Discussion

1. Define: real GNP, velocity, and aggregate supply.
2. Why does total income equal total output in the economy?
3. What makes federal government finance particularly different from state and local government finance?
4. If the economy were always at full employment, operating at its capacity, what would be the approximate value of the elasticity of the price level with respect to changes in total expenditures?
5. Suppose the people in a particular economy decided:
   a. They want to build up their cash balances.
   b. They are against borrowing to do so.

Discuss what will happen to this economy in terms of the general equilibrium equation: $(I - S) + (L - B) + (H - \Delta M) = 0$.

● Exercises

1. If the marginal propensity to consume out of total income were 70% and investment increased by $1 billion, by how much does the equilibrium level of expenditures rise?

2. Given the following macroeconomic model:

$$Y_t = C_t + I_t + G_t; \quad C_t = (.7)Y_{t-1}; \quad I_t = (.2)Y_{t-1}; \quad \text{and } G_t = 100,$$

   where

   Y_t = total income and expenditure,
   C_t = consumption expenditures,
   I_t = investment expenditures,
   G_g = government expenditures.

   a. What is the equilibrium level of total expenditures, Y_e?
   b. What is the magnitude of the government expenditures multiplier, $\Delta Y_e / \Delta G_t$?
   c. What would the value of the government expenditures multiplier be if the accelerator coefficient (which is shown as .2) were zero?

3. In a simple growth model of the type discussed in this chapter:
   a. If an economy has a marginal propensity to consume of .8 and a capital-output ratio of 10, what is the warranted rate of growth?
   b. If the actual rate of growth in investment were to exceed the warranted rate of growth, what would be the result? And why?

4. If the federal government runs a cash deficit of $100 billion and the public's holdings of government securities rises by only $40 billion:
   a. What happens to the monetary base?
   b. If that increase in the monetary base causes a 20% increase in the money supply, what happens to nominal and real GNP if velocity falls by 5% and prices go up by 5%?

5. Consider an economy in which consumers will spend 70% of their after-tax income and the only tax is a 30% income tax.
   a. Calculate the magnitude of the simple investment multiplier.
   b. Assume the tax rate is reduced to zero while everything else stays the same. Now calculate the magnitude of the simple investment multiplier.

6. If you were paid $100 to read this chapter and you then spent 75% of it with a recipient who would also spend 75% of what he received by paying it to others who would spend 75% of that, and so on, what would be the eventual total expenditures resulting from the initial $100?

7. If GNP rose by 10% in conjunction with a rise in the GNP Price Index of 7% and an increase in velocity of 3%, what must have been the approximate percentage change in:
   a. The quantity of real output (price deflated GNP)?
   b. The money supply?

8. Consider the following growth model:

Aggregate Demand	Aggregate Supply
$Y_t = C_t + I_t$	$a = K_t/Y_t =$ constant
$C_t = b\ Y_t$	
$I_t = (1+r)I_{t-1}$	

a. What must r equal for noninflationary (and nondeflationary) equilibrium growth?

b. If $b = .8$, $a = 10$, and $r = 5\%$, will this economy have an inflationary or deflationary problem?

● Source Note

[1]Growth models of this type were formulated independently by the English economist Sir Roy Harrod and the American Evsey Domar. For a comparison of the two formulations, see Harrod's "Domar and dynamic economics." *The Economic Journal,* September 1959, pp. 451–64.

● Selected Additional Readings

Dornbusch, Rudiger, and Fischer, Stanley. *Macroeconomics* (2nd ed.) New York: McGraw-Hill, 1981. Chapters 2 and 3.

Gordon, Robert J. *Macroeconomics* (2nd ed.) Boston: Little, Brown, 1981. Chapters 2 and 3.

Harrod, R. F. "Domar and dynamic economics." *The Economic Journal.* September 1959.

Keynes, John Maynard. *The General Theory of Employment Interest and Money.* New York: Harcourt, Brace, 1936. Book III.

Monetary Theory

4

What Is Money?

A platitude as true as it is trite says, "Money is as money does." Money is whatever happens to be the generally accepted means of exchange in a particular economic system. Historically it has been everything from rocks to cattle. Èconomists generally list a few or many of a whole host of characteristics that are desirable in a particular tangible good if it is to be used as money. Today most money is a bookkeeping entry in the banking system — paper currency and coin are a small fraction of most of the usual definitions of the money supply.

We define money by its functions. Most texts list a number of functions in addition to serving as the medium of exchange, serving as a *store of value,* serving as a *unit of account,* and so on. However, any commodity that is generally acceptable in exchange for other goods will necessarily be useful in these other roles as well. The function of money is to be exchanged. The prime requisite of money is that it be exchangeable for other goods at exchange ratios that have some degree of certainty. The ratio of money to other goods are their *prices* in money terms. If, as in cases of hyperinflation, this ratio becomes wildly unstable, money ceases to serve as an acceptable medium of exchange. It thereby ceases to be money regardless of what the government with the printing press may contend.

The requirement that money be readily acceptable in exchange for other goods at an exchange ratio (or price) that has some degree of certainty is merely to say that money has what economists have come to call *liquidity.* Of course, all goods with some economic value have *some* liquidity and thereby some degree of "moneyness." Everything from real estate to a pile of iron ore has some exchange value and can serve as a store of value through time. Indeed one can think of a spectrum of economic assets from the most to the least liquid. Currency is pure liquidity. Inflation and recession notwithstanding, one is more confident of the value of $1,000 cash three months or three years hence than $1,000 worth of stock listed on the New York Stock Exchange. The listed stock is undoubtedly more liquid than real estate, but less liquid than a deposit in a savings account.

The definition of what constitutes the *money supply* for a particular economy at a particular point in history is necessarily a somewhat arbitrary judgment call. In the United States we have numerous definitions, the most common of which is currency in circulation plus deposits on which people may write checks ($M1$). We extend that to include savings and time deposits held by individuals ($M2$), and so on, to include all the liquid assets held by the public ($M3$). For our purposes in this chapter we will define the money supply as currency in circulation and deposits subject to check.

Although we can define what is to be considered money and what is to be considered just another liquid financial asset, we must recognize that *all* credit transactions involve the creation of liquidity and thereby the creation of a money substitute. Probably one of the greatest sources of liquidity in the economy is trade credit among corporations (when one company sells to another on open book account). One can imagine that if all the business firms in the economy suddenly required "cash on delivery," the money supply would have to be expanded a great deal or trade would grind to a halt.

Similarly, even a personal loan from one individual to another creates a money substitute. One student may have $20 on a particular Friday and no prospects for social activity until the middle of next week. Another student may have money arriving from home on Monday but a pressing desire (if not need) for financial resources this weekend. If the $20 is loaned from the first student to the second on the basis of a simple I.O.U., a money substitute has been created. The lender has what he feels is a liquid asset, since he expects it to turn into cash next Tuesday. If he did not believe that, he presumably would not have lent the money. The holder of the I.O.U. has his liquid store of value and the borrower has $20 to spend this weekend. The velocity of the money supply will be increased by the creation of this money substitute since the $20 that would have lain idle in the wallet of the lender will now circulate among some of the local bars or whatever.

Where Does the Money Come From?

In Chapter 3 we noted that the government creates money simply by printing it and spending it. Of course, in a modern economy the government does not usually even have to bother printing the money. They just add more zeros to Treasury checks. The best way to understand the theory of money creation is to follow the mechanics of the bookkeeping. First, the government sells itself a bond or other evidence of government indebtedness. In the United States the Federal Reserve acquires a Treasury security. We can illustrate this with an abbreviated balance sheet of the central bank (Table 4.1). In exchange for the Treasury security the Federal Reserve Bank credits the Treasury's checking account.

TABLE 4.1   Federal Reserve Bank Balance Sheet

Assets		Liabilities	
Government security	$1,000,000	$1,000,000	Treasury's checking account

Next, the government spends the money. In the United States the Treasury writes a check on its account at the Federal Reserve. The recipient of the check deposits it in a local commercial bank. We see the bookkeeping here in Tables 4.2 and 4.3. The commercial bank (First Bank) gives the customer a deposit in exchange for the Treasury check. The bank then sends the check to the Federal Reserve for payment. The Federal Reserve pays First Bank by crediting its account for the amount of the check. It charges the check against the Treasury's checking account.

This reserve account that First Bank now has with the Federal Reserve can be used as legally required reserves and working balances to support loans it might make. A commercial bank must be prepared to meet requests by its depositors for currency and requests by other banks for payment of checks deposited with them but drawn on it. Both claims can be met with a reserve deposit at the Federal Reserve Bank. If a commercial bank needs currency, its local Federal Reserve Bank will provide currency in exchange for part of the bank's reserve account deposit. Similarly, if one of the bank's depositors writes a check to a store that keeps its deposit in another bank, the Federal Reserve, as part of the check clearing process, will reduce the reserve account of the bank on whom the check is written, and raise the reserve account of the bank in which the check was deposited.

We have half the answer to our question of where the money comes from. The government prints it and spends it. This is called *monetization* of the government deficit. The money supply will always go up dollar for

TABLE 4.2   Federal Reserve Balance Sheet

Assets		Liabilities	
$1,000,000	Government security	$1,000,000	First Bank's reserve account

TABLE 4.3   First Bank's Balance Sheet

Assets		Liabilities	
$1,000,000	Reserves	$1,000,000	Deposit

dollar with an increase in the monetary base. When the government monetizes a deficit, the money supply will increase, because someone ends up with a deposit in a commercial bank. The recipient can also choose to hold all or part of the government expenditures in the form of cash. If the recipients of the $1,000,000 in our illustration chose to hold this amount of cash, the bookkeeping steps would be as indicated in Table 4.4. Yes, it is true — governments do carry their currency outstanding as a liability, although most of them certainly have no intention of redeeming it. In the United States a $20 Federal Reserve note presented to the government for payment will get you two tens or four fives.

If the public does choose to hold the increase in the monetary base in the form of currency, the monetary expansion is ended. Assuming more realistically that at least some proportion of the increase in the monetary base ends up as an increase in bank reserves, additional money might be created as a result of the monetization of bank loans. Just as the bank created a demand deposit in exchange for a government check, it can create a demand deposit in exchange for a business firm's I.O.U. The limitation on this activity is that each individual bank must have sufficient balances with the central bank and currency in its vault to be able to redeem its deposits on demand in currency. Also, banks in this country have statutory reserve requirements that must be met with deposits with the Federal Reserve. If a bank were so superconservative as to plan for 100% of its deposits to be withdrawn, it could never make any loans. Recall the bank's balance sheet after the deposit of the Treasury's check (see Table 4.5). If the bank expected all deposit holders to come in tomorrow and demand cash — or, what amounts to the same thing, to write checks that get deposited in other banks — it had better keep a ratio of reserves to deposits of 100%. Actually bankers discovered early in the economic history of the world that everybody does not want their money at the same time. So the reserve ratio can be something less than 100%. Specifically, banks discover

TABLE 4.4 Federal Reserve's Balance Sheet

Assets	Liabilities
Step 1	
Government security $1,000,000	$1,000,000 Treasury's checking account
Step 2	
No change	−$1,000,000 Treasury's checking account
	+$1,000,000 Federal Reserve notes (currency)
Step 3	
Government security $1,000,000	$1,000,000 Federal Reserve notes

TABLE 4.5 First Bank's Balance Sheet

Assets	Liabilities
Reserves $1,000,000	$1,000,000 Deposit

through experience some prudent ratio of reserves to deposits that will ensure that they will be able to meet their commitments. What is prudent is dictated by the combination of legal reserve requirements, the volatility of their deposits, and the liquidity of their other assets.

For illustrative purposes let us assume the reserve ratio to be 20%. The required reserves are therefore 20% of deposits. Anything above that is excess reserves. If a bank lends out an amount equal to its excess reserves, it is in the reasonably prudent position where the proceeds of all loans can be totally withdrawn from the bank and it will still have enough reserves to meet its reserve requirement.

Consider First Bank. The deposits of $1,000,000 and the 20% reserve requirement generate an amount of required reserves of $200,000. The bank has $1,000,000 of reserves on deposit with the Federal Reserve, giving it $800,000 of excess reserves. If the bank makes loans equal to its excess reserves its balance sheet will initially be as shown in Table 4.6, since bankers never hand borrowers money, just deposit slips.

Suppose First Bank's worst fears are realized and all borrowers spend their money in such a way that it ends up in another bank to whom First Bank must pay with a check drawn on its reserve account. After First Bank pays out the reserves for the checks and charges the checks against the borrowers' accounts, it has the balance sheet shown in Table 4.7. As indicated earlier, by lending an amount exactly equal to excess reserves, First Bank ends up with exactly the 20% required reserve ratio if all the loan proceeds are withdrawn.

But what about the deposit in the other bank? A major theorem of monetary theory is, "Everybody gotta be somewhere." These loan proceeds were paid to somebody. The recipients of these payments have the choice of holding currency or keeping a deposit in the banking system. If they

TABLE 4.6 First Bank's Balance Sheet

Assets		Liabilities	
Reserves	$1,000,000	$1,000,000	Original deposits
Loans	800,000	800,000	Borrowers' deposits
	$1,800,000	$1,800,000	

TABLE 4.7 First Bank's Balance Sheet

Assets	Liabilities
Reserves $200,000	$1,000,000 Deposits
Loans 800,000	
$1,000,00	$1,000,000

cash their checks and hold the $800,000 in the form of currency, the money supply will have increased by a total of $1,800,000 as a result of the $1,000,000 increase in the monetary base. The first $1,000,000 was created when the government deficit was monetized — at the moment the public deposited the Treasury check and obtained a bank deposit in exchange. The additional $800,000 was created when the bank monetized private debt by making a loan. The important thing to note is that in the United States and in all other industrialized capitalistic countries around the world, money gets created in two separate and distinct ways: (1) by the government printing press as deficits are monetized; and (2) by monetization of private debt as bankers take highly illiquid I.O.U.'s from businesses and give out in exchange a liability of the bank (a deposit) that is sufficiently liquid to be counted as part of the money supply. Critically important, however, is that (2) cannot take place without (1) having gone before. If the government had not injected any reserves into the system and bankers had gone ahead with their lendings they very likely would not sleep too well with a balance sheet such as shown in Table 4.8. Suppose a depositor wanted to cash a check, or deposited a check with another bank. *No* liquidity is available with which to meet this withdrawal unless there is a market in which this banker can sell some of the loans.

To summarize to this point, printing press money, known as the monetary base, will increase the money supply dollar for dollar whether it is held as currency or deposited in the banking system and increases bank reserves. If it is deposited in the banking system, the increase in reserves may lead to a further increase in the money supply if the reserves are used for the purpose of monetizing private debt.

TABLE 4.8 Balance Sheet of a Bank with a Problem

Assets	Liabilities
Loans $800,000	$800,000 Deposits

In our example we assumed the bank receiving the original deposit of the Treasury check loaned out its excess reserves of $800,000. Let us now assume that when the proceeds of those loans were withdrawn from First Bank they were deposited in Second Bank instead of being converted to cash. The balance sheet for Second Bank would look like Table 4.9. The deposit of the checks drawn on First Bank, which Second Bank turned over to the Federal Reserve to build its reserve account, generated deposits of an equal amount in Second Bank. The total reserves of Second Bank increased by $800,000 but its required reserves went up by only 20% of that amount, or $160,000. This leaves Second Bank with $640,000 of excess reserves that it may prudently lend. The sequence of balance sheets for Second Bank are shown in Table 4.10 and 4.11. Table 4.11 shows the results from Second Bank's worst fears being realized in which all the loan proceeds are withdrawn. But of course the $640,000 that was withdrawn from Second Bank "gotta be somewhere." If the recipients of the payments from the borrowers do not choose to hold it in cash, it will be deposited somewhere in the banking system. For purposes of illustration let us say that it all gets deposited in Third Bank, which now has a balance shown in Table 4.12. Third Bank now has excess reserves of $512,000 (total reserves of $640,000

TABLE 4.9   Second Bank's Balance Sheet(a)

Assets	Liabilities
Reserves $800,000	$800,000 Deposits

TABLE 4.10   Second Bank's Balance Sheet(b)

Assets		Liabilities	
Reserves	$800,000	$800,000	Original deposit
Loans	640,000	640,000	Deposited loan proceeds
	$1,440,000	$1,440,000	

TABLE 4.11   Second Bank's Balance Sheet(c)

Assets		Liabilities	
Reserves	$160,000	$800,000	Deposits
Loans	640,000		
	$800,000	$800,000	

TABLE 4.12 Third Bank's Balance Sheet

Assets	Liabilities
Reserves $640,000	$640,000 Deposits

less the required reserves of $128,000). If the loan demand is sufficiently strong, this progressive monetization of bank loans will proceed in the sequence shown in Table 4.13. Table 4.13 illustrates the *maximum* impact of a $1,000,000 increase in the monetary base in a contemporary monetary system. "Change in Reserves" indicates the final position of each bank after all the assumed transactions have taken place. Since each bank is completely "loaned up," the "Change in Total Deposits" is exactly five times the "Change in Reserves." In each case the bank will have engaged in lending activity, shown under "Change in Bank Loans," equal to the difference between its change in deposits and the growth in its reserves.

If the process is continued until the ever-decreasing excess reserves get close enough to zero to ignore, we can total up the full monetary impact of the $1,000,000 government deficit. Each bank keeps a portion of the original $1,000,000 reserves as they pass through, but the full amount of this monetary base stays in the system. It should come as no surprise, then, that the total for the "Change in Reserves" is $1,000,000. The "Change in Total Deposits" adds up to $5,000,000, indicating the increase in that component of the money supply. The *money multiplier,* in this case 5, is always equal to the reciprocal of the effective reserve requirement. In our case that is assumed to be 20%.

A balance sheet for the entire *banking system* gives a fairly clear picture of the process. (See Table 4.14.) The deposit component of the money

TABLE 4.13 Maximum Deposit Expansion

Bank	Change in Reserves	Change in Total Deposits	Change in Bank Loans
First	$200,000	$1,000,000	$800,000
Second	160,000	800,000	640,000
Third	128,000	640,000	512,000
Fourth	102,400	512,000	409,600
.	.	.	.
.	.	.	.
.	.	.	.
Last	0	0	0
Totals	$1,000,000	$5,000,000	$4,000,000

TABLE 4.14 Balance Sheet for Entire Banking System

Assets	Liabilities
Reserves $1,000,000	$5,000,000 Deposits
Loans $4,000,000	
$5,000,000	$5,000,000

supply has been increased by $5,000,000 but this total increase is the result of two distinct forms of money creation: $1,000,000 of printing press money in the form of U.S. Treasury checks deposited in the banking system, and $4,000,000 of monetization of private debt that came about when bankers issued highly liquid deposits in exchange for highly illiquid commercial loans.

We have assumed that all loan proceeds stayed in the banking system (no cash withdrawals), and even more unrealistically we assumed that there was such strong loan demand that all available reserves were utilized. The truth is that in modern monetary systems of this type an increase in the monetary base of $1 will have an impact on the money supply of something between $1 and the full money multiplier effect. There are always some unused excess reserves in the system. The full multiplier effect is most closely approximated in a business cycle boom when loan demand is strong and both bankers and borrowers are optimistic about the business outlook. Times of recession and depression will see a substantial amount of unused excess reserves in the system, and an increase of $1 in the monetary base increases the money supply not much more than $1.

Classical Monetary Theory

Early theorists believed money was only a "veil" that covered "real" economic transactions. We now feel money is a good deal more important. Nevertheless, classical monetary theory contains enough truth to be worthy of study. Indeed, in a full employment, inflationary economy, the classical approach comes close to being more relevant than the more recent Keynesian approach.

The classical economists recognized that although one cannot eat or otherwise consume money, it most certainly is useful to its holder. They believed the demand for money was primarily for transaction or cash register purposes, although in an uncertain world people might want to hold some precautionary cash balances. The required balances would depend on the number of transactions required, T, and the price level at which the transactions were to take place, P. The demand for the services of money would be the product of the price level and the number of transactions, $(P)(T)$.

The supply of money services is the product of the stock of money, M, and its velocity, V. Setting the supply of money services, $(M)(V)$, equal to the demand for money services, $(P)(T)$, gives the famous old quantity theory equation

$$(M)(V) = (P)(T).$$

Contemporary quantity theorists use real GNP as a proxy for the number of transactions and so substitute Q for T. This gives us the equation we derived in Chapter 3 when we defined velocity.

$$(M)(V) = (P)(Q) = \text{GNP},$$
$$(M)(V) = \text{GNP},$$
$$V = (\text{GNP})/(M).$$

The simple classical model develops the so-called quantity theory of money by making two important assumptions:

1. Changes in the money supply do not affect the level of real output, Q.
2. The velocity of the money supply, V, is fixed or changes so slowly with changes in payment mechanisms as to be effectively fixed.

Referring to the equation in Chapter 3,

$$\% \Delta \text{GNP} = \% \Delta M + \% \Delta V,$$
$$\% \Delta \text{GNP} = \% \Delta P + \% \Delta Q,$$
$$\% \Delta P + \% \Delta Q = \% \Delta M + \% \Delta V.$$

The two assumptions of the simple classical model imply that

1) $\% \Delta Q = 0$, and 2) $\% \Delta V = 0$.

This means $\% \Delta P = \% \Delta M$. The naive quantity theory states that an equal percentage change in prices will result from any given change in the money supply: a 10% increase in the money supply causes GNP to rise by the full 10% since the velocity is constant. The 10% rise in GNP is fully reflected in inflation since the quantity of real output is fixed.

If there *were* changes in velocity due to the development of money substitutes or changes in the public's desire to hold idle precautionary balances, the change would impact on the price level. The classical model assumes a vertical aggregate supply curve ($\% \Delta Q = 0$), so that any change in total expenditures is fully reflected in prices ($\% \Delta P = \% \Delta \text{GNP}$).

In terms of general equilibrium, the classical model matches any excess supply of money with an excess demand for goods; that is, if $\Delta M > H$, then $I > S$ in our equation $(I - S) + (L - B) + (H - \Delta M) = 0$. If people find that they have money balances larger than they desire, they will buy goods (not bonds) with the excess. They will spend the extra money for real investment or consumption. Hence we get a price and not an interest rate effect. As we will see, the Keynesian model assumes that excess money balances will be used to buy bonds instead of goods and hence will result in falling interest rates instead of rising prices.

The early British economists formulated the quantity theory of money in a slightly different way. They reached identical conclusions but their model is somewhat more useful in studying the dynamics of the impact of changes in the money supply. Instead of assuming velocity to be constant, they assumed the *stock* of money that the public desired to hold was a constant proportion of GNP, k. The so-called Cambridge k (England, not Massachusetts) was defined as

$$M = (k)(\text{GNP}),$$
$$k = (M)/(\text{GNP}).$$

In mechanical definitional terms k is simply the reciprocal of velocity. The idea, however, that the desired stock of money is a function of the level of GNP has a bit more behavioral content than simply assuming a constant velocity.

We can rewrite the Cambridge quantity theory equation to isolate the price-deflated value of the money stock as

$$k = (M)/[(P)(Q)],$$
$$(k)(Q) = (M)/(P).$$

The demand for "real" money balances is a constant proportion, k, of real GNP, Q. The supply of real money balances is, of course, the money supply divided by the price level as given on the right-hand side of the equation, $(M)/(P)$.

We can now see an important truth in the quantity theory by observing how the public's desire (or lack of it) for holding cash balances impacts on the price level. Indeed, in the pure quantity theory the public essentially sets the price level in seeking to achieve the desired level of cash balances.

Let us say $Q = 100$ and $k = .25$. If the money supply were \$25 the price index would be 1. The money supply in real terms is equal to 25 units of output. As a subsidiary piece of information, let us note that wheat is selling for \$3 per bushel. One dollar is worth one-third of a bushel of wheat in real terms.

Now let us say that collectively the public decides that instead of cash balances equal to 25% of real GNP ($k = .25$), they only want cash balances equal to 12 1/2% of real GNP ($k = .125$). Each person can only draw down his or her cash balances by spending the money, in which case someone else will be holding it. Collectively the public's desire for smaller cash balances is not going to reduce the total number of dollars in circulation. If we stick to our classical assumptions that excess money balances are used only to buy goods (not bonds), and the total amount of output in the economy is fixed, then prices must rise as people try to get rid of their excess money balances.

In this case we started with

$$(.25)(100) = (25)/(1),$$

and our new equilibrium will be

$$(.125)(100) = (25)/(2).$$

The price level is now 2 instead of 1. If the price of wheat doubled along with everything else, then it is now $6 per bushel. A dollar is now worth only one-sixth of a bushel of wheat. The excess money balances are now gone — they were removed not by reducing the number of dollars in circulation but by reducing their value. Although this is far from the whole story as far as money is concerned, it does contain some important truths. The public's demand for money influences total expenditures directly, inflation will tend to be self-limiting as the value of a fixed money supply declines, and so on.

An important point to reiterate here is that we have two different ways to say the same thing and economists tend to bounce back and forth between them: money stocks and velocity. We can say a credit transaction increases the stock of liquid assets and lowers the demand for the existing (narrowly defined) stock of money — the Cambridge k gets smaller. Or we can say a credit transaction enables us to use the existing money stock more efficiently by turning it over more times — velocity gets larger. In either case there is an increase in the supply of money or a decrease in the demand for it and inflationary pressure is generated. Sometimes the discussion is facilitated by speaking of the stock of money and liquid assets and sometimes the concept of velocity is more illuminating. We shall use both.

At this point we reiterate the primary theorem of monetary theory, "Everybody gotta be somewhere." Money is not used up in transactions. The total existing money stock must be held by someone. Ex post, the supply must equal the demand. In the classical model, if ex ante the supply is greater than the demand, an excess demand for goods will result in upward pressure on the price level. The price level will rise and reduce the real value of the money stock until ex ante supply is equal to demand. The equilibrium price level is determined by the money supply and the public's desire to hold it.

Keynesian Monetary Theory

The classical economists believed money was held only for transaction purposes. Keynes contended money was also held as an investment for "speculative" purposes. The classical economists felt that any idle balances would be converted into real or financial assets to earn the owner some rate of return. In formulating his monetary theory Keynes considered the major alternative to holding cash balances to be other financial assets, say bonds. In other words, if ex ante the supply of money were greater than the demand for it, the holders of the excess money balances would lend the excess by buying bonds. In our general equilibrium equation this implies that if $\Delta M > H$, then $L > B$.

Keynes accepted the classical economist contention that the transaction demand for cash balances would be dependent on the level of economic activity. He contended that speculative demand was a function of the level of interest rates. Specifically, he envisioned speculators as perpetually trying to decide whether to hold cash or bonds. If speculators felt bond prices were likely to rise in the near future (interest rates likely to fall), they would want to shift from cash to bonds. Conversely, if speculators felt the next move in bond prices were likely to be down (interest rates up), then they would shift out of bonds and into cash. Strictly in terms of interest rates, one can say that if speculators think interest rates are about to fall, they want to reduce their cash balances now and "lock in" those nice high rates. If rates are expected to rise, they stay in cash until rates go up and then lend.

The Keynesian theory takes the position that participants in the money and bond markets have an idea of some average level around which interest rates will fluctuate. The higher the rates rise the more likely they are about to fall. The lower they go, the more speculators think the next move has to be up. Making the demand for cash balances a negative function of interest rates is based on two assumptions.

1. Speculators will want to hold bonds if they expect rates to fall and cash if they expect rates to rise.

2. The higher rates rise the more speculators feel rates must soon fall, and the lower rates go the more it is felt they must soon rise.

Referring to Fig. 4.1, if interest rates were relatively high at r_1 the demand for money would be relatively low at M_1 because holding bonds would be considered attractive. If, on the other hand, rates were very low, say r_2, the demand for cash balances would be relatively high at M_2. Bonds are unattractive at these low rates because of the feeling that rates must rise soon. Bond prices will fall and a gain will have been made by having held cash.

The dynamics of the Keynesian framework are similar to the classical except that interest rates (the price of bonds) adjust instead of the price of goods. As indicated in Fig. 4.2, we can depict this as a simple supply-demand model with the supply of money fixed. If we are in equilibrium with the money supply at M_1 and the interest rate at r_1 when suddenly the

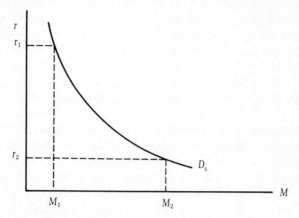

FIGURE 4.1 A Money Demand Curve.

money supply is increased to M_2, the supply curve will shift from $S_\$$ to $S'_\$$. The comparative statics of the matter is that the interest rate falls from r_1 to r_2. Let us consider the dynamics of this move in the interest rate. When money supply is increased, holders of cash find their balances excessive. In Keynesian analysis the public tries to reduce excess cash balances by lending them out, buying bonds. As noted previously, in our general equilibrium equation,

$$(I - S) + (L - B) + (H - \Delta M) = 0,$$

we have $\Delta M > H$ being offset by $L > B$. The excess supply of money is matched by an excess demand for bonds. As the price of bonds is bid up interest rates fall. As interest rates fall more and more speculators believe

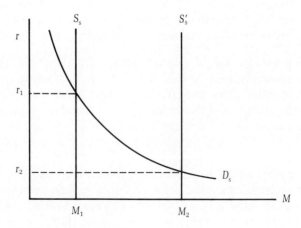

FIGURE 4.2 A Shift in the Money Supply.

that holding money is a good investment. A new equilibrium is reached when the demand for cash balances moves from M_1 to M_2, which can only happen when the interest rate moves from r_1 to r_2.

As in the classical model, the public cannot really get rid of excess cash balances. In trying to do so they generate a demand for cash bonds. This process keeps up until ex ante demand has risen to match the available supply.

We noted earlier that the Keynesians do accept the transaction demand for cash balances. Part of the demand for money therefore depends on the level of interest rates, and part of it depends on the level of economic activity. Hence, if we draw our demand curve on a graph with the rate of interest on the vertical axis, we must have a different demand curve for each level of GNP. Figure 4.3 illustrates this with GNP_2 being a higher level of economic activity than GNP_1. At the lower level of economic activity the total demand for money (transactions and speculative) is M_1. With an increase in GNP to GNP_2 the speculative demand would remain unchanged if the interest rate stayed at r_1. The transaction demand required to support the new level of economic activity would increase the total demand by enough to increase it from M_1 to M_2.

Figure 4.4 depicts a situation in which the money supply is held constant as the level of economic activity rises from GNP_1 to GNP_2. The comparative statics indicate that the interest rate will rise from r_1 to r_2. The interest rate increase is required in order to *reduce* the speculative demand for money so that the transaction demand can *increase* sufficiently to finance the higher level of economic activity.

The dynamics of this mechanism are of interest. As the level of transactions demand for cash balances rises along with the rise in the level of economic activity, the ex ante demand for money exceeds the supply. Those requiring additional transactions balances seek to borrow the difference so

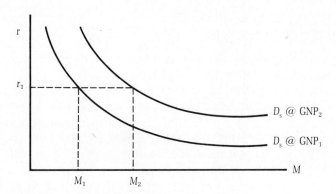

FIGURE 4.3 A Shift in Transactions Demand.

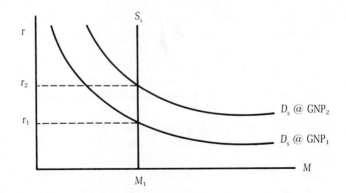

FIGURE 4.4   A Shift in Demand, Fixed Supply.

that ex ante borrowing exceeds lending at the original rate of interest. In attempting to obtain funds the borrowers sell bonds at cut-rate prices, the rate of interest rises, the speculative demand for money falls, and this makes additional balances available for transactions. In the new equilibrium the total supply and demand of money are unchanged but the composition of the demand is changed. Money has been moved from speculative balances to transaction balances by a rise in the interest rate.

We have discussed Keynesian monetary theory strictly in terms of the cash balances approach. As noted earlier, cash balances demand and velocity are really just different ways of looking at the same thing. We could formulate Keynesian monetary theory in terms of velocity just as well. The Keynesian theory amends the classical assumption of fixed velocity to make velocity a positive function of the interest rate. If interest rates rise velocity will rise. A higher level of GNP can be supported with a fixed money supply if interest rates are allowed to rise. The higher rates will provide the incentive for the public to move the money around faster.

Term Structure of Interest Rates

We have been referring to *the* interest rate of "the level of interest rates" as a single variable. There are, of course, a whole multitude of interest rates. At any point in time, rates on different credit transactions may vary because of: risk of default (people think the government has a greater ability to repay a loan than a college professor), tax status (state and local government bonds are generally exempt from federal income tax), and the *term to maturity*. This last classification refers to the length of time for which the money is borrowed. Even the same borrower will pay a different rate on a loan which is to be repaid in three months than on one to be repaid in thirty years.

To depict the term structure of interest rates we generally use a *yield curve:* a graphic presentation of the rates paid on loans that differ in maturity but are otherwise identical. The most common yield curve is one showing yields on U.S. government securities from three-month Treasury Bills to thirty-year bonds. Some historical yield curves are shown in Fig. 4.5.

The term structure of interest rates is being introduced at this point because the predominant theory of term structure, the *expectations theory,* is similar to the Keynesian theory of the demand for money. One criticism of Keynesian monetary theory is that it makes no distinction between a financial asset maturing in three days and one maturing in thirty years. The security maturing in three days, however, is considerably more liquid than is one maturing in thirty years. Keynes's contention was that interest was payment for relinquishing liquidity. If we extend this theory to the term structure of interest rates, we would expect long-term securities to have a higher rate of interest than short-term securities. This would result in a positively sloped yield curve like those for 1977 and 1978 in Fig. 4.5.

A positively sloped yield curve is in fact referred to as "normal," although it is obvious that actual yield curves come in a wide variety of shapes. A plot of yield curves for some homogeneous group of securities in the United States over the last forty years looks something like a bowl of spaghetti. However, out of very diverse experience one can discern some degree of common cyclical behavior. Usually in periods of "easy money" and recession (periods of reduced levels of economic activity), the yield curve will be positively sloped (1977 and 1978). In periods of "tight money" and economic boom (periods of increased levels of economic activity), the yield curve may well be negatively sloped (1974 and 1979).

Why these curves are shaped like this at these particular points in the business cycle can be at least partly explained in terms of speculators who behave very much like the Keynesian money market participants we discussed. You will recall that those speculators bounced back and forth between cash and bonds depending on whether they expected rates to rise or fall. The same sort of behavior is expected of an investor considering whether to buy a three-month Treasury Bill or a thirty-year bond. If one buys the bond and rates rise, the price of the bond will fall. The change in interest rates would be irrelevant if one held the bond to maturity thirty years hence. But if one has to sell the bond prior to maturity, one would have to take a capital loss. With the three-month Treasury Bill, however, the investor is sure to get his or her principal back intact at the end of three months regardless of what happens to interest rates in the interim.

As indicated in Fig. 4.5, the short-term rates fluctuate a great deal more than the long-term rates: from over 10% to 4.5% for short-term rates, compared to 9 1/4% to 7 3/4% for long-term rates. Despite the fact that short-term *rates* fluctuate more than long-term *rates,* long-term bond *prices* fluctuate a great deal more than short-term *prices*. This is partly explainable

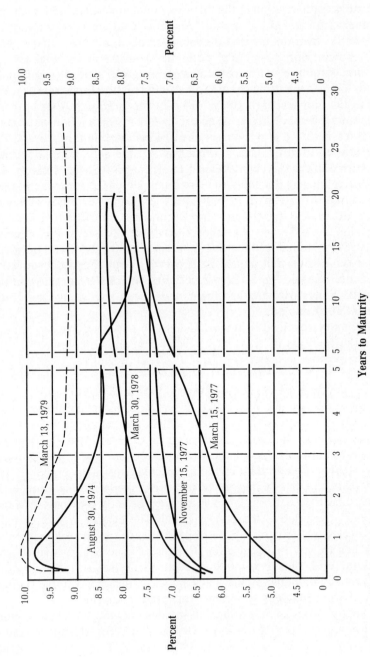

FIGURE 4.5   Yields on U.S. Government Securities. (Prepared by the Federal Reserve Bank of St. Louis.)

in terms of the arithmetic of bond prices. A small change in yield will alter the price on a short-term security only by a small amount. On a 20-year security the price will change a great deal. For example, if a security has one full year to maturity and has a coupon rate of 5% (pays $5 per $100 per year), it need only fall to $99 per $100 to yield 6%. A bond with 20 years to maturity must fall to $88 to raise its yield from 5% to 6%. To lower the yield from 5% to 4% the 1-year security need only rise to $101, but the 20-year security must go to $114. The possible gain from a 1% fall in rates is only 1% on a 1-year security. It is 14% on a 20-year security. A 1% rise would only lower the price of a 1-year security by the same 1%. Holding a 20-year security risks a 12% loss for the same change in yield to maturity. Additionally, within one year the shorter-term security will mature with no loss, regardless of how high rates rise. In later chapters we will look in more detail at actual historical changes in short- and long-term rates. At this point we need only note that calculations of actual realized yields for holding a security for any given period show increased variation with increased term to maturity.

Such variations in price mean that short-term securities are more liquid than long-term securities. Assuming liquidity to be a desirable characteristic in a financial asset, why would anyone want long-term securities? There are two possible reasons.

1. The investor feels that interest rates are about to fall; long-term bond prices will rise creating large profits for their holders.
2. The investor prefers certainty of yields over the long-term to liquidity.

Let us consider each of these in turn. The first is the explanation of the term structure we referred to earlier, the expectations theory. The second refers to what is known as the *market segmentation* theory.

The expectations theory assumes, quite reasonably, that speculators will want to buy long-term securities when they think rates are more likely to fall than to rise. Conversely, when they feel rates are more likely to rise than fall, they would prefer to hold short-term securities. The buyers of securities are the lenders. They are only half the market. We must also consider the source of the supply of the securities, the borrowers. They would like to minimize their interest costs through time. To do this they want to issue long-term securities when rates are low. When rates are high they want to borrow short-term to maintain their ability to refinance at lower rates later. Ex post, the borrowers and lenders must get together for transactions to transpire.

What happens when both lenders and borrowers have similar expectations? Refer again to Fig. 4.5, and the high interest rate, tight money yield curves of 1974 and 1979. We said that this structure prevails at the peak of the business cycle. Interest rates are generally believed to be at all-time high levels. Both potential borrowers and potential lenders feel that there will soon be a general decline in rates. If short-term and long-term rates were equal, the borrowers would all want to borrow short-term in order to refinance at lower rates later. If short-term and long-term rates were equal, the lenders would all want to buy long-term securities in order to lock in those high rates or obtain the capital gains resulting from the rise in long-term securities prices as rates fell. At the peak of the business cycle we have the demand for funds concentrated in the short-term market and the supply of funds concentrated in the long-term market. Ex ante demand for funds exceeds supply in the short-term market and supply exceeds demand in the long-term market. The relative levels of the short-term and long-term rate must generate an equilibrium. Obviously, short-term rates will rise to the level required to discourage some borrowers and encourage some lenders. In the long-term market we have to have rates that are low relative to the short-term so that some borrowers will prefer to go into the long-term market and some lenders will prefer the higher short-term rate.

The low interest rate easy money yield curves in Fig. 4.5 in 1977 and 1978 exist because of widespread expectations that rates will be higher in the future. If short-term rates equalled long-term rates there would be an excess supply of short-term funds and an excess demand for long-term funds. The borrowers would want to borrow long-term while rates were low. Lenders would want to invest in short-term securities until rates rose. Ex post, we find equilibrium achieved by short-term rates being low relative to long-term rates. This premium of long-term rates over short-term rates will encourage some lenders to invest in long-term securities for the higher yield and discourage some would-be long-term borrowers.

It is important to recognize that the role of expectations in influencing the shape of the yield curve is *not* dependent on the accuracy of the forecast implied by these expectations. It has frequently been the case in the U.S. economy during the last thirty years that the yield curve would imply rates falling in the next year, and in fact they would rise. Just as we assume the participants in all the markets we analyze behave in the manner they *believe* will maximize their economic welfare, this does not mean they succeed. That would require perfect forecasting, which you will surely realize is impossible by the time you finish this book.

The expectations theory of the term structure of interest rates was discussed entirely in terms of the supply and demand for funds. We leave it as an exercise for the student to recast the entire exposition using the supply and demand for financial assets.

Earlier we noted there were two reasons for sacrificing the liquidity of a short-term investment by lending long-term. The first was the expectation that rates are about to fall and we discussed the expectations theory. The other reason for lending long-term is to obtain what the British economist

Joan Robinson calls "income certainty" as opposed to "capital certainty." Capital certainty is really another name for liquidity and is obtained by investing short-term. Very small price fluctuations and a return to cash every time the short-term security matures assures the investors that should they want to withdraw their capital anytime over the next twenty years, the principal would be available with little or no chance of loss. However, the investor in short-term financial assets certainly does not have income certainty. If you were to ask investors in short-term financial assets what rate of return they will earn over the next twenty years they would likely have to reply that they had no idea. Investors in twenty-year securities are in exactly the opposite position. They have income certainty but no capital certainty. Investors in twenty-year government bonds can tell you at the time of investment exactly what they will earn over the next twenty years. They cannot, however, tell you what they will realize from their investments if they should have to sell the securities on the open market before they mature. That depends on what happens to interest rates.

Some investors desire income certainty more than liquidity. They seek to minimize their risk to interest rate fluctuations by matching up the term to maturity of their assets and liabilities — and they happen to have long-term liabilities. Pension funds and insurance companies commit themselves today to pay a fixed dollar amount in ten, twenty, or thirty years, in exchange for a fixed number of dollars paid to them today. It would be very risky indeed for them to be exposed to the fluctuations of short-term interest rates over this time period. Instead they assure themselves of, say, a 7% return for twenty years, by investing in a twenty-year security. They can thereby promise to pay a certain amount of money twenty years hence. They might be able to earn a higher rate by investing in short-term securities if rates rose. They could then meet their commitment and make extraordinary profits besides. Then again, rates might fall and they would earn less and be thrown into bankruptcy (if not jail) for failing to meet their commitments.

It is therefore reasonable to expect segments of the market, groups of borrowers and lenders, to have strong preferences for long- or short-term borrowing and lending. The market segmentation theory of the term structure of interest rates merely contends that the relative levels of long- and short-term rates are determined by the supply and demand pressure generated by these groups in each segment of the market.

All term structure theorists generally feel that there is on average a positive liquidity preference. "All other things being equal," investors would rather invest short-term and borrowers would rather borrow long-term. In fact, the yield curve has historically been positively sloped more of the time than it has been negatively sloped. On average, long-term securities yield more than short-term securities — hence, the term "normal" for the positively sloped yield curve.

● Questions for Discussion

1. Should consumer credit, represented by plastic cards, be counted as part of the money supply? Should we consider counting total credit extended or total credit available but not yet used? Why?

2. Why is a foreign car a more liquid asset than a set of surgical tools costing an equal amount?

3. Why is a short-term security more liquid than a long-term security?

4. Discuss what you think would happen if Congress passed a law requiring that reserve requirements be reduced to zero for all member banks and other financial institutions required to keep reserves with the Federal Reserve system.

5. In what two distinct ways is "money" created in the U.S. economy?

6. Illustrate the quantity theory of money using the following equation: $Y = (P)(Q) = (M)(V)$. Specify the two necessary assumptions. How close do you think they come to being met in reality? In the short run? In the long run?

7. In a strict classical system, total expenditures cannot increase without an increase in the money supply. In a Keynesian system total expenditures may increase without an increase in the money supply. How? Where does the additional liquidity required for the additional transactions come from?

8. If you expect a general increase in interest rates, would you prefer to buy a ninety-day Treasury bill or a thirty-year U.S. government bond? Why?

● Exercises

1. Assume a banking system such as that in the United States. The legal reserve requirement on deposits is 20%. Consider the two simplified balance sheets for a *banking system* as shown in Case A and Case B:

Case A			Case B	
Assets	Liabilities		Assets	Liabilities
Reserves $200	$500 Deposits		Reserves $100	$500 Deposits
Loans $300			Loans $400	

1. Starting in the condition shown, if loan demand suddenly increased to such an extent that all reserves were fully utilized, what would be the maximum possible *increase* in loans and deposits in each case?

2. Assume:

   Required bank reserves against demand deposits are 10%;
   Required reserves against time deposits are 7 1/2%;
   For every $1 of demand deposits, the public will hold $1 in cash and $2 of time deposits; and
   The banks stay "loaned up," no excess reserves.

   If there is an increase in the monetary base of $2,000,000, what happens to:
   a. Demand deposits

b. Time deposits?
c. Public's cash holdings?
d. M1?
e. M2?
f. Total bank loans?

3. Assume:

All banks must keep 20% reserves against demand deposits and a 5% reserve against time deposits;
The public keeps 1/3 of its 3 most liquid assets in the form of currency, 1/3 in demand deposits, and 1/3 in the form of time deposits with commercial banks; and
The banks keep no excess reserves.

If government fiscal and monetary policy expand the monetary base by $1,000,000, what happens to:
a. Demand deposits?
b. Time deposits?
c. Currency in the hands of the public?
d. Total bank loans?

4. State whether each of the following is True or False *and why:*
   a. The banking system creates money just like the federal government creates money.
   b. In a recession it is to be expected that short-term interest rates would fall more rapidly than long-term rates.
   c. The Federal Reserve together with the Treasury determines the amount of currency in the hands of the nonbank public.

● Source Note

[1]Joan Robinson, *The Rate of Interest.* London: MacMillan, 1952.

● Selected Additional Readings

Bernstein, Jeffrey I., and Fisher, Douglas. The demand for money and the term structure of interest rates: A portfolio approach. *Southern Economic Journal* Vol. 48, No. 2 (October 1981).

Dornbusch, Rudiger, and Fischer, Stanley. *Macroeconomics* (2nd ed.) New York: McGraw-Hill, 1981. Chapters 4, 7, and 8.

Gordon, Robert J. *Macroeconomics* (2nd ed.) Boston: Little, Brown, 1981. Chapter 4.

Kessel, Reuben A. *The Cyclical Behavior of the Term Structure of Interest Rates.* New York: National Bureau of Economic Research, 1965.

Keynes, John Maynard. *The General Theory of Employment Interest and Money.* New York: Harcourt, Brace, 1936. Chapter 17.

Lutz, Friedrich A. *The Theory of Interest.* Chicago: Aldine, 1968.

Tobin, James. "Commercial banks as creators of 'money.'" In Deane Carson, ed. *Banking and Monetary Studies*. Homewood, Ill.: Richard D. Irwin, 1963. Reprinted in Ronald L. Teigen, ed. *Readings in Money, National Income and Stabilization Policy*. Homewood, Ill.: Richard D. Irwin, 1978.

_____. The interest elasticity of the transaction demand for cash. *Review of Economics and Statistics*. August 1966.

Theory of Monetary and Fiscal Policy

5

Definitions

Much debate centers on the relative effectiveness of monetary and fiscal policy without very precise definitions of what is meant. We defined monetary policy earlier as manipulating the money supply in order to influence the level of economic activity, and fiscal policy as the manipulation of government expenditures and taxes for the same purpose. In Chapter 3 we showed how the two are connected by what we might call the government's budget constraint. The government must fund all its expenditures in one of three ways: taxes, borrowing, or expanding the monetary base. In algebraic terms

$$G = T + \Delta D + \Delta MB.$$

We can rearrange the terms to put the fiscal policy variables, G and T, on one side and the monetary policy variables, ΔD and ΔMB, on the other:

$$G - T = \Delta D + \Delta MB.$$

What then *is* fiscal policy, as distinct from monetary policy? Changing only G and T? If so, fiscal policy would always require a balanced budget. If government expenditures, G, are increased and you do not want any monetary impact, you must increase taxes, T, by an equal amount. Otherwise some change is implied for ΔD and ΔMB. In strictly mechanical terms let us see exactly what the government's policy alternatives are. Since the equation above must hold for each and every accounting period, any change in one variable implies a change in at least one other. The simplest governmental policy we can consider must involve at least two of the four variables. There are six possible pairs of these four variables. The matrix in Table 5.1 lays out the six possible policies. In the matrix we have given each policy a name and a number. Also, we have indicated whether the two variables involved must move together ($+$), or in opposite directions ($-$). For example, *pure fiscal policy* (1), involves government expenditures, G, and taxes, T. If one is increased or decreased, the other must be moved in the same direction by the same amount if we want to keep the policy confined to these two variables. Since they move in the same direction we

TABLE 5.1 Monetary and Fiscal Policy Alternatives

	G	T	ΔD	ΔMB
G		(1) Pure (+) Fiscal Policy	(2) Dept- (+) Financed Expenditures	(3) New- (+) Money–Financed Expenditures
T			(4) (−) Tax/Debt Substitution	(5) (−) Tax/Money Substitution
ΔD				(6) Pure (−) Monetary Policy
ΔMB				

have a (+) in the matrix. On the other hand, *pure monetary policy* (6), has a (−) since if we increase the monetary base, ΔMB, we must be decreasing the publicly held debt, ΔD. We now want to discuss each alternative policy in turn and examine what each one's impact on the level of aggregate demand might be.

Pure Fiscal Policy

As we noted, pure fiscal policy is a balanced budget change in government expenditures and taxes. Conventional economics presumes that an equal increase in government expenditures and taxes will increase aggregate demand. The total impact will be the sum of a stimulative impact of the increase in government expenditures and the negative or depressing impact of an increase in taxes. The orthodox economics is that the positive government expenditures multiplier, $(\Delta Y)/(\Delta G)$, will be larger than the negative tax multiplier, $(\Delta Y)/(\Delta T)$.

That the *balanced budget multiplier,* as this mechanism is called, is positive, seems reasonable. Money is being taken from taxpayers who presumably have a propensity to consume less than 100%, and it is placed in the hands of a government that will spend every cent of it. A balanced budget expansion of government expenditures does imply a propensity to consume 100%. Although it is likely that much of the money to pay the taxes will come from reduced consumption expenditures, some of it most likely will come from reduced savings. To the extent that taxes are paid by reducing savings, a policy of a balanced budget change in government expenditures and taxes will have an impact on aggregate demand in the same direction as the change in government expenditures.

The other way to look at this policy is with a decrease in government expenditures and taxes. The cut in expenditures reduces aggregate demand while the tax cut increases it. By similar reasoning, the decline in the expenditures by the government will not be completely offset by the expenditures stimulated by the tax cut, since some of the proceeds from the tax cut would be saved instead of spent. Hence, an equal cut in expenditures and taxes would be deflationary.

Debt-Financed Expenditures

With this policy, a change in government expenditures, G, is matched by a change in the publicly held debt, ΔD. For example, a stimulative policy would presumably be to increase government expenditures without a corresponding increase in taxes, T, or the monetary base, ΔMB. In this case, also, we have potentially offsetting effects on the level of aggregate demand. Certainly the increase in government expenditures will increase total expenditures and thereby aggregate demand, but the sale of the government securities to the public will presumably raise interest rates. The increased level of interest rates will discourage private investment, which will reduce aggregate demand.

The depressing effect on investment of increased government expenditures financed by debt is known as the *crowding-out effect*. The magnitude of the crowding-out effect depends sequentially on:

How much the interest rate is increased by the increase in debt, $(\Delta r)/(\Delta D)$,

How sensitive investment is to the interest rate, $(\Delta I)/(\Delta r)$, and

The size of the investment multiplier we discussed in Chapter 3, $(\Delta Y)/(\Delta I)$.

Algebraically, the effect on aggregate demand, ΔY, of an increase in debt, ΔD, can be summed up as the product of these effects:

$$(\Delta Y)/(\Delta D) = (\Delta r/\Delta D)\,(\Delta I/\Delta r)\,(\Delta Y/\Delta I).$$

The effect is clearly negative since the first and last terms are positive and the middle term, $(\Delta I/\Delta r)$, is the negative slope of the marginal efficiency of capital schedule.

Regarding the total effect of this policy of debt-financed expenditures, the question is: Is the positive fiscal policy effect, $(\Delta Y)/(\Delta G)$, greater than the negative monetary policy effect, $(\Delta Y)/(\Delta D)$? Algebraically, we can phrase this question as

$$(\Delta Y)/(\Delta G) - (\Delta r/\Delta D)\,(\Delta I/\Delta r)\,(\Delta Y/\Delta I) > 0?$$

If we assume the multiplier effect of government expenditures, $(\Delta Y)/(\Delta G)$, is the same size as the private investment multiplier, $(\Delta Y/\Delta I)$, then we can rewrite our algebraic question as

$$(\Delta Y)/(\Delta G) \, [1 - (\Delta r/\Delta D) \, (\Delta I/\Delta r)] > 0?$$

The entire expression will be positive if the expression inside the brackets is positive; that is, if

$$1 - (\Delta I)/(\Delta D) > 0, \text{ which requires that } \Delta D > \Delta I.$$

For any given time the increase in the debt necessary to finance an increase in government expenditures will be equal in amount to the expenditures' increase; that is, $\Delta D = \Delta G$. Our conclusion is that the impact of this policy will be positive if the increase in government expenditures is greater in dollar amount than the decrease in private investment brought about by the rise in interest rates, $\Delta G > \Delta I$. Whether the monetary policy side, the crowding-out effect, offsets the stimulative impact of the fiscal policy side depends on whether an increase in government expenditures of $1 will discourage less than $1 worth of private expenditures. It will necessitate the issuance of $1 worth of debt, but will that debt increase interest rates so much that private investment is reduced by $1 or more?

The crowding-out effect is generally assumed to be less than 100% in the short run. A debt-financed increase in government expenditures is believed to be inflationary. A cut in government expenditures for goods and services and a corresponding reduction in the national debt is believed to be deflationary.

New-Money–Financed Expenditures

New-money–financed expenditures are probably the most potent of the six possibilities available to the government, since it combines a fiscal policy action and a monetary policy action in such a way that they are both affecting aggregate demand in the same direction. If the government increases its expenditures for goods and services, it is directly increasing aggregate demand. Financing these expenditures with an increase in the monetary base will create an excess supply of money. If you are a classical economist, you will expect the excess money supply to manifest itself in an excess demand for goods, a direct increase in aggregate demand. If you are a Keynesian, the excess supply of money will create an excess demand for financial assets (lending), which will drive down interest rates and bring forth increased investment expenditures.

Taking the Keynesian approach we can express the impact of this policy as the following sum of two terms:

$$(\Delta Y/\Delta G) + (\Delta r/\Delta MB) \, (\Delta I/\Delta r) \, (\Delta Y/\Delta I).$$

The first term is the fiscal policy effect of the simple government expenditures multiplier, $\Delta Y/\Delta G$. The second term is the monetary policy component and algebraically reduces to the effect of a change in the monetary base on the level of aggregate demand, $\Delta Y/\Delta MB$. We have broken the monetary policy component down into the following parts: the effect of the change in the monetary base on the interest rate, $\Delta r/\Delta MB$; the effect of the interest rate on the level of investment, $\Delta I/\Delta r$; and, finally, the investment multiplier, $\Delta Y/\Delta I$.

Both $\Delta Y/\Delta G$ and $\Delta Y/\Delta MB$ are clearly positive, so it is obvious what constitutes a stimulative or restrictive policy in this case. If we want to increase aggregate demand, we increase government expenditures and the monetary base. If we want to restrain aggregate demand, we reduce government expenditures and the monetary base.

Tax/Debt Substitution

Tax/debt substitution is different from the preceding three policies in that the two variables involved must move in opposite directions, as indicated by the $(-)$ in the matrix. If we cut taxes to stimulate aggregate demand but do not want to change government expenditures or the monetary base, we must offset the tax cut with an increase in the stock of government debt outstanding. The fiscal policy side of this move, the tax cut, is clearly stimulative. The monetary policy side, the increase in government borrowing, can potentially raise interest rates, discourage investment, and restrain aggregate demand. The stimulative impact of the tax cut might be partly or totally offset by the increase in government borrowing.

Algebraically, we can state the impact of this policy as the sum of the following two terms:

$$(\Delta Y/\Delta T) + (\Delta r/\Delta D)\,(\Delta I/\Delta r)\,(\Delta Y/\Delta I).$$

The fiscal policy part of this expression, $(\Delta Y/\Delta T)$, is negative. If taxes are cut, aggregate demand will rise and vice-versa. The monetary policy portion, which reduces to $(\Delta Y/\Delta D)$, is also negative since it is made up of the product of two positive and one negative term. If the government's debt goes up, aggregate demand will go down and vice-versa. As indicated by the three parenthetical expressions, this negative relationship between government borrowing and aggregate demand can be broken down into the effect of the increased supply of debt on the interest rate, $(\Delta r/\Delta D)$; the effect of the increased interest rates on the level of investment, $(\Delta I/\Delta r)$; and the investment multiplier, $(\Delta Y/\Delta I)$. The first and last are both positive. The middle expression, the slope of the marginal efficiency of capital schedule, is negative.

Although both the monetary and fiscal policy effects are negative in this case, we have ambiguous results because the policy variables must move in opposite directions. A cut in taxes requires an increase in debt and an increase in taxes allows a reduction in debt. Again we have the potential of a crowding-out effect from the monetary policy side offsetting the effect of a tax change on the fiscal policy side. As with debt finance expenditures, the rise in interest rates might discourage enough investment to offset the stimulative effects, in this case, of a tax cut. We can phrase the question of whether the fiscal policy effect will dominate as

Is $(\Delta Y/\Delta T) + (\Delta r/\Delta D)\,(\Delta I/\Delta r)\,(\Delta Y/\Delta I) > 0$, if $\Delta T < 0$ and $\Delta D > 0$?

In this case we cannot reduce the problem to any simpler terms since there really are no grounds for assuming the tax multiplier, $\Delta Y/\Delta T$, and the investment multiplier, $\Delta Y/\Delta I$, are of the same size. If anything, we suspect $\Delta Y/\Delta I$ is larger than $\Delta Y/\Delta T$ since part of any tax cut is likely to be saved. Despite the obvious ambiguities, the economics profession generally believes that the link between a change in interest rates and the level of investment, $\Delta I/\Delta r$, takes a sufficiently long time and/or is sufficiently weak that the fiscal policy effect will prevail in the short run. We believe that for purposes of stabilization policy, a debt-financed tax cut is probably inflationary. Conversely, a tax increase used to reduce the national debt is probably deflationary in the short run.

Tax/Money Substitution

Tax/money substitution is another policy for which the policy variables must move in opposite directions as indicated by the $(-)$ in the matrix. If we cut taxes and do not wish to cut government expenditures or increase the national debt, we must increase the monetary base. Similarly, a tax increase not used to finance increased government expenditures or reduce the national debt will result in a decrease in the monetary base.

This policy, however, has no ambiguity as to the direction of its impact. Both a tax cut and an increase in the monetary base will be stimulative. A tax increase and a reduction in the monetary base will both tend to restrict aggregate demand. Algebraically, we have the sum of the two terms that will always be of the same sign

$(\Delta Y/\Delta T) + (\Delta r/\Delta MB)\,(\Delta I/\Delta r)\,(\Delta Y/\Delta I).$

If the selected fiscal policy part of the package is a reduction in taxes, the first term will be positive as the tax cut stimulates consumer and other expenditures. The monetary policy part of the package will then have to be an increase in the monetary base, which will lower interest rates since $\Delta r/\Delta MB$ is negative. The lower interest rates will encourage investment via the marginal efficiency of capital schedule, $\Delta I/\Delta r$. The last parenthetical expression is, of course, the investment multiplier, the impact of which will serve to reinforce the impact of the tax cut.

Pure Monetary Policy

This last policy alternative also has a $(-)$ in the matrix to indicate that if the monetary base is increased the level of government debt will have to be decreased. We could just as well have called this policy money/debt substitution, since that is what the government is doing when engaging in pure monetary policy.

In this case also it is obvious what will be a stimulative and what will be a restrictive policy. If the government buys back its own bonds with printing press money, both the increase in the supply of money and the demand for bonds will drive up the price of bonds — interest rates will fall. Algebraically, we can express the result as the sum of two very similar terms

$$(\Delta r/\Delta MB)\,(\Delta I/\Delta r\,(\Delta Y/\Delta I) + (\Delta r/\Delta D)\,(\Delta I/\Delta r)\,(\Delta Y/\Delta I),$$

or we can combine the two terms as

$$[(\Delta r/\Delta MB) + (\Delta r/\Delta D)]\,[(\Delta I/\Delta r)\,(\Delta Y/\Delta I)].$$

In this case we are merely saying that both the change in the monetary base and the change in the outstanding government debt, which must be in the opposite direction, will move the interest rate in the same direction. The interest rate will then impact on investment, which will in turn have the multiplier effect on aggregate demand. Increasing the monetary base while decreasing the publicly held debt will stimulate aggregate demand. Selling government debt to the public to reduce the monetary base will restrict aggregate demand.

In addition to the effect of the interest rate on investment, the neoclassical or monetarist economist would include a direct impact on aggregate demand of changes in the monetary base. As we noted in Chapter 4, this school of thought emphasizes that an excess money supply will be reflected in an excess demand for goods; people with extra cash balances might well try to get rid of them by buying goods as well as by trying to lend. Buying goods increases aggregate demand directly. Buying bonds increases aggregate demand indirectly, via lower interest rates and increased investment.

● Questions for Discussion

1. Comment on the statement that "If monetary policy is to be independent of fiscal policy, then the budget must be balanced."

2. Which of the following two policies do you think would have the greater impact on aggregate demand, and why?
   a. A $20 billion increase in government expenditures financed by an increase in the publicly held debt.
   b. A $20 billion increase in government expenditures financed by an increase in taxes.

● Exercises

1. Consider the policy action given on the left of Table 5.2. In the body of the table indicate what you think would happen to the variable described at the

TABLE 5.2 Direct Effects of Policy

Policy Action	Demand for goods minus the supply of goods $(D_g - S_g)$	Demand for bonds minus the supply of bonds $(D_b - S_b)$	Demand for cash balances minus the supply of money $(D_\$ - S_\$)$	Eventual impact on GNP
Government purchases and taxes increased by an equal amount	( )	( )	( )	( )
Government cuts expenditures for goods and services and uses the money to buy back government bonds from the nonbank public	( )	( )	( )	( )
Government increases its expenditures for goods and services and obtains the money by selling Treasury securities to the Federal Reserve System	( )	( )	( )	( )
Government cuts taxes and makes up the loss in revenue by issuing Treasury securities to the nonbank public	( )	( )	( )	( )
Government raises taxes and uses the proceeds to pay off Treasury securities held by the Federal Reserve Bank	( )	( )	( )	( )
The Federal Reserve Banks buy outstanding Treasury securities	( )	( )	( )	( )

TABLE 5.3 Policy Variables

Policies	Government expenditures	Tax revenues	Change in govt. debt	Change in monetary base	Change in the (demand)-(supply) of		
					Goods	Bonds	Money
1	( )	( )	( )	( )	( )	( )	( )
2	( )	( )	( )	( )	( )	( )	( )
3	( )	( )	( )	( )	( )	( )	( )
4	( )	( )	( )	( )	( )	( )	( )
5	( )	( )	( )	( )	( )	( )	( )
6	( )	( )	( )	( )	( )	( )	( )

Did you remember that you are trying to *restrain* the economy, *not* stimulate it?

top of each column. An increase should be indicated by a plus (+), a decrease by a minus (−), and a case in which the outcome is uncertain with the information given should be indicated with a question mark (?).

2. Consider the six federal government stabilization policies being used to *reduce* aggregate demand. Indicate in Table 5.3 what should be done to the policy variables to restrain the level of economic activity and the *direct* effects on the net demand for goods, bonds, or cash balances. Place a (+) in the parenthesis for an increase, a (−) for a decrease, and (0) for no change. Put *something* in each space.

Policies:

    1 Pure Fiscal Policy

    2 Debt-Financed Expenditures

    3 New-Money–Financed Expenditures

    4 Tax/Debt Substitution

    5 Tax/Money Substitution

    6 Pure Monetary Policy

● Selected Additional Readings

Christ, Carl F. A simple macroeconomic model with a government budget restraint. *Journal of Political Economy,* Vol. 76, No. 1 (January/February 1968).

Hiller, Brian. Does fiscal policy matter? The view from the government budget restraint. *Public Finance,* Vol. 32, No. 3 (1977).

Steindl, Frank G. Money and income: The view from the government budget restraint. *Journal of Finance,* Vol. 29, No. 4 (September 1974).

Some Theories of
the Business Cycle

6

Theories of the business cycle are so numerous and diverse that it is obvious that economic history has not revealed *the* theory. This is partly because no two business cycles are exactly alike. A particular theory may have great relevance for one cycle, but be almost irrelevant for another.

We mentioned in Chapter 1 that since one person's expenditure is another person's income it is not surprising that different sectors of the economy move together. If, for whatever reason, one sector of the economy starts to decline, other closely connected sectors of the economy will suffer also. This *diffusion* of the business cycle throughout the economy, whether a recession or a boom, has long been recognized and is well-documented statistically. Wesley Claire Mitchell, the founder of the National Bureau of Economic Research and an early student of the business cycle, began collecting the relevant statistics shortly after World War I, long before the government had any interest in such activities.[1] He was also an exponent of the *leading indicator* approach to business cycle forecasting, which we will discuss in Chapters 9 and 10.

The cumulative rise or fall in the general level of economic activity is very similar in most business cycle theories. The difficult part of constructing a theory is explaining the turning points. (Similarly, the difficulties with forecasting are the turning points.) When *will* the boom end and a recession begin? Clearly, at a turning point the system is not in equilibrium.

Another early business cycle theorist, Joseph Schumpeter, whose theories we will discuss in more detail later, defines equilibrium as "That . . . position . . . which, as long as the given data are maintained, tends to repeat itself in every period."[2] The term *equilibrium* has been used with widely varying meanings, but there is a common element in all its uses. That common element is repetition or constancy of some economic magnitude. Nothing is constant over the business cycle and nothing ever really returns to its starting place. That is what makes each business cycle unique. The economy grows and changes with each cycle — new products, new firms, new consumers. As Schumpeter observed, "As a matter of history, it is to physiology and zoology, not to mechanics, that our science is indebted for an analogous distinction which is at the threshhold of all clear thinking about economic matters."[3] The economy *grows* and changes. Certainly complete equilibrium in the physical universe would seem to be a cold, grey, stationary state of matter that can only be characterized as dead. We have growth and change and thereby fluctuations.

Nonrecurring fluctuations are the essence of disequilibrium and turning points are the essence of fluctuations. In looking at various business cycle theories we shall be particularly interested in how the turning points come about. To have a business cycle theory one must have inherent in the system a reason why each step upward helps bring about the necessary conditions for a downward movement; each decline into recession or depression must sow the seeds of recovery.

Schumpeter's Theory of Innovations

Schumpeter's approach to business cycle theory was to construct in great detail an economy that was in virtually complete macroeconomic equilibrium, the so-called *stationary state*. Business produces and people consume the same products year after year — without even any new ways invented to produce the old products. Of course, the population has to be stable and there can be no institutional changes whatsoever. Very likely a pretty dull economy in which to live but also probably one in which we would have nothing that could be called a business cycle.

Schumpeter then contrasts the real world with his stationary state to try to isolate the sources of economic fluctuations. He concludes that what most of us consider "progress" is at the source of the problem. Schumpeter feels that as "entrepreneurs" come up with new ways of doing things ("innovations") this disturbs equilibrium and creates fluctuations. Schumpeter distinguishes between "inventions" (which may gather dust for years) and "innovations," which are commercial applications of previous inventions. Historically in this country, new types of farm implements, the railroad, the auto, and the supply and use of electricity, have all been important innovations. In more modern times, important innovations have been transistors, computers, copying machines, communication satellites, and so on.

An innovation need not be a new product per se. A new method of marketing, distribution, or processing will have the same effect of disturbing the previous equilibrium as the introduction of a brand new product. In recent decades such innovations as discount stores, mutual funds, and fast food franchises have all had substantial impact.

Schumpeter felt that if these innovations came along randomly in a more or less steady stream we would not have the modern-day business cycle. However, such developments tend to be bunched up. There tend to be none; then there are a great many at once. The reason these instigators of change, the entrepreneurs, tend to be successful in clusters is because, as Schumpeter put it, "The appearance of one or a few entrepreneurs facilitates the appearance of others, and these the appearance of others, and these the appearance of more, in ever increasing numbers."[4] When you get electricity you create a market not just for light bulbs, but also for milking machines. When you have transistors you can build efficient computers; interstate highways bring motels and a real estate boom, and so on.

All innovations require investment, and, as noted earlier, investment has a greater short-run impact on aggregate demand than on aggregate supply. Moreover, the investment in a new industry will by its very nature tend to be cyclical. Initially, the level of investment will go from zero to whatever rate the entrepreneurs can promote to establish the required capital stock for this new industry. Afterwards, it will fall to the rate equal to the replacement of worn-out capital and the long-term growth rate of the economy. This is best illustrated by examining the concept of the *accelerator*.

Clark's Principle of Acceleration

In 1917 an eminent American economist by the name of J. M. Clark published an article entitled "Business Acceleration and the Law of Demand: A Technical Factor in Economic Cycles."[5] His technical factor was the observation that with a fixed capital-output ratio, a small percentage change in final sales would give rise to a large percentage change in investment.

Consider the simple example of 10 machines producing widgets. Each machine produces 100 widgets per year, and in this equilibrium state the demand for widgets is exactly 1,000 widgets per year. Each machine lasts ten years, at which point it must be replaced. In our equilibrium condition we have an industry of 10 machines with 1 wearing out each year. Demand for the industry that manufactures the machines, gross investment, is just 1 machine per year. Let us assume that suddenly demand for widgets increases 20% to 1,200 per year. To produce the extra 200 units per year, the widget industry would need 2 additional machines. Demand for widget-making machines would rise temporarily to 3 machines in one year and then fall back to 1.2 machines per year for replacement. Specifically, the time path of final sales and demand for investment goods would be as shown in Table 6.1. Graphically, the time path for sales of consumer goods and producer goods would be as shown in Fig. 6.1. Table 6.1 and Fig. 6.1 should make it apparent that if you are in the business of selling producer goods, you will experience the business cycle even if consumers only have a simple one-shot increase in demand.

This particular phenomenon is, of course, relevant to Schumpeter's business cycle theory. Each new innovation generates a temporary demand

TABLE 6.1 The Principle of Acceleration

Time Period	Sale of Widgets to Consumers		Sale of Machinery to Producers	
	Level	% Change	Level	% Change
1	1,000		1	
2	1,000	0	1	0
3	1,000	0	1	0
4	1,200	+ 20	3	+ 200
5	1,200	0	1.2	- 60
6	1,200	0	1.2	0

for the required investment goods. Once the initial investment has been made, the replacement market requires a lower rate of investment.

There are two additional complications. First, the distribution of information regarding the size of the market is far from perfect and the optimism in boom times of entrepreneurs is boundless. The creation of productive facilities for a new product or service typically overshoots the level required to meet the underlying demand. The demand for a resin to make a particular new plastic may seem insatiable to every chemical company

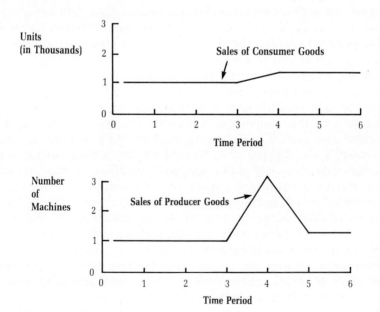

FIGURE 6.1 The Principle of Acceleration.

that decides to build a plant to produce it. However, when they all come on stream more or less simultaneously there is then *excess* capacity and no need for even replacement capacity for a number of years. Hence, the drop in demand is even more dramatic than that shown in Fig. 6.1, which depicts a case of no excess capacity.

Second, we have ignored the fact that these investment expenditures will, through the multiplier effect discussed in Chapter 3, create additional consumer demand. This additional consumer demand can in turn, via accelerator relationships in other industries, generate additional investment demand, and so on.

Samuelson's Multiplier-Accelerator Model

The interaction of the multiplier and the accelerator in a simple macroeconomic model was explored as long ago as 1939, in an article by Paul Samuelson, and is now included in most macroeconomic texts.[6] Under the particular formulation used by Samuelson, the level of aggregate demand is eventually described by a second-order difference equation; i.e., Y_t is a function of Y_{t-1} and Y_{t-2}. Depending on the assumptions regarding the size of the propensity to consume (which determines the size of the multiplier) and the capital-output ratio (which determines the accelerator), it is possible to obtain all the possible forms of cyclical behavior we discussed earlier in conjunction with first-order difference equations in Chapter 2. Small multiplier-accelerator values give a stable system that will return to equilibrium smoothly or with cycles of diminishing magnitude. Large values for the propensity to consume and the ratio of capital to output will give an unstable system that will depart even further from equilibrium.

Let us take a brief look at the algebra of Samuelson's multiplier-accelerator model as we will want to use an amended form of it to discuss the business cycle theory of the British economist, Sir John Hicks. We can briefly summarize such a model with three equations: (1) a statement of aggregate demand, (2) a consumption function, and (3) the accelerator relationship between induced investment and changes in the level of consumption.

(1) $Y_t = C_t + I_t + A_t$.

(2) $C_t = \alpha Y_{t-1}$.

(3) $I_t = \beta (C_t - C_{t-1})$.

A_t in equation (1) represents all autonomous expenditures. All government expenditures would fall into this category as well as consumption and investment expenditures that are independent of the level of economic activity, that is, consumption and investment expenditures not dependent on other parts of the economy. The parameter, α, is the propensity to consume out of income and β is the increment to the capital stock, I_t, required for an increase in consumption.

If we substitute equations (2) and (3) into equation (1) we obtain

(4) $Y_t = \alpha(1 + \beta)Y_{t-1} - (\alpha)(\beta)Y_{t-2} + A_t$.

The equilibrium level of Y_t is the value at which $Y_t = Y_{t-1} = Y_{t-2}$,

$Y_e = (A_t)/(1 - \alpha)$.

Notice the accelerator coefficient β does not influence the equilibrium level since in equilibrium the level of induced investment is zero. If $Y_{t-1} = Y_{t-2}$, then $C_t = C_{t-1}$ and $I_t = 0$.

Without going into all the details of the mathematical conditions for differing cyclical behavior, we can simply note at this point that if the product of the propensity to consume and the accelerator coefficient, (α) (β), is greater than 1.00 the system will be unstable. Once it departs from equilibrium it will depart ever further either cyclically or monotonically. If α and β are small enough so that their product is less than 1.00 the system will tend to move toward equilibrium either cyclically or smoothly.* The unstable multiplier-accelerator model was used by a British economist, Sir John Hicks, to create a complete business cycle theory.

Hicks's Theory of the Trade Cycle

In his book *The Trade Cycle*, J. R. Hicks assumed that the economy could be represented by a multiplier-accelerator mechanism with values for α and β such that the system was unstable.[7] However, for two good reasons he did not use the multiplier-accelerator mechanism to generate the turning points in the cycle. First, any simple difference-equation model would generate nice, neat cycles of constant periodicity, and economies obviously do not behave that way. Second, since he assumed values of the propensity to consume and the accelerator coefficient such that the system was unstable, cyclical movements would have to become ever larger in amplitude and, not being a Marxist, he did not feel that was an accurate description of modern industrialized economies either. Hicks assumed values for α and β such that if Y_t rose above its equilibrium value, it would continue to rise at an accelerating rate. Conversely, if the level of economic activity fell significantly below its equilibrium level for two periods, it would fall indefinitely.

A multiplier-accelerator model that is monotonically unstable does generate the cumulative upward or downward movement one observes in cyclical

---

*Whether or not one gets cycles depends on whether or not α is less than $(4\beta)/(1 + \beta)^2$; if so, the system will fluctuate.

activity, but it does not explain the turning points. Hicks created an upper turning point by the simple but reasonable assumption that there is some limit, a ceiling, above which the level of economic activity cannot go — the maximum operating capacity of the economy. This generates an upper turning point because it is inherent in the multiplier-accelerator model that if output fails to rise as indicated by equation (4) for two periods, the below-equilibrium levels of Y_{t-1} and Y_{t-2} will initiate a cumulative downward movement.

The lower turning point is explained in a similar fashion by assuming there is some amount of absolutely autonomous demand for goods that will remain, regardless of the level of other economic activity. This includes many government expenditures and consumers' expenditures for absolute necessities — and perhaps on an irregular basis the speculative investment activity of Schumpeter's first new entrepreneurs as well. This autonomous expenditure, A_t in equation (4), is assumed to grow at some positive rate, r. Thus the long-term equilibrium level of income is higher every year. Also with this built-in growth, aggregate income and expenditures cannot fall indefinitely. Specifically, Hicks's model can be described algebraically as

$$Y_t = (1 + \beta)Y_{t-1} - (\alpha)(\beta)Y_{t-2} + A_t,$$

where $A_t = A_0(1 + r)^t$ and Y_t must always be less than some ceiling, Y_c. In equilibrium $Y_t = Y_{t-1} = Y_{t-2}$, so

$$Y_e = A_0(1 + r)^t/(1 - \alpha).$$

The growing equilibrium level of the economy will be the autonomous expenditures times the multiplier resulting from the marginal propensity to consume.

Graphically, the underlying Hicksian model would be as shown in Fig. 6.2. The economy hits a trough of economic activity at time T as the decline is arrested by the growth in the floor level of economic activity, Y_f, as autonomous expenditures, $A_0(1 + r)^t$, continue to rise at $r\%$ per year. Once economic activity begins to rise, the multiplier and the accelerator interact in such a way as to sustain the boom until time P, at which point economic activity reaches a peak. The peak comes about due to capacity limitations, the ceiling on the level of economic activity, Y_c.

Although the model described above is Hicks's basic model, he believes that real world economies depart quite substantially from the simple mechanics of this model. For example, he feels the size of the parameter, β, is smaller in a period of declining economic activity than in a boom. "It seems safe to conclude that the accelerator, in the form in which it persists into the slump, is a mere ghost of what it was in the boom."[8] Investment's smaller reaction to declines in consumption than to increases results from the fact that only inventories of finished goods and raw materials can be quickly used up. One can "disinvest" in plant and equipment only by allowing it

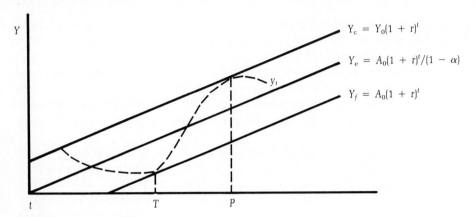

FIGURE 6.2 Hicks's Trade Cycle.

to depreciate and wear out. Hence, negative investment is constrained to be very much smaller than positive investment. This makes each cycle different depending on the form of the investment of the preceding boom. As Hicks phrased it,

> The main hope for an end to the depression will then have to be based upon . . . the disinvestment process. How long it will take to come to the rescue depends upon the nature of the capital equipment installed in the preceding boom. If the investment in that boom was mainly on investment in stocks, it is possible that they will be worked off fairly quickly; if it consisted of the installation of a large amount of very durable equipment, the process of disinvestment may be very slow indeed.[9]

Hicks also made the concept of maximum capacity, or a ceiling level of economic activity, more realistic by recognizing that there are really multiple ceilings — there is a capacity level for the construction industry, for the automobile industry, and so on. Hicks distinguishes between the consumption goods and investment goods industries. He notes that if the consumption goods ceiling is hit first, some general inflation is likely to take place before the downturn.[10]

Hicks also allows for the effects of the monetary system on his model. He feels monetary phenomena will not only change the value of the accelerator coefficient but also lower the floor level of economic activity by lowering the level of autonomous investment. ". . . Really catastrophic depression is most unlikely to occur as a result of the simple operation of the real accelerator mechanism; it is likely to occur when there is profound monetary instability — when the rot in the monetary system goes very deep."[11] Hicks felt this to be the case in the collapse of world economies in 1930–34. Consistent with this position, Hicks was somewhat optimistic about the efficacy of monetary policy, contending that if wisely applied, "Booms would be quiet affairs, and the slumps would be far short of being major disasters."[12] On the other hand, "If autonomous investment is seriously unsteady, the most that can be hoped from interest rate policy does not go very far."[13] As we turn our discussion to the monetary theories of the business cycle, we can note that Hicks reaches the eclectic conclusion that

> A more general, and more convincing, approach would be to assume that both sources of instability are, at least potentially, at work — that monetary instability, of the kind we have just considered, is superimposed upon the real instability which we analyzed in the earlier chapters of this book.[14]

Monetary Theories of the Cycle

Practically no theorists espouse a purely monetary explanation of the business cycle, but as we found with Hicks, all theorists include monetary phenomena as an exacerbating factor. Certainly it is easy to see that with a monetary system based on the monetization of private debt, in a boom the money supply will tend to expand rapidly, and when the recession comes the contraction in private loan demand will cause a contraction in the money supply.

Historically, money "panics" have heralded the arrival of recessions and depressions. All booms end with high interest rates, tight money, and something of a "crash" in the credit markets. But does this mean the financial phenomena "caused" the end of the boom and the ensuing recession? Not really. It is similar to the absolutely correct statement that each and every business failure and bankruptcy can be said to have resulted from the fact that "they ran out of money," but that is not much of an explanation of what happened.

In Chapter 4 we introduced the original quantity theory equation, $MV = PT$. We updated it by replacing T, total transactions, with Q, the quantity of real output in the economy, to get $MV = PQ$. We then derived the so-called quantity theory of money, which is really a monetary theory of prices. The contention that a given percentage change in the money supply will cause an equal percentage change in the price level was based on the assumptions of fixed real output and fixed velocity of money. Of course, if the quantity of real output does not change, one has no business cycle with which to be concerned. As a result, many early economists, like Irving Fisher, the originator of the quantity theory equation, simply were not concerned with the business cycle. This was in the tradition of the early British economists Mill, Ricardo, and others.

One can develop a naive theory of the business cycle using the quantity theory approach. If one assumes that instead of the quantity of real output,

Q, being fixed, the price level, P, is fixed, then the level or output will be totally responsive to changes in the money supply. The quantity theory as originally formulated assumes the aggregate supply curve to be vertical, so only prices change in response to changes in aggregate demand. Our naive monetary explanation of the business cycle assumes the aggregate supply curve to be horizontal, so only the quantity of real output can change. Of course, both theories assume that the elasticity of change in aggregate demand to change in the money supply is 100%.

More realistically, anyone concerned with the study of the business cycle accepts the proposition that the elasticity of price and real output with respect to changes in aggregate demand is somewhere between zero and 100%. The aggregate supply curve is neither vertical nor horizontal. A change in aggregate demand will be partly reflected in a change in real output and partly in a change in the price level, with relatively more inflation associated with an increase in aggregate demand near the peak of a business cycle and more of an increase in real output if aggregate demand is increased in a recession. At any particular point in history there is always heated argument about the exact magnitudes of these elasticities for a particular economy.

Note that in the classical theory of cyclical fluctuations based on the money supply nothing was said regarding interest rates. That is because the classical economists believed interest rates played little or no role in fluctuations in the level of economic activity. However, some early economists gave a central role to the interest rate. Early in this century a Swedish economist, Knut Wicksell, argued that the quantity theorists, like the American Irving Fisher, had things backwards. Increases in the money supply did not cause increases in the price level. Rather, increases in prices caused the money supply to increase. Wicksell reasoned that the rate of return on investment was a function of current and expected prices of goods. If the price of commodities were high relative to the price of credit, businesses would borrow and invest in order to produce more goods. The borrowing from the banks would result in the monetization of private debt, thereby expanding the money supply. Hence, high prices result in an increase in the money supply.[15]

Specifically, Wicksell contended that if the "natural" rate of interest rose above the "bank" rate of interest, the money supply would begin to increase and prices would begin to rise. This would continue until something happened to lower the natural rate or raise the bank rate. In contemporary terms the natural rate of interest is the marginal efficiency of capital, what businesses expect to earn on real investment. The bank rate is the return on financial assets in general and commercial bank loans in particular. The boom begins when, for whatever reason, the cost of borrowing gets significantly below expected returns on investment. This difference between the rate of return on real and financial assets generates a demand for bank loans by investors seeking to exploit the opportunity for profit. The banks respond by monetizing private debt, thereby increasing the money supply. The excess money balances create an excess demand for goods.

Obviously at some point the bank rate will start to rise and/or the real rate will start to fall. When the expected rate of return on real investment falls below the rate at which funds can be borrowed the process will begin to reverse itself and the recession is on. As bank loans are paid off (or defaulted on), bank credit is reduced, and the money supply falls accordingly.

The critical element in this process is the lag in the response of the bank rate. Irving Fisher, the father of the quantity theory of money, observed that at the peak of the business cycle the "loss of confidence and failure are all due to the *belated* rise of the interest rate."[16] Wicksell's theory has been referred to as the "doctrine of the Trailing Bank Rate."[17] If one specified the lag in the bank rate algebraically, one could depict this process mathematically as a cobweb theorem model of the type discussed in Chapter 2. With respect to the marginal efficiency of capital, the "real" rate, one could use a Hicksian multiplier-accelerator model, which would result in ever-increasing prospects for the likelihood of high yields on real investment. With such a structure, expected yields on investment would rise more rapidly than the bank rate and the boom would be self-sustaining.

The entire mechanism can be reversed to describe a self-sustaining recession or depression. As the prospective yields on investment collapse in an unstable multiplier-accelerator model, a "sticky" bank rate responds only with a lag. Bank credit is unattractive; its growth stops or reverses with a corresponding effect on the money supply.

Among modern theorists the mechanics of the monetary mechanism of the cumulative process, up or down, is pretty much the same. The difference, as is usual in business cycle theories, comes in the explanation of the turning points — the peaks and troughs. The modern quantity theorists mostly blame government policies, while others allow for instability originating in the private sector.

If one bases a business cycle theory on excess supply or demand for money impacting on the other sectors of the economy, however, one must have fluctuations in the supply or demand for money balances. The modern quantity theorists emphasize supply changes resulting from what are essentially political considerations. Recall the impact of the federal government deficit on the monetary base, $G - T = \Delta D + \Delta MB$. If governments choose to run deficits, which most do at one time or another and the U.S. government chooses to do most of the time, they must either increase the outstanding publicly held debt, ΔD, or the monetary base, ΔMB. Increasing the government debt by any significant amount increases the supply of financial assets enough to lower their price and thereby increase interest rates. Politically, governments do not like to be responsible for raising interest rates anymore than they like to be responsible for raising taxes. Just as the desire not to raise taxes created the deficit in the first place, the desire not to increase interest rates will cause the deficit to be financed by an increase in the monetary base.

Monetarists feel that the upward swing of the cycle is initiated by the monetization of government deficits. It is then sustained by the monetization of private credit. Regardless of the starting point, eventually the increase in aggregate demand creates an accelerating rate of inflation. The rate of inflation will at some point become politically intolerable and the government will be forced to do something about it. It must remove some of the excess supply of money in order to remove some of the excess demand for goods, which is causing the ratio at which money exchanges for goods, the price level, to rise.

Although it was the monetization of the government deficit resulting from a reluctance to raise taxes that created the problem in the first place, the policy response to the resulting inflation is typically not a tax increase. Instead, the government sells securities to the public to reduce the monetary base, a negative ΔMB for a positive ΔD. Eventually, the decrease in the supply of money balances brought about by the policy of restricting the growth of the monetary base halts the increase in aggregate demand. The boom ends with a "credit crunch."

We can discuss the mechanics of excess cash balances generating an excess demand for goods in terms of the general equilibrium equation we discussed in Chapter 3:

$$(I - S) + (L - B) + (H - \Delta M) = 0.$$

Recall that this equation is true both ex post and ex ante. If the first parenthetical expression is greater than zero, $I > S$, there is an excess demand for goods; if ex ante lending is greater than borrowing, $L > B$, there is an excess demand for financial assets; or if the desire to hoard money exceeds the increase in the money supply, $H > \Delta M$, there is an excess demand for cash balances. Quantity theorists contend that when the money supply is increased and creates an excess supply of money, $\Delta M > H$, the holders of the excess money balances will seek to reduce them by demanding goods and services with their excess money balances, creating an excess demand for goods, $I > S$. The negative term represented by the last parenthetical expression on the right in the general equilibrium equation is matched by a positive term of the first parenthetical expression on the left.

The increase in aggregate demand for goods originally results from the excess supply of money, $\Delta M > H$, creating an excess demand for goods, $I > S$. The restrictive monetary policy now counteracts this by an excess supply of government bonds, $B > L$, manifesting itself as an excess demand for cash by the government, $H > \Delta M$.

In addition, the rise in prices is in itself important in reducing the excess supply of money balances. As nominal GNP goes up, the transaction demand for cash increases proportionately, helping to bring the supply and demand for cash balances into equality. As a result, the increase in the money supply need not be reversed to end the increase in aggregate demand; it need only be stopped.

The direct link between demand for goods and services and the stock of money assumed by the quantity theorists is, in reality, just the assumed constant velocity of the money supply. The validity of both assumptions depends on excess money balances being spent for goods and services and not for financial assets. As previously noted, buying financial assets does not directly increase the demand for goods and services. Keynesian monetary theory contends that a significant proportion of excess money balances will be spent to buy financial assets, increasing the price of financial assets, thereby lowering interest rates and making people content with larger idle cash balances. Of course, larger idle cash balances imply a reduced velocity.

Rational Expectations and the Business Cycle

The most recent theoretical debates in business cycle theory revolve around something referred to as the theory of *rational expectations.*[18] In some ways this latest controversy is merely a continuation of a debate that has existed for at least 30 years.* The argument centers on whether a capitalist, market-oriented economy is inherently stable or unstable. More precisely, the question is: How much of the instability in the economy results from exogenous shocks, in particular, government monetary and fiscal policy, and how much from the miscalculation and overreaction by business firms and consumers, and hence is endogenous to the system?

On one side are what might be called classical economists, old or new, who are convinced that the economy is inherently stable. They contend that, historically, government policy has destabilized it in a perverse fashion. On the other side are what might be called Keynesians, who feel that psychological shifts in consumers' purchasing and portfolio preferences and in business's confidence are a substantial source of instability.

The rational expectations terminology comes from the basic assumption of the neo-classical group today that in all markets the participants are using all available information in an attempt to maximize their economic

---

*For example, Gottfried Haberler wrote in a survey article in 1956 that "At the one extreme we have the purely monetary explanations of the cycle which assume that the real economic system is inherently stable and that instability is introduced by misbehavior or mismanagement of money." *Banca Nazionale de Lavoro Quarterly Review*, Vol. 9, September 1956. Reprinted in Gordon and Klein, eds. *Readings in Business Cycles*, Homewood, Ill.: Richard D. Irwin, A.E.A., Vol. 10, pp. 130–152. The quotation is from page 135 of the *Readings*.

welfare. That is not an unreasonable assumption. The debate starts when the assumption is extended to imply that the individuals and business firms in the economy all have such a good understanding of the impact of policy changes and other exogenous events that they are able to develop rational and accurate predictions of what will happen. Given a little time they adjust completely to the change. This implies that all markets fluctuate around their long-run equilibrium values. The policy implication of this conclusion is that capitalism cannot be made any more efficient or the economy more stable by any form of government intervention. The government can redistribute wealth and income but cannot increase the total produced over time. In other words, the long-run level of such macroeconomic variables as the unemployment rate are set by market forces. The government may be able to lower the unemployment rate temporarily but only at the expense of raising it later by an approximately offsetting amount. (We will return to this particular aspect of the debate in detail in Chapter 11.) Unemployment or inefficient employment of labor or other resources result only from errors in planning and forecasting.

One naturally responds by asking that if the government cannot improve the performance of the economy, how can it hurt it? The rational expectations school contends that if government policy is consistently predictable by the economic participants, it will have little or no effect. People will simply adjust. However, erratic and unexpected shifts in policy or other factors in the economic environment are responsible for the business cycle. The government cannot make the economic engine run smoother, but it can throw a wrench into it.

This book takes a position midway between the two extremes. We do believe with the rational expectations theorists that the impact of policy varies greatly depending on whether it is expected or is a surprise. In forecasting the impact of policy, one must consider the fact that people are going to anticipate and adjust to that policy. On the other hand, there is merit to the Keynesian position, which leans heavily on imperfect markets and "sticky" wages and prices. Although we do not have a good body of theory to explain it, empirical observations clearly show that the responsiveness of prices to supply and demand conditions varies tremendously among markets. In the 1982 recession, for example, the price of steel and the wages of steelworkers hardly fell at all while at least 50% of the labor and capital in that industry were unemployed. On the other hand, farm prices, crude oil, and other raw materials prices all fell dramatically from lack of demand. An increase in aggregate demand would apparently have raised output of steel and raised the price of raw materials.

The open questions in business cycle theory today revolve mostly around why we get price changes in some markets and quantity changes in others if all the participants are acting rationally.[19]

● Questions for Discussion

1. What is the difference between an invention and an innovation as defined by Schumpeter?
2. Why does one successful innovation pave the way for others?
3. What does the capital-output ratio have to do with the principle of acceleration?
4. In Hicks's *Theory of the Trade Cycle* is the product of the marginal propensity to consume and the accelerator coefficient assumed to be greater or less than one?
5. What sets the minimum level of economic activity in Hicks's model?
6. Describe a typical expansionary sequence in the economy resulting from the businesspeople's expected rates of return on investment exceeding the "bank rate." What could bring about an upper turning point?
7. Compare and contrast the impact of excess money balances when the behavior pattern of the holders of those balances results in:
   a. An excess demand for goods.
   b. An excess demand for financial assets.

● Exercise

Consider the following Hicks-type model:

1. $Y_t = C_t + I_t$
2. $C_t = c_y(Y_{t-1})$
3. $I_t = i_0 + i_y(Y_{t-1})$
4. $Q_t = Q_0(1 + r)^t$
5. $Y_t = (P_t)(Q_t)$

Assume the sum of the marginal propensity to consume and the accelerator coefficient $(i_y + c_y)$ is greater than 1.00. If this system receives an exogenous shock upwards, what rate of growth will Y_t and P_t asymptotically approach?

● Source Notes

[1]Arthur F. Burns, ed. *Wesley Claire Mitchell: The Economic Scientist*. New York: NBER, 1952.

[2]Joseph Schumpeter, (Pronounced Shum pāter). *The Theory of Economic Development*. New York: Oxford University Press, 1961, p. 29. First published by the Department of Economics of Harvard University as Vol. 46 in the Harvard Economic Studies Series, 1934.

[3]Joseph Schumpeter, *Business Cycles*. New York: McGraw-Hill, 1939, Vol. 1, p. 37.

[4]*The Theory of Economic Development*, p. 228.

[5]J. M. Clark, Business acceleration and the law of demand: A technical factor in economic cycles. *Journal of Political Economy*. Chicago: University of Chicago, March 1917.

[6]Paul Samuelson, Interactions between the multiplier analysis and the principle of acceleration. *The Review of Economic Statistics*, Vol. 21, No. 2, May 1939, pp. 75–78.

[7]J. R. Hicks, *The Trade Cycle*. London: Oxford University Press, 1958.

[8]*Ibid.*, p. 104.

[9]*Ibid.*, p. 119.

[10]*Ibid.*, p. 134.

[11]*Ibid.*, p. 163.

[12]*Ibid.*, p. 165.

[13]*Ibid.*, p. 166.

[14]*Ibid.*, p. 153.

[15]Knut Wicksell, *Lectures on Political Economy*. Vol. 2. London: George Routledge, 1935. Reprinted. New York: Augustus M. Kelly, 1967.

[16]Irving Fisher, *Purchasing Power of Money*, Chapter 3. New York: MacMillan, 1926.

[17]Howard S. Ellis, *German Monetary Theory 1905–1933*. Cambridge, Mass: Harvard University Press, 1934, p. 300.

[18]Robert E. Lucas, and Thomas J. Sargent, eds. *Rational Expectations and Econometric Practice*. Minneapolis, Minn.: University of Minnesota Press, 1981; and Lucas, Robert E. *Studies in Business Cycle Theory*. Cambridge, Mass.: MIT Press, 1981.

[19]For a short popularized discussion of this, see Are the new economic models the answer? *Brookings Review*. Washington, DC: The Brookings Institution, Fall 1982.

● Selected Additional Readings

Clark, J. M. Business acceleration and the law of demand: A technical factor in economic cycles. *The Journal of Political Economy*, March 1917.

Hicks, J. R. *The Trade Cycle*. London: Oxford University Press, 1950.

Niehans, J. Interest rates, forced savings and prices in the long run, *Review of Economic Studies*, No. 32 (1965).

Samuelson, Paul A. Interaction between the multiplier analysis and the principle of acceleration. *The Review of Economic Statistics*, Vol. 21, No. 2 (May 1939).

Schumpeter, Joseph A. *The Theory of Economic Development*, New York: Oxford University Press, 1961. First published by the Department of Economics, Harvard University as Vol. 46 in the Harvard Economic Studies Series, 1934.

——————. *Business Cycles*. New York: McGraw-Hill, 1939.

Time Series Analysis

7

Decomposition of Time Series

A *time series* is a set of data points such as monthly housing starts for the nation, weekly retail sales for a shopping center, or one's daily beer consumption.* It is a set of numbers that gives the level of some economic activity for a given period. Historically, analysts have sought to break time series into the following four components:

1. *Seasonal* movements are defined as movements that are repeated in a particular time of the year, month, or other subdivision of the calendar. The rise of toy sales in December is a seasonal movement. Seasonal movements need not, however, repeat only once each year. Each month banking transactions rise dramatically at month-end. Airport traffic has a weekly pattern: high on Friday afternoon and low on Saturday morning.

2. *Trend* movements are the result of long-term growth or decline. A rigid logical definition is difficult since what is meant by a trend movement is a "significant" positive or negative correlation with time. To have a trend, a time series should be to some extent forecastable on the basis of the passage of time. For example, the U.S. population has grown at various rates over the past 200 years, but it obviously has had a positive trend. Although we expect fluctuations in the rate of population growth in coming years, a forecast each year that the population will rise would appear justified on the basis of trend movement alone. Indeed, most economic time series denominated in money have such a strong trend due both to economic growth and inflation that a forecast of "more" or "higher" is a fairly safe one each year.

3. *Cyclical* movements are those movements that are highly correlated with movements in the general level of economic activity. This does not mean that each time series hits a peak or trough at the same time as the general level of economic activity. As we will discuss in some detail later, some time series "lead" the economy (turn up or down

*If you have not recently had an introductory course in statistics, the appendix to this chapter is recommended before continuing.

sooner). Others "lag," or turn later than the general level of economic activity.

4. *Random* movements are fluctuations in time series that we cannot explain as seasonal, trend, or cyclical. "Random" is the catchall term for our ignorance. By definition, one cannot predict the next number in a series of random numbers. Time series with a large random component, such as day-to-day changes in stock prices, are impossible to predict.

The decomposition or breaking down of time series into the seasonal, trend, and cyclical components is usually done by sequentially removing the seasonal and trend components. We then call what is left the cycle, with the fervent hope that the random component is not so large as to obscure our view of the cyclical movement.

We will first consider some artificially constructed time series containing no unexplained or random component. Not only will we deal with time series with no random component, we will also *know* the size of each component and its interaction with the others — knowledge certainly unavailable to us in analyzing the real world. Table 7.1 and Fig. 7.1 present three hypothetical time series. In time series 1 of Table 7.1, "Simple Additive," the observed time series, Y, is the sum of the trend, t, the seasonal, S_1, and the cycle, C_1, as shown. One could go a long way toward forecasting

TABLE 7.1 Some Hypothetical Components of Economic Time Series

				Cross-effects between S and t $Y = t + S_2 + C$ $S_2 = tS_1$ $Y = t(1 + S_1) + C$				Cross effects between both S and t and between C and Y: $Y = t + S_2 + C_2$ $C_2 = C_1t$ $Y = t(1 + S_1 + C_1)$			
Simple additive: $Y = t + S_1 + C$											
t	S_1	C_1	Y	t	S_2	C_1	Y	t	S_2	C_2	Y
1	1	10	12	1	1	10	12	1	1	10	12
2	2	9	13	2	4	9	15	2	4	18	24
3	3	8	14	3	9	8	20	3	9	24	36
4	4	7	15	4	16	7	27	4	16	28	48
5	1	6	12	5	5	6	16	5	5	30	40
6	2	5	13	6	12	5	23	6	12	30	48
7	3	6	16	7	21	6	34	7	21	42	70
8	4	7	19	8	32	7	47	8	32	56	96
9	1	8	18	9	9	8	26	9	9	72	90
10	2	9	21	10	20	9	39	10	20	90	120
11	3	10	24	11	33	10	54	11	33	110	154
12	4	11	27	12	48	11	71	12	48	132	192

Y = the observed data; t = the trend component; S = the seasonal component; C = the cyclical component. We assume quarterly data (the seasonal repeats every four periods).

this time series with knowledge of the trend and seasonal. The trend is a +1 per time period and the seasonal is a repetition of the series 1, 2, 3, 4 every four time periods. With this information one could "detrend" and "seasonally adjust" the data and concentrate on forecasting the cycle. We will discuss these procedures in more detail later.

Time series 2 and 3 illustrate cross-effects between the seasonal and trend, and between the cycle and trend. Whereas in series 1 the seasonal movement is the same each year, in series 2 there is a cross-effect between seasonal and trend — there is a trend in the seasonal. As a result, the seasonal growth from the first quarter to the fourth quarter is 15 (from 1 to 16) in the first year, but it is 27 in the second year (from 5 to 32). Similarly, the seasonal drop from the fourth quarter of one year to the first quarter of the next grows from 11 (16 to 5) between the first and second year to 23 (32 to 9) between the second and third year.

In series 3 the trend interacts with both the seasonal and the cyclical movement. The strong trend effect on the cyclical converts the V-shaped cycle of series 1 and 2, labeled C_1, in Table 7.1 and Fig. 7.1, to a growth cycle. As is apparent from the graph in the lower right-hand corner of Fig. 7.1, labeled C_2, the downward phase of the cycle in the first year and a half is just a reduced rate of growth as compared to the upswing in the last year and a half.

As mentioned earlier, most analyses seek to break down a time series into its components of seasonal, trend, and cyclical. The purpose is most often to study and attempt to forecast the cyclical movement. In the three time series just studied we know the exact formulation of the trend and seasonal. As a result we can easily isolate the cyclical movement as follows:

Series 1 $Y = t + s_1 + C_1.$

         $C_1 = Y - t - S_1.$

Series 2 $Y = t + tS_1 + C_1.$

         $C_1 = Y - t - tS_1.$

Series 3 $Y = t + tS_1 + tC_1.$

         $C_1 = (Y)/(t) - 1 - S_1.$

Note that isolating the cycle in series 1 and 2 requires subtracting trend and seasonal movements from the observed time series. In series 3, however, the original time series must be divided by the trend value. In the first two cases the cycle is a simple additive function and can be isolated by subtracting out the other components. In the third case the relationship is multiplicative (trend times cycle) and so must be reversed by division.

Of course in practice, all one has is the observed series and must guess at the underlying structure. Consider the two time series, 4–A and 4–B, given in Table 7.2 and shown in Fig. 7.2. Both 4–A and 4–B fit the simple

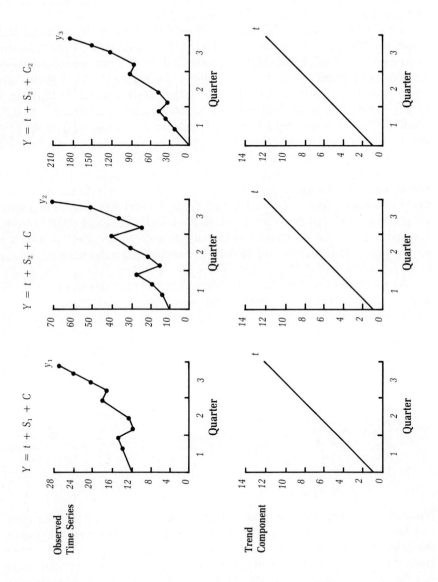

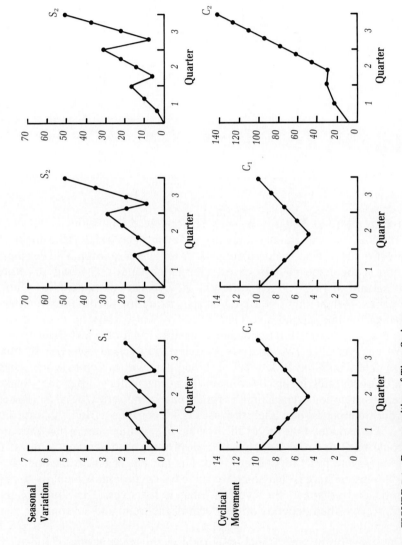

FIGURE 7.1 Decomposition of Time Series.

109

TABLE 7.2 Two Views of One Observed Time Series

4--A				4--B			
t	S	C	Y	t	S	C	Y
3	5	1	9	2	5	2	9
6	10	2	18	4	10	4	18
9	5	3	17	6	5	6	17
12	10	4	26	8	10	8	26
15	5	5	25	10	5	10	25
18	10	6	34	12	10	12	34
21	5	7	33	14	5	14	33
24	10	6	40	16	10	14	40
27	5	5	37	18	5	14	37
30	10	4	44	20	10	14	44
33	5	3	41	22	5	14	41
36	10	2	48	24	10	14	48

additive structure of $Y = t + S + C$. The observed time series is the same in each case, but the trend values are different. The trend value for 4--A is $+3$ per quarter. The trend value for 4--B is $+2$ per quarter. The seasonal variation is the same in both cases, alternating values of 5 and 10. Note at the bottom of Fig. 7.2 how different the cyclical components turn out. Time series 4--A has an inverted V-shape, rising for the first six quarters and falling for the second six. Time series 4--B also shows a cyclical rise for the first six quarters but then holds constant at 14 for the last six quarters.

We can visualize two analysts studying the cyclical behavior of time series 4. They both have identical observed data with which to work. They are both successful in discovering the seasonal pattern. But they make different assumptions regarding the time trend in the series. Analyst A uses a $+3$ per time period and analyst B uses a $+2$ per time period. As a result, analyst A concludes that the cyclical value of this time series has gone up and come back down to its original level of three years earlier. Analyst B claims the cycle has "topped out" but has not yet begun to decline. The important lesson here is that since we solve for cyclical movement by taking out trend and seasonal, the cycle is what is left over. The shape of the observed cycle then depends on the form of the trend and seasonal chosen by the analysts!

The question of which analyst is right in this case is one of those "it depends" situations. Although it depends on a number of things — including the purpose of the analysis — it may not make any difference. The most critical determinant of which structure is more appropriate for the analysis of time series 4 depends on the behavior of the time series in the years

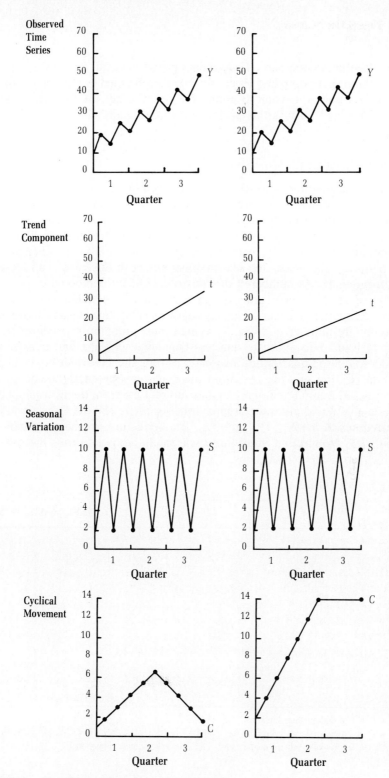

FIGURE 7.2 Two Ways to Decompose the Same Series.

after those presented here. Twelve data points are really not enough to say much about a time series. Hopefully, if one obtained twelve more (or 144 more) data points it would become obvious whether the time trend is $+2$ or $+3$. We will discuss this problem in more detail below.

Seasonal Adjustment

Most macroeconomic time series are published in *seasonally adjusted* form. Seasonal adjustment is the process of taking out the change from one period to the next resulting from the change in the seasonal component. For example, in time series 4 we have the seasonal component of alternating 5s and 10s, but the only really necessary information is the change from one period to the next. The seasonal movement in this case is an increase of 5 from each odd-numbered quarter to each even-numbered quarter and the decrease of 5 each time we go from an even-numbered to an odd-numbered quarter. We can seasonally adjust, or offset this seasonal movement, in an infinite number of ways. The three most common procedures would be to: (1) add 5 to alternate quarters beginning with the first quarter ($+5$ to odd-numbered quarters); (2) subtract 5 from alternate quarters beginning with the second quarter (-5 from the even-number quarters); or (3) add 2.5 to the odd-numbered quarters and subtract 2.5 from the even-numbered quarters. Table 7.3 gives the original time series, Y, and the three seasonally adjusted series as Y_{a1}, Y_{a2}, and Y_{a3}. The series are presented graphically in Fig. 7.3. Notice that in all three seasonally adjusted series the quarter-

TABLE 7.3   Time Series 4

Y	Y_{a1}[a]	Y_{a2}[b]	Y_{a3}[c]	$\Delta Y_{a1} = \Delta Y_{a2} = \Delta Y_{a3}$
9	14	9	11.5	
18	18	13	15.5	4
17	22	17	19.5	4
$\underline{26}$	$\underline{26}$	$\underline{21}$	$\underline{23.5}$	$\underline{4}$
25	30	25	27.5	4
34	34	29	31.5	4
33	38	33	35.5	4
$\underline{40}$	$\underline{40}$	$\underline{35}$	$\underline{37.5}$	$\underline{2}$
37	42	37	39.5	2
44	44	39	41.5	2
41	46	41	43.5	2
$\underline{48}$	$\underline{48}$	$\underline{43}$	$\underline{45.5}$	$\underline{2}$

[a] $Y_{a1} = Y + 5$ to odd-numbered quarters.
[b] $Y_{a2} = Y - 5$ from even-numbered quarters.
[c] $Y_{a3} = Y + 2.5$ to odd-numbered quarters and -2.5 from even-numbered quarters.

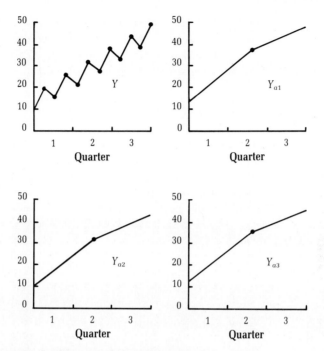

FIGURE 7.3   Seasonal Adjustment Three Different Ways.

to-quarter movements are the same. Graphically, their movements are all parallel. The second seasonally adjusted series is the same as the first except it is 5 units lower. The third seasonally adjusted series is the average of the other two.

The most common form of seasonal adjustment is multiplicative rather than additive. The seasonal adjustment factors are generally given in the form of an index. The observed time series must be divided by this index to obtain a seasonally adjusted series. Table 7.4 is an appendix to the U.S. government publication *Business Conditions Digest,* July 1979. This table contains the seasonal adjustment factors for a number of time series. Note that although all but one of the adjustment factors are multiplicative, series number 33, Net Change in Mortgage Debt, is additive. The factor is the millions of dollars that must be subtracted from the observed time series to obtain the seasonally adjusted time series.

Table 7.5 illustrates the seasonal adjustment procedure for a multiplicative seasonal adjustment factor, with series number 13, New Business Incorporations, and the procedure with the additive factor for series number 33, Net Change in Mortgage Debt (both from Table 7.4). Note that the multiplicative seasonal factor is, as with an index, multiplied by 100. For example, the observed data for the number of New Business Incorporations

TABLE 7.4 Current Adjustment Factors

Series	1979											
	Jan.	Feb.	Mar.	Apr.	May	June	July	Aug.	Sept.	Oct.	Nov.	Dec.
13. New Business Incorporations[a]	104.6	89.8	110.9	102.0	107.6	105.0	99.7	103.7	89.7	103.4	90.2	93.5
15. Profits (after Taxes) per Dollar of Sales, Manufacturing[b]	...	92.8	...	...	109.4	...	...	98.7	...	...	98.7	...
33. Net Change in Mortgage Debt[a,c]	−1535	−1709	−20	131	922	1308	156	1022	−30	−307	−162	352
72. Commercial and Industrial Loans Outstanding	100.4	99.2	100.0	100.3	100.2	100.2	99.8	99.1	99.1	99.8	100.7	101.3
517. Defense Department Gross Obligations Incurred[a]	107.0	89.0	91.3	100.5	85.8	94.6	86.5	84.3	118.8	135.8	110.9	94.9
525. Defense Department Military Prime Contract Awards	94.5	77.4	93.8	89.8	89.4	91.0	72.0	72.6	163.9	144.7	107.0	102.9
543. Defense Department Gross Unpaid Obligations Outstanding	105.4	104.1	101.2	101.7	99.0	97.1	95.0	92.1	95.5	101.0	103.7	104.0
570. Employment in Defense Products Industries	100.7	100.0	99.6	99.7	99.8	100.1	99.9	99.7	100.1	99.9	100.0	100.4
580. Defense Department Net Outlays[a]	94.8	98.0	106.3	96.3	101.2	104.0	94.1	103.5	103.8	98.4	103.9	92.9
604. Exports of Agricultural Products	104.0	97.2	107.3	104.1	102.4	94.9	87.5	87.1	89.4	107.8	110.8	107.4
606. Exports of Nonelectrical Machinery	95.1	94.7	110.5	106.3	107.3	103.0	95.4	91.2	93.2	100.8	99.1	103.3
614. Imports of Petroleum and Products	104.3	92.8	104.8	105.8	91.9	103.3	100.1	105.2	103.1	93.9	93.3	101.4
616. Imports of Automobiles and Parts	101.7	96.1	117.8	110.6	105.0	111.0	92.2	79.1	84.7	97.4	100.3	103.8

Note: These series are seasonally adjusted by the Bureau of Economic Analysis or the National Bureau of Economic Research, Inc., rather than by the source agency. Seasonal adjustments are kept current by the Bureau of Economic Analysis. Seasonally adjusted data prepared by the source agency will be used in *Business Conditions Digest* whenever they are available. For a description of the method used to compute these factors, see Bureau of the Census Technical Paper No. 15, *The X-II Variant of the Census Method II Seasonal Adjustment Program.*

[a]Factors are the products of seasonal and trading-day factors.

[b]Quarterly series; factors are placed in the middle month of the quarter.

[c]These quantities, in millions of dollars, are subtracted from the month-to-month net change in the unadjusted monthly totals to yield the seasonally adjusted net change. These factors are computed by the additive version of the X-11 variant of the Census Method II seasonal adjustment program.

TABLE 7.5 Application of Seasonal Factors

1979	Multiplicative Seasonal			Additive Seasonal		
	New Business Incorporations, Number			Net Change in Mortgage Debt Millions of Dollars		
	Observed Data	Seasonal Factor	Adjusted Data	Observed Data	Seasonal Factor	Adjusted Data
Jan.	44,361	104.6	42,410	99,555	− 1,535	101,090
Feb.	37,987	89.8	42,302	81,011	− 1,709	82,720
Mar.	47,422	110.9	42,761	88,420	− 20	88,440
Apr.	43,895	102.0	43,034	75,391	131	75,260
May	47,231	107.6	43,895	93,252	922	92,330
June	45,196	105.0	43,044	96,448	1,308	95,140
July	44,521	99.7	44,655	98,006	156	97,850
Aug.	44,499	103.7	42,911	85,762	1,022	84,740
Sept.	40,084	89.7	44,687	87,430	− 30	87,460
Oct.	48,058	103.4	46,478	107,033	− 307	107,340
Nov.	40,420	90.2	44,811	74,198	− 162	74,360
Dec.	40,747	93.5	43,579	52,302	352	51,950
Total	524,420	1,200.1	524,567	1,038,808	128	1,038,680
Means	43,702	100.0	43,714	86,567	11	86,556
Standard Deviation	3,227		1,240	14,611		14,691

for January 1979 was 44,361. To obtain the seasonally adjusted figure of 42,410 we must divide 44,361 by 1.046 since January business incorporations generally run 4.6% above the typical monthly level. Note also that the sum of the seasonal factors is 1,200 for an average value of 100.0. This makes the total and average levels for the adjusted and unadjusted data virtually identical. It is desirable that seasonal adjustment not change annual totals or year-to-year comparisons, but only that it smooth out the monthly seasonal fluctuations to reveal the trend and cyclical movements.

In the case of the additive seasonal adjustment of the Net Change in Mortgage Debt, the seasonal factor indicates that the increase in mortgage debt in January is, on average, $1,535 million below the typical month. To obtain a seasonally adjusted figure we must add the $1,535 million to the observed datum of $99,555 million to get $101,090. The adjusted and unadjusted figures for the year do have approximately the same mean values at $86,556 and $86,567. The $11 million difference is, of course, the average value of the seasonal adjustment. Ideally, the sum and average value for the seasonal adjustment factors should be zero. In this case the $10 million is small enough. As a proportion of the average values, it is equal to only one one-hundredth of one percent.

The adjustments of both time series meet the requirement that the annual averages and totals not be significantly disturbed. An additional question is whether it is really necessary that both these series be adjusted for seasonal variation. The question of when to adjust is a very important one that is frequently not even asked. By definition, seasonal movement is a regularly occurring departure of the data relative to some base, which may be a particular month or the average of all months. If January is always below December (as with retail sales) then there is obviously seasonal movement from December to January. We will be able to perceive trend and cyclical movements better if we smooth out the time series either by adding the appropriate amount to January or by subtracting it from December. It really does not matter which. But suppose on the basis of many years' data it appears that January is above December about half the time and below it about half the time (such as with stock market prices). Statistical tests, of course, can measure whether there is a statistically significant difference between the average value for December and January.[1] Such tests are almost never done and much data is seasonally adjusted pointlessly.

Consider the two time series in Table 7.5. The adjustment of New Business Incorporations converts a January to December fall in the unadjusted data of about 10% to a slight increase in a much smoother time series of the adjusted data. The standard deviation of the time series over the twelve months is 3,227 for the unadjusted data, but is reduced to 1,240 by the seasonal adjustment process. The adjustments are fairly large in percentage terms, ranging from +10.9% for March to −10.3% for September. The adjustment process would contribute to the analysis of the trend and cyclical movements of this time series.

On the other hand, the seasonal adjustment of the Net Change in Mortgage Credit appears to have not been worth the trip. The largest adjustment of $1,709 million for February is only equal to less than 2% of the average for the year and many of the other adjustments are very small indeed. The adjustment procedure does not do much to smooth out the monthly movements, since the standard deviation for the year rises slightly from $14,611 for the unadjusted series to $14,691 for the adjusted series — essentially no change. Although not conclusive, this indicates that this series contains no statistically significant seasonal movement.*

The problem with seasonal adjustment when there is no significant seasonal movement to be removed is not that it is just a waste of time and

---

*To reach a firm conclusion we would need to take a number of years' data and run a statistical test on the hypotheses that the mean value of the individual months are significantly different from the overall mean.

effort — it can be positively harmful to time series analysis, especially if the procedure is the one used for seasonal adjustment by most departments and agencies of the U.S. government. The government uses a computer program (called the "X-II Variant of the Census Method Seasonal Adjustment Program") that derives seasonal adjustment factors by comparing unadjusted data to a moving average of the data. In other words, a 12-month moving average is assumed to represent seasonally adjusted data. The program uses the last five years' data to generate what is considered typical at present and to allow for seasonals that change through time. The problem is that although running a moving average through a time series will indeed smooth the series, to the extent that random movements are present, the process will generate meaningless cycles where none existed before. The effect of something called the *Slutsky proposition* tells us that a moving average of a random series will have a cyclical movement.[2] As an econometrician named Valavanis noted more than twenty years ago, the effect of using the moving average technique as a seasonal adjustment will (to the extent that there are random movements in the series) result in an oscillation that "will be confounded with the amplitude of the true seasonal. This will manifest itself in two ways: either the seasonal will seem to shift or, if it does not shift, it will contain the cyclical properties of the cumulated random effects."[3]

Obviously you should not automatically seasonally adjust any and all data with which you work. A simple test for the need of seasonal adjustment is to take the average value for each seasonal time period with which you are concerned (month, quarter, or whatever) for the entire time for which the data are available. Then check the average values to determine, intuitively or statistically, whether there *is* a significant difference between, say, January and February. If there is no significant difference, do not seasonally adjust.

If there is a significant difference in the average values, these average values can be used to derive simple but effective seasonal adjustment factors of either the multiplicative or additive form. Let us say the data in the first column in Table 7.6 are the average retail sales for a small shopping center. If these averages are derived from, say, twelve years' data, we might feel that the averages represent a typical value for each month relative to the others. The second column in the table gives the ratio of each monthly average to the overall average. The third column gives the difference of each from the overall average. It appears intuitively obvious that the overall average monthly value of $14,636,000 differs significantly from most of the other individual monthly averages.

The column labeled Ratio to Overall Mean contains multiplicative seasonal factors. Of course, as mentioned earlier, seasonal adjustment factors are, like index numbers, typically multiplied by 100 so that we would publish the January seasonal as 71.96 and so on through December at 165.69. These factors indicate that on the basis of historical experience, January is typically 28.04% below the average month and December is typically 65.69% above

TABLE 7.6 Seasonal Adjustment of Hypothetical Average Monthly Sales

Month	Monthly Averages Sales in Thousands	Ratio to Overall Mean	Difference from Overall Mean in Thousands
Jan.	$10,532	.7196	− $4,104
Feb.	12,640	.8636	− 1,996
Mar.	13,575	.9275	− 1,061
Apr.	13,422	.9170	− 1,214
May	12,998	.8881	− 1,638
June	14,502	.9908	− 134
July	13,212	.9027	− 1,424
Aug.	13,650	.9326	− 986
Sept.	14,721	1.0058	85
Oct.	15,012	1.0257	376
Nov.	17,119	1.1696	2,483
Dec.	24,250	1.6569	9,614
Total	175,633	12.0000	0
Means	14,636	1.0000	0

the average month. Note that the factors add up to 12.00 and thereby have an average value of 1.00. This ensures that seasonal adjustment using these factors does not alter the total for the year significantly. If, on average, you multiply each month by 1.00, raising some and lowering others, you will end up with approximately the same total for the adjusted and unadjusted data.

The last column on the right in Table 7.6, Difference from Overall Mean, is a set of additive seasonal adjustment factors obtained by calculating how much, on average, each month differs from the typical monthly value. The numbers in this column indicate, for example, that on average, January is a slow month running $4,104,000 below norm, and things really hum during December, which typically runs $9,614,000 above the average month. Note that the additive seasonal adjustment factors sum to zero in the same way and for the same reason that the multiplicative factors sum to 12. The total sales for the year will be the same after adjustment with these additive factors as they were before the adjustment since our adjustments net out to zero.

Time Trends

Just as seasonal movements are some significant relationship between the season of the year and the value of the observed variable, a time trend is some significant relationship between the observed variable and the mere passage of time. This presents the same sort of choices and problems we had with seasonal adjustment. We must decide what we think is a "significant" relationship; we have our choice between various additive and multiplicative relationships.

In a simple additive trend the variable simply rises by so much per time period and the relationship can be expressed algebraically as $Y_t = k + Y_{t-1}$ or $Y_t - Y_{t-1} = \Delta Y_t = k$, where k is some constant. In continuous form we could write $Y_t = (k)(t) + Y_0$, where Y_0 is the initial value at time period zero and Y_t is the value of time t. Graphically, the relationship between time and the dependent variable is a simple straight line with a slope of k.

In the multiplicative form of a time trend the value of the dependent variable in each time period is some multiple of itself in the previous time period. If the multiplier is greater than 1.00, we have a positive rate of growth; if the multiplier is less than 1.00, we have a negative rate of growth. Algebraically, $Y_t = (1+r)Y_{t-1}$ or $(Y_t)/(Y_{t-1}) = (1+r)$. In this case if $r = .05$, we would be multiplying each time period's value by 1.05 to obtain the trend value for the next time period, a growth rate of 5%. If $r = -.05$, $(1+r) = .95$, and Y_t would be 95% of Y_{t-1} for a negative growth rate of 5%. We can generalize this formulation of trend as $Y_t = (1+r)^t(Y_0)$ or $(Y_t)/(Y_0) = (1+r)^t$, where Y_0 is where you started from and Y_t is where you are at time t.

To calculate a trend value one needs only two data points. If the first year in a 10-year time series is 232 and the last year's value is 432, we can fit either our additive or multiplicative relationship to these data. Given $Y_t = 432$, $Y_0 = 232$, and $t = 10$, then in the additive case

$$Y_t = (k)(t) + Y_0,$$
$$432 = (k)(10) + 232,$$
$$(10)(k) = 432 - 232 = 200,$$
$$k = 20,$$
$$Y_t = 20t + Y_0.$$

The trend value is 20 units per period. It *is* a true statement that, in some sense, this variable has grown on average by 20 units per time period. The question of whether we have found a meaningful trend we will return to shortly.

To fit the multiplicative trend relationship to these data, we insert the values given in the additive case:

$$Y_t = (1+r)^t(Y_0),$$
$$432 = (1+r)^{10}(232),$$
$$(1+r)^{10} = (432)/(232) = 1.862069,$$
$$(1+r) = \sqrt[10]{1.862069} = 1.0641,$$
$$Y_t = (1.0641)^t(Y_0).$$

Again, it is certainly proper to say that, on average, this variable has grown at 6.41% per year compounded annually. By fitting the beginning and ending to a constant percentage growth line we derive a particular growth rate, but this does not mean it is a trend.

In the case of both the additive and multiplicative trend values, the question of whether or not we have a meaningful trend involves a number of considerations, the analysis of which requires some science and some art. Certainly if the value of this variable had been 232 for years 1 through 9 and then the jump to 432 had come in one year, we would not regard either the additive value of +20 per year or the multiplicative rate of 6.41% per year as particularly meaningful. We would not even regard the statement that the variable had an average growth rate of 20 units or 6.41% per year as very informative. What we are saying is that we would want a better "fit" of the trend line to all ten data points before we would feel the relationship between the dependent variable and time to be meaningful. How good a fit is a question of long standing in statistics and depends largely on the purpose of the analysis and the alternatives open to the investigator. Strictly speaking, in statistical terms we are seeking to reject the hypothesis that k or r is equal to zero. If we do reject the hypothesis, we presumably accept the alternative hypothesis that there is a statistically significant time trend. Determining statistical significance and goodness of fit involves the measurement of the movements in the variable that are not explained by the mere passage of time — the quantification and study of the "error terms." This is a subject we will return to in the next chapter.

The problem of deciding between the additive and multiplicative time trend is similar to the problem of deciding if there is a trend at all. We want to use whichever relationship seems to fit the data better. We can plot the data around the fitted trend line and "eyeball" it. Actually a straight line on plain (arithmetic) graph paper indicates an additive trend. A straight line on semilogarithmic paper indicates a multiplicative, constant percentage trend. More precise measurement of goodness of fit is possible by running a simple regression. For the additive trend, regress all the data points on consecutive integers representing time in the following equation: $Y_t = a + (k)(t)$. The value of a is irrelevant but will, of course, be the value for Y_t when $t = 0$, usually a pretty strange number if you use contemporary years for time as in 1970, 1971, and so on.

In the case of the multiplicative trend we can convert the relationship to standard linear form by taking logarithms of that equation

$$Y_t = (1+r)^t (Y_0)$$
$$\log Y_t = \log Y_0 + [\log (1+r)] (t).$$

The regression is run by correlating the logarithms of the time series with the consecutive integers representing time. The coefficient obtained will be the logarithm of $(1+r)$. One then takes the antilog and subtracts 1.00 to obtain the trend rate of growth. Again, the intercept, log Y_0, is of no particular interest unless you want to know the trend value when $t = 0$.

There are, of course, an infinite number of more complex relationships between time and a set of economic data. Extrapolating anything other than a simple additive or constant percentage change has historically proven to be a highly unreliable activity. In any case, in deciding if there is a meaningful trend and in deciding which particular formulation is the most appropriate, regression analysis is probably the best approach. In most real-world situations any standard statistical measure of goodness of fit, R^2, standard error of the estimate, and so on, should indicate fairly clearly whether the data contain a meaningful time trend and the most appropriate formulation.

Having decided a time series has a meaningful trend we can use the trend relationship to *detrend* the data in a process similar to seasonal adjustment or we can use the relationship as all or part of a forecasting model. Let us first consider the process of detrending a time series. As we mentioned earlier, a frequent analytical approach is to seasonally adjust and detrend the data with the hope of observing the cyclical behavior of the residual if the random component is not so strong as to obscure cyclical movements.

Detrending is merely removing the trend movements in much the same way we remove, or adjust for, seasonal movements. Let us consider a time series containing only trend and cyclical movements. We want to isolate the cycle. In the case of an additive trend we would have the following relationships:

$$Y_t = T_t + C_t,$$
$$T_t = Y_0 + (k)(t).$$

Solving for the cyclical value, C_t, we obtain

$$C_t = Y_t - T_t = Y_t - Y_0 - (k)(t).$$

The cyclical movement from one month to the next, ΔC_t, would be

$$\Delta C_t = C_t - C_{t-1} = Y_t - Y_{t-1} - k,$$
$$\Delta C_t = \Delta Y_t - k.$$

The cyclical movement is the movement in the observed time series minus the trend value, k. Detrending consists of subtracting k each time period.

If we assume a multiplicative model we have the following relationships:

$$Y_t = (T_t)(C_t),$$
$$T_t = (1 + r'(Y_0)).$$

Solving for the cyclical value, C_t, we obtain

$$C_t = (Y_t)/(T_t) = [Y_t]/[(1 + r)'(Y_0)].$$

This equation tells us that to detrend a time series containing a multiplicative trend, we must divide the observed data by the trend value. If we want to look at the rate of growth from one period to the next of a detrended value, we must "discount" the observed data by one plus the trend rate of growth, $(1+r)$. The ratio of the detrended data from one period to the next, $(C_t)/(C_{t-1})$, is

$$(C_t)/(C_{t-1}) = [(Y_t)/(Y_{t-1})]/(1+r).$$

For example, let us say the observed data for two years is 100 and 110. We have ascertained there is a trend of 6% per year. Intuition would tell us the detrended value is a growth from 100 to about 104 — the 110 minus the 6% of the first year's value. The exact calculation from our algebraic relationships is

$$(C_t)/(C_{t-1}) = [(110)/(100)]/(1.06),$$
$$(C_t)/(C_{t-1}) = (1.10)/(1.06) = 1.038.$$

The detrended rate of growth is only approximately 4%, 3.8% to be exact. The difference is the effect of compounding. If the first year's value were 103.8 and it grew by 6%, it would indeed grow to 110 since $103.8 \times 1.06 = 110$. The .2 difference between the 3.8 and the 4% is the 6% rate of growth of the 3.8.

A Word of Caution on Decomposition of Time Series

It is important to recognize that the concepts of seasonal, trend, and cyclical movements are inventions of analysts and thereby as much analytical conveniences as descriptions of reality. There are time series *without* any seasonal movement. There are time series, such as temperature, that are immune to the business cycle. (Speaking of temperature, scientists carry on an endless debate on whether there is a positive or negative trend in the world's temperature.) One should not automatically assume all three categories of movement in analyzing all time series. Certainly proper statistical procedure would indicate one should assume the hypothesis that there are no such movements (that the series is random) and then seek analytically to reject the null hypothesis on solid logical grounds.

● Questions for Discussion

1. Evaluate the statement: "Always seasonally adjust your data; it can't hurt and it might help."

2. After we seasonally adjust and detrend a time series, what do we have left?

3. What is seasonally adjusted annual data?

● Exercises

1. If my company's sales were $10,283,461 for October 1973, and $26,672,649 for October 1983, what is the annual rate of growth on average:
   a. In absolute terms?
   b. In percentage terms?

2. If these two data points are representative of a trend, what is the equation for the trend value:
   a. As a constant, linear, additive trend?
   b. As a constant percentage rate of growth per year?

● Source Notes

[1]For example, see: John R. Stockton, and Charles T. Clark. Difference between two sample means. *Introduction to Business and Economic Statistics,* 6th ed., Cincinnati, Ohio: Southwestern Publishing Co., 1980, p. 204.

[2]Eugene Slutsky, The summation of random causes and the source of cyclical processes. *Econometrica,* April 1957, pp. 105–146.

[3]Stefan Valavanis, *Econometrics.* New York: McGraw-Hill, 1959, p. 178.

● Selected Additional Readings

Austin, John S. How to use and interpret seasonal factors. *Business Economics,* Vol. 16, No. 4 (September 1981).

Granger, C. W. J. *Forecasting in Business and Economics.* New York: Academic Press, 1980.

Pindyck, Robert S., and Daniel L. Rubinfeld. *Econometric Models and Economic Forecasts.* New York: McGraw-Hill, 1981.

Zellner, Arnold, ed. *Seasonal Analysis of Economic Time Series.* Washington, D.C.: U.S. Department of Commerce, Bureau of Census, 1978.

APPENDIX: __An Introduction to Several Statistical Concepts__

Means, Medians, and Modes

The most frequently calculated value of economic time series discussed in this text is the *arithmetic mean* or *average* value. Arithmetic mean is used here to indicate a simple average calculated by adding up all the numbers in the series and dividing by the number of data points. Algebraically, the arithmetic mean is defined as

$$\overline{x} = (x_1 + x_2 + x_3 + \ldots + x_n)/n = \left(\sum_{i=1}^{n} x_i \right)\Big/ n.$$

There are other means, such as the geometric (where you multiply all the data points together and then take the *nth* root), the hormonic (where you sum the reciprocals), and so on, but in this and most other texts the arithmetic mean is what is meant when the term "average" is used without being further qualified.

As a measure of what is supposed to be a typical value, the average value can be very misleading if there are a few very large or very small data points. The standard example is with personal income. If you calculated the average income of a group of 30 people in which one individual had an annual income of $15 million while all the others had incomes between $10 and $30 thousand the average would be something more than $500 thousand — not a very representative figure for the group. Thus you will find most personal income data presented as the *median*.

The median is defined as that value above (and below) which 50% of the values fall. In the example above, the median would have to fall somewhere between $10 and $30 thousand depending on the distribution. The mechanics of calculating a median value are to array the data from the largest to the smallest and come down exactly half way on the number of data points. If you have an odd number of data points, say 31, you can use the 16th largest (which is also the 16th smallest) as the median value. There will be 15 values larger and 15 values smaller. If you have an even number of data points, say 30, then all you can really say is that the median value falls between the values for the 15th and 16th data points in the array. Common practice is to take the mean of these two as the median, although more complex estimates are sometimes used.

In a third approach to what is a typical value of an economic statistic, one can take the most frequently occurring value or the range of values in which more values fall than any other range of equal size. This is called the *mode* or *modal value*. For example, suppose we have information on individual incomes by $5,000 increments and more people in our group fall in the $20,000 to $25,000 category than in any other segment. The $20,000 to $25,000 range may include only 38% of the group, but if no other $5 thousand range has as many as 38% of the group, then the modal value for income is between $20 and $25 thousand.

Measures of Dispersion: Average Absolute Deviation, Variance, Standard Deviation, and Coefficient of Variation

In analyzing economic time series we frequently wish to have some measure of just how typical the average value is, some measure of the dispersion of the individual observations around the mean. Summing up all the deviations from the mean value will not tell us anything since the sum of the deviations of any set of numbers from their mean value will always equal zero. If we consider the series 9, 6, and 12, the mean is 9 and the deviations are 0, -3, and $+3$. Algebraically, we can show that the sum of the differences between the mean value and all the individual data points is zero as follows:

$$\sum(x_i - \bar{x}) = \sum x_i - n\bar{x} = \sum x_i - n(\sum x_i/n) = \sum x_i - \sum x_i = 0.$$

So what can we use as the typical deviation from the mean? We can't use the arithmetic average of these deviations. If the sum of the deviations is zero, the average deviation is zero. We can take the *mean absolute deviation*, MAD, also called the *average absolute deviation*. To calculate this measure we simply sum up the deviations without regard to sign and divide by how many we have. In the case of our 9, 6, and 12 series the absolute sum would be $0 + 3 + 3 = 6$. The average absolute deviation is 6 divided by 3, or 2.

A more common way to measure dispersion is to square the deviations before summing and, thereby, obtain the *variance* and *standard deviation*. Squaring, of course, converts all the deviations (plus or minus) to positive numbers. In the case just mentioned, the deviations 0, -3, and $+3$ would become 0, $+9$, and $+9$ when squared. The sum of the three would be 18 and the average value 6. The average squared deviation from the mean for a set of numbers is called the *variance*. The square root of the variance is the *standard deviation*. In this case the standard deviation is the square root of 6, or 2.45. We can get a feel for the information content of these measures of dispersion by contrasting our first set of data points (9, 6, 12) with another set having the same mean but greater dispersion. Consider the set 9, 3, and 15. The mean is still 9, but the deviations from it are 0, -6, and $+6$. The mean absolute deviation is $12/3 = 4$. The variance is $(36 + 0 + 36)/3 = 24$ and the standard deviation is the square root of 24, or 4.90. We doubled our deviations and the average absolute deviation doubled from 2 to 4. The variance went up by 2 squared, or 4, since it went from 6 to 24. The standard deviation also doubled from 2.45 to 4.90.

Algebraically these measures of dispersion are defined as follows:

$$\text{MAD} = \text{mean or average absolute deviation} = \sum \left| (x_i - \bar{x}) \right| / n,$$

$$\sigma^2 = \text{variance} = \sum (x_i - \bar{x})^2 / n, \text{ and}$$

$$\sigma = \text{standard deviation} = \sqrt{\sum (x_i - \bar{x})^2 / n}.$$

We must note that in contexts other than simple measures of dispersion, there are valid statistical reasons for calculating the variance and standard deviation using one less than the number of data points as the denominator, that is, dividing by ($n - 1$) instead of by (n). Obviously this makes a great deal of difference if the set of numbers is small and very little difference if (n) is very large. In this text when the mean and standard deviations are presented as strictly descriptive measures of the typical value and the dispersion of a time series around it, (n) is always used and not ($n - 1$).

We should consider one additional measure of dispersion. It is the *coefficient of variation*, the ratio of the standard deviation to the mean. When we compare the sets of numbers (9, 6, 12) and (9, 3, 15) we find we have doubled the dispersion in both absolute and percentage terms. A rise in the standard deviation by a factor of 2 accurately describes it. However, we would get the same result if we contrasted the first set of numbers (9, 6, 12) with the set (109, 103, 115). The latter set has an average value of 109 and deviations from the mean of 0, -6, and $+6$. The mean absolute deviation, variance, and standard deviation are all the same as in our second set of numbers (9, 3, 15). The mean absolute deviation is 4, the variance is 24, and the standard deviation is 4.90. But do we really want to say that the series (109, 103, 115) is as volatile as the set (9, 3, 15)? They do both have the same standard deviation, but intuitively 4.90 as a typical departure from a mean value of 109 does not seem as large as the same deviation from a mean value of 9. Moreover, of course, it is not as large in percentage terms. In recognition of this, in an effort to be more descriptive we frequently take the standard deviation

TABLE 7A.1 Three Short Time Series

	Series 1		Series 2		Series 3	
	X	X − X̄	X	X − X̄	X	X − X̄
Observation 1	9	0	9	0	109	0
Observation 2	6	− 3	3	− 6	103	− 6
Observation 3	12	+ 3	15	+ 6	115	+ 6
Arithmetic mean, average, x̄	9		9		109	
Average absolute deviation, mean absolute deviation, MAD	2		4		4	
Variance, σ^2	6		24		24	
Standard deviation, σ	2.45		4.90		4.90	
Coefficient of variation, $\sigma/\bar{x}$	.272 (27%)		.544 (54%)		.045 (4 1/2%)	

as a percentage of the mean. As we defined it above, this ratio is called the *coefficient of variation*. In our three examples, the coefficient of variation is 27% in the first case, 54% in the second case, and 4-1/2% in the third case. Table 7A.1 summarizes these measures with these three very small data sets.

The Correlation Coefficient

The correlation coefficient is a measure of the association between two series of numbers, a measure of how closely their movements parallel one another. If two time series move in the same direction at the same time, we say there is a positive correlation. If they consistently move in opposite directions, then there is negative correlation. If there is no apparent linear relationship between movements in the two series, there is zero correlation.

More precisely stated, the correlation coefficient measures similarity of movement in two series deviations from their mean value. The correlation coefficient is calculated by taking the square root of the ratio of the *covariance*, σ_{12}, of two time series to the product of their standard deviations. Algebraically, the correlation coefficient between x_1 and x_2, r_{12}, is defined as follows:

$$r_{12} = \sqrt{(\sigma_{12}^2)/(\sigma_1)(\sigma_2)},$$

where

$$\sigma_{12}^2 = \left[\sum (x_1 - \bar{x}_1)(x_2 - \bar{x}_2) \right] / (n).$$

If each time period, x_1 and x_2, have very similar departures from their respective means, the numerator of the correlation coefficient will be large and the correlation coefficient will be close to 1.00. If either x_1 or x_2 were a constant and so had zero departures from its mean, of course, the correlation coefficient would be zero. Also,

TABLE 7A.2 Four Time Series

Year	Series 1		Series 2		Series 3		Series 4	
	x	$(x - \bar{x})$	x	$(x - \bar{x})$	x	$(x - \bar{x})$	x	$(x - \bar{x})$
1	2	−2	7	−2	4	+2	4	−1
2	4	0	9	0	2	0	6	+1
3	6	+2	11	+2	0	−2	5	0
4	5	+1	10	+1	1	−1	4	−1
5	3	−1	8	−1	3	+1	6	+1
$\bar{x}$	4		9		2		5	
σ^2	2		2		2		.8	

if the cross-products of the two sum to zero, the covariance will be zero, and the correlation coefficient will be zero.

Consider the four short (five years) time series in Table 7A.2. Series 1 has a perfect positive correlation with series 2 ($r_{12} = 1.00$), a perfect negative correlation with series 3 ($r_{13} = -1.00$), and no correlation with series 4 ($r_{14} = 0$). Figure 7A.1 shows the relationships in graphic form. The left-hand panel of the graph shows each pair of time series plotted against time. One can readily observe the synchronization of movements in series 1 and 2, the converse movements in series 1 and 3, and the lack of consistency in movements in series 1 and 4. The right-hand panel shows the pairs plotted against each other. Here we see on the first panel at the top that perfect positive correlation ($r_{12} = 1.00$) is a positively sloped straight line. Conversely, the second panel shows perfect negative correlation ($r_{13} = -1.00$) as a negatively sloped straight line. The lower right-hand panel shows that zero correlation ($r_{14} = 0$) plots as a wide-ranging scatter diagram.

Of course these time series have been artificially constructed to give these extreme results. All the real world falls somewhere between $+1.00$ and -1.00 with many a forecasting scheme floundering on a correlation coefficient that came out very close to zero. We will come back to the question of how far away from zero is meaningful below when we discuss statistical significance.

Linear Regression

Linear regression consists of explicitly deriving the straight line relationships shown in Fig. 7A.1. Specifically, the regression lines in Fig. 7A.1 are:

$$x_2 = 5 + x_1 \quad \text{and} \quad x_3 = 6 - x_1.$$

If we had knowledge of the value of x_1 for any one of these five years, we could, through the use of these equations, determine x_2 or x_3. If we had good analytical reasons to believe these relationships would hold up in the future, we could base forecasts for x_2 and x_3 on known or forecasted values of x_1. Of course, such a perfect fit among economic time series is never found in the real world. Hence, let

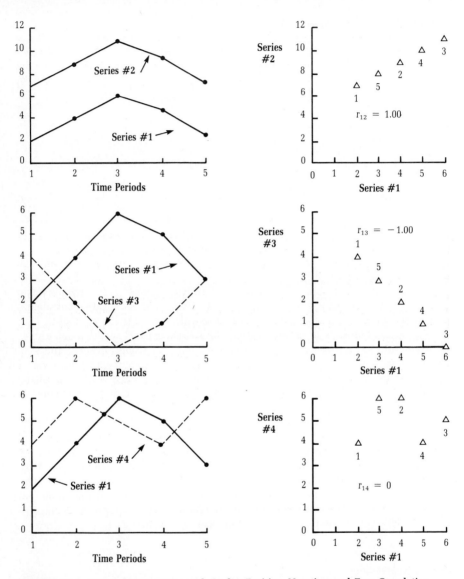

FIGURE 7A.1 Pairs of Time Series with Perfect Positive, Negative, and Zero Correlation.

us be more realistic and consider some series with correlation coefficients other than $+1.00$ or -1.00.

Let us create series 5 and 6 by alternately adding and subtracting 2.00 to series 2 and 3 as shown in Table 7A.3. The plot of x_1 against x_5 and x_6 is shown in Fig. 7A.2. Although some positive and negative associations are still apparent, they are far from perfect. How do we estimate this relationship? How do we measure how accurately a line relating the two variables describes their relationship? In fact,

TABLE 7A.3   Three Correlated Time Series

	Year	X_1	X_5	X_6
	1	2	9	6
	2	4	7	0
	3	6	13	2
	4	5	8	−1
	5	3	10	5
Mean, $\bar{x}$				
		4	9.4	2.4
Variance, σ^2				
		2	4.2	7.4

what criteria do we use in computing the line supposed to describe the relationship between the two variables? For a lot of good theoretical and practical reasons that we will not discuss here, the prevalent practice is to solve for the relationship between the two variables that would minimize the squared error term if you were using x_1 to predict x_5 or x_6. In this context x_1 is called the *independent variable* and x_5 or x_6 is the *dependent variable*. Customarily independent variables are indicated by the use of x's and dependent variables by the use of y's. As in the text we will indicate forecasts, predictions, or estimates with a "hat" or accent circumflex, $\hat{y}$.

The equation that minimizes the sum of the squared error terms is called the *least-squares line*. A derived relationship between a dependent variable and time as the independent variable is called a *least-squares trend line*. The formula for estimating the parameters of a least-squares regression equation is:

$$y = a + bx; a = \bar{y} - b\bar{x}; b = (\sigma_{xy}^2) / (\sigma_x^2).$$

The *regression coefficient*, b, is the ratio of the covariance between the dependent and the independent variable to the variance of the independent variable. Like the correlation coefficient, the regression coefficient will be a large positive or a large

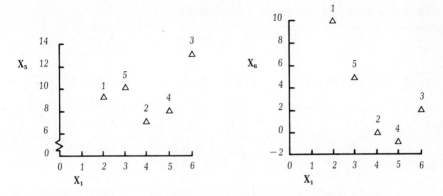

FIGURE 7A.2   Time Series with Less than Perfect Positive and Negative Correlation.

negative number if the covariance between the two variables is a large positive or negative. In the case of using x_1 to estimate x_5 and x_6 the regression equations and correlation coefficients are:

$$\hat{x}_5 = 7 + .6\,(x_1) \qquad r_{15} = .41$$
$$\hat{x}_6 = 8 - 1.4\,(x_1) \qquad r_{16} = -.73.$$

At this point let us note two important characteristics of ordinary least-squares estimating equations:

1. Such a relationship is different depending on which variable is decreed to be the dependent variable. Although r_{12} does equal r_{21}, b_{12} does not equal b_{21} in

$$\hat{x}_1 = a_1 + b_{12}x_2$$
$$\hat{x}_2 = a_2 + b_{21}x_1.$$

2. A least-squares estimate will be unbiased in the sense that the summation and average value for the estimated values will equal the actual values for the data on which the equation is based; i.e.,

$$\sum \hat{y} = \sum y \text{ and } \overline{\hat{y}} = \overline{y}.$$

The Coefficient of Determination and Other Measures of Forecasting Accuracy

Let us look closer at using x_1 to forecast x_5 and x_6. The forecasts generated with the least-squares equations given and their error terms are shown in Table 7A.4.

Let us now consider the question of just how good x_1 is as a forecaster of x_5 and x_6. As indicated earlier, we know that we obtain an unbiased estimate since the average estimate is equal to the average of the actual time series. The question of how good a forecasting procedure is can be thought of, as indicated in the text, as to how bad the error terms are. The most common criterion for the evaluation

TABLE 7A.4 Least-Squares Estimates of Two Time Series

	Year	x_1	$\hat{x}_5 = 7 + .6(x_1)$			$\hat{x}_6 = 8 - 1.4(x_1)$		
			x_5	$\hat{x}_5$	$x_5 - \hat{x}_5$	x_6	$\hat{x}_6$	$x_6 - \hat{x}_6$
	1	2	9	8.2	.8	6	5.2	.8
	2	4	7	9.4	−2.4	0	2.4	−2.4
	3	6	13	10.6	2.4	2	−.4	2.4
	4	5	8	10.0	−2.0	−1	1.0	−2.0
	5	3	10	8.8	1.2	5	3.8	1.2
Mean, $\overline{x}$		4	9.4	9.4		2.4	2.4	
Variance, σ_x^2		2	4.2	.7		7.4	3.9	

of forecasts and forecasting techniques is to apply one of our measures of dispersion to the error terms. Instead of measuring the deviation of a series from its mean, we measure the deviation of the forecast from the actual or (what amounts to the same thing) the deviation of the error term from zero. We can use mean absolute deviations, MAD, defined as

$$\text{MAD} = \sum |Y_t - \hat{Y}_t| / n = \sum |e_t| / n.$$

We can also use the *root mean squared error*, RMSE, defined as

$$\text{RMSE} = \sqrt{\sum (Y_t - \hat{Y}_t)^2 / n} = \sqrt{\sum e_t^2 / n}.$$

When we are using a technique such as least squares that gives us an unbiased estimate (mean value of the error terms equal to zero), the RMSE is the standard deviation of the error term. In regression analysis the RMSE can be adjusted for the number of degrees of freedom to generate the *standard error of the estimate*, SEE, defined as

$$\text{SEE} = \sqrt{\sum e_t^2 / (n - 2)}.$$

As indicated, the adjustment is to divide by $(n - 2)$ instead of (n).

In the exercise above with x_1 being used to forecast x_5 and x_6, we have rigged the data so the two series of error terms are identical. In both cases the mean absolute deviation is the same at 1.76, the root mean squared error is the same at 1.88, and the standard error of the estimates are equal at 2.43. But is x_1 really as useful in forecasting x_5 as it is in forecasting x_6? Remember that $r_{15} = .41$ while $r_{16} = -.73$. The correlation coefficients indicate that the association between x_1 and x_6 is a bit closer than between x_1 and x_5. In fact, the square of the correlation coefficient is called the *coefficient of determination*. The square of a particular correlation coefficient, say r_{15}^2, measures the proportion of the variance of the dependent variable, x_5, that can be "explained" by the use of the independent variable, x_1. The total variance of x_5 is $\sum (x_5 - \overline{x}_5)^2 / n$ and would be the variance of the error terms if one always used the mean value as a forecast. Using the regression equation based on x_1 improves on using the mean value as a forecast, but the variance that is not explained by the regression equation is the variance remaining in the error terms, $\sum (x_5 - x_5) / n$. Skipping a great deal of algebraic manipulation, another way to write the correlation coefficient squared is as follows:

$$r_{15}^2 = 1 - \left[\sum (x_5 - \hat{x}_5)^2 / \sum (x_5 - \overline{x}_5)^2 \right] = 1 - \sigma e^2 / \sigma_5^2.$$

The variance of x_5, σ_5^2 would be the average squared error term if you could make no better forecast than just to guess the mean value, $\overline{x}_5$, for every time period. If you did not improve on this with the regression analysis, then $\sigma_e^2 = \sigma_5^2$ and $r_{15}^2 = 0$. To the extent that you improve on this, $\sum e^2$ goes down and r^2 goes up. The usual terminology is that σ_5^2 is the "total variation" in x_5, σ_e^2 is the "unexplained variation"; so $\sigma e^2 / \sigma_5^2$ is the proportion of the variation not explained. Therefore, its complement, $r_{15}^2 = 1 - \sigma e^2 / \sigma_5^2$, is the "explained variation." In our example,

x_1 can be used to "explain" only 17%, $(r_{15}^2 = .168)$, of x_5's variation but slightly over 53% of x_6's, $(r_{16}^2 = .533)$.

Statistical Significance and Hypothesis Testing

The subtitle of this section actually contains a pair of synonyms since questions of statistical significance and hypothesis testing are really one and the same thing. For example, when you consider the question of whether you think a particular forecasting procedure is biased, you are actually asking whether it does on average generate significant positive or negative errors. In looking for statistical significance one is actually testing the hypothesis that the statistic with which one is concerned is equal to zero. If you find grounds for rejecting that hypothesis, the statistic is said to be significant.

As another example, I would predict that an honestly tossed coin would generate 50% heads and 50% tails. My forecast for the proportion of heads out of any given number of tosses would have to be that half of them would be heads. If, in fact, the results over some sample period were 75% heads and 25% tails, I might suspect something strange is happening. More precisely, I would want to inquire as to whether the 75% is, for the number of trials I have, significantly different from 50%.

Let us use this example to define a number of standard statistical terms. First, my *null hypothesis* is that the difference between the proportion of heads "in the long run" (number of tosses approaches infinity) and 50% is zero. If on the basis of my sample statistic of 75%, I can find grounds for rejecting the null hypothesis, I may choose to accept the *alternative hypothesis* that the long-run value for heads is greater than 50%. Notice I do not really "prove" the alternative hypothesis but turn to it by rejecting the null hypothesis. It is properly said that nothing is ever proved with statistics; one only disproves things.

The most important missing piece of information in our example is the number of tosses. Say our sample consisted of only four tosses, three of which happened to be heads. On the basis of this small sample we might not be ready to accuse the flipper of running a dishonest game. However, if out of 4,000 tosses 75% were heads, we probably would prefer to bet our money on heads for any given toss.

The case of only two possible outcomes and testing the hypothesis that each outcome is equally likely is a statistical problem in which the theory is fairly simple. The outcome is governed by the *binomial distribution*. On the four-toss sample we can calculate that if the outcomes were, in fact, equally likely, there is one chance in four of three heads by pure chance. If we declare the game dishonest, we run a 25% chance of falsely accusing the flipper. If we continue to believe the game to be honest we run a 75% chance of being cheated. The first type of error, rejecting the null hypothesis when we should not, is called *Type I error*. The second type of error, failing to reject the null hypothesis when we should have, is called *Type II error*. With a sample of 4,000 tosses the probability of Type I error is quite small, less than a fraction of 1%.

To repeat, statistically speaking, we do not prove anything in the positive sense. We can only *reject* hypotheses. In many cases the rejection of one hypothesis causes us to accept the alternate hypothesis, but in no way have we "proved" the alternate hypothesis. Empirical scientific truth consists of hypotheses that we have been unable to reject.

In regression analysis we seek to reject the hypothesis that the correlation and regression coefficients are equal to zero. If we fit a regression line of the form $\hat{Y} = a + bX$, we are seeking to reject the following hypotheses:

$b = 0$, $r_{xy} = 0$, and $r_{xy}^2 = 0$.

These three algebraic statements are all equivalent statistically. If X and Y are independent, $r_{xy} = 0$, $r_{xy}^2 = 0$, and $b = 0$. Of course, this means that $\hat{Y} = a = \overline{Y}$. Recall that $a = \overline{Y} - b\overline{X}$. If X and Y are independent, your best forecast of Y is its mean value, $\overline{Y}$.

The computed means, correlation coefficients, variances, and standard deviations are all taken to be empirical estimates of their theoretical counterparts and used to reject or not reject various hypotheses. The *confidence level* of a test of statistical significance refers to the estimated probability of making Type I error, rejecting a hypothesis when you should not. In our case of 4,000 tosses of the coin, we are more than 99.9% confident that we are not making a mistake by saying that 75% heads is so unlikely to happen by chance that we reject the hypothesis that 50% is the true long-term value.

In the case of the coin toss, and the implied binomial distribution, we know the kind of chance behavior with which we are dealing. Most importantly we know what the dispersion around 50% should be by chance if the game were honest. In other more complex situations, we are frequently not so sure. We use the computed variance and standard deviation to estimate statistical confidence levels. Most commonly the chance outcomes are assumed to be distributed according to the *normal distribution* which gives the computed standard deviation, using $(n - 1)$, special significance. In general, the testing of a hypothesis that something is equal to zero consists of deriving the best possible estimate of the standard deviation of the probable outcomes and calculating the number of standard deviations the observed result is from zero. If a normal distribution of results is assumed, the odds of something falling by chance more than one standard deviation from zero are 1 chance in 3.15. The odds of it falling more than two standard deviations away from the expected value are 1 in 23. At three standard deviations we are up to 1 in 370. In terms of confidence of not making Type I error: at one standard deviation we can reject the null hypothesis with 68% confidence; at two standard deviations, 95% confidence; and with three standard deviations, 99.7% confidence.

Although, in fact, the exact conditions for the use of the normal distribution are rarely met completely in practice, there are good theoretical reasons to believe the normal distribution is a good approximation for a wide range of conditions, especially if the sample is large, say a hundred or more data points.

The calculated standard deviation has a descriptive and analytical utility independent of the assumption of the normal distribution or any other particular distribution. It can be shown that it is impossible to have *any* set of numbers in which less than 89% of them will fall within three standard deviations of the mean as calculated from the set of numbers. As a generalization, any set of numbers will have a percentage of its members within k standard deviations of its mean equal to at least $(1 - 1/k^2)$. In theoretical terms, even if you know nothing about the underlying distribution except its standard deviation, you can still reject the null hypothesis with 89% confidence if you get a sample statistic three standard deviations away from its expected value. These results flow from a statistical theorem known as *Chebyshev's inequality*.[1]

● Source Note

[1]For more explanation and some examples in statistical application see: Edwin Mansfield, *Statistics for Business and Economics*. New York: W. W. Norton, 1980, pp. 114–115.

Autoregressive Forecasting Techniques

8

An autoregressive forecasting technique is a method of forecasting future values of a time series by using only the past history of the time series. Some forecasting methods of this type are very simple. If you *always* drink exactly two beers each and every day, your beer consumption would be a dull time series to analyze and an easy one to forecast. The forecasting mechanism would be $\hat{Y}_t = Y_{t-1} = 2$. The forecast of your beer consumption today, $\hat{Y}_t$, will equal your beer consumption yesterday, Y_{t-1}, which is equal to 2. Forecasting toy sales in December could be done with the autoregressive technique of using the history of the time series, which could tell us the typical seasonal change from November to December, the recent annual rate of growth from one December to the next, and so on. If, however, you took account of what had happened to people's income (how much money they had available to spend on toys), you would no longer be using a purely autoregressive forecasting technique, since people's income is another time series to be related to the one you are trying to forecast.

The Use of the Error Term in Selecting and Improving Forecasts

One surety about a forecast is that it is going to be wrong most of the time. The question is not whether your forecast will be right or wrong. The only question is how wrong you will be. When forecasting a particular time series we measure how wrong we are by the difference between what we forecast and what actually happens. The size of the error term for the period t, e_t is defined as

$$e_t = Y_t - \hat{Y}_t, \quad \text{where} \quad \hat{Y}_t = \text{our forecast, and}$$
$$Y_t = \text{the actual value.}$$

The first thing one should do with error terms is look for some consistent bias. If we have a forecasting technique that gives us consistently negative error terms, $\hat{Y}_t > Y_t$, we know this forecasting procedure has a positive bias. We can reduce the size of the error terms and thereby improve the accuracy of the forecast by simply lowering each forecast by the average negative value of the error term. Mathematically this will result in a set of forecasts that add up to the same total as the actual values over the sample period. The average value of the estimates will be the same as the actuals, and the error term will have a total and average value of zero — the definition of an unbiased forecast. Similarly, if the sum of the error terms gives a positive number, we know our forecast has a downward bias and can be improved by raising each forecast by the average amount of the error term.

Let us consider two hypothetical forecasts and their error terms. Table 8.1 gives us 12 data points for forecasting technique A, 12 for forecasting technique B, the actual value of the variable we are trying to forecast, and the error terms. We should note that 12 monthly data points are really not sufficient to evaluate monthly sales forecasting techniques, especially since we would want to check for seasonal fluctuations; but our purpose here is to keep the sample small enough so that the mechanics of the procedures are easy to follow.

From an inspection of the error terms in the two right-hand columns of Table 8.1, it is obvious that forecasting technique A has a positive bias (tends to forecast too high), and technique B has a negative bias (tends to forecast too low). The average value of forecast A at 17.92 is 2 units higher than the actual value of 15.92. The average value of forecast B at 14.92 is 1 unit below the average actual. Both techniques can be improved by simply adding or subtracting the amount required to remove the bias. Table 8.2

TABLE 8.1 Two Hypothetical Forecasts and Their Error Terms

Time Period	Sales Forecast A	Sales Forecast B	Actual Sales	Error Terms	
				A	B
Jan.	13	7	10	−3	3
Feb.	12	11	12	0	1
Mar.	17	15	14	−3	−1
Apr.	18	16	17	−1	1
May	20	18	19	−1	1
June	27	20	23	−4	3
July	27	20	23	−4	3
Aug.	20	18	17	−3	−1
Sept.	19	15	15	−4	0
Oct.	15	14	15	0	1
Nov.	14	10	12	−2	2
Dec.	13	15	14	1	−1
Total	215	179	191	−24	12
Average	17.92	14.92	15.92	−2.00	1.00

TABLE 8.2 Two Hypothetical Forecasts Corrected for Bias

Time Period	Unbiased Forecast A	Unbiased Forecast B	Actual Sales	Error Terms	
				A	B
Jan.	11	8	10	−1	2
Feb.	10	12	12	2	0
Mar.	15	16	14	−1	−2
Apr.	16	17	17	1	0
May	18	19	19	1	0
June	25	21	23	−2	−2
July	25	21	23	−2	2
Aug.	18	19	17	−1	−2
Sept.	17	16	15	−2	−1
Oct.	13	15	15	2	0
Nov.	12	11	12	0	1
Dec.	11	16	14	3	−2
Total	191	191	191	0	0
Average	15.92	15.92	15.92	0	0

shows the results of subtracting 2.00 from each forecast by technique *A* and adding 1.00 to each technique *B* forecast.

The adjustment of the forecasts results in totals and averages for both forecasts equal to the total and average values for the actual sales. The error terms for each forecasting technique now add up to zero. Neither forecast is consistently too high or low.

Now that we have two unbiased forecasts, how do we decide between them? The most direct approach to measuring the accuracy of a forecast is simply to go "MAD," an acronym for *Mean Absolute Deviation*. We simply add up the error terms without regard to whether they are plus or minus and then divide the total by how many of them we have. This gives us the average of the absolute value of the error term. For forecasting technique *A*, the total of the errors is 18, which when divided by 12 gives us a mean absolute deviation of 1.50. In the case of *B*, the total is 14 for a mean absolute deviation of only 1.17. Technique *B* would presumably be the preferred forecasting procedure due to its smaller average error term.

By far the most popular measures of forecasting accuracy are derived from the standard deviation of the error term. The standard deviation of a time series, σ_y, is a measure of the width of the dispersion around the mean value, $\bar{y}$, as indicated by the following formula:

$$\sigma_y = \sqrt{\Sigma(y - \bar{y})^2/n}.$$

In the case of the error term of an unbiased estimate where the mean value, $\bar{e}$, is equal to zero, the formula for the standard deviation of the error term would be

$$\sigma_e = \sqrt{\sum e^2 / n}.$$

The standard deviation of the error term will measure the dispersion of the errors around zero and hence the accuracy of the forecasts. The lower the standard deviation of the error term, the better the forecasts. What we are doing computationally is taking the square root of the average squared error term as a representative measure of the "typical" error. Measuring the accuracy of the two forecasting techniques shown in Table 8.2 we find that

$$\sum e_A^2 = 34 \qquad\qquad \sum e_B^2 = 25$$
$$\sigma_{eA} = \sqrt{(34)/(12)} = 1.68 \qquad \sigma_{eB} = \sqrt{(25)/(12)} = 1.44.$$

Again, technique B appears to be the better of the two forecasting procedures since this measure of the typical error is also smaller. It is not a coincidence that we obtained the same ranking of the two techniques using MAD or the standard deviation. It would take a truly strange set of data to give opposing results with these two measures. The mean absolute deviation is easier to compute and intuitively more appealing, but the standard deviation is more commonly used because it is very closely related to the Standard Error of the Estimate used in regression analysis and a whole host of other statistical measures.*

First Differences and Diffusion Indexes as Leading Indicators

One form of autoregressive forecasting is to use the first difference or percentage rate of change as a leading indicator. By *leading indicator,* we mean a time series that will reach a turning point before the time series we are trying to forecast. Ideally, a leading indicator would always turn up or down the same number of periods in advance of a peak or trough and never have a turn that was not followed by a turn in the series to be forecast. No such perfect indicators exist, but first differences and diffusion indexes do appear to contain some information regarding the future course of events for some time series.

---

*The Standard Error of the Estimate in regression analysis is simply the standard deviation of the error term adjusted for the number of degrees of freedom lost in making the estimate. Instead of dividing by n before taking the square root, one divides by $n-k$ where k is the number of degrees of freedom lost in the estimation process. In simple two-variable regression analysis (one dependent and one independent) $k = 2$ and it goes up by 1.00 with each additional independent variable in multiple regression analysis.

Using a first difference or percentage change as a leading indicator is something that we all do intuitively. A person in business feels that when the annual or monthly rate of increase in sales goes from 10% to 7% to 3%, sales may soon stop rising altogether and perhaps even begin to decline. A declining rate of increase may indicate that there will soon be a decrease. This sort of relationship between the rate of change and the underlying time series is inherent in the arithmetic of any series that has a fairly smooth cycle. Consider the time series Y, and its first difference ΔY, shown both numerically in Table 8.3 and graphically in Fig. 8.1.

The first difference of a time series makes a good leading indicator of peaks and troughs because, mathematically speaking, the original time series has a zero first difference at a peak or trough. In our example we start with the time series rising and thereby the first difference is above the zero line. However, since the first difference must get back to zero in order to go negative as the underlying time series peaks at $t = 7$, the first difference must turn down well before that time; in this case at $t = 4$. Similarly, as Y falls, ΔY is below zero but must turn in advance of the turn in Y since ΔY must cross zero when Y stops falling and starts rising. In this case, ΔY only leads Y by one time period.

Generally speaking, the first difference will act as a good leading indicator of any fairly smooth time series — or a series that can be made smooth by seasonal and trend adjustment. A time series that slows its rate of increase before it begins to fall is by definition a series with a smooth cyclical movement. A highly erratic time series that changes direction with large discrete jumps will not generate a first difference that tells you much about where it is going.

A variation of the first difference as a leading indicator approach involves what are sometimes called *pressure curves,* where one uses the percentage rate of change to measure upward or downward "pressure" on the future behavior of the time series. Such indicators are usually plotted as indexes computed by taking the ratio of, say, this month's sales to the sales for the same month last year. If this year June's sales were $120 million and

TABLE 8.3 A Time Series and Its First Difference

t	Y	ΔY	t	Y	ΔY	t	Y	ΔY
1	10		6	29	3	11	24(T)[b]	−1
2	13	3	7	30(P)[a]	1	12	25	1
3	17	4	8	29	−1	13	27	2
4	22	5(P)[a]	9	28	−2	14	30	3
5	26	4	10	25	−3(T)[b]	15	34	4

[a](P) = peak.
[b](T) = trough.

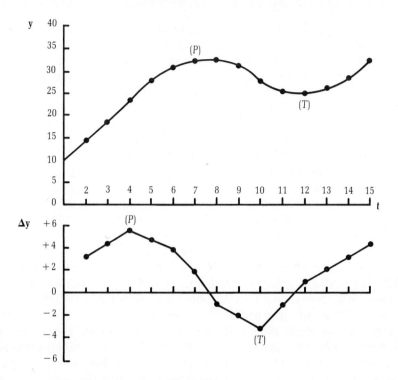

FIGURE 8.1   A First Difference as a Leading Indicator.

last June's sales were $100 million, the "1/12 index" would be 120. The index was computed by taking the ratio of this June's sales to last June's, 1.20, and multiplying by 100 as is customary with indexes.

Alternatively, pressure curve indexes are computed by using the percentage increase over the last twelve months, (12/12), the last quarter, (3/3), or just month-to-month changes, (1/1). For example, for a (12/12) pressure curve one sums up the sales for the most recent twelve months and takes that total as a ratio to the twelve months previous to that. Similarly, a (3/3) curve is computed by taking the ratio of the most recent three months to the three months before that.

Table 8.4 shows a (1/1) pressure curve for the data shown in Table 8.3 and graphed in Fig. 8.1. Note that in this particular case the pressure curve peaks and troughs one period earlier than the straight first difference. This is not a mathematical necessity but only a peculiarity of this particular data. Of course, a pressure curve index will tend to lead the underlying data for the same reasons and under the same conditions as any first difference model.

Whether the index is above or below 100 is significant in that it indicates whether the most recent time period is above or below the time period to

TABLE 8.4 A Time Series and Its (1/1) Pressure Curve Index

t	y	Index	t	y	Index	t	y	Index
1	10		6	29	112	11	24(T)[b]	96
2	13	130	7	30(P)[a]	103	12	25	104
3	17	131(P)[a]	8	29	97	13	27	108
4	22	129	9	28	97(T)[b]	14	30	111
5	26	118	10	25	89	15	34	113

[a](P) = peak.
[b](T) = trough.

which it is being compared. In this case the 103 in period 7 indicates a 3% increase from period 6 to period 7. The value of 97 in period 8 indicates a 3% decrease in Y from period 7 to period 8.

Another popular autoregressive leading indicator is what is called a *diffusion index*. To be susceptible to this approach the variable we are seeking to forecast must be a composite index of some type, such as the GNP. If we note that GNP is made up of the four components of consumption, investment, government expenditures, and net exports, we can construct a diffusion index on the basis of the proportion of these components that are rising. For example, if from one quarter to the next consumption and investment expenditures rose but government expenditures and net exports fell, the diffusion index would equal 50. Half, or 50%, of the components of GNP were rising. In this case, with only four components, our diffusion index could only take the values of 0, 25, 50, and 100. Time series with more components such as the industrial production index, the consumer price index, or a finer breakdown of GNP can of course take on a larger number of discrete values.

Diffusion indexes do tend to be leading indicators of the time series from which they are constructed for the same reasons as first differences. When most or all the components of a series are rising (a diffusion index near 100), a variable will usually be rising at a rapid rate. As the rate of increase slows as the variable approaches a cyclical peak, the number of components reporting increases will tend to fall, causing the diffusion index to peak in advance of the underlying series. Similarly, as the rate of decline in some series slows before a trough, it is likely that some of its components will actually begin to rise, causing the diffusion index to reach a trough before the primary variable. As with other first difference indicators, there is no mathematical necessity for this type of relationship unless the cyclical movement is relatively smooth.

Although diffusion indexes can be analytically informative regarding how pervasive a movement is in a composite index, there is no statistical proof that they serve any better as a leading indicator than a simple first difference model based either on the absolute or percentage change. The diffusion index does answer the straightforward question of what percentage of the components is rising. This author feels, however, that diffusion indexes are a less reliable leading indicator than first differences because they do not distinguish between a very rapid and a very slow rate of increase of, say, 80% of the components.

Simple Naive Forecasts

In discussing first differences, pressure curves, and diffusion indexes we discussed procedures used only as broad indicators of the possibility of a coming turning point. Those indicators could be used in simple or multiple regression analysis to generate a specific forecast for the underlying variable, but other more direct approaches are generally used to generate a specific autoregressive forecast.

We now turn to procedures for using a time series to generate a specific forecast of itself, not just a general indication of the expected direction of movement. One general class of forecasts is referred to as *naive* forecasts. These techniques are given that name because they are based on the rather naive but frequently very useful assumption that the next time period will be the same as the current one. This assumption can refer either to the absolute level of the primary variable or to its rate of change, and we can treat the rate of change as either a straight first difference or as a percentage change. For example, if this month's sales were up by $10,000 to a level of $100,000, we could forecast sales to be $100,000 next month. We could forecast another increase of $10,000 and forecast a level of $110,000. Or we could note that the $10,000 was an 11% increase over the previous month's level of $90,000 and forecast a level of $111,000 for next month. Each approach would be classed as a naive forecasting technique. The first assumes a constant level of sales, the second a constant absolute increase, and the third a constant percentage increase.

Let us apply each of our three naive approaches to the time series given in Tables 8.3 and 8.4. We will evaluate the accuracy of each approach on the basis of mean absolute deviations. The time series, the forecasts, and their error terms are shown in Table 8.5. Note that two of the procedures do not give us unbiased estimates for the 13 periods for which we have estimates. We have only 13 usable data points, since we lose the first two points in calculating our first estimate, based either on a constant absolute rate of change or a constant percentage change.

From Table 8.5 we can observe that the average actual value for the 13 periods forecast was 26.6. The forecast averages were 25.0, 26.6, and 27.0. The mean absolute deviations turn out to be 2.5, 1.5, and 1.3. If we choose to rank the accuracy of these techniques on the basis of this criterion, we would conclude that the assumption of a constant level is the worst,

TABLE 8.5 Naive Forecasts and Their Error Terms

t	Y_t	$\hat{Y}_t = Y_{t-1}$		$\hat{Y}_t = Y_{t-1} + \Delta Y_{t-1}$		$\hat{Y}_t = (Y_{t-1})(1 + \% \Delta Y_{t-1})$	
		$\hat{Y}$	e	$\hat{Y}$	e	$\hat{Y}$	e
1	10[a]						
2	13[a]						
3	17	13	4	16	1	16.9	.1
4	22	17	5	21	1	22.2	−.2
5	26	22	4	27	−1	28.5	−2.5
6	29	26	3	30	−1	30.7	−1.7
7	30	29	1	32	−2	32.3	−2.3
8	29	30	−1	31	−2	31.0	−2.0
9	28	29	−1	30	−2	28.0	0.0
10	25	28	−3	27	−2	27.0	−2.0
11	24	25	−1	22	2	22.3	1.7
12	25	24	1	23	2	23.0	2.0
13	27	25	2	26	1	26.0	1.0
14	30	27	3	28	2	29.2	.8
15	34	30	4	33	1	33.3	.7
Absolute							
Total	346	325	33	346	20	350.4	17.0
Average	26.6	25.0	2.5	26.6	1.5	27.0	1.3

[a]Not included in computation of total or average.

the same change next month is better, and the same percentage change assumption is the best. Incidentally, if we rank the three approaches using the standard deviation of the error term, we get the same ranking with calculated standard deviations of 2.40, 1.62, and 1.52.

We should also consider another measure of forecasting accuracy called the *Theil Coefficient* (also sometimes known as "Theil's Inequality Coefficient"), which implicitly measures forecasts against a simple naive model. The Theil Coefficient is calculated by taking the square root of the ratio of the sum of the squared error terms to the sum of the squared first differences; i.e.,

$$\sqrt{\sum(Y_t - \hat{Y}_t)^2 \Big/ \sum(Y_t - Y_{t-1})^2} = \sqrt{\sum e_t^2 \Big/ \sum \Delta Y_t^2}.$$

Of course, if one is using a simple naive model, $\hat{Y}_t = Y_{t-1}$, the Theil Coefficient will always equal 1.00. If the Theil Coefficient is less than 1.00, then you are doing better than a simple naive model. If it is greater than 1.00, you would have been better off with the simple naive model. In the case of our three naive models the Theil Coefficients are 1.00, .56, and .54, respectively.

The naive forecasting methods are among the oldest of forecasting techniques and are in many ways just what their name implies. But they have been shown to be of substantial value. One of their major values is as a benchmark against which any more complex technique can be measured. In many recorded cases these relatively simple techniques have been shown to be superior to complex mathematical forecasting models. Unless there is some significant gain from a more complicated model, the simple naive models are generally preferred, since they do not involve complicated computations by electronic computer and skilled statisticians. At the very least, when outside consultants or inside geniuses come to you with their great "new" discovery for forecasting, you can usually dispense with them quickly by determining that they have either (1) rediscovered a naive model or (2) used a more complex model that does not do as well. The first step in evaluating a forecasting technique should always be to compare it to whatever naive model seems most appropriate. Most techniques will not be able to show any significant superiority to a naive model when rigorously compared on the basis of mean absolute deviations or some other quantitative measure of accuracy.

Exponential Smoothing

Exponential smoothing is the name of a widely used technique of autoregressive forecasting that is closely related to the naive models we just considered. It is somewhat more complex than the straight naive models, but more flexible. This approach is based on the intuitively appealing idea of correcting one's forecast for the coming period by the size and direction of the error in this period's forecast. Specifically,

$$\hat{Y}_{t+1} = Y_t + \alpha(Y_t - \hat{Y}_t),$$

where

$$Y_{t+1} = \text{the forecast for the coming period},$$
$$\hat{Y}_t = \text{the forecast for the current period},$$
$$Y_t = \text{the actual value for the current period}.$$

Note that the right-hand side of the equation consists of the current period's forecast **plus** the error term for the current period. This means that if our error is **negative,** the forecast was too high ($\hat{Y}_t > Y_t$), and we will lower our forecast for the coming period. Conversely, if we underestimate the variable in the current period and the error term is **positive** ($\hat{Y}_t < Y_t$), we will raise our forecast for the coming period.

How much we correct for our error depends on the size of the coefficient α. If $\alpha = .80$ we will change our forecast by 80% of the error term. If $\alpha = .20$ we will only adjust by 20%. At one extreme, if $\alpha = 0$ then $\hat{Y}_{t+1} = \hat{Y}_t$ and our forecast remains unchanged regardless of what happens to the time series. (A constant forecast would make sense if we believed the series consisted of random variation around a mean value equal to $\hat{Y}_t$.) At the other extreme, if $\alpha = 1.00$ we adjust for 100% of the error and we have reverted to a naive forecast.

$$\text{If } \alpha = 1.00,$$
$$\text{then } \hat{Y}_{t+1} = \hat{Y}_t + (Y_t - \hat{Y}_t) = \hat{Y}_t - \hat{Y}_t + Y_t,$$
$$\text{and } \hat{Y}_{t+1} = Y_t.$$

The forecast for the coming period is equal to the value of the variable during the current period. This is the absolute level naive forecast discussed earlier.

Another way to look at the exponential smoothing model is to rearrange the terms as follows:

$$\hat{Y}_{t+1} = \hat{Y}_t + \alpha(Y_t - \hat{Y}_t) = \hat{Y}_t - \alpha\hat{Y}_t + \alpha Y_t,$$
$$\hat{Y}_{t+1} = \alpha Y_t + (1 - \alpha)(\hat{Y}_t).$$

In this form it is obvious that the forecast for the coming period, $\hat{Y}_{t+1}$, is a weighted average of the actual for the current period, Y_t, and our estimate for the current period, $\hat{Y}_t$. The weightings are α and $(1 - \alpha)$, respectively. As with any weighted average the sum of the coefficients is equal to 1.00. If $\alpha = .80$, we give 80% of the weighting to the current actual value and

20% to our forecast. If $\alpha = .30$, we would be giving a 30% weighting to the current actual value and 70% to our current forecast in constructing our new forecast.

But from where did the forecast $\hat{Y}_t$ come? If we have been using this forecasting procedure for a large number of time periods, the current forecast contains the influence of all the history of this time series. We can see this by expanding the forecasting equation into an infinite geometric progression.

$$\hat{Y}_{t+1} = \alpha Y_t + (1 - \alpha)(\hat{Y}_t),$$

$$\hat{Y}_t = \alpha Y_{t-1} + (1 - \alpha)(\hat{Y}_{t-1}),$$

$$\hat{Y}_{t-1} = \alpha Y_{t-2} + (1 - \alpha)(\hat{Y}_{t-2}),$$

$$\cdots\cdots\cdots\cdots$$

$$\cdots\cdots\cdots\cdots$$

$$\cdots\cdots\cdots\cdots$$

$$\hat{Y}_{t-n} = \alpha Y_{t-n-1} + (1 - \alpha)(\hat{Y}_{t-n-1}).$$

If we substitute the second equation into the first for Y_t and then the third into the resulting equation for Y_{t-1}, and so on, we obtain

$$\hat{Y}_{t+1} = \alpha Y_t + \alpha(1 - \alpha) Y_{t-1} + \alpha(1 - \alpha)^2 Y_{t-2}$$
$$+ \alpha(1 - \alpha)^3 Y_{t-3} + \ldots + \alpha(1 - \alpha)^n Y_{t-n}.$$

Of course, as n gets very large $(1 - \alpha)^n$ gets very small. What we have for our forecast in the $t + 1$ period is a weighted average of all the actual values of the variable that went before. Regardless of the value of α, the more recent values will be more heavily weighted than those in the more distant past. How much more depends on the size of α. The larger α is, the more weight is given to the more recent data.

Let us look at what proportion of the total weighting of 100% is in the coefficients of the four most recent data points for some illustrative values of α. (See Table 8.6.) In the case of $\alpha = .80$ the most recent four data

TABLE 8.6 Exponential Smoothing as a Weighted Average of Past Four Values

Coefficient of	Algebraic Coefficient	Numerical Coefficient		
		$\alpha = .20$	$\alpha = .50$	$\alpha = .80$
Y_t	α	.2000	.5000	.8000
Y_{t-1}	$\alpha(1 - \alpha)$	.1600	.2500	.1600
Y_{t-2}	$\alpha(1 - \alpha)^2$	.1280	.1250	.0320
Y_{t-3}	$\alpha(1 - \alpha)^3$	.1024	.0625	.0064
Total of First Four Coefficients		.5904	.9375	.9984

points determine 99.8% of the forecast. When $\alpha = .20$ the most recent four data points only determine 59% of the forecast, with the other 41% to be determined by earlier history.

What is the basis for deciding whether α should be large or small? Of course one wants to use the α that results in the best forecasts over an extended period of time. That generally means that with highly erratic time series one wants a small α, and with a smooth time series a large α. With highly erratic series one does not want to respond too quickly to an apparent cyclical turn, because it may not be one. On the other hand, if one has a time series that moves in smooth, long cyclical swings a high α is justified.

Let us use the same time series we used in our first difference models for a brief illustration of this method, although only 15 data points is a bit short. Table 8.7 shows the actual time series along with estimates and error terms for exponential smoothing with α's of .20, .50, and .80. To obtain a starting estimate we use the simple naive forecast with $Y_2 = Y_1$. As we can see from the earlier graph in Fig. 8.1, this time series has a rather pronounced upward trend except for a slight dip centered at $t = 11$. Hence, the slow reaction forecast, $\alpha = .20$, is always below the actual. The error terms are all positive. As we increase the size of α to .50, and .80, we get

TABLE 8.7 Exponential Smoothing Forecasts and Their Error Terms

t	Y_t	$\hat{Y}_t = \hat{Y}_{t-1} + \alpha(e_{t-1})$					
		$\alpha = .20$		$\alpha = .50$		$\alpha = .80$	
		$\hat{Y}_t$	e_t	$\hat{Y}_t$	e_t	$\hat{Y}_t$	e_t
1	10[a]						
2	13	10.00	3.00	10.00	3.00	10.00	3.00
3	17	10.60	6.40	11.50	5.50	12.40	4.60
4	22	11.88	10.12	14.25	7.75	16.08	5.92
5	26	13.90	12.10	18.13	7.88	20.82	5.18
6	29	16.32	12.68	22.06	6.94	24.96	4.04
7	30	18.86	11.14	25.53	4.47	28.19	1.81
8	29	21.09	7.91	27.77	1.23	29.64	− .64
9	28	22.67	5.33	28.38	− .38	29.13	− 1.13
10	25	23.74	1.26	28.19	− 3.19	28.23	− 3.23
11	24	23.99	.01	26.60	− 2.60	25.65	− 1.65
12	25	23.99	1.01	25.30	− .30	24.33	.67
13	27	24.19	2.81	25.15	1.85	24.87	2.13
14	30	24.75	5.25	26.07	3.93	26.57	3.43
15	34	25.80	8.20	28.04	5.96	29.31	4.69
Absolute Total	359	271.78	87.22	316.97	54.98	330.18	42.12
Average	25.64	19.41	6.23	22.64	3.93	23.58	3.01

[a]Not included in the computation of total or average.

a more accurate forecast — and a few negative error terms. Note that the mean value of each is below the mean value of the actual time series, 25.64. The mean values of the forecasts are 19.40, 22.64, and 23.58. All three forecasting techniques have a negative bias due to the positive trend in the time series.

We could improve these forecasts by adding a positive constant to raise the average value of the forecast enough so that the error terms sum to zero. More properly, we could explicitly recognize the positive trend and detrend the data before searching for our optimum α. What sort of trend formulation should we use? If we refer back to Table 8.5 where we compared various forms of the naive forecast, we find the percentage rate of change to be better than either a first difference or absolute level naive forecast. Very likely a percentage trend would give the best fit. But let us turn to a longer data sample to illustrate the behavior of an exponential smoothing forecast with a relatively large and relatively small α.

Figure 8.2 depicts a time series divided into two distinct periods. For the first 25 data points the series is a set of random numbers; pure noise with a mean value of 444 and a standard deviation of 277. The second 25 data points contain a definite linear trend with a positive slope of 44 units per time period and a standard error of the estimate of 67.

This particular example has a certain element of realism. In many circumstances a variable is essentially fluctuating around a fixed value, but one would like to be alerted if in fact a particular trend does develop. For example, say a manufacturer of nuts and bolts has hundreds of individual products being sold for a wide variety of uses. He schedules production on the basis of sales forecasts generated by exponential smoothing equations. Should he use a relatively small α, say .20, or a relatively large α, say .80? On the graph in Fig. 8.2 the 0's show estimates generated with an $\alpha = .20$, while the Δ's show estimates based on $\alpha = .80$. Estimates of $\alpha = 1.00$ are not shown but would merely be the original time series lagged one period. For the first 25 periods when the time series is fluctuating around a fixed value, the accuracy of the estimate is about the same regardless of the value of α. It really does not make much difference whether α is .20, .80, or 1.00. The mean absolute deviations for these three values of α are 263, 265, and 264 — not significantly different.

Since all three values of α are equally inaccurate, does it make any difference which one is used? Yes. It is a question of how sensitive you want the alarm that is supposed to alert you to a developing trend to be. A very sensitive alarm is not without its cost. The actual level of sales fluctuates quite a bit, a standard deviation of 277 as noted. Presumably, inventories are used to smooth out the production on a month-to-month basis. Over the time period each value for α does generate a monthly average forecast and thereby a production schedule approximately equal to the actual monthly sales of 444. The difference in the size of α is that

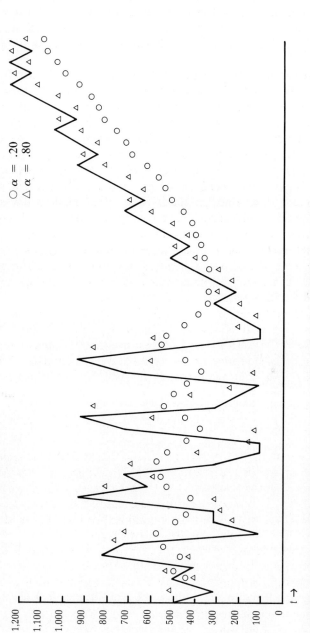

FIGURE 8.2 Exponential Smoothing Forecasts Based on 20% and 80% Adjustment Factors.

every time sales jump with α = .80, production is increased by 80% of the last error, just in case the increase is the beginning of a trend or a cyclical turning point. If it is not, production must be cut dramatically in the next time period. On the other hand, with α = .20 we believe that "one robin doesn't mean spring is here." As can be seen on Fig. 8.2 when the upward trend does in fact begin in the second half of the entire period, the α = .20 estimates (the 0's) are much later in responding to it than the α = .80 estimates (the Δ's).

So we can say that a large α will alert us to a turning point sooner than a small one, but we pay a price. Note the magnitude of the fluctuations of the estimates. The standard deviation of the level of ordered production with α = .80 for the first 25 periods would be 218, almost as large as the standard deviation of actual sales of 277. On the other hand, if we will accept a forecast that is not so sensitive to either random fluctuations or an incipient trend, we can use α = .20, and have a standard deviation of our production schedule of only 54. In Fig. 8.2, note the wide fluctuations of the Δ's and the relatively small fluctuations of the 0's.

● Questions for Discussion

1. Is simple trend extrapolation an autoregressive forecasting technique?
2. Define the following terms
   a. Pressure curves.
   b. Diffusion index.
   c. Naive forecast.
3. Is the following statement true or false and why? "You should expect an autoregressive forecasting technique to show a negative bias when a series is rising, especially if it is rising at an increasing rate." Discuss the converse contention concerning a time series declining.

● Exercise

Given below is a time series for a 13-month period. Use the exponential smoothing technique to forecast the last 12 months, beginning with August. Use the first July value, 867, as your August forecast. Try α = .20, α = .50, and α = 1.00. Calculate the error terms for each α and evaluate the results.

July	867	Jan.	993
Aug.	971	Feb.	791
Sept.	1,032	Mar.	838
Oct.	1,009	Apr.	897
Nov.	1,019	May	764
Dec.	974	June	679
		July	691

● Selected Additional Readings

Alexander, Sidney S. Rate of change approaches to forecasting — Diffusion indexes and first differences. *Economic Journal,* Vol. 68 (June 1958).

Granger, C. W. J. *Forecasting in Business and Economics.* New York: Academic Press, 1980.

McCuistion, Tommy J. *Business Cycle Forecasting.* Cleveland: Parker Hannifin, 1979.

Pindyck, Robert S., and Daniel L. Rubinfeld. *Econometric Models and Economic Forecasts.* New York: McGraw-Hill, 1981.

An Introduction to Some Macroeconomic Indicators

9

In this chapter we will first look at the mathematical relationship between nominal (current dollar) measures such as GNP and "real" (price deflated) values for the same variable. We will then turn our attention to aggregate price indexes and discuss the so-called *index number problem* inherent in the calculation of all such measures. Next we will look at the most politically potent macroeconomic measures — the consumer price index and the unemployment rate. Finally, we will look at the official classification of economic indicators as "leading," "lagging," or "coincident." In Chapter 10 we will examine each component of GNP as to its definition, cyclical behavior, and the success or lack of it we have had in forecasting each of them.

Relationship Between Percentage Changes in Real and Nominal GNP

In Chapter 3 while discussing macroeconomic theory we defined "real GNP," Q, as current dollar GNP, Y, divided by some price index, P. We divided the percentage change between price and real changes. For example, we considered a 5% increase in Y (from 100 to 105) composed of a 3% increase in the price index (from 100 to 103) and a 2% increase in real output (from 100 to 102). It is important to note that the percentage increase in a nominal value can only *approximately* be broken up into a price effect and a change in real output. In this case, since $Y = (P)(Q)$, the nominal value, Y, is (1.03) (102). This is approximately 1.05 for a 5% increase but it is *exactly* equal to 1.0506 for an increase of 5.06%. The 5.06% came about because the exact mathematical formulation for the percentage change in a product is

if $Y = (P)(Q)$, then $\%\Delta Y = (\%\Delta P) + (\%\Delta Q) + (\%\Delta P)(\%\Delta Q)$.

The last term on the right, $(\%\Delta P)(\%\Delta Q)$, is (.03)(.02) in this example. The product of these two numbers is .0006 or .06%. In this case the cross-product of the two percentage changes is not particularly significant. Frequently, however, it is large enough to matter. For example, in 1978 GNP in the United States went up by 12%. This resulted from a 7.3% increase in the price level and a 4.4% increase in real output. For purposes of public argument one might say that of the 12% increase in GNP, 7 1/2% of it was inflation and 4 1/2% of it was an increase in real output. Of course, any serious student of macroeconomics (like you) knows that the mathematically exact statement regarding the percentage changes in these three variables was

$$\% \, \Delta Y = (\% \Delta P) + (\% \Delta Q) + (\% \Delta P)\,(\% \Delta Q),$$
$$.120 = (.073) + (.044) + (.073)\,(.044),$$
$$.120 = (.117) + (.003).$$

The Index Number Problem

We have been referring to the GNP price index without being too precise about exactly what it is. The concept at a basic level is clear enough — we want something that measures the rate of inflation. It is easy to measure the rate of change in the price of a single commodity. If apples cost $1.00 per basket last year and cost $1.10 this year, we can say unambiguously that the price itself or any index derived therefrom should show a 10% increase over the time period. Problems arise when one wants to speak of the rate of price change for a "basket of goods" such as the GNP of an economy. One can say that the price of apples went up by 10% and that the price of oranges went up by 5%, but what can one say about the "price level" of apples *and* oranges?

Of course, we are going to take some average to obtain a price level index, but we must take into account the relative importance of the two products. If production of apples is twice as important to the economy as the production of oranges we would want to weight the apple price increase by two-thirds and the orange price increase by one-third and say the average change in prices was 8-1/3% computed as follows:

$$(10\% + 10\% + 5\%)/(3) = (25)/(3) = 8\text{-}1/3\%.$$

The essence of the index number problem is that the importance to the economy of various products is always changing. There is no totally satisfactory answer to this problem. Suppose that apples were twice as important to the economy as oranges in the first year, but oranges were twice as important in the second year. What then? Another way to look at the index number problem is to consider how one would go about measuring total real output in this fruity economy. If 10 apples and 5 oranges were produced in the first year and 5 apples and 10 oranges in the second, can one make any statement about which year had the larger real output? If you like apples and hate oranges, the first year is "more." If your tastes run the other way, the second year is more.

Let us recap the production and prices in such a simple two-fruit economy (Table 9.1) and see what our choices are in trying to measure inflation and real output. It is apparent that total output measured in current dollars increased by 6.67% as a result of a 45% fall in the value of apple production and a 110% rise in the value of orange production. We have two choices for measuring inflation in this economy. We can either:

1. Assume that real output stayed the same from year 1 to year 2 and measure the change in the value of total output resulting strictly from price changes; or
2. Assume that the same goods were produced in year 1 as were in fact produced in year 2 and see what happens to the total value of output as a result of the price changes.

Alternative 1 will give us a price index that weights apples and oranges in the proportion of their production in year 1. Alternative 2 will weight them according to their production in year 2.

The technical terminology calls an index that uses base year (year 1) weights a *Laspeyres index* and an index that uses current year (year 2) weights a *Paasche index*. In our case we can calculate a Laspeyres price index as follows:

$$L_P = (\Sigma P_2 Q_1)/(\Sigma P_1 Q_1) = [(\$11)(10) + (\$10.50)(5)]$$
$$[(\$10)(10) + (\$10)(5)]$$
$$= (\$110 + \$52.50)/(\$100 + \$50) = (\$162.50)/(\$150) = 1.0833.$$

Multiplying by 100, as is customary, we have a Lespeyres price index of 108.33, which indicates the inflation rate in this economy is 8-1/3% from year 1 to year 2. To calculate the growth in real output we need to deflate the dollar value of total output for the second year by dividing it by the price index as follows:

Real output = $(\$160)/(1.0833) = \$147.70$.

TABLE 9.1 Total Output and Prices in a Two-Commodity Economy

| Year | Apples | | | Oranges | | | Total Dollar Value of Output |
	Output	Price	Value	Output	Price	Value	
1	10	$10.00	$100	5	$10.00	$50	$150
2	5	$11.00	$ 55	10	$10.50	$105	$160
%Δ	−50%	+10%	−45%	+100%	+5%	+110%	+6.67%

Output in year 2 stated in "year 1 dollars" is $147.70, which is 1.5% less than the value of the dollar output in year 1 of $150. Using a Laspeyres price index as a deflator indicates that real output fell by approximately 1.5%. In terms of the percentage change relationship previously discussed we have:

$$\%\Delta Y = \%\Delta P + \%\Delta Q + (\%\Delta P)(\%\Delta Q),$$
$$.0667 = .0833 - .0153 + (.0833)(-.0153),$$
$$.0667 = (.0680) + (-.0013).$$

Very roughly speaking, current dollar output was up by almost 7% as a result of an 8-1/2% rise in prices offset by a 1-1/2% decline in real output.

Let us now try the alternative of the Paasche index, which isolates price effects by assuming the composition of output holds constant with the mix of year 2.

$$P_p = (\Sigma P_2 Q_2) / (\Sigma P_1 Q_2) = [(\$11)(5) + (\$10.50)(10)] /$$
$$[(\$10)(5) + (\$10)(10)] = (\$55 + \$105) / (\$50 + \$100) =$$
$$(\$160) / (\$150) = 1.0667.$$

The Paasche index comes out to be 106.67% indicating a price rise of 6.67%, somewhat less than the 8.33% indicated by the Laspeyres index. The price of apples went up twice as fast as the price of oranges. The Laspeyres index based on year 1 production weights apples more heavily, since apple production fell from year 1 to year 2. The Paasche index weights oranges more heavily, since it is based on year 2 production. The price of oranges went up by only 5%, so we get a lower estimated inflation rate.

Using the Paasche index to deflate the value of year 2 production to obtain real output we get ($160)/(1.0667) = $150, which indicates no change in real output. The total dollar value went up by 6.67%, and it was all due to inflation.

We have dealt strictly with the computation of price indexes and then obtained the change in the quantity by using the price index to deflate the dollar value. This is the customary and intuitively appealing way to go about such computations. However, we can calculate quantity indexes in the same way we just computed price indexes by either:

1. Assuming prices held constant from year 1 to year 2 and calculate the change in the value of total output resulting exclusively from changes in quantity; or

2. Holding prices constant at their values for year 2 and calculating the impact on total value resulting from changes in the quantities produced.

Option 1 is a Laspeyres quantity index. It establishes the importance of apples and oranges on the basis of their price in year 1. Option 2 is a Paasche quantity index.

Measuring price changes with a Paasche index and then using it to determine the price deflated change in real output is the same as computing a Laspeyres quantity index. For example,

$$P_q = (\Sigma P_2 Q_2)/(\Sigma P_2 Q_1) = (\$160)\,(\$162.50) = .985.$$

The Paasche quantity index is 98.5 for year 2, indicating a fall in real output of 1.5%. This is the same result we obtained by deflating with a Laspeyres price index. Conversely, a Laspeyres quantity index would be

$$L_q = (\Sigma P_1 Q_2)/(\Sigma P_1 Q_1) = (\$150)/(\$150) = 1.00.$$

The value of the Laspeyres quantity index is 100, indicating that real output did not change from year 1 to year 2 — the same result we obtained by deflating with a Paasche price index.

Let us summarize the index number problem and its alternative solutions. In obtaining the "average" price increase for a bundle of goods one must take some sort of weighted average. The problem is the assignment of the weights. The Laspeyres index weights the items by their importance in the base year. The Paasche index weights them by their importance in the current year. The Laspeyres index measures inflation by asking, "If we were to buy exactly the same goods this year as last year, how much more would they cost?" The Paasche index seeks to measure inflation by asking, "If last year we had bought the same goods as we are buying his year, how much more would we be paying this year than last?"

The Cost of Living or Consumer Price Index

The consumer price index of the United States or any other country represents an attempt to measure the price level for some typical consumer's market basket of goods. Before discussing some other problems with the consumer price index, let us consider the impact of the index number problem on the computation of a consumer price index. The problem can be stated in the same form as we discussed it before. To obtain a weighted index of the rate of change in prices we must assign weights to the various items in the basket. We can weight the items by their importance in the consumer's total expenditures in the base year or the current year.

The choice of a Laspeyres index (base year weighting) or a Paasche index (current year weighting) runs into the problem that consumers can and do substitute goods as prices change. These changes are not random. The substitution is done in such a way as to impart a predictable bias to the indexes. Suppose pork and chicken are regarded as substitutes by some consumers. The price of pork goes up by 20% and the price of chicken does not go up at all. One would expect that people would consume more chicken and less pork. As a result, pork would be relatively more important in the base year and chicken would be relatively more important in the current year. Assuming substitution in an economically rational manner, the item whose price goes up the fastest will be more important in the base year and the one whose price goes up less will be more important in the current year. Using base year weights with a Laspeyres index will show a relatively high rate of inflation. Using current year weighting with a Paasche index will indicate a lower rate of inflation. The base year weights emphasize goods whose prices rose most. Current year weights will give less weight to those items whose prices rose rapidly over this time period. As a result we will find that a Laspeyres index overstates inflation relative to a Paasche, and vice-versa.

We can illustrate this with the same numbers used in the previous section to discuss the measurement of the output of an entire economy. Instead of "output" of apples and oranges we are now discussing "consumption." Instead of trying to determine whether real output increased, we are now trying to determine whether or not our typical consumer was able to "keep up with inflation." Using the same apples and oranges example we used earlier, but with the column labels changed, we can construct Laspeyres and Paasche consumer price indexes. (See Table 9.2.)

From our previous calculations we can state what happened to our consumer depending on whether we use the Laspeyres or Paasche price index.

	Laspeyres	Paasche
Change in Total Consumption Expenditures	+6.67%	+6.67%
Inflation Rate	+8.33%	+6.67%
Change in Real (Price Deflated) Consumption	−1.53%	0

The computations indicate that if the consumers had continued their consumption pattern the way they did in year 1, 10 apples and 5 oranges, they could not have maintained their level of consumption with the increase in expenditures being only 6.67%. To consume 10 apples and 5 oranges at year 2 prices would have required $162.50, an increase of 8.33%. The

TABLE 9.2 Total Consumption and Prices in a Two-Commodity Economy

	Apple Consumption			Orange Consumption			Total Consumption Expenditures
Year	Quantity	Price	$	Quantity	Price	$	
1	10	$10	$100	5	$10.00	$50	$150
2	5	11	55	10	10.50	105	160
%Δ	−50%	+10%	−45%	+100%	+5%	+110%	+6.67%

Laspeyres price index indicates the consumer to be 1.5% worse off in terms of real consumption in year 2.

Of course, microeconomic theory and common sense tell us that there is some number of oranges consumed that will leave individuals economically just as well off with a decrease in apple consumption. We do not really know what this trade-off rate is for consumers without looking into their heads and examining their "utility function"; but we can infer something from the fact that consumers switched from apples to oranges as the price of apples rose faster than that of oranges. The Paasche index says the consumers could have had in year 1 the same consumption pattern they, in fact, chose in year 2 with their total expenditures at that time. Their total expenditures are up by 6.67% and the cost of the year 2 basket of goods is up by 6.67%. Therefore are they no worse off? Not really. Presumably, if consumers had wanted the year 2 basket of goods in year 1 they would have bought it with the total expenditure of $150. But they obviously preferred more apples. They were forced by the rising price of apples to substitute oranges for apples and are presumably somewhat worse off as a result.

The Paasche index, by showing no decline in real consumption, understates the impact of inflation because it assumes no loss in utility from being forced to substitute oranges for apples. The Laspeyres index overstates the impact of inflation by assuming that it is impossible to substitute one good for another.*

The consumer price index (CPI) published monthly in this country is a Laspeyres index with the market basket updated periodically (every five to ten years).† A Paasche index, available on a quarterly basis as part of the GNP accounts, is known as the personal consumption expenditures price deflator (PCE). As we would expect, the CPI generally shows a greater rate of inflation, since it assumes no substitution away from expensive items. The PCE assumes people have always been buying more of the items whose prices have not gone up so rapidly. We have to say that the CPI as a Laspeyres index *usually* shows a higher rate of inflation than the PCE and not *always,* since there are substantial other differences in the methods of computing these two indexes. Due to these differences the PCE can show a higher rate of inflation for short periods of time. Consider the years 1976 through 1979 in Table 9.3.

---

*In microeconomic theory, being "no worse off" means remaining on the same indifference curve. It can be shown that compensating consumers for a price rise computed with a Laspeyres index will allow them to reach a higher indifference curve (overestimation of inflation). Compensating with the use of a Paasche index will not be enough to keep them on their original indifference curve (underestimating inflation). See any standard intermediate microeconomics text for an algebraic and geometric presentation of this point.

†Both the consumer price index (CPI) and the Paasche index are included in *Economic Indicators,* published monthly by the U.S. Government Printing Office, Washington, D.C.

TABLE 9.3   CPI Versus PCE

Year	Consumer Price Index	Personal Consumption Expenditures Deflator	Difference (CPI) − (PCE)
1976	5.8%	5.1%	0.7%
1977	7.6%	5.7%	1.9%
1978	11.4%	6.8%	2.2%
1979	13.4%	8.9%	4.5%

Note that as we would expect, the CPI shows a higher rate of inflation than the PCE for these years. In fact, the gap seems to have increased rather dramatically from 0.7% in 1976 to 4.5% in 1979. The reason for this increasing divergence is due largely to the fact that two items whose prices went up spectacularly over this time period are much more heavily weighted in the CPI than the PCE. One is "shelter," the cost of housing, which includes the effect of mortgage interest rates. The CPI weights shelter at 29.8% of total consumption. The PCE weighted it at only around 17% in 1979. The other significant item is "energy," including gasoline. The CPI, on the basis of 1972–73 consumption patterns, weights energy consumption at 8.5%. The PCE weighting in 1979 was only 6%.

However, as we mentioned, for short periods of time it is possible for the CPI to show a lower rate of inflation than the PCE. For example, in the third quarter of 1980 mortgage interest rates fell temporarily and energy prices paused in their ascent. As a result, for the third quarter of 1980 the CPI showed a rate of inflation of only 6.8%, versus 9.3% for the PCE. This could not occur if the same data were used to construct both indexes. In fact, there are a number of significant differences in the construction of the two indexes. The CPI is constructed from a sample survey. The PCE is estimated (as are all the GNP accounts) from everything from sales tax receipts to trade association reports. We will take a closer look at the construction of the CPI, but the explanation for the third quarter 1980 reversal of the usual relationship between the two indexes was, as indicated, mainly due to energy and mortgage rates. The construction of the CPI implicitly assumes that people refinance their homes every month at current mortgage rates. The PCE estimates the cost of actual expenditures for shelter. This particular difference leads to a significant downward bias in the CPI relative to the PCE in periods of declining interest rates, such as mid-1980, and an upward bias in periods of rising interest rates, such as 1979.

The popularly stated goal of constructing the CPI is to measure the "cost of living." A significant question is, therefore, *whose* living. It is apparent that the change in the cost of living for those buying tuxedos and champagne will be different from those whose budget is devoted to blue jeans and beer. The difference will depend on the rate of change in the prices of these items that are not likely to all have the same rate of inflation. Originally, the U.S. Department of Commerce set out to measure the cost of living of the "clerical/industrial worker in an urban environment." Since such workers constitute only about 40% of the population of the United States, in 1972 the index was broadened to include the consumption pattern of "all urban households." About 80% of the U.S. population lives in households defined to be in urban areas. The market basket of goods is selected by conducting a survey of consumer spending patterns. The last survey determined the market basket of goods purchased by the "average" urban consumer in 1972–73. So what we have is a Laspeyres index with the market basket of goods being those goods people were buying in 1972 and 1973.

Having determined what proportion of their income consumers spend for eggs, bacon, entertainment, and so on, the government sends out approximately 400 shoppers to around 40,000 retail establishments each month to buy these goods. If the complete basket of consumer goods costs 1% more from one month to the next, we compound that and report that the cost of living rose at an annual rate of 12.7% per year, since $(1.01)^{12} = 1.127$.

Given the changing consumption patterns we discussed, which took place in less than 10 years, one can see how meaningless a comparison of the "cost of living" over a 30 or 40 year period is. How much was a video recorder in 1934? A nonsense question deserving a nonsense answer. A 1981 automobile is obviously a different (and more expensive) product than a 1931 automobile. It is literally impossible to separate how much the price difference is due to inflation and how much is due to the change in the product purchased by the consumer.

The next time you are asked if you realize the dollar is worth only 23¢ you could give the questioner a lecture on the complexities of measuring the cost of living. Your time would probably be more efficiently spent if you merely offered to buy all the dollars he had on him at the quoted value of 23¢. This is, of course, fighting nonsense with nonsense. However, it is possible that as the questioner ponders exactly what you mean by your offer, he might also ponder what, if anything, he means by his statement. If he means a dollar today buys less "happiness" (economists read "utility") today than it did in Granddaddy's day, he has embarked on an argument about the "quality of life" that is not likely to be settled in any scientific way.

There is a little experiment widely used by economics professors to emphasize the abuse and misunderstanding of the consumer price index when it is used as the inverse of a "happiness index" across the generations. One selects a student from among those in the lecture room for Economics

101 and has him or her come forward to make a buying decision. The facts for this decision are in the form of two mail-order catalogues. One is this year's and the other is one of those very old ones that have been reprinted for collectors of such memorabilia. The question to the student is, "If you have $1,000 to spend, in which catalogue would you prefer to spend it? In which could you obtain the most happiness per dollar?" If the professor has had the misfortune to have chosen a student who is really into acquiring kerosene cans, hoe handles, horse-drawn plows, and so on, the experiment just fell apart. If, as is more likely, the student is really in the market for the latest stereo set with headphones, he will most surely prefer today's selection of merchandise to what was available in Granddaddy's day. From this experiment one can naively conclude that the dollar buys more utility today than 50 years ago. The value of money is up! Prices are down! Again, we are fighting nonsense with nonsense. Ask meaningless questions and you will get ambiguous answers.

To reiterate, the CPI measures the short-run inflationary pressures on a selected market basket of consumer goods purchased at retail. Being a Laspeyres index, the market basket is fixed some years earlier by surveys of what urban wage earners were buying at that time. It contains information regarding the rate of change in these prices and no more.

The Unemployment Rate

The only statistic to rival the consumer price index for attention from the media and the politicians is the unemployment rate. It probably also suffers an equal amount of abuse and misunderstanding. A substantial amount of the misunderstanding arises from concentrating on a single statistic to try to comprehend the complexities of the labor market. The unemployment rate, as calculated and published by the U.S. government, is the percentage of people estimated to be unemployed out of the civilian labor force. The *civilian labor force* is defined as total civilian employment plus those who are unemployed. (See Table 9.4.)

Table 9.4 presents part of the employment picture for the years 1974, 1975, and 1976 as the economy entered and recovered from a recession. It is only part of the employment picture, leaving out many other statistics, such as claims for unemployment compensation, the length of the average workweek in manufacturing, and so on. Table 9.4, however, is the data on which the national unemployment rate is calculated. By analyzing these data we will have a pretty clear picture of what the national unemployment rate means, and what it does not mean.

As the economy entered the depths of the 1974–1975 recession we had an increase in the total noninstitutional population 16 years of age and over of 2.622 million. Technically, this many people were potentially added to

TABLE 9.4 Labor Force and Employment Data, 1974–1976 (Numbers in Thousands)

	1974	1975	Change	1976	Change
Population 16 and over	150,827	153,449	2,622	156,048	2,599
Armed Forces	2,229	2,180	−49	2,144	−36
Civilian Employment	85,935	84,783	−1,152	87,485	2,702
Unemployed	5,076	7,830	2,754	7,288	−542
Civilian Labor Force (3) + (4)	91,011	92,613	1,602	94,773	2,160
Not in Workforce	57,587	58,656	1,069	59,131	475
Unemployment Rate (4) ÷ (5)	5.6%	8.5%	+2.9	7.7%	−.8
Employment Rate [(2) + (3)] ÷ [(1)]	58.5%	56.7%	−1.8	57.4%	+.7
Labor Force Participation Rate [(2) + (5)] ÷ [(1)]	61.8%	61.8%	-0-	62.1%	+.3

the workforce. (All figures are averages for the year.) At the same time the number of people in the armed forces fell by 49,000 and civilian employment fell by 1.152 million. Potentially, we could have had in excess of 3.8 million more people joining the ranks of the unemployed. This would have given us an unemployment rate of something in excess of 12%. In fact, in 1975 unemployment rose by only a bit less than 2.8 million and the unemployment rate rose to only 8.5%. What happened to the other million people? As indicated in the table, those "not in the workforce" rose by over one million. People simply took retirement, went back to school, or for whatever reason, stopped looking for work. This is typical of a recessionary period. The increase in the not in workforce category of 1,069 is equal to 41% of the increase in the population.

On the other hand, in 1976 the not in workforce category grew by only 475 thousand, or only 18% of the population growth. The population 16 and over grew by 2.6 million. Employment grew by 2.7 million. With the 475 thousand not joining the workforce the rise in employment reduced unemployment by over half a million. Of course, in 1976 if *all* the increase in employment had come from the ranks of the unemployed, the level of unemployment would have been reduced to around 5 million for an unemployment rate of 5.4% instead of the 7.7% actually recorded. There is something of the "we must keep running to just stand still" with regard to the unemployment rate when there is a positive trend in the number of people in the workforce.

Another way to observe the cyclical fluctuation in the rate of growth in the labor force is to look at the labor force participation rate shown at the bottom of Table 9.4. This ratio takes those in both civilian and military employment plus those unemployed as a percent of the population 16 years of age and over. Notice that this ratio held constant at 61.8% for the recession years of 1974 and 1975, but rose to 62.1% in 1976. The movement in the *marginal* labor force participation rate is more dramatic. Taking the incremental participation in the labor force from 1974 to 1975 as a percent of the growth in the population gives us only 59%. However, from 1975 to 1976 the increase in the workforce was an impressive 82% of the increase in population.

Given the practical and conceptual problems of defining who is in the workforce and who is not, which we will discuss in more detail below, many analysts prefer the employment rate to the unemployment rate. The employment rate is *not,* as you might think, the complement of the unemployment rate. If the unemployment rate is 8.5%, the employment rate is not 91.5%. As indicated at the bottom of Table 9.4, *the* employment rate published by the government is Armed Forces and civilian employment as a percentage of the population. The employment rate fell from 58.5% in 1974 to 56.7% in 1975 as the economy went into the recession and then rose from 56.7% to 57.4% in the recovery year of 1976. The appeal of the employment rate is that it does avoid any fluctuations resulting from variation in the labor force participation rate. Since it takes employment as a percentage of the entire population age 16 and over, it is not influenced by whether people drop out of, or rejoin, the labor force.

The compilation of the underlying employment statistics requires some difficult judgment calls. The basic data are the result of surveys conducted each month. The Department of Labor, Bureau of Labor Statistics, sends people out to knock on doors of something in excess of 55,000 households each month to inquire about the employment status of residents. The surveyor fills out a questionnaire of some pages, but nowhere on the questionnaire is the question, "Are you unemployed?" The surveyor asks what an occupant's permanent employment, if any, might be. If the respondent has just been laid off by the local automobile plant and is merely sitting on her front porch hoping to be called back, she is *not* unemployed. To be unemployed she must be actively seeking employment. The fact may be that the worker feels that seeking employment would be pointless since she is sure that she will be called back in a couple of weeks and no one would hire her knowing she would be a very short-term employee. However, if she is not working and not actively seeking employment, she is not part of the workforce.

Actually, it would be extremely unlikely for a laid-off worker not to at least be going through the pretense of seeking alternative employment, since in all states such activity is a necessary condition for receiving state unemployment compensation. In all likelihood, our hypothetical interviewee would report her conscientious trips to the State Employment Office each week. She may not examine the job listings carefully or be that enthusiastic if sent out for a job interview, but for national reporting purposes she is legitimately in the ranks of the unemployed. She will be reported as unemployed unless she gets caught by one of the other questions that might elicit the information that she is helping out at her father-in-law's furniture store about 25 hours a week while awaiting her return to the assembly line. In that case she is most certainly in the workforce and she is employed.

The procedure for developing the statistics from which the national and local unemployment rates are developed is to collect the survey data of this type. Then the officials at the Bureau of Labor Statistics apply various "rules of thumb" to decide whether or not particular people are in the labor force, and if they are, whether they are employed or unemployed.

As you can see, these statistics were not designed as a social indicator to measure the human misery of unemployment. Some individuals are officially classified as unemployed who are better off economically than when they were employed. They are receiving 80 or 90% of their previous take-home pay from a combination of private and government unemployment benefits. Of course, they are in no way seriously seeking alternative employment until these payments decline or end. So one can argue that the national unemployment rate vastly overstates the social problem.

On the other hand, it is well documented that there is a large group of "discouraged workers" that looked for work for some months or years and then gave up. Since they are not actively seeking employment they are not counted as unemployed. Obviously, many of them would take a job if they could find one. Note how the labor force participation rate rises in a period of recovery such as 1977. One could argue that the unemployment rate grossly understates the social problem of unemployment. We will return to but not settle this controversy later, in our discussion of the Phillips curve.

Leading, Lagging, and Coincident Indicators

The premier business cycle publication of the U.S. government, *Business Conditions Digest*, currently publishes 111 economic time series classified by whether they lead, lag, or are coincident with the peaks and troughs in the level of general business activity. (See Fig. 9.1.) We will look at the most prominent of the indicators, but first we must consider a problem. The concept of the timing of individual time series relative to the general level of business implies some dating of *the* business cycle. How does one establish the peaks and troughs for the business cycle? To say whether a series leads or lags one must have some frame of reference; hence, *the* business cycle is referred to as the *reference cycle* and its peaks and troughs as *reference turning points*.

The reference turning points are established by the National Bureau of Economic Research (NBER), the nonprofit research organization we have

Timing at Business Cycle Peaks

Cyclical Timing \ Economic Process	I. EMPLOYMENT AND UNEMPLOYMENT (18 series)	II. PRODUCTION AND INCOME (10 series)	III. CONSUMPTION, TRADE, ORDERS, AND DELIVERIES (13 series)	IV. FIXED CAPITAL INVESTMENT (18 series)	V. INVENTORIES AND INVENTORY INVESTMENT (9 series)	VI. PRICES, COSTS, AND PROFITS (17 series)	VII. MONEY AND CREDIT (26 series)
LEADING (L) INDICATORS (62 series)	Marginal employment adjustments (6 series) Job vacancies (2 series) Comprehensive employment (1 series) Comprehensive unemployment (3 series)	Capacity utilization (2 series)	New and unfilled orders and deliveries (6 series) Consumption (2 series)	Formation of business enterprises (2 series) Business investment commitments (5 series) Residential construction (3 series)	Inventory investment (4 series) Inventories on hand and on order (1 series)	Stock prices (1 series) Commodity prices (1 series) Profits and profit margins (7 series) Cash flows (2 series)	Money flows (3 series) Real money supply (2 series) Credit flows (4 series) Credit difficulties (2 series) Bank reserves (2 series) Interest rates (1 series)

ROUGHLY COINCIDENT (C) INDICATORS (23 series)	Comprehensive employment (1 series)	Comprehensive output and real income (4 series) Industrial production (4 series)	Consumption and trade (4 series)	Backup of investment commitments (1 series) Business investment expenditures (5 series)			Velocity of money (2 series) Interest rates (2 series)
LAGGING (Lg) INDICATORS (18 series)	Duration of unemployment (2 series)			Business investment expenditures (1 series)	Inventories on hand and on order (4 series)	Unit labor costs and labor share (4 series)	Interest rates (4 series) Outstanding debt (3 series)
TIMING UNCLASSIFIED (U) (8 series)	Comprehensive employment (3 series)		Trade (1 series)	Business investment commitments (1 series)		Commodity prices (1 series) Profit share (1 series)	Interest rates (1 series)

FIGURE 9.1 Cross-Classification of Cyclical Indicators by Economic Process and Cyclical Timing. (*Business Conditions Digest*, June 1984.)

Timing at Business Cycle Troughs

Economic Process / Cyclical Timing	I. EMPLOYMENT AND UNEMPLOYMENT (18 series)	II. PRODUCTION AND INCOME (10 series)	III. CONSUMPTION, TRADE, ORDERS, AND DELIVERIES (13 series)	IV. FIXED CAPITAL INVESTMENT (18 series)	V. INVENTORIES AND INVENTORY INVESTMENT (9 series)	VI. PRICES, COSTS, AND PROFITS (17 series)	VII. MONEY AND CREDIT (26 series)
LEADING (L) INDICATORS (47 series)	Marginal employment adjustments (3 series)	Industrial production (1 series)	New and unfilled orders and deliveries (5 series) Consumption and trade (4 series)	Formation of business enterprises (2 series) Business investment commitments (4 series) Residential construction (3 series)	Inventory investment (4 series)	Stock prices (1 series) Commodity prices (2 series) Profits and profit margins (6 series) Cash flows (2 series)	Money flows (2 series) Real money supply (2 series) Credit flows (4 series) Credit difficulties (2 series)
ROUGHLY COINCIDENT (C) INDICATORS (23 series)	Marginal employment adjustments (2 series) Comprehensive employment (4 series)	Comprehensive output and real income (4 series) Industrial production (3 series) Capacity utilization (2 series)	Consumption and trade (3 series)	Business investment commitments (1 series)		Profits (2 series)	Money flow (1 series) Velocity of money (1 series)

	Unfilled orders (1 series)	Business investment commitments (2 series) Business investment expenditures (6 series)	Inventories on hand and on order (5 series)	Unit labor costs and labor share (4 series)	Velocity of money (1 series) Bank reserves (1 series) Interest rates (8 series) Outstanding debt (3 series)
LAGGING (L) INDICATORS (40 series)	Marginal employment adjustments (1 series) Job vacancies (2 series) Comprehensive employment (1 series) Comprehensive and duration of unemployment (5 series)				
TIMING UNCLASSIFIED (U) (1 series)					Bank reserves (1 series)

Figure 9.1 (Continued)

mentioned previously. This organization, originally under the guidance of Wesley Claire Mitchell, pioneered business cycle research in the late 1920s. Today the NBER's decisions on the reference cycle are taken as gospel, although they are, in fact, quite subjective. No single time series or group of time series is decreed to be *the* reference cycle. A committee of professional business cycle analysts convened by the NBER establishes the official peaks and troughs in accordance with the following definition:

> Business cycles are a type of fluctuation found in the aggregate economic activity of nations that organize their work mainly in business enterprises: a cycle consists of expansions occurring at about the same time in many economic activities, followed by similarly general recessions, contractions and revivals which merge into the expansion phase of the next cycle; this sequence of changes is recurrent but not periodic; in duration business cycles vary from more than one year to ten or twelve years; they are not divisible into shorter cycles of similar character with amplitudes approximately their own.[1]

With slight modification, this definition has been used since 1927. Although most of the definition is self-explanatory, it is not all that rigorous. It does not say, for example something like, if real GNP falls at an annual rate of 1% for two consecutive quarters we have entered a recession. The definition does say unambiguously that business cycles are "recurrent but not periodic." The only real constraint in the definition is that if you define a business cycle, say peak to peak, you should not be able to find another cycle of equal amplitude between those two peaks. If so, you did it wrong. The preeminent business cycle analyst alive today, Geoffrey H. Moore, long with the NBER, elaborates on the problems of setting and using the reference dates.

> All these materials then aid in the formulation of a judgment as to the date of a business cycle peak. Sometimes they point quite clearly to a single month: sometimes the evidence is conflicting and presents a difficult choice. We have, however, felt that it was best to choose a single month in each case rather than to indicate a zone within which the peak probably lies or to specify alternative monthly dates. Users of the chronology should be aware, however, that a degree of uncertainty attaches to any particular date and that revisions of the underlying statistical materials may later suggest a different choice. Indeed, the National Bureau has from time to time reviewed the dates and revised some of them by a month or two or three. . . . One of the advantages of basing them on a wide variety of evidence is that it reduces the possibility of error and the need for subsequent revision.[2]

We must keep in mind that all that is established with regard to *the* business cycle is the peak and trough of each cycle. This determination tells us absolutely nothing about the rate of rise or fall in the general level of economic activity, nothing about the magnitude of the boom or the severity of the recession. There is a composite index of coincident indicators that one might use to measure the magnitudes of cyclical fluctuations. The composite index of coincident indicators has coincided with the reference trough five of the last six recessions, but it has coincided with only one of the last six references peaks. The most commonly used series as a proxy for the business cycle when more than just turning points is required is real GNP if one can get by with quarterly data, or the industrial production index if monthly data are required. The industrial production index is a component of the composite index of coincident indicators, but corresponds slightly better with the reference cycle. The industrial production index had the same score as the composite index on troughs — five out of six. It did better on the peaks, only missing three out of the last six by being slightly early. As might be guessed from the attention we have given them, the consumer price index and the unemployment rate are commonly used measures of the severity of the business cycle problem, especially by the media. Neither corresponds very closely to the reference cycle. We will consider details of their timing and interaction later.

The classification of series by their timing, the idea that the sequence in which economic indicators reach a cyclical peak or trough has some consistent pattern, implies a "typical" business cycle. As we mentioned in Chapter 1, each business cycle has its own unique characteristics, but has enough common elements to be worthy of study. A large part of the common elements of different business cycles is the sequence of peaks and troughs in the various time series. (Note that in Fig. 9.1 there is one matrix for peaks and another for troughs, since a series may lead at the peak and lag at the trough.)

Three widely followed time series are composites made up of the best of those that lead, lag, and are coincident. In our chapter on macroeconomic forecasting we will consider the use of these in forecasting. To determine which individual series should be used in the composite indexes, the government and the NBER joined forces to evaluate the full 111 time series and assigned them numerical scores. In the words of any recent issue of *Business Conditions Digiest*, stated on page one:

> All cyclical indicators have been evaluated according to six major characteristics: economic significance, statistical adequacy, consistency of timing at business cycle peaks and troughs, conformity to business expansions and contractions, smoothness, and prompt availability. A formal detailed weighting scheme was developed and used to assess each series by all the above criteria.[3]

After scoring each series, the ones having the highest scores were used to construct a composite leading, lagging, and coincident index.

Table 9.5 presents the components of each of the three indexes and the weights assigned to each component. The weights were assigned in proportion to the scores received in the evaluation already described. It is interesting to note that the weighting is not that different from what absolutely equal weighting would be. In the case of the index of leading economic indicators there are twelve components, so equal weighting would be 8.3%. The actual weights assigned range from a high of 9.1% to a low of 7.4%.

TABLE 9.5   Components of Composite Leading, Coincident, and Lagging Economic Indicators

Series	Weight
Index of Leading Economic Indicators	
Change in Total Liquid Assets, Smoothed[a]	9.1%
Layoff Rate, Manufacturing (Inverted)	8.9
Stock Prices, 500 Common Stocks	8.9
Money Supply, M2, in 1972 Dollars	8.9
Average Workweek, Production Workers, Manufacturing	8.6
Net Change in Inventories on Hand and on Order, 1972 Dollars, Smoothed[a]	8.6
New Orders for Consumer Goods and Materials, 1972 Dollars	8.3
Net Business Formation	8.0
New Building Permits, Private Housing Units	7.9
Contracts and Orders for Plant and Equipment, 1972 Dollars	7.8
Vendor Performance, Percent of Companies Receiving Slower Deliveries	7.6
Change in Sensitive Crude Materials Prices, Smoothed[a]	7.4
	100.0%
Index of Coincident Economic Indicators	
Employees on Nonagricultural Payrolls	26.0%
Industrial Production, Total	25.7
Personal Income Less Transfer Payments, 1972 Dollars	25.5
Manufacturing and Trade Sales, 1972 Dollars	22.8
	100.0%
Index of Lagging Economic Indicators	
Average Duration of Unemployment (Inverted)	17.8%
Average Prime Rate Charged by Banks	16.8
Ratio, Consumer Installment Credit to Personal Income	16.8
Manufacturing and Trade Inventories, 1972 Dollars	16.6
Commercial and Industrial Loans Outstanding, Weekly Reporting Large Commercial Banks	16.6
Labor Cost per Unit of Output, Manufacturing	15.4
	100.0%

Source: Computed from data found in *Business Conditions Digest*, March 1979, p. 106.

[a]"Smoothed" means the series is a weighted four-month moving average, with weights of: one-sixth, one-third, one-third, and one-sixth.

The standard deviation of the weights is only .55% or less than 7% of the mean value of 8.3%. For the index of coincident economic indicators, equal weighting would be 25% each since there are only four components. The weights assigned range from a low of 22.8% to a high of 26.0% for a standard deviation of 1.28% or only 5% of the mean value. Equal weighting for the index of lagging economic indicators would give each of the six selected a weight of 16.7%. The actual weighting ranges from 15.4% to 17.8% with a standard deviation of only .70% or just over 4% of the mean value. Although the extensive evaluation of the time series in terms of the six characteristics was undoubtedly important in selecting the 22 out of the 111 to be used in the composite indexes, the results of these tests were not that important in assigning weights to the individual components of each index. The scores of all the series qualifying to be in the composite indexes were all sufficiently close together that the weighting is not that different from just weighting each series in the composite equally.

Let us take a closer look at the indicators listed in Table 9.5. Looking first at the twelve indicators found to lead consistently on turning points, notice how many are in terms of rates of change. Fully half, or six out of the twelve leading indicators are first differences. This should not be surprising if you recall our discussion in Chapter 8 of how the first difference of a series will inherently lead the series if the series is reasonably smooth. Note that the indicator with the highest score and, thereby the highest weight, is the rate of change in a series that has been smoothed by using a four-month moving average, change in total liquid assets, smoothed. The second series, the layoff rate, manufacturing (inverted) is, of course, a component of the change in the level of employment, a coincident indicator. That the layoff rate in manufacturing leads the business cycle in an inverse fashion does tell us that in the typical cycle the number of employees laid off from manufacturing jobs begins to rise well before the onset of the recession and ceases before the recovery begins.

Stock prices, the third-ranked leading indicator, have a history as a leading economic indicator that is older than the NBER. Stock prices do reflect investors' expectations of the state of business. Stock prices should fall when the psychology of business becomes pessimistic and rise when optimism runs rampant. They are a consensus forecast with all the failings that implies. The fact that stock prices rank among the most consistent of the leading economic indicators is as much the result of the low level of consistency of the behavior of other indicators as it is proof of the information content of stock prices. The stock market has missed numerous turns in the economy (notably during 1929 when it lagged) and it has predicted even more turns that did not occur.

The fourth of the leading indicators, money supply, $M2$, in 1972 dollars, is closely related to the first series, change in total liquid assets. In fact, the money supply, $M2$, is one of the liquid assets whose change is measured in the first series. The $M2$ definition of the money supply is composed of currency in the hands of the public plus demand deposits and personal time deposits in commercial banks. Total liquid assets include $M2$ and a lot of other liquid assets held both by individuals and corporations. We will look closer at the definitional problems in this area in Chapter 15 when we consider the measurement of monetary policy. In these two series we have one measure of the level of liquidity in real terms and a measure of the change in the level of liquid assets in nominal terms. They do both lead, with leads that are long and variable. Not surprisingly, the first-difference series (the change in liquid assets) is more volatile and usually leads by more than the measure of the level of the real money supply. Their movements indicate that as a boom matures the rate of growth in liquid assets begins to decline well before the decline in the general level of business activity. Similarly, as the economy approaches a peak, the rate of inflation begins to exceed the expansion of the money supply so that the real value of $M2$ begins to fall. These two indicators are fairly volatile and, thereby, give a number of false signals — especially the change in total liquid assets. However, each qualifies as one of the better leading indicators by virtue of the fact that via the highly regulated banking system the figures are available promptly with a minimum of revision.

Although one could think of the average workweek, production workers, manufacturing, as part of the first difference in the number of hours worked in manufacturing, the fact that it leads the business cycle does tell us something about business behavior in the typical cycle. The fact that this indicator moves early tells us that in the typical business cycle businesses adjust the workweek before hiring or firing people. The overtime begins to disappear before unemployment begins to rise. Conversely, on the upswing the workweek will lengthen before employment rises, as employers do away with shorttime and even temporarily go to some overtime before hiring new employees. Businesses like to see if the increased demand is temporary or real.

The next two indicators are very similar to each other and do not tell us anything particularly surprising about the behavior of the economy. The net change in inventories on hand and on order, 1972 dollars, smoothed, is sensitive to new orders as is new orders for consumer goods and materials, 1972 dollars. Both are price deflated and the first is smoothed with a four-month moving average. It is not surprising that before a boom approaches a peak the rate of increase in the price level begins to exceed the rate of increase in orders for both inventory and consumer goods. Likewise, a recovery from recession is signaled in advance by the rate of new orders rising in real terms.

Net business formation is the rate of change in the population of business firms. Firms disappear with bankruptcy and voluntary dissolution and come into being with new incorporations. As the economy approaches a peak, bankruptcies begin to exceed new incorporations and after the recession has been underway the situation is reversed. The existing population of business firms is a coincident indicator of the level of business activity, and its rate of change is a leading one.

It is fairly obvious why the next two indicators of advance paperwork lead the actual level of economic activity. New building permits, private housing units and contracts and orders for plant and equipment, 1972 dollars, both represent a firm commitment by someone to undertake a rather large expenditure. We will have more to say about expenditures for residential construction and business plant and equipment expenditure in Chapter 10 when we discuss these components of aggregate demand.

The fact that vendor performance, percent of companies receiving slower deliveries, is a consistent leading indicator tells us that deliveries get much more prompt as production catches up with orders before a recession begins. Similarly, before the boom really gets underway in a recovery, some companies start receiving slower deliveries as producers are pleasantly surprised by orders exceeding their expectations.

The advance rise and fall in the rate of change in sensitive crude materials prices, smoothed, primarily reflects price movements in the industrial commodities markets such as copper, scrap iron, plywood, and so on. These markets are notoriously volatile and the reported series is necessarily smoothed. We will return to the behavior of various prices over the cycle. It is important to note that although the sensitive prices move prior to the general business cycle, labor cost per unit of output is a lagging economic indicator. With materials prices up early and labor cost lagging, profit margins rise in the early stages of recovery and fuel the upward movement. Conversely, before the peak these prices break and begin to fall, but labor costs continue to rise. If one is manufacturing plywood, the profit squeeze is on.

Turning to the index of coincident economic indicators presented in Table 9.5, nothing is included that is any great surprise. General economic activity consists of production, employment, and income. The four coincident indicators included in the composite index are simply those that tend to show a good bit of coincident cyclical volatility. The number of people employed is the source of personal income. In the next chapter we will discuss why sales and employment in manufacturing are more cyclical than in agriculture or the service industries. Transfer payments are removed from the personal income series because many of them, including unemployment compensation, are specifically designed to move countercyclically. In the composite index of coincident economic indicators the four series pick up the entire circular flow of employment, production, and income.

In considering the index of lagging economic indicators we must note that frequently it is questionable whether a particular economic time series is considered a lagging or leading indicator. If it lags the current cycle by long enough, who is to say it is not leading the next turn in the cycle? In terms of theory, it depends on which way one thinks the causal affects are running. In most economic models causation runs both ways. The price causes the quantity supplied or demanded to change and the quantity supplied or demanded causes the price to change.

Let us consider this problem of whether an indicator should be considered a leading or lagging one, with the second of those to be chosen as a component of the lagging index, average prime rate charged by banks. The economic rationale for including this as a lagging indicator is that the typical business cycle boom is well underway when the demand for bank credit becomes so strong that the interest rate on bank loans is driven up significantly. Similarly, the recession is usually well underway before loan demand falls off so much that bankers must reluctantly lower the prime rate. Note that this approach has causation going from the level of economic activity, demand for bank loans, to the level of interest rates, with a positive correlation between the two. Of course, as we have mentioned before and will return to again, an effect runs the other way, from the level of interest rates to the level of economic activity. This relationship is negative; higher rates make investment less attractive and slow the level of economic activity. Low interest rates encourage investment and increase the level of economic activity. In this context we would, of course, think of the level of interest rates as a leading indicator. High interest rates do occur well before the end of a boom and rates must necessarily fall before one can ever expect that recovery is on the way. Some interest rates move more quickly than the prime rate, but none are officially classified as leading indicators. Treasury Bond and Bill yields are, however, classified as coincident at the peak. The student of business cycle movements should realize that this classification is just as ambiguous as the answer to the question: Does the level of economic activity set the level of interest rates or does the level of interest rates influence the level of economic activity? The proper answer is, of course, that both effects are present and we will consider them in more detail when we look at the application of monetary policy in Chapters 13 and 14.

The same analysis we have just applied to interest rates can be applied to the third indicator in the composite lagging index, ratio, consumer installment credit to personal income. It is classified as a lagging indicator with a positive relationship. As the boom matures and the rate of growth in personal income begins to slow, this ratio rises. In a recession, as people stop buying consumer durables the growth in consumer credit falls to zero or goes negative, and this indicator belatedly falls. Of course, in addition to this lagging positive relationship, we want to recognize the leading negative relationship also. As consumers assume more and more debt in a boom, they are setting the stage for the coming recession. A higher and higher percentage of their income must go to repay this debt and is, therefore, not available for additional current expenditures. As a leading indicator, when this indicator goes up, look for the coming downturn in the economy. Conversely, in a recession, as the ratio of consumer debt to income falls, we have a leading indicator of the coming recovery in business.

The lagging indicator receiving the highest score and thereby weighted the heaviest, average duration of unemployment, has a fairly unambiguous basis for its negative relationship. The economy slows and unemployment rises at the same time, but it is some time before the average duration of unemployment rises significantly. On the upswing, the long-term unemployed are the last to return to work.

The fourth and fifth components of the composite lagging index are closely connected. Manufacturing and trade inventories, 1972 dollars, must be financed by commercial and industrial loans outstanding, weekly reporting large commercial banks. In the typical cycle, inventories and the loans to finance them rise late in the boom and cannot be reduced until the recession is well underway.

Perhaps the lagging indicator that tells us most about the business cycle is the last one, labor cost per unit of output, manufacturing. We already mentioned the role this indicator has in propelling the boom. The major component of manufacturing cost is labor. Probably the most consistent behaviors over the cycle are that prices rise faster than costs in the recovery and give us the increasing profits required to propel the boom; and costs rise faster than prices at the peak and give us the declining profits of a recession.

The Indicators over the Typical Business Cycle

Let us conclude this chapter on indicators with a brief description of their behavior during the typical business cycle. Of course, the average sequence of events hides as much as it reveals about any given business cycle, but to study is to simplify. First, let us simplify the description of the business cycle itself. The researchers at the National Bureau of Economic Research and various other analysts discuss the business cycle by breaking it down into nine stages. Stages 1, 2, and 3 are the expansion; 4, 5, and 6 are centered around the peak; 7, 8, and 9 encompass the recession and trough — with stage 9 of one cycle being stage 1 of the next. This classification system has really not caught on, probably because it is more detailed than required. In our discussions we will just consider four stages, each of which blends into the next in a continuous fashion. We will speak in terms of: (1) the expansion, using the term recovery for the early stages and boom for the latter stages; (2) the peak of the cycle when the general level of economic activity stops rising and begins to fall; (3) the recession or, if particularly severe, the depression; (4) the trough at which point the level of economic activity has stopped falling but has not yet begun to rise. This is merely a more formal statement of the terminology we have already been using.

Now let us consider the behavior of broad categories of indicators in the typical cycle. As indicated above, production and employment statistics are the business cycle, and thereby coincident indicators. Rates of change in these will, of course, lead the underlying series. Production and employment in raw materials producing industries move first, then the consumer goods industries, and the capital goods industries move last. We will discuss this in some detail in the next chapter on the components of aggregate demand.

The behavior of prices over the cycle is an important causative factor in the cycle in terms of the cost of labor per unit of output. With the exception of sensitive commodity prices, the prices of factors of production (including labor) lag the prices of final goods and services. As the economy begins its recovery from a recession, the prices of final goods and services rise relative to the cost of factors of production. This, of course, opens up profit margins and makes increased production and the required capital investment more attractive. Business hires more people, unemployment falls, and orders are placed for additional plants and equipment. Interest costs are low and loan funds are readily available.

As the boom matures, interest rates, labor costs, and other factor prices belatedly move up to match the general rise in prices. This squeezes profit margins, making some of the plans for expansion of capacity with additions to plant and equipment look a bit overly optimistic. Inventories suddenly seem high and the stage is set for the recession.

As the recession begins and markets for final goods become weak, interest rates, wages, and other factor costs continue to rise — and everybody asks economists, "What happened to the law of supply and demand? It's not working any more." The profit squeeze causes cutbacks in production and employment. Incomes slow or stop their rise. Inventories are liquidated, orders for plant and equipment are cancelled, and bank loans are paid off.

We mentioned earlier that the difficult part of business cycle theory is finding a rationale for turning points. We can see that as production falls, incomes fall, sales fall, and production will be cut further; but why does this movement not only eventually end, but reverse itself? Probably every turning point, both at the bottom and at the top, is more unique to a particular cycle than the pure rise or fall, but some endogenous factors are at work to reverse the movement. As inventories are liquidated and bank loans paid off, interest rates fall and make heretofore unattractive investments attractive. The population grows and generates buying needs. Psychologically, after things have been substantially down for some period of time, business's idea of "normal" changes. Any positive blip will be interpreted as the beginning of the recovery and business will react accordingly.

We discussed earlier the Schumpeterian push for recovery from new innovations requiring large amounts of investment. We will discuss the possible push from deliberate monetary and fiscal policy actions in coming chapters. Also, as we noted earlier, economists continue to debate how stable the economy is inherently, and how much deliberate economic policy can do to stabilize it.

• Questions for Discussion

1. What is meant by the statement, "The dollar is worth only 23¢."
2. Which is better as a "cost of living" index, the CPI (Laspeyres) or the PCE (Paasche)?
3. Explain how the *unemployment rate* rose by 2.9% from 1974 to 1975, but the *employment rate* fell by only 1.8% over the same period?
4. Why do you think that most of the twelve leading economic indicators used in the official index are first differences?
5. Relate the microeconomic concept of diminishing returns discussed in Chapter 2 to the behavior of costs and profits over the typical business cycle.

• Exercises

1. If nominal GNP went up by 11.3% in a particular year and real GNP went up by exactly 5%, what was the inflation rate as measured by the GNP price index? (Don't forget the cross-product.)
2. The U.S. government's latest revision of the national income statistics indicates that they estimate current dollar GNP to have gone from $1,918.3 billion in 1977 to $2163.9 in 1978 while the GNP price index went from 140.05 to 150.42.
   a. In percentage terms, how much "real growth" was there in the economy from 1977 to 1978?
   b. How much inflation was there over the same time period?
3. The GNP of the National Republic of Berea consists of only two products, beer and sausage. The output and prices in two successive years were as follows:

   > Year 1 beer output = 100 units at $110 per unit.
   >   sausage output = 50 units at $10 per unit.
   > Year 2 beer output = 110 units at $121 per unit.
   >   sausage output = 10 units at $38.50 per unit.

   Calculate the: a. Percentage increase in nominal GNP.
                  b. Rate of growth in real GNP.
                  c. Inflation rate as measured by the GNP price index.
   (There are two sets of correct answers for b. and c. so make sure you have a mutually consistent pair.)

● Source Notes

[1]Arthur F. Burns and Wesley C. Mitchell. *Measuring Business Cycles*. New York: NBER, 1946, p. 3.
[2]Geoffrey H. Moore. *Business Cycles, Inflation and Forecasting*. Cambridge, Mass.: Ballinger Publishing Co. for the NBER, 1980, p. 18.
[3]For the technical details of their scheme, see articles in *Business Conditions Digest,* May and November 1975, and March 1979.

● Selected Additional Readings

Blinder, Alan S. The consumer price index and the measurement of recent inflation. *Brookings Papers on Economic Activity*. No. 2. Washington, D.C.: The Brookings Institution, 1980.

Braithwait, Steven D. The substitution bias of the Laspeyres price index: An analysis using estimated cost of living indexes. *American Economic Review*, Vol. 70, No. 1 (March 1980).

Zarnowitz, Victor, and Geoffrey H. Moore. Sequential signals of recession and recovery. *The Journal of Business*, Vol. 55, No. 1 (January 1982).

The Components of
Aggregate Demand

10

As indicated in Chapter 3 in our discussion of macroeconomic theory, the bookkeeping for total output for the economy uses the categories of consumption goods, investment goods, and those goods and services claimed by government, $C + I + G$. If we then add the net shipments of goods out of the country, exports minus imports, we would have the current definition of total output, Gross National Product. When we add net exports, N_x, we have GNP $= C + I + G + N_x$. Table 10.1 gives the government's estimates of total output of the economy in nine recent years.

On an ex-ante basis these components of total output shown in Table 10.1 would be the components of aggregate demand. The sum of what the consumers plan on buying, what business plans on investing, and so on, is what makes the economy go. The actual data in the table are, of course, ex-post data. Our goal in this chapter is to define each component of aggregate demand, examine its behavior over the business cycle, and comment on the success, or lack of it, economists have had in forecasting each segment.

Consumption Expenditures

The data on consumption expenditures presented in Table 10.1 are divided into expenditures for durable goods and other consumer expenditures. The latter category is made up of expenditures for services and nondurable goods. *Durable goods* are defined by the government as those goods having a useful life of more than three years. These are all the hard goods: television sets, cars, refrigerators, and so on. *Nondurable goods* are food, clothes, and so on. *Services* are such things as haircuts and the doctor telling you to take two aspirin and go to bed. All the figures in the table are in current dollar terms. None are price deflated except real GNP.

In the consumption category it is obvious that the cyclical variation is concentrated in the durable goods component. Over the nine-year time span presented here, the year-to-year change in durable goods expenditures ranges from less than 1% in 1980 to 18.6% in 1976. Other consumption expenditures

TABLE 10.1 Recent Data on the U.S. Economy* (Dollars in Billions)

	1975			1976			1977		
	Level	Change Amount	Change Percent	Level	Change Amount	Change Percent	Level	Change Amount	Change Percent
Consumption									
Durable Goods	132.2	10.7	8.8	156.8	24.6	18.6	178.8	22.0	14.0
Other**	844.2	77.6	10.1	927.5	83.3	9.9	1026.7	99.2	10.7
Total	976.4	88.3	9.9	1084.3	107.9	11.1	1205.5	121.2	11.2
Investment									
Business Fixed	157.7	1.1	0.7	174.1	16.4	10.4	205.5	31.4	18.0
Res. Const.	55.3	−2.6	−4.5	72.0	16.7	30.2	95.8	23.8	33.1
Inventory Change	−6.9	−21.0	—	+11.8	+18.7	—	+21.0	+9.2	—
Total	206.1	−22.6	−9.9	257.9	51.8	25.1	322.3	64.4	25.0
Government									
Federal Defense	83.0	6.0	7.8	86.0	3.0	3.6	93.3	7.3	8.5
Other Federal	39.7	5.8	17.1	43.2	3.5	8.8	50.6	7.4	17.1
Total Federal	122.7	11.7	10.5	129.2	6.5	5.3	143.9	14.7	11.4
State and Local	217.2	24.1	12.5	232.9	15.7	7.2	250.6	17.7	7.6
Total Government	339.9	35.8	11.8	362.1	22.2	6.5	394.5	32.4	8.9
Net Exports	+26.8	+13.4	—	+13.8	−13.0	—	−4.2	−18.0	—
Total GNP	1549.2	115.0	8.0	1718.0	168.8	10.9	1918.0	200.0	11.6
"Real" GNP (1972 $)	1233.9	−14.1	−1.1	1300.4	66.5	5.4	1371.7	71.3	5.5
GNP Price Index	125.56	10.64	9.3	132.11	6.55	5.2	139.83	7.72	5.8
Unemployment Rate	8.5%	2.9%	—	7.8%	−0.7%	—	7.0%	−0.8%	—
Consumer Price Index	161.2	13.5	9.1	170.5	9.3	5.8	181.5	11.0	6.5
T-Bill Rate, Average	5.82	−2.05	−26.0	5.00	−0.82	−14.1	5.26	+0.26	+4.9

*This is what the Department of Commerce thinks happened as of February 1984; they will change their minds and there will be revisions.

**This figure is obtained by subtracting durable goods expenditures from total consumption expenditures as reported for GNP accounting.

TABLE 10.1 (Continued)

	1978			1979			1980		
	Level	Change Amount	Percent	Level	Change Amount	Percent	Level	Change Amount	Percent
Consumption									
Durable Goods	200.2	22.0	12.3	213.4	13.2	6.6	214.7	1.3	0.6
Other**	1146.3	120.1	11.7	1293.8	147.5	12.9	1453.4	159.6	12.3
Total	1346.5	142.1	11.8	1507.2	160.7	11.9	1668.1	160.9	10.7
Investment									
Business Fixed	248.9	43.7	21.3	290.2	41.3	16.6	308.8	18.6	6.4
Res. Const.	111.2	15.4	16.1	118.6	7.4	6.7	102.9	−15.7	−13.2
Inventory Change	+26.5	+3.5	—	+14.3	−12.2	—	−9.8	−24.1	—
Total	386.6	62.5	19.3	423.0	36.4	9.4	401.9	−21.1	−5.0
Government									
Federal Defense	100.3	7.5	8.1	111.8	11.5	11.5	131.2	19.4	17.4
Other Federal	53.3	2.7	5.3	56.5	3.2	6.0	65.9	9.4	16.6
Total Federal	153.6	10.2	7.1	168.3	14.7	9.6	197.0	28.7	17.1
State and Local	278.3	27.9	11.1	306.0	27.7	10.0	340.8	34.8	11.4
Total Government	431.9	38.1	9.7	474.4	42.5	9.8	537.8	63.4	13.4
Net Exports	−1.1	+2.9	—	+13.2	+14.3	—	+23.9	+10.7	—
Total GNP	2163.9	245.6	12.8	2417.8	253.9	11.7	2631.7	213.9	8.8
"Real" GNP (1972 $)	1438.6	68.9	5.0	1479.4	40.8	2.8	1475.0	−4.4	−0.3
GNP Price Index	150.42	10.37	7.4	163.42	13.00	8.6	178.42	15.0	9.2
Unemployment Rate	6.0%	−1.0%	—	5.8%	−0.2%	—	7.1%	+1.3%	—
Consumer Price Index	195.3	13.8	7.6	217.6	22.3	11.4	246.8	29.2	13.4
T-Bill Rate, Average	7.22	+1.96	+37.3	10.04	+2.82	+39.1	11.51	1.47	14.6

*This is what the Department of Commerce thinks happened as of February 1984; they will change their minds and there will be revisions.

**This figure is obtained by subtracting durable goods expenditures from total consumption expenditures as reported for GNP accounting.

TABLE 10.1 (Continued)

| | 1981 | | | 1982 | | | 1983 | | |
| | Level | Change | | Level | Change | | Level | Change | |
		Amount	Percent		Amount	Percent		Amount	Percent
Consumption									
Durable Goods	236.1	21.4	10.0	244.5	8.4	3.6	278.6	34.1	13.9
Other**	1621.1	167.7	11.5	1747.4	126.3	7.8	1880.0	132.6	7.6
Total	1857.2	189.1	11.3	1991.9	134.7	7.3	2158.6	166.7	8.4
Investment									
Business Fixed	352.2	43.4	14.1	348.3	−3.9	−1.1	347.7	−0.6	−0.2
Res. Const.	104.3	1.4	1.4	90.8	−13.5	−12.9	130.5	39.7	43.7
Inventory Change	+18.5	+28.3	—	−24.5	−43.0	—	−6.9	+17.6	—
Total	474.9	73.0	18.2	414.5	−60.4	−12.7	471.3	56.8	13.7
Government									
Federal Defense	154.0	22.8	17.4	179.4	25.4	16.5	200.3	20.9	11.6
Other Federal	75.2	9.3	14.1	79.3	4.1	5.5	74.9	−4.4	−5.5
Total Federal	229.2	32.2	16.3	258.7	29.5	12.9	275.2	16.5	6.4
State and Local	366.5	25.7	7.5	390.5	24.0	6.5	415.0	24.5	6.3
Total Government	595.7	57.9	10.8	649.2	53.5	9.0	690.2	41.0	6.3
Net Exports	+26.3	+2.4	—	17.4	−8.9	—	−10.6	−28.0	—
Total GNP	2954.1	322.4	12.3	3073.0	118.9	4.0	3309.5	236.5	7.7
"Real" GNP (1972 $)	1513.8	38.8	2.6	1485.4	−28.4	−1.9	1534.8	49.4	3.3
GNP Price Index	195.14	16.72	9.4	206.88	11.74	6.0	215.63	8.75	4.2
Unemployment Rate	7.6%	+0.5%	—	9.7%	+2.1%	—	9.6%	−0.1%	—
Consumer Price Index	272.4	25.6	10.4	289.1	16.7	6.1	298.4	9.3	3.2
T-Bill Rate, Average	14.08	2.57	22.3	10.69	−3.39	−24.0	8.62	−2.07	−19.4

*This is what the Department of Commerce thinks happened as of February 1984; they will change their minds and there will be revisions.

**This figure is obtained by subtracting durable goods expenditures from total consumption expenditures as reported for GNP accounting.

184

are considerably less volatile, varying only between a low of 7.6% in 1983 to a high of 12.9% in 1979.

The expenditures for nondurable goods and services are sufficiently stable that forecasting their growth from one year to the next with some degree of accuracy is not that difficult. Indeed, a simple naive percentage change model would have worked reasonably well over this period. If one had assumed that for each year from 1976 through 1983 the percentage change in these expenditures would be the same as in the previous year, one would have had a mean absolute deviation from the actual of only 1.00%. Given some knowledge of the inflation rate and the state of disposable personal income, a forecast of this component of aggregate demand can be fairly reliable. Consumers will continue to buy such necessities as groceries and school shoes even as incomes slow their rise and inflation accelerates at the peak of the cycle. Note that our largest percentage increase of 13% came in 1979 as inflation accelerated from 7.6% to 11.4% as measured by the consumer price index. The growth in real GNP, and, hence, price deflated incomes, tapered off to 3.2% in 1979 from 4.8% in the previous year. Also, we can note that the smallest percentage change in expenditures for nondurable goods and services, 7.6%, was in the recession year of 1983 when the inflation rate of the CPI had declined to 3.2%.

Forecasting consumer behavior has been especially important in recent years. In the absence of major fluctuations in federal defense expenditures, fluctuations in consumption expenditures seem to be the major factor in the timing of the business cycle. Consumption expenditures are, as we noted in Chapter 9, a coincident economic indicator. They always amount to more than 60% of total GNP. When we examine the business cycle history of the United States in Chapter 16 we will see that since World War II the precipitating causes of fluctuations in economic activity have been either changes in federal defense expenditures (the Korean and Vietnam Wars), or apparently autonomous changes in consumption expenditures. And the fluctuations in consumption expenditures are primarily due to fluctuations in expenditures for durable goods.

If we were to apply a naive percentage change model to forecasting expenditures on durables for the last eight years of this nine-year period, we would experience a mean absolute deviation of our forecast from actual of 11.0%. This 11.0% average change in the growth rate from one year to the next can be compared to the 1.00% year-to-year average change for other consumer expenditures. Clearly the expenditures for durable goods is the source of considerable instability in the economy. In fact, over the last fifteen years these expenditures appear to have dominated the business cycle. When the economy is booming, consumer durable-goods industries will be booming. When the economy is in a recession, consumer durables will not be selling well. If they were, we would not be in a recession. The largest year-to-year increase in consumer expenditures on durable goods over the nine-year period, 18.6%, was in 1976 as the economy recovered from the 1974–1975 recession. The smallest change was the .60% in 1980 as the economy went into the recession of 1980–1981.

As a result of the importance of durable-goods consumption expenditures on the cyclical behavior of the economy, economists have devoted considerable effort attempting to forecast consumer behavior in this area. One significant concentration of people working on this problem is the Survey Research Center at the University of Michigan, where researchers spend much time collecting what is called *anticipatory data*. They conduct surveys asking consumers about their buying plans. The researchers seek ex ante data in the responses to the question of whether the consumer plans to buy a particular durable good in the next 3, 6, 9, or 12 months. This group also has an index of consumer sentiment as an overall measure of how the consumer feels about the state of the economy. Regrettably, neither the anticipatory data on buying intentions or the index of consumer sentiment have turned out to be very useful in forecasting actual buying behavior. This is an area that needs, and is receiving, substantial additional research attention.

In summary we can say that fluctuations in consumer expenditures are a major factor in the business cycle. The fluctuations are concentrated in the durable goods portion and we are not very good at forecasting them.

Total Investment

In our circular flow model in Chapter 3, we had the level of investment playing a primary role in determining the equilibrium level of income and output. In Chapter 6 in which we examined some theories of the business cycle, we found investment played a very large role either directly or indirectly in all theories of the business cycle. So it should come as no surprise that changes in the level of total investment are highly correlated with changes in the general level of economic activity. In Table 10.1 we can see that the only three years in which total investment expenditures declined were the recession years of 1975, 1980, and 1982 with decreases of 9.9%, 5.0%, and 12.7%, respectively. The most rapid rise in the level of investment expenditures was in the strong recovery years of 1976 and 1977, with an increase of approximately 25% each year.

As Schumpeter and others quite properly observed, investment underlies much of the business cycle, and the magnitude of the change in investment expenditures typically determines the magnitude of the cyclical fluctuation. For example, the recession of 1975 was much more severe than that of 1980. Average unemployment rose by 2.9% and real output fell by 1.1% in 1975. In 1980 the average unemployment rate rose by only 1.4% and real output fell by almost nothing, 0.1%. As we noted, the 1975 decline in total investment was 9.9%. In 1980 it was about half that, 5.0%. If using data for the eleven years 1970–1980 inclusive, one runs a simple correlation between the percentage change in total investment and the percentage change in real GNP, one gets a simple correlation coefficient of .96. If one uses the resulting regression equation to predict the percentage change in real GNP on the basis of being given the percentage change in total investment, the forecasts are sufficiently accurate to give a standard error of the estimate of less than .80%.* (Now, if we could only forecast total investment.)

Business Fixed Investment

This component of total investment is composed of expenditures by business on factories, warehouses, and all the machinery and equipment that go in them. It is another component of aggregate demand on which anticipatory data are collected. There are a number of surveys of business plans for the acquisition of plant and equipment. Unlike the consumer surveys, however, the anticipatory data from business on investment plans have substantial predictive value. It is not too difficult to understand why this is so. Most corporations go through rather long and involved capital budgeting procedures. Also, many expenditures of this type require extensive engineering studies before they can be undertaken. These activities generate fairly firm numbers as to corporate investment expenditures plans. On the basis of these data, it is possible to make fairly accurate forecasts of expenditures for business fixed investment.

However, being able to forecast business fixed investment does not, as it turns out, happen to be a great forecasting feat. As you will recall from Chapter 9, this series is a lagging economic indicator, which is not too difficult to comprehend if one keeps in mind that the national income accounts procedures seek to estimate plant and equipment actually put in place and structures actually built and paid for rather than plans or new orders for such activities. On the upswing in a recovery period, such as late 1975 and early 1976, business decision makers no doubt observed that business was getting better. Consumer durable expenditures were up by 18.6% and the CPI inflation rate was down to 5.8%. But reacting to this with actual expenditures on new plant and equipment takes time. The activities that generate the fairly reliable anticipatory data also require the lags in business fixed investment expenditures: engineering studies, capital appropriations procedures, financing arrangements, and so on. Note that although the rate of change in consumer durable goods expenditures had

---

*The equation is:

$$\%\Delta Q = .702 + .220 \ (\%\Delta I), \quad R^2 = .92, \quad SEE = .72.$$

dropped to 14% in 1977 from 18.6% in 1976, business fixed investment expenditures rose from a rate of increase of 10.4% to 18%. Most of the decisions regarding the 18% increase in investment expenditures in 1977 were made in 1976, but actually were implemented after a lag of some duration.

Business fixed investment expenditures generally lag in a similar fashion on the downturn but not so reliably. Of course, many investment projects cannot, or at least for economic reasons, should not, be halted abruptly. One really should get the roof on a new warehouse before one halts construction even if the prospective user has just gone bankrupt in the current recession. But business is surprisingly quick to take the ax to capital expenditure projects. Orders are quickly canceled for equipment and, on occasion, construction *does* stop before the roof is done. As a result, the government's official classification system classifies business fixed investment in plant and equipment as a coincident indicator at the peak and a lagging indicator at troughs. The other component of business fixed investment, structures, is classified as lagging at both the peak and the trough.

Investment in Residential Construction

This component of investment expenditures is not strictly the home buyer's judgment of the economic outlook. Some homes do get built "on speculation," in the hopes that buyers will be available when the houses are completed. But most expenditures on housing are the ultimate result of consumers having the willingness and ability to make what is probably the biggest expenditure of their lives. For the last 30 years consumers have been willing, and the primary determinant of expenditures for residential construction has been the availability of mortgage money. Up until the 1979–1980 peak, as soon as interest rates in each cycle would begin to rise, the availability of mortgage money would drop precipitously, and expenditures on residential construction would decline commensurately. This would result in residential construction turning down substantially before the general level of economic activity. Conversely, at the beginning of a recession, business loan demand drops dramatically and the Federal Reserve usually follows aggressive easy money policies. The resulting decline in interest rates has historically caused residential construction to respond rapidly enough for it to be the leading sector as the economy begins to come out of the recession.

Historically, residential construction reliably led the rest of the economy. That is how it used to be. It now appears that the cycle in residential construction has been largely synchronized with the rest of the economy by the removal of certain regulations and increasing consumer sophistication. A primary reason for the rapid disappearance of mortgage money in the early stages of a boom used to be that deposit inflows would practically cease for the major mortgage lenders. These were Savings and Loan Associations nationally and Mutual Savings Banks in the East. The dramatic drop in deposit flows came about because a federal regulation ("Reg. Q") put a ceiling on the rate of interest these and other institutions could pay depositors. When rates went above that level, savers bought 9% U.S. Treasury Bills instead of obtaining 5-1/2% on a savings account — hardly irrational behavior. In the tight money periods of 1966, 1969, and 1974, the Savings and Loan Associations and Mutual Savings Banks did not just increase the rate they charged on mortgages, but in many cases ceased mortgage lending altogether. No mortgage money at *any* price.

Things changed in 1979, however, with the introduction of the "money market certificates" that these and other financial institutions may now issue in exchange for a savings deposit. The legal ceiling interest rate that may be paid on this form of deposit is adjusted each week to be above the level of U.S. Treasury Bills and is, therefore, always competitive. The result was that in the tight money period of 1979–1980 mortgage money was always available — at a price.

One can see the change that has taken place by tracing the impact of interest rates on residential construction. In 1974 Treasury Bills averaged a yield of 7.9% (not shown in Table 10.1), but declined to 5% by 1976 (as indicated in Table 10.1). As the table shows, residential construction rebounded strongly in 1976 and 1977, +30% and 33%, after being squeezed severely by the tight money of 1974. The next time around, when the average Treasury Bill rate rose from 7.22% in 1978 to 10.04% in 1979, residential construction merely slowed its rate of growth to 6.7%. In 1980, when the Bill rate averaged 11.63%, expenditures on residential construction finally declined, but only by 13.2%. By contrast, when Treasury Bill yields increased from an average of 7% in 1973 to 7.9% in 1974, residential construction expenditures declined by 17%.

The more recent time period was different in the cyclical behavior of residential construction both in terms of the magnitude and the timing of the decline. Residential construction did not lead the rest of the economy into the recession by declining in 1979 with the coming of high interest rates. Instead, it went down with everything else in the recession of 1980. And, of course, the magnitude of the decline was much less than one would have expected on the basis of historical experience. With the opportunity to pay competitive rates to savers the mortgage lenders stayed in the market at ever higher rates. The availability of mortgage money did not slow the demand by consumers for residential construction as it had previously. Mortgage money was available at ever higher rates. Finally, at mortgage rates of 16 to 19%, residential construction was slowed because the monthly payment required to pay off the mortgage had increased significantly. A true supply-demand situation prevailed instead of the artificially regulated one of earlier periods, when mortgage money was simply cut off when interest rates reached a certain level.

Economists generally believe that residential construction will still be sensitive to interest rates. But it will not necessarily be a leading indicator. It is likely that residential construction will be more nearly coincident with the general business cycle, although independent movements in this component of aggregate demand are certainly possible if exogenous forces drastically change the availability of mortgage money.

Inventory Changes

Changes in the level of inventories is conceptually one of the more difficult components of aggregate demand. First, change can be either positive or negative, which removes any meaning there might be to percentage changes. Note there are no percentage changes shown for this item in Table 10.1, since such computations would have little meaning. What is the percentage change of an item that goes from $-\$1$ billion to $+\$1$ billion from one year to the next? Or worse yet, what is the percentage change from zero to \$5 billion?

The reason this component may be either positive or negative is, as indicated by what we call it, that it is the *change* in the level of inventories. If businesses were perfectly happy with their inventories and succeeded in holding them constant from one period to the next, this component of aggregate demand would be zero.

The conceptual basis for GNP is an attempt to try to measure what the economy produced in a given accounting period. If the consumers consume 100 widgets in a particular time period but 20 of them were taken out of inventory, the economy produced only 80 widgets during that time period. In the GNP accounts we would want to enter: consumption $= +100$ and change in inventories $= -20$. Conversely, if consumers consumed 100 widgets in a year and we increased our stock of widgets in inventory by 20, we would have produced 120 widgets that year. The GNP computations would include consumption of 100 and inventory change of $+20$. Of course, if these two time periods were consecutive years, we could say that the output of widgets changed by 40 units (from 80 to 120) from one year to the next and all the variation came about through changes in inventory, since the consumption of widgets held constant at 100.

In Table 10.1 we show the impact of inventory swings under the change column only in dollar terms. For example, in 1975 the table indicates an inventory change as a component of GNP of $-\$6.9$ billion. This means that businesses reduced the *level* of inventories by that amount below what they were in 1974. Under the column labeled change, amount, we show

−$21.0 billion for 1975. This is a measure of the change in the rate of accumulation or liquidation on total GNP. It is the *second* difference in the level of inventories. Since businesses liquidated inventories at an annual rate of $6.9 billion in 1975 and this is a negative swing of $21 billion, we know that in 1974 businesses must have *accumulated* inventory at an annual rate of $14.1 billion.

It is apparent from the figures for recent years that changes in the rate of inventory accumulation are a source of considerable cyclical instability. In the example just given, total investment fell by $22.6 billion from 1974 to 1975 and the shift from inventory accumulation to liquidation accounted for $21 billion of it. As a component of GNP over the nine-year period presented in Table 10.1, inventory change has varied from a high of +$26.5 billion in 1978 to a low of the −$24.5 billion in 1982. The severity of a recession is highly correlated with the decline in total investment. In addition, the correlation is highest between this particular component of investment, inventory change, and the severity of a recession. Note that the inventory change went negative in 1975, 1980, and again in 1982. But in 1980 the rate of inventory liquidation was only $3 billion per year, as compared to $6.9 billion in 1975 and $24.5 billion in 1982. In 1975 and 1982 real GNP fell by 1.1% and 1.9% and the unemployment rate rose by 2.9% and 2.1%. In 1980 real GNP declined by only 0.1% and the unemployment rate rose by only 1.4%.

Historically, inventory changes have had such a high correlation with the fluctuation in the general level of business that students of the business cycle who come up with various classifications of business cycles always have one classified as the "inventory cycle." Recall our discussion of the accelerator relationship in Chapter 6. We noted how a small change in final consumer demand of, say 10%, could lead to a cyclical movement in the demand for investment goods rising from zero to something like 30%, and back down again. Inventories are investment goods and they are more easily adjustable up or down than are plants and equipment. If your customer keeps $3 of inventories for each $1 of sales, an increase in sales of $1 will temporarily create a demand for $4 worth of your product — $1 to replace the sold item and $3 to bring inventories up to the new higher desired level.

That word "desired" in the previous sentence is of particular importance. Inventory policy in many cases is a judgment call businesses must make on the basis of their sales forecasts. If they have too much inventory they get stuck with goods left over. If they are too low they miss some sales because they are "out of stock." This means that a change in the psychology of businesses regarding the economic outlook, in general, and their sales forecasts, in particular, can create substantial inventory fluctuations and, thereby, significant impacts on aggregate demand.

The inventory cycle is fairly easy to describe but rather difficult to detect until after the fact. We can begin a description of an inventory cycle at the beginning of a recovery. Businesses are voluntarily increasing inventories as the sales increase. At some point, as the peak of the cycle approaches, the sales forecast will have been too optimistic and the voluntary accumulation of inventories will turn into involuntary accumulation. The national statistics, ex post, will still show inventories rising, but now it will not be because the business is happily building up the stock of goods in anticipation of rising sales. Rather, the unpleasant surprise of surplus goods must be faced. This, of course, sets the stage for voluntary liquidation. When the liquidation of inventories begins, the recession is on. As businesses retrench, at some point they will overshoot the mark in the other direction. The sales forecast will have been too pessimistic. Suddenly their voluntary liquidation becomes involuntary liquidation. Actual inventories are now below the desired level of inventories, ex ante, and the stage is set for the subsequent recovery. The cycle then begins again as inventories are voluntarily accumulated. As stated, the inventory cycle is easier to describe than to detect. It is difficult to tell when inventory accumulation or liquidation shifts from being voluntary to being involuntary.

Another point to remember regarding the inventory change component of GNP is that one must recognize that "inventories" are not just finished goods piled up in a warehouse waiting to be sold. At the national level this category includes raw materials and goods in process as well. Of course, one manufacturer's finished goods may be the customers' raw material. In any case, in manufacturing it is technologically impossible to increase production without increasing inventories at all stages of the production process. We expect inventories to rise as output increases in the economy. It cannot be otherwise for any length of time. What is of interest is how fast inventories are going up relative to output. Hence, the government collects and publishes various inventory/sales ratios. The government classifies this ratio for manufacturing as a lagging indicator, but the real liability of its use in forecasting is the lag in publication and the frequent substantial revisions of the inventory figures.

Government

The claims of the various levels of government on the output of the economy are a significant component of aggregate demand. These claims constitute something between 19% and 22% of total output. For purposes of measuring the impact through the circular flow of income and output, it makes no difference whether the expenditures are by the federal government or by some unit of the state and local governments. However, the financial implications are likely to be sufficiently different, so that the overall impact on the economy is quite different. As we mentioned before, the federal government can spend money it neither taxed nor borrowed by, in effect, printing it, and thereby increasing the monetary base.

In Chapter 12 we will consider the federal government's activities on both the expenditure and revenue side as we consider the measurement and practice of fiscal policy. At this point we will only consider the 33¢ out of each dollar of the federal government's expenditures that are a direct component of aggregate demand. For example, in 1980 the federal government spent approximately $600 billion. Only about $200 billion went for the purchase of goods and services and is thereby directly part of GNP. In this chapter we are concerned only with the expenditures for wages to people who work for the federal government or payments for goods ranging from paper clips to battleships. The other expenditures by the federal government allow someone else to increase their component of aggregate demand. The year 1980 was fairly typical of recent years. The approximately $600 billion in total expenditures was distributed as follows:

Purchase of goods and services	$200 billion
Transfer payments	250
Grants-in-aid to state and local governments	87
Net interest paid	53
Net subsidies	12
Total	$602

The largest item after the purchase of goods and services, transfer payments, is the federal government's expenditures for unemployment compensation, Social Security payments, payments out of the Interstate Highway Trust Fund, and so on. These payments do have an inflationary impact on aggregate demand, but not because the G in $C + I + G$ goes up. An increase in Social Security or unemployment benefits increases consumption expenditures in the GNP accounts, not government expenditures. The next largest item, grants-in-aid to state and local governments, obviously enables those political units to increase their demands on the output of the economy. Interest paid to holders of government securities increases their income and potentially their expenditures. Some part of the last category, subsidies, could be classified as direct demand for goods, to the extent that an activity is subsidized by the government buying some industrial or agricultural output and storing it. Although historically that approach has been used, most subsidy programs today simply make direct payments to the beneficiaries. We will consider all the expenditures of the federal government when we discuss fiscal policy in Chapter 12. As noted above, in this chapter we will restrict ourselves to the purchase of goods and services.

In the decade of the 1970s the federal government's direct claim on the output of the economy declined precipitously. This does not mean that the impact of the budget has declined commensurately (we will consider that later); but the fact is that in real, price deflated terms, total expenditures by the federal government for goods and services has *fallen* by an average of 3.3% per year compounded annually. In 1970 the federal government purchased 9.6% of GNP. By 1980 that had fallen to 7.6%. The decline was concentrated totally in defense expenditures, which fell from 7.4% of GNP to 5%. Nondefense expenditures for goods and services actually rose slightly as a percent of total output, from 2.2% to 2.5%. There are indications that in the 1980s we are seeing this pattern reversed. In 1983 total federal government expenditures were back up to 8.3% of GNP and defense expenditures back up to 6%.

Federal Defense Expenditures

Historically, "wars and threats of wars" have been a source of great cyclical instability in all economies. The U.S. economy is no exception. We began our national existence with the inflation caused by the issuance of the eventually worthless continental currency — hence, the expression, "Not worth a continental." We had war-time inflation followed by recession or depression in conjunction with the War of 1812, the Civil War, World Wars I and II, and the Korean and Vietnam Wars. We will consider some of these in detail later, when we look at the business cycle history of this country.

In the recent past one cannot really make a case against defense expenditures as contributing to cyclical instability or the increasing inflationary pressures of recent years. The percentage growth in defense expenditures compared to the increase in GNP (see Table 10.1) are as follows:

	Defense (in percent)	GNP (in percent)
1975	7.8	8.0
1976	3.6	10.9
1977	8.5	11.6
1978	8.1	12.8
1979	11.5	11.7
1980	17.4	8.8
1981	17.4	12.3
1982	16.5	4.0
1983	11.6	7.7

Defense expenditures increased by less than total GNP for five years. This means that the percentage of total output claimed by this component declined for the five years 1975 through 1979. Only when defense expenditures jumped by 17.4% in 1980, as the economy slowed in the recession, did the share of GNP for defense rise. The jump in 1980 did have the effect of cushioning the recession. The timing of the very large increase in defense expenditures in 1980 was probably more the result of there being an incumbent president running for re-election than the result of a deliberate policy of economic stabilization.

In 1981 a new president came into office with an announced commitment to increase defense expenditures. For the last three years of the data given, the growth rate of this component of aggregate demand has substantially exceeded the growth rate of GNP.

Defense expenditures are determined by world and domestic political considerations. Although considerable data exist on appropriations, defense contracts, and so on, we have frequently failed to forecast this component of GNP very well at all. Obviously, forecasting world and domestic politics is even less of a science than business cycle forecasting. It appears that although we have been lucky in the recent past, for the foreseeable future defense expenditures have the potential of being a major destabilizing force, through both inflationary pressure and procyclical fluctuations.

Federal Nondefense Expenditures

In recent years this component of GNP has been somewhat more erratic than defense expenditures and generally has risen at a faster rate than GNP. The percentage rates of growth for nondefense expenditures by the federal government and GNP (see Table 10.1) are as follows:

	Nondefense (in percent)	GNP (in percent)
1975	17.1	8.0
1976	8.8	10.9
1977	17.1	11.6
1978	5.3	12.8
1979	6.0	11.7
1980	16.6	8.8
1981	14.1	12.3
1982	5.5	4.0
1983	− 5.5	7.7

A simple average of these rates of growth for 1975 through 1980 gives 12.2% for the nondefense expenditures and only 10.6% for GNP. These expenditures gave us the worst of both worlds. They contributed to inflationary pressure by rising more rapidly than total GNP and they grew in a very erratic fashion. One might charitably say that the jumps in the rate of growth in these expenditures in 1975 and 1980 were meant to counter the recessions in those years. But that still leaves the 1976, 1977, 1978 sequence as a pure disturbance with sequential rates of growth of approximately 9%, 17%, and 5%.

The last three years' data depict a marked deceleration in the rate of growth in the federal government's demand for goods and service for non-defense purposes. Again, it is probably not just a coincidence that there was a change in the occupant of the White House in 1981. The absolute decline in 1983 is not likely to be a permanent reversal of a trend, but as the first current dollar decline in this category since 1956, it does dramatize a shift in emphasis.

State and Local Government

Again, as with the federal government, when we consider state and local government expenditures as a component of GNP, we are talking about state and local governments hiring people and buying things. Transfer payments do not count. Welfare and unemployment compensation increase aggregate demand by increasing the recipients' demand for consumption goods.

To obtain the proper perspective on state and local government expenditures, we have to take a longer view than the nine years given in Table 10.1. Table 10.2 presents data for 1950, 1960, 1970, 1975, 1980, and 1983.

From the end of World War II until 1975, state and local governments were truly growth industries. For the 25 years from 1950 through 1975, state and local government expenditures for goods and services rose in *real* terms at an average annual rate of 4.9%. As indicated on Table 10.2, their share of GNP more than doubled, from 6.9% to 14%. State and local governments' demand for employees and materials seemed limitless, but their capacity to finance this growth was not.

It was in 1975 that New York City brought home forcefully to investors that state and local governments do not have the right to print money to cover their deficits. Prior to 1975, investment in general obligations of state and local governments had been treated by the financial community as

TABLE 10.2 State and Local Government Expenditures

Year	Current Dollars (billions)	Percent Change Per Year from Previous Figure	Percent of GNP	1972 Dollars (billions)	Percent Change Per Year
1950	$19.8		6.9%	$50.8	
1960	46.5	8.9%	9.2	82.4	5.0%
1970	124.4	10.3	12.5	140.5	5.5
1975	217.2	11.8	14.0	167.8	3.6
1980	335.5	9.1	12.8	177.9	1.2
1983	415.0	6.3	12.5	175.4	−0.5

virtually risk free. The legal language of the obligations virtually gave the bondholders the right to go in and levy taxes. In most cases there was an explicit statement that payment to the bondholders took precedence over everything else, including the wages of policemen and firemen. *That* should make sure the bondholders were paid! In 1975, what should have been obvious all along became apparent. No judge, state or federal, was going to create anarchy in a major metropolitan area by paying bondholders in lieu of the police and fire departments.

As a result of the realities demonstrated by New York City, there has been since 1975 something of a revolution in state and local government finance. These units of government have for the first time had to hire public accounting firms to establish bookkeeping systems that can be audited. Investors now demand cash-flow projections! The impact of expenditures has been dramatic. As can be seen in Table 10.2 state and local government expenditures have dropped from 14% of GNP in 1975 to 12.8% in 1980. Real growth has been a mere 1.2% per year for the five-year period 1975–1980, after averaging 4.9% for the previous twenty-five years. The demand for goods and services by local governments has actually fallen in real terms for the first three years of the 1980s, at an annual rate of .5%.

While state and local government expenditures generated a steady upward pressure on aggregate demand from 1950 through 1975, they were not the source of any great cyclical instability. If anything, they have been a stabilizing force in the economy. Again, as with federal government expenditures, forecasting the future course of these expenditures probably requires a political forecast. It appears that fluctuations in this component of aggregate demand will not be as great in the 1980s as they were in the 1970s. It also appears that they will not return to the real growth rates of the 1950s and 1960s. However, we will probably see a return to some positive rate of growth of between 1 and 2%, just on the basis of population growth.

Net Exports

With this component of aggregate demand we have the same conceptual problems we had with inventory change, since it also can be either plus or minus. Note the absence of percentage change figures in Table 10.1. The reason this item can go negative is because we include imported goods in the other components and, since we did not produce them, they must be subtracted to get GNP. For example, if the consumers bought 100 widgets and we imported 20 of them (and exported none), this economy only produced 80 widgets. The GNP computations should have the value of 100 widgets under consumption and −20 under net exports. On the other hand, if we had exported 20 widgets (and imported none) and consumers bought 100, the economy obviously produced 120. The GNP computations should include the value of 100 widgets in consumption and 20 in net exports.

In general, net exports are not a major source of cyclical instability in the U.S. economy. For reasons we will explore in some detail in Chapter 18, fluctuations in this component of aggregate demand are *caused* more *by* the business cycle, rather than a factor *causing* the business cycle. Net exports tend to fall with a rapid rise in real GNP and rise in recessions when economic growth slows. The percentage rate of growth in real GNP and the level of net exports for the period 1975–1983 as given in Table 10.1 will make the pattern clear.

	Percent Change in Real GNP	Net Exports (billions)
1975	−1.1	$ 26.8
1976	5.4	13.8
1977	5.5	−4.2
1978	5.0	−1.1
1979	2.8	13.2
1980	−0.3	23.9
1981	2.6	26.3
1982	−1.9	17.4
1983	3.3	−10.6

In the recession year of 1975, net exports were $26.8 billion. As the economy grew at a real rate of approximately 5.5% in 1976 and 1977, net exports first fell to $13.8 billion and then went negative at −$4.2 billion in 1977. As the growth in real GNP slowed in 1978 and 1979 net exports began to rise again, until with the recession of 1980, they had returned to the level of $24 billion. The recovery of 1981 was short (twelve months) and weak, and our continued export surplus was atypical. Apparently, before the impact of the recovery of 1981 was felt we were back into the recession of 1982. The recovery of 1983 has had the usual negative impact on net exports. The countercyclical movement in net exports makes this component of aggregate demand a stabilizing force. Actually, what it means is that we "export" some of the fluctuations in our economy to our trading partners by buying more from them and selling less to them in boom times and reversing the process in recessions.

The magnitude of net exports is really not large enough for it to have been a substantial factor in the fluctuations of the U.S. economy in recent years. The relatively large $26.8 billion level in 1975 was only 1.7% of GNP. This oversimplifies the problem somewhat and the size and fluctuations in net exports may well increase in coming years. We will take a closer look at this problem in Chapter 18. At this point we may say that the net export component of aggregate demand is fairly predictable on the basis of the stage of the business cycle. The exceptions to the predictability of net exports occur when there are basic shifts in world trade patterns, such as those brought about by an unusually bad wheat crop in the rest of the world (we export a lot of wheat) or a precipitous jump in the price of coffee or petroleum (we import a lot of both). Otherwise, in this country we do not look to net exports for an explanation of cyclical fluctuations.

● Questions for Discussion

1. Why is the cyclical variation in consumer expenditures concentrated in durable goods?
2. What is the inventory cycle?
3. How is it that in 1980 the federal government spent more than $600 billion, but the federal government component of GNP shows only about $200 billion?

● Exercise

1. If seasonally adjusted expenditures for residential construction as reported in the GNP accounts were at an annual rate of $120 billion in one quarter of the year and at $90 billion the next quarter, what is the annualized rate of decline in percentage terms?

● Selected Additional Readings

Blinder, Alan S. Retail inventory behavior and business fluctuations. *Brookings Papers on Economic Activity,* No. 2, 1981. Washington, D.C.: The Brookings Institution, 1981.

Dornbusch, Rudiger, and Stanley Fischer. *Macroeconomics.* (2nd ed.) New York: McGraw-Hill, 1981. Chapter 2.

Jaffee, Dwight M., and Kenneth T. Rosen. Mortgage credit availability and residential construction. *Brookings Papers on Economic Activity,* No. 2, 1979. Washington, D.C.: The Brookings Institution, 1979.

King, Donald A. Accuracy of quarterly GNP estimates. *Business Economics,* Vol. 7, No. 3 (May 1982).

National Economic Policy, the Goal of Noninflationary Full Employment

11

Goals of Economic Policy

The goals of economic policy most often considered by both policymakers and economists are:

1. Price stability.
2. Full employment.
3. Economic growth.
4. A "satisfactory" international balance of payments position.

Goals 1 and 2 clearly dominate policy discussions; hence, the extensive discussion of the CPI and the unemployment rate in Chapter 9. In fact, it is not much of an oversimplification to say that goals 3 and 4 receive considerable lip service but have almost no real impact on policymakers. We will consider goal 4, a "satisfactory" international balance of payments position, in detail in Chapter 18. As indicated by the quotation marks, there is some question regarding what constitutes a "satisfactory" balance of payments position at a particular time.

Goal 3, economic growth, receives considerable superficial attention, but if one looks closely at the rhetoric, one usually finds the real concern is for goal 1 or 2. For example, in a recession or depression politicians, businesspeople, and labor leaders will all call for greater economic growth—to create more jobs to lower the currently high unemployment rate. In a boom the same spokespeople will observe that the problem of inflation is "too many dollars chasing too few goods." Hence we need greater economic growth for more goods—to help fight inflation.

The truth is, of course, that at the macroeconomic policy level the only way to encourage economic growth is to increase the proportion of the output of the economy that is saved and invested instead of being consumed. We need to decrease the proportion of our output going to consumption. The person calling for maximum economic growth is calling for a minimum level of consumption, which is not likely to be a very politically popular position. In some totalitarian, centrally controlled economies deliberate policies are taken to hold consumption to the bare minimum so that the highest possible proportion of the output will be available for investment (or armaments). In the United States we are not really interested in maximum economic growth.

The primary goal of national economic policy seems clearly to be full employment with price stability. We state it now as a single goal, which raises the problem of combining the two. Can we have price stability and full employment together? A large part of this chapter is devoted to that question.

In terms of measuring success, or lack of it, in achieving the goals of economic policy, the country seems regrettably to have sunk into a single number syndrome for each goal. Price stability is measured by the monthly change in the CPI and full employment is measured (inversely) by the monthly unemployment rate. As these statistics are published each month, public opinion analysts keep tabs on the degree of concern of the body politic for each. This means the policymakers know at each point in time whether people are more concerned about the inflation rate or the unemployment rate. Policymakers generally react accordingly.

A Trade-off Between Full Employment and Price Stability?

Let us consider the inflation rates, unemployment rates, and the course of the business cycle over the selected ten-year periods 1954–1963 and 1964–1973. During the first of these periods, there were three recessions; 1953–1954, 1957–1958, and 1960–1961. During the latter ten-year period there was only one rather mild recession in 1970–1971. If we average the annual rates of inflation and unemployment over these two ten-year periods we obtain results shown in Table 11.1.

Clearly, the early time period had lower inflation rates and higher unemployment than the latter time period. During the ten years during which we had the three recessions, 1954–1963, we had an average annual rate of increase in the consumer price index of only 1.4%. In fact, during 1954 and 1955 the rate of increase averaged out to zero, going up by about 0.5% in 1954 and down by 0.5% in 1955. The worst year during this time period

TABLE 11.1 Two Contrasting Periods of Inflation and Unemployment

	1954–1963	1964–1973
Average Annual Percent CPI	1.4%	3.8%
Average Unemployment, Percent	5.4	4.6

was 1957, with an inflation rate of 3.6%. In the more recent period, 1964–1973, during which we had only one recession, the average annual rate of increase in the CPI was 3.8%. The best we did was the first year of the period, 1964, when the CPI went up by only 1.3%. Significantly, the worst year was the last one of this ten-year period, 1973, with an average inflation rate of 6.2% as measured by the CPI.

The other side of the coin, the level of unemployment over these two time periods, tends to support the idea of an inflation-unemployment trade-off. During the earlier low inflation period of 1954–1963 we experienced an average unemployment rate of 5.4%. There was only a 4.6% rate in the latter ten-year period. During the first period unemployment reached a high of 6.8% for the yearly average in the recession of 1958. In the latter period the highest annual average was only 5.9% in 1971. The lowest average rate for any year in 1954–1963 was 4.1% in 1956. In 1969 the unemployment rate averaged only 3.5%. Indeed, the unemployment rate fell to 4% in January of 1966 and never reached that level again until over four years later, in February of 1970, when it rose to 4.2%. Of course, in 1966 the CPI increased only 2.9% and by 1969 it was going up at an annual rate of 5.4%.

The Concept of the Phillips Curve

One can see from the foregoing how the idea that we might have a two-way choice on how we want to run the economy could arise. We apparently could run either a low-pressure economy with frequent recessions as in 1954–1963 and have low inflation and high unemployment, or we could have a high-pressure economy with few or no recessions and have low unemployment at the price of a higher inflation rate as in 1954–1973. The concept of a trade-off between goals of full employment and price stability is refined in the form of the Phillips curve. A hypothetical curve is shown in Fig. 11.1.

The Phillips curve was originated by an Australian economist using British data. His original idea was to relate the average annual rate of increase in wages to the unemployment rate. He proposed the not unreasonable hypothesis that when unemployment was very low labor would be able to bargain for relatively high rates of wage increases. Alternatively, when unemployment was very high, he felt that wage increases would be more moderate. Hence, he proposed a negative relationship between the percentage rate of increase in wages and the level of the unemployment rate. His original studies covering the years 1862–1957 for the United Kingdom generally supported his hypothesis.[1]

The contemporary Phillips curve, found not only in scholarly journals but in the popular financial press as well, corrupts the original idea by using the rate of price inflation rather than the rate of increase in wages. In the

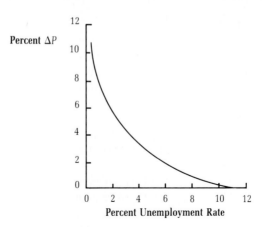

FIGURE 11.1   A Hypothetical Phillips Curve.

United States the GNP price index or the CPI is generally related to the unemployment rate. As we will see, a hypothetical relationship between inflation and the rate of unemployment in the United States fit the data quite well over the 1960s and then fell apart in the 1970s. (See Figs. 11.2 and 11.3.).

Before we discuss why we feel that we cannot find a stable relationship between the rate of inflation and the level of unemployment, let us first examine what sort of socioeconomic problems we would still have even if the Phillips curve could be pinned down. Consider the hypothetical Phillips curve depicted in Figure 11.1. Some parts of the curve are not totally hypothetical. In particular, the ends reflect some accepted behavior patterns in this economy. The lower right-hand end where the curve crosses the

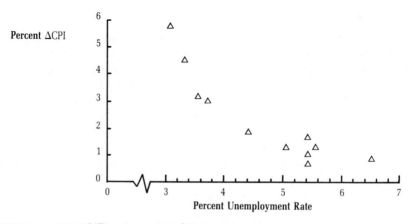

FIGURE 11.2   U.S. Phillips Curve, Actual Data, 1959–1969.

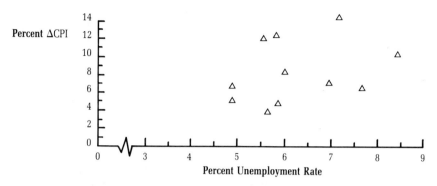

Percent ΔCPI

FIGURE 11.3   U.S. Phillips Curve, Actual Data, 1970–1980.

axis does seem to be in accord with much empirical work done on the U.S. economy. In other words, we do feel that if we ran the unemployment rate up to something in excess of 10% and kept it there for three or four years, the CPI and GNP price indexes would probably show something close to a zero rate of increase. (Of course, politically we are probably not ready to pay that kind of price to stop inflation.) We also think that the curve not crossing the vertical axis at all contains some truth. Note that, as the mathematicians say, the curve only "asymptotically approaches" the vertical axis. No matter how strong the inflationary pressure has been in this economy we have never gotten the measured rate of unemployment down to zero. Even during World War II, with massive excess demand, wage and price controls, rationing, and an apparent labor shortage, we still had some measurable unemployment.

Although we think the ends of the curve reflect something about reality, the rest of the curve is strictly hypothetical for reasons that we will discuss later. Right now let us assume the world is sufficiently simple that the economists have found *the* Phillips curve, presented it to Congress, and said, "Tell us what combination of inflation and unemployment you want, and we will direct the policymakers to move in that direction." This procedure by the economists is as it should be, since a permanent trade-off between unemployment and inflation would pose problems that are essentially political, not economic.

When this question is posed to Congress we can imagine typical members of Congress recognizing that they should confer with their constituents. It is, after all, impossible to serve the public if one is not in office. If the members of Congress confer with their constituents in the order of the size of their individual campaign contributions, a most likely person to be asked first is a wealthy one. Let us assume this voter has maximized his claim on the output of the economy by obtaining a large block of capital and earns his daily bread by clipping coupons off various tax-exempt and corporate securities. With his income fixed in dollar terms this voter will be a "sound money man" (or woman). Indeed, if this voter had read Chapter 15 of this text in which we review the business cycle history, he may well propose the curve be extended into the lower quadrant, where the inflation rate presumably becomes negative. He can correctly observe that in the early 1930s, with the unemployment rate between 10% and 30%, prices frequently fell. The real value of fixed dollar payments went up.

Although our example was one of a wealthy individual suffering losses from inflation, we must hasten to point out that no generalities on this matter regarding income class can really be made. Our members of Congress might also ask a retired school teacher trying to survive on a very meager, fixed dollar teachers' retirement fund. They would get the same answer they got from the bondholder. To the extent that the retired school teacher was looking out for her own best economic interest, she, too, would say, "What's a little unemployment; this inflation is killing me." In general, anyone whose income is fixed in dollar terms and is not subject to a high probability of being unemployed in recession or depression will vote for the lower end of the curve.

As our Congressmembers check with their labor union support they will find some sentiment for moving somewhat farther up on the curve. The manufacture of consumer durables is a heavily unionized industry, and as we discussed earlier, is subject to cyclical variation. These voters presumably would be willing to endure some inflation to reduce the probability of their being unemployed. Perhaps they would vote for the midpoint of 4% inflation and 4% unemployment—it at least has a certain symmetrical appeal.

The support for the high rates of inflation and very low unemployment rates would come from those concerned with the "unemployables." It is a fact that despite all the good reasons given for "structural unemployment," when a boom (and inflation) really get going many "unemployables" suddenly are employed. The social worker in the inner city whose main concern is badly educated minority youths would undoubtedly think double-digit inflation a worthwhile price to pay for the benefits received.

Our reason for examining these political positions along the Phillips curve is to point out the social and political problems that would still remain even if the world were so simple as to be subject to representation by a stable Phillips curve. We will now turn to the reasons why the world is not even this simple.

The Downfall of the Phillips Curve

As we mentioned, it was during the 1960s that economists thought they had found a stable Phillips curve. Figure 11.2 shows why. The data for the years 1959 through 1969 seem to depict a smooth Phillips curve of the type we have discussed. In fact, the trade-off did not even look that bad. Apparently we could have a 1% inflation rate with only about a 6.5% unemployment rate. We could reduce unemployment to 4% with only about a 2.5% rate of inflation in the CPI. The simple correlation between the two variables is a −.85, implying that a linear relationship would "explain" 73% of the variation in the CPI with the unemployment rate.* The years 1959–1969 certainly seem to depict a meaningful Phillips curve and many were the unfortunate souls ready to forecast on the basis of it.

Consider Fig. 11.3 depicting the data for 1970 through 1980. If there is *any* significant relationship between the two variables, it certainly is not readily apparent. In fact, the simple correlation between the two is positive, +.26. It is not significantly different from zero. It would be delightful if the Phillips curve were positively sloped. Lower unemployment associated with lower rates of inflation would present us with no political problem whatsoever. Everyone would agree which way we wanted to go, toward the lower rates of inflation *and* unemployment.

Obviously, the more recent data destroy any illusions one might have about the existence of a stable Phillips curve. When we examine exactly how increasing inflation did work its magic of reducing unemployment in the 1960s, we discover why the relationship fell apart in the 1970s. Consider again our hypothetical Phillips curve in Fig. 11.4. Let us say the economy has been operating at the nicely symmetrical point of 4% inflation and 4% unemployment. The curve indicates that if we were to increase the inflation

---

*The linear equation is: $\%\Delta CPI = 8.0 - 1.2\%Un$. Of course, an appropriate nonlinear relationship would give an even better fit.

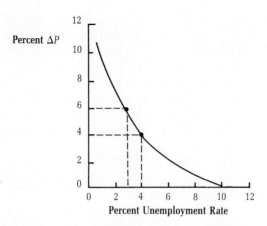

FIGURE 11.4   Moving from 4% to 3% Unemployment with 6% Inflation.

rate of 6% the unemployment rate would fall to 3%. How does this come about? Recall that wages and other costs lag, but prices of finished goods are coincident with the cycle.

If 4% has been the inflation rate for a number of years, it stands to reason that long-term contracts in general, and labor contracts in particular, have been signed with the expectation that the inflation rate over the life of the contract will be 4%. In other words, we are in something of a dynamic equilibrium with 4% unemployment and a 4% expected and actual inflation rate. Now let us assume that the government stimulates aggregate demand sufficiently to raise the inflation rate from 4% to 6%. The 6% inflation rate, of course, comes as a surprise. The real, price-deflated wage turns out to be lower than both employers and employees expected it to be. The cost of labor per unit of output falls. Microeconomic principles tell us that any resource available at a lower price will have the quantity demanded increased. What businesspeople see is the price of their product going up more rapidly than their labor costs. Their profit margin opens up. They decide to produce more, hire more labor, increase employment, and reduce the unemployment rate. That is how an increase in the inflation rate from 4% to 6% could, in our example, reduce the unemployment rate from 4% to 3% as we move along the 1960s type Phillips curve.

Note that an important element in the functioning of the Phillips curve is the element of surprise. The people signing the contracts for labor and other resources have to be surprised by that 6% inflation. They were expecting 4%. But, of course, after the 6% inflation rate has been around for awhile people will come to expect 6%. If the economy was in some sort of equilibrium at point A in Fig. 11.5 when people were expecting 4% and the actual rate

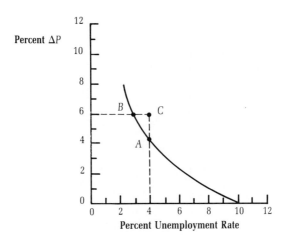

FIGURE 11.5 Two Inflation Rates, One Unemployment Rate.

was 4%, why should things be different if people come to expect 6% and the actual rate turns out to be 6%? In other words, while we could reduce the unemployment rate from 4% to 3% by going from point *A* to point *B*, this is dependent on people expecting 4% inflation. As people come to expect 6%, the unemployment rate is going to tend to drift out toward point *C*. In fact, as we show in Fig. 11.6, we will have a new Phillips curve when the expected inflation rate, $E\%\Delta P$, rises to 6%. If the inflation rate stays at 6%, the unemployment rate will begin to drift back out to 4% as people begin to anticipate the 6% inflation rate and act accordingly. Union wage demands do reflect recent inflationary experience.

Of course, the government does have an alternative to allowing the unemployment rate to rise. When the market participants come to expect 6%, surprise them with 10%. Point *D* is a point which will hold the unemployment rate down to 3% as long as people only expect 6%. But eventually people will come to expect the 10% and a still higher rate of inflation will be required to hold the unemployment rate down to 3%.

What economists have concluded is that the Phillips curve is essentially a short-run phenomenon. It does exist, but its precise location depends on inflationary expectations. Expectations are changing all the time and are heavily influenced by recent experience. When we combine the transitional nature of the Phillips curve with the political nature of federal government stabilization policies we get what has come to be called a "Phillips loop."

Figure 11.7 depicts a simplified description of a complete policy cycle. The sequence of inflation rates and unemployment rates of which the Phillips loop is composed is indicated by the arrows and numbers. The numbers indicate the sequence and the arrows indicate the direction of movement.

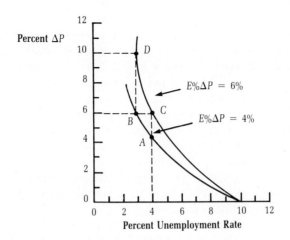

FIGURE 11.6   Two Phillips Curves from Two Levels of Inflationary Expectations.

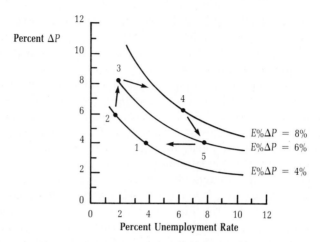

FIGURE 11.7 A "Phillips Loop" from Three Phillips Curves.

We begin at point 1 with the unemployment rate and the inflation rate both equal to 4%. Let us assume that the voters are screaming that unemployment is too high. The government responds to this pressure with policies designed to stimulate aggregate demand and reduce the unemployment rate. As a result of the increase in aggregate demand the inflation rate goes from 4% to 6%. This higher inflation rate is unexpected, and so are all those effects on real wages, profits, and employment discussed earlier. The increased employment lowers the unemployment rate to 2%. As indicated by point 2, we have moved from 4% inflation and 4% unemployment to 6% inflation and 2% unemployment. The government policies are temporarily successful. However, as people come to expect 6% inflation, they begin to negotiate labor and other supply contracts accordingly. Then the government finds it must stimulate the economy even more just to hold the rate of unemployment at its current lower level. Our example in the figure indicates an increase in the inflation rate from 6% to 8% would be required as shown by point 3. As we move from point 2 to point 3 we get a higher rate of inflation with no change in the unemployment rate since we are only compensating for increased inflationary expectations. This policy will be continued as long as the public opinion polls and the election results show people to be more concerned with unemployment than with inflation. At some point, however, the accelerating inflation rate will come to be "public enemy number one." Price stability will displace full employment as the primary goal of economic policy. There will be a period during which policy will result in a meaningful restraint in aggregate demand. This will very likely result in a recession, during and after which the public will be surprised by an inflation rate that is lower than was expected. This sequence is depicted in Fig. 11.7 by the moves from point 3 to 4 and then to 5. Over this time period people had come to expect 8% inflation and suddenly got 6%. Then they came to expect 6% but got only 4%. Of course, as we mentioned earlier, when the inflation rate turns out to be *less* than anticipated, the Phillips curve effects that lowered the unemployment rate before are reversed and serve to raise the unemployment rate now. Labor costs go up faster than prices, profit margins are squeezed, production and employment are cut back, and unemployment rises—the typical recessionary sequence. In Fig. 11.7 we see the unemployment rate rise to a level of between 6% and 7% as the inflation rate falls from 8% to 6%. At an unexpectedly low inflation rate of 4% unemployment rises to 8%. When the people become convinced the 4% rate of inflation is here to stay, the unemployment rate actually falls, with no increase in inflation as we move from point 5 back to point 1.

We need to emphasize again that the foregoing is a greatly oversimplified version of the interaction of inflation and the unemployment rate over the business cycle, but it does contain enough truth to be useful. Consider the actual data from 1972 through 1980 plotted in Fig. 11.8. There is obviously more going on than we have described, but the clockwise movement of the Phillips loop is readily apparent.

Let us reiterate the state of affairs with respect to the Phillips curve. The popularity of the concept is much diminished because it has been discovered that the Phillips curve is not stable; it will not stay put. Its location depends on the inflationary expectations of the market participants, which will change based on their recent experience. This means that in the long run the Phillips curve does not exist, because as people adapt to a higher rate of inflation, unemployment will drift back to its long-run equilibrium rate. Conversely, if unemployment is increased because of a determined and successful effort to reduce the rate of inflation, the unemployment rate will eventually fall back to its lower long-run equilibrium level as people come to expect the lower rate of inflation and act accordingly.

There is still considerable controversy among economists regarding the following two questions:

1. How long is the long run and the short run in this mechanism? How long does it take the labor market to adapt to changed rates of inflation?
2. Is the long-run equilibrium unemployment rate stable? If not, what determines its level?

We will consider the problems raised by the second question in some detail in the next section of this chapter.

Let us close our discussion of the Phillips curve by pointing out that it does have relevance for macroeconomic policy. Although the Phillips curve jumps around in response to changing expectations, we are always on *some* Phillips curve. This means that, at the macroeconomic policy

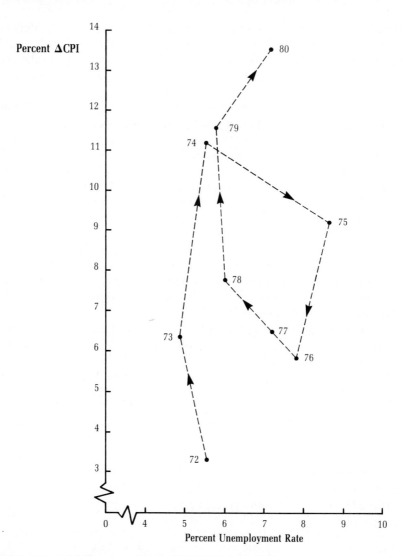

FIGURE 11.8   A "Phillips Loop," Actual U.S. Data, 1972–1980.

level, anything done to reduce unemployment will result in a higher rate of inflation than there otherwise would have been. If one cuts taxes, lowers interest rates, increases government expenditures, or whatever one does at the macroeconomic policy level to decrease unemployment, one will make some contribution to increasing inflation. Conversely, any macroeconomic policy designed to fight inflation will result in greater unemployment than we otherwise would have had. Politicians have the propensity to enunciate the obvious untruth that they will "stop inflation without creating unemployment." This is most certainly impossible. Perhaps in the long run, by lowering the expectations of inflation, one can reduce inflation without increasing unemployment, but over the cycle, inflation never abates until unemployment rises.

The Noninflationary or Inflation Threshold Unemployment Rate

Empirical observation regarding the inflation rate has impressed economists with the utility of a naive forecasting model. In short, we have come to the conclusion that the major cause of inflation is inflation! The scholarly journal articles speak of "complex autoregressive mechanisms," but the business cycle theory and sequence is quite simple. When prices go up, this eventually makes wages go up; wages are a large component of costs so costs go up, which causes prices to go up again. In other words there is a great deal of inertia in the system. Whatever rate of inflation we have been having in the recent past is the best forecast of the rate for the immediate future. Rapid changes in aggregate demand, up or down, will initially be reflected in output and employment, not prices.

We are thus victims of our own history. If we have been running a 4% inflation rate, it is no great policy trick to hold inflation between 3% and 5%. On the other hand, if we have been running a 10% inflation rate, it is impossible to have an inflation rate between 3% and 5% without massive unemployment.

Although all the empirical studies do show a high degree of autocorrelation for inflation-rate time series, the naive forecast can be improved on by including the unemployment rate. In our discussion of the Phillips curve we described a mechanism by which unexpected increases in the rate of inflation cause unemployment to fall. The direction of causation goes from the inflation rate to the unemployment rate. However, we noted that if the unemployment rate were held at this lower level, the inflation rate would increase. After a lag, the causation runs from the unemployment rate to the inflation rate. A low unemployment rate in this case requires an accelerating inflation rate.

Current macroeconomic theory concludes that the unemployment rate will alter the *rate of change* in the inflation rate. If inflation has been running at 6% or 12% this year, next year it is likely to be closer to whichever level we have been experiencing. However, we do somehow move from 6% to 12% (or vice versa) slowly over a period of years, and that is where the unemployment rate comes in. Economists do not now spend their computer time and other peoples' research funding looking for the exact location of the full range of values for the Phillips curve. Instead they seek to determine what was originally called the *noninflationary unemployment rate*. The expression is something of a misnomer since if the economy is at the noninflationary unemployment rate, we can still have inflation. A more recent and descriptive term is the *inflation threshold* unemployment rate.[2]

We can have any number of possible rates of inflation depending on our recent history. The definition of the inflation threshold unemployment rate, U_{ni}, is that unemployment rate at which the inflation rate would have no tendency to rise or fall. If we are at 6% inflation, we will stay there; if we are at 12% or 4% we will stay there if the unemployment rate is at the "threshold" level. If we push the unemployment rate below the U_{ni}, the inflation rate will begin to rise. That is how we get from 6% to 12%. If we have a recession and the unemployment rate rises above the U_{ni}, the inflation rate will begin to fall. The U_{ni} is roughly analogous to the long-run equilibrium unemployment level considered in our discussion of the dynamics of the Phillips curve.

If the economists have now ceased looking for a stable Phillips curve and are now seeking the inflation threshold unemployment rate, have they found it? Not exactly, since they have found that it tends to move also. In particular, "the evidence suggests that several independent and related forces have been operating since the early 1960s to push up the U_{ni} quite sharply."[3] The research indicates that the U_{ni} was in the range of 4 to 4.5% in the mid-1960s and has now risen to 5.5 to 6%. This means that back in the 1960s the inflation rate did not begin to accelerate until unemployment fell below 4.5%, whereas in the late 1970s any unemployment level below 6% apparently caused the inflation rate to begin to rise.

The obvious question is: What has changed in the structure of the U.S. economy to give us a 1.5% higher unemployment rate, all other things being equal? Basically, there appear to be two primary reasons for the rise in the U_{ni} over the last fifteen years. The first is the population distribution. The post–World War II baby boom graduated from high school and college and joined the workforce over this period. The rates of growth for five-year periods of the entire population and the population 16–26 years of age are shown in Table 11.2.

TABLE 11.2 Percentage Change in Population Total U.S. and 16–24-Year-Old Age Group

Period	Total U.S. Population	16–24 Year Olds
1949–1954	9.28%	−4.88%
1954–1959	9.08	8.70
1959–1964	7.91	22.76
1964–1969	5.62	20.28
1969–1974	4.55	12.95
1974–1979	4.10	6.32

As the figures make clear, the period from 1959 through 1974 saw the number of 16–24 year olds increasing substantially faster than the general population. Compared to the 1950s the shift was spectacular. For the 15-year period 1959–1974 the 16–24 age group increased by 67%, or at an average annual compound rate of 3.5%. The total population increased by only 19%, or at an average annual rate of only 1.2%, less than a third as fast as the growth rate of the 16–24-year-old group. As might be expected, new entrants to the workforce run higher rates of unemployment than the rest of the population. For example, in January of 1981 the unemployment rate for 16–19 year olds was 19%. It was only 7.4% for the total civilian workforce. In short, during the 1960s and early 1970s the economy had an invasion of new, untrained, uncommitted workers dumped on it. This should certainly have given the economy a higher unemployment rate than it otherwise would have had. Alternatively, one could say in Phillips curve terms that a higher rate of inflation would be required to hold the unemployment rate down to a given level. More precisely, we now feel that a major factor in causing the U_{ni} to rise from the 4.5% range in the early 1960s to 6% by the late 1970s was the influx of new entrants to the labor market as a result of demographic patterns.

We are optimistic with respect to the demographic factors for the immediate future. Over the next 20 years the 16–24-year-old age group will decline as a percentage of the population. As we have shown, the difference between the rates of growth of the younger age group and the total population had already begun to narrow by the 1974–1979 period. In fact, for the year 1979 the rate of growth in the total population, at 0.85% for the year, had already exceeded that of the 18–24 year old group, at 0.45%. The available statistics and demographic studies indicate clearly that the number of new entrants to the workforce will decline in the next two decades. This should be a factor in lowering the unemployment rate. We can probably have a reasonable degree of confidence in these population forecasts, since in some ways demographers have an easier forecasting job than business cycle analysts. They can get a count of who is already born and all they have to do is forecast how many will die before making it to age 16.

Another factor raising the inflation threshold unemployment rate for the past 20 years is the participation rate of women in the workforce. This factor is probably more properly classed as sociological rather than demographic. Regardless of the classification of the phenomenon, the numbers make fairly clear that since as far back as 1949, the proportion of women in the workforce has been rising steadily. This by itself would tend to raise the unemployment rate, since women have consistently experienced higher unemployment rates than men. In addition, over this time period the amount by which the female unemployment rates exceed the male rates has also increased. The relevant numbers are shown in Table 11.3. Note the steep decline from 1959 to 1979 in the amount by which the male labor force

TABLE 11.3 Comparison of Men versus Women in Workforce

	Labor Force Participation Rates			Unemployment Rates		
	Male	Female	Difference	Male	Female	Difference
1949	86.4%	33.1%	53.3%	5.9%	6.0%	− 0.1%
1954	85.5	34.6	50.9	5.3	6.0	− 0.7
1959	83.7	37.1	46.6	5.3	5.9	− 0.6
1964	81.0	38.7	42.3	4.6	6.2	− 1.6
1969	79.8	42.7	37.1	2.8	4.7	− 1.9
1974	78.7	45.6	33.1	4.8	6.7	− 1.9
1979	77.9	51.0	26.9	5.1	6.8	− 1.7

Source: *Economic Report of the President*, January 1981, pp. 264–66.

participation rate exceeds that of the female rate from 47% to 27%. The amount by which the female unemployment rate exceeds the male unemployment rate held fairly constant from 1954 to 1959, at around 0.6%, but rose substantially and permanently from 1959 to 1964. From 1959 to 1964 the male unemployment rate fell by 0.7%. The female unemployment rate actually rose by 0.3%. Between those years the male labor force participation rate fell by 2.7% while the female rate rose by 1.6%. It appears that as a higher and higher proportion of women have joined the workforce an increasing proportion of them are technically classified as unemployed.

Summary

In this chapter we first established that the primary goals determining economic policy are price stability and full employment. We then observed that over the years from the early 1950s to the mid-1960s we had frequent recessions, relatively high rates of unemployment, but delightfully low rates of inflation. For the decade 1965–1975 we had only one recession, very low rates of unemployment, but a problem with an accelerating rate of inflation.

The association of high unemployment with low inflation and vice versa is formalized in the concept of the Phillips curve. We noted that even if the macroeconomic mechanism were so simple that we could find *the* Phillips curve, we would still have some difficult social and political decisions regarding economic policy. How much inflation and how much unemployment is likely to be a question on which many groups in our economy will disagree.

Of course, the data on inflation and unemployment from 1970 to 1980 destroy any hope of a stable Phillips curve. We were not terribly surprised by this after we took a close look at what makes the Phillips curve work.

For the inflation rate to reduce the unemployment rate it must come as a surprise. Apparently, people have come to expect ever higher rates of inflation over the last twenty years.

With inflationary expectations changing very slowly, any given inflation rate tends to become firmly entrenched in the system, which makes the current rate of inflation the primary determinant of the future rate of inflation. A naive forecasting model works very well. We did relate the unemployment rate to the inflation rate, but only at the first difference level. High rates of unemployment are associated with a slow decline in the rate of inflation. A very low unemployment rate is associated with an increasing rate of inflation. We defined the inflation threshold unemployment rate, U_{ni}, as the unemployment rate which would lead to no increase or decrease in the rate of inflation. If the economy is at the U_{ni} and the inflation rate is 4% or 12%, it will stay at 4% or 12%. The inflationary rate moves from 4% to 12% if the unemployment rate is below the U_{ni} for long enough. Similarly, the rate will move from 12% to 4% if the unemployment rate is above the U_{ni} for long enough.

Although the economics profession is far from certain on these matters, it appears that the U_{ni} has risen from about 4.5% unemployment in the mid-1950s to around 6% in 1980. This increase means that under similar levels of aggregate demand, today we will have about 1.5% higher unemployment rate than we would have had twenty years ago.

There are two demographic-sociological reasons for this rise in the U_{ni}: the large influx of new entrants to the labor force resulting from high birth rates in the 1940s and the increase in the female labor force participation rate. The rate of growth in the 18–24-year-old age group went from being less than that of the general population in the 1950s to a rate of growth more than three times as fast in the 1960s. During the same time period the female labor force participation rate went from 35% to 51%. The amount by which the female unemployment rate exceeds the male unemployment rate rose from 0.7% to 1.9%.

For the future, one can be optimistic about the impact on unemployment of the rate of inflow of new entrants into the labor force, based on current demographic patterns. However, attaining the goal of noninflationary full employment is likely to remain quite difficult.

● Questions for Discussion

1. What would be the implications of the United States adopting a policy of maximum economic growth as its only and overriding goal?

2. If the economy were faced with a known Phillips curve, what position would you think would be optimal for you when you graduate from college? After being employed for ten years? As a retired person?

3. Why do economists contend that for inflation to result in increased output and decreased unemployment it must come as a "surprise"?

4. Discuss some of the factors that may have contributed to a secular rise in the measured unemployment rate over the last 30 years.

5. Add recent years' data on the percentage change in the CPI and the unemployment rate to Figs. 11.3 and 11.8 and discuss the result in terms of the pattern of cyclical behavior discussed in this chapter.

● Source Notes

[1] A. W. Phillips. The relation between unemployment and the rate of change of money wage rates in the United Kingdom, 1862–1957. *Economica*, 25 (1958), pp. 283–99.
[2] *Economic Report of the President*, February 1983, p. 37.
[3] Michael L. Wachter. Some problems in wage stabilization. *The American Economic Review*, Vol. 66, No. 2, May 1976, p. 65.

● Selected Additional Readings

Dornbusch, Rudiger, and Stanley Fischer. *Macroeconomics* (2d ed.) New York: McGraw-Hill, 1981. Chapters 9, 12, 13, and 15.

Fama, Eugene F. Inflation, output and money. *The Journal of Business*, Vol. 55, No. 2 (April 1982).

Friedman, Milton. The role of monetary policy. *American Economic Review* (March 1968).

Gordon, Robert J. *Macroeconomics*. (2d ed.) Boston: Little, Brown, 1981. Part III.

Hall, Robert E. Employment fluctuations and wage rigidity. *Brookings Papers on Economic Activity*, No. 1, 1980. Washington, D.C.: The Brookings Institution, 1980.

Levi, Maurice D., and John H. Makin. Inflation, uncertainty, and the Phillips Curve: Some empirical evidence. *American Economic Review*, Vol. 70, No. 5 (December 1980).

Phillips, A. W. The relation between unemployment and the rate of change of money wage rates in the United Kingdom, 1861–1957. *Economica* (November 1958).

Resley, David H. The formation of inflation expectations. *Review* of the Federal Reserve Bank of St. Louis, Vol. 62, No. 4 (April 1980).

Sachs, Jeffrey. The changing cyclical behavior of wages and prices, 1890–1976. *American Economic Review*, Vol. 70, No. 1 (March 1980).

Samuelson, Paul, and Robert Solow. Analytical aspects of anti-inflation policy. *American Economic Review* (May 1960).

Schultze, Charles L. Has the Phillips Curve shifted? Some additional evidence. *Brookings Papers on Economic Activity*, Vol. 2, 1971. Washington, D.C.: The Brookings Institution, 1971.

———. Some macro foundations for micro theory. *Brookings Papers on Economic Activity,* No. 2, 1981. Washington, D.C.: The Brookings Institution, 1981.

Summers, Lawrence H. Measuring unemployment. *Brookings Papers on Economic Activity*, No. 2, 1981. Washington, D.C.: The Brookings Institution, 1981.

Wallace, Myles S. A backward bending supply of labor schedule and the short run Phillips curve. *Southern Economic Journal*, Vol. 48, No. 2 (October 1981).

Fiscal Policy

12

Measures of Fiscal Policy

As noted earlier, fiscal policy is defined as that part of national economic policy made up of government expenditures and receipts, and the resulting surplus or deficit. The most commonly used measures of fiscal policy are the figures for the federal government's budget computed on a basis consistent with the GNP accounts we discussed earlier. The *national income accounts budget*, as it is called, is somewhat less comprehensive than the unified budget alternative, but the magnitude and direction of change in the surplus or deficit is very close for the two. (Also, the national income accounts budget is constructed on the basis of the calendar year whereas the unified budget is based on the government's fiscal year, October 1 through September 30.*)

The first thing we must do to obtain a meaningful measure of the level of government expenditures and revenues is, in effect, to detrend these numbers in the same way we would any time series that rises every year. We should not be surprised to find that both total expenditures and revenues of the federal government go up almost every year. Expenditures have gone up 31 out of the last 34 years (1947–1980). The three year-to-year declines in expenditures compare to six declines in revenues over the same time period. Revenues last declined in 1970 and expenditures have risen each year since 1955. Given that government expenditures and revenues generally grow with inflation and the growth of the economy, the question for the measurement of fiscal policy is their growth relative to the overall level of economic activity. Hence, it is common to detrend government expenditures and receipts by dividing them by current dollar GNP. The resulting values can be expressed as percentages of GNP. Expenditures and receipts as a percentage of GNP measure the level of the government's economic activity relative to the growth of the economy both in inflationary and real terms.

---

*Prior to 1977 the fiscal year ran from July 1 through June 30. A fiscal year is referred to by the name of the year in which it ends; i.e., fiscal year 1981 ended at midnight September 30, 1981.

Table 12.1 presents both the current dollar values and the ratio to GNP of federal government expenditures, receipts, and surplus or deficit for the years 1947–1983.

Recalling our previous discussions of fiscal policy, we noted in Chapter 3 that government expenditures inject income into the circular flow of income and expenditure without any corresponding production of consumer goods. Government expenditures have an inflationary impact in the same way as private investment expenditures. Conversely, we noted that the collection of taxes withdraws money from the circular flow of income. The members of the household sector of the economy work to earn income by producing goods, but must pay taxes with it instead of spending it for goods. Taxes have a deflationary impact similar to voluntary savings. Goods are produced, income is earned, but no demand for goods is exercised. Taxes are frequently referred to as involuntary savings.

In Chapter 5, when we looked at the underlying definitions and theory of monetary and fiscal policy we noted that "pure fiscal policy" would require a balanced budget. A surplus or deficit has monetary implications via a change in either or both the government debt and the monetary base. We also noted the impact of the balanced budget multiplier. The inflationary impact of a $1 increase in expenditures is usually assumed to be greater than the deflationary impact of $1 of taxes. Hence a balanced budget expansion of the government's economic activities is inflationary. In the terms we want to discuss the problem here, if the government's share of economic activity increases, even with a zero or constant deficit, there will be an inflationary impact. The government expenditures will stimulate aggregate demand more than the taxes will retard it, since part of the tax burden will be carried by reducing savings instead of reducing consumption.

Consider the long-term picture of fiscal policy presented in Table 12.1. In 1947 federal government expenditures and receipts were approximately 13% and 19% of GNP, respectively, resulting in a surplus of about 6% of GNP. In 1983 federal government expenditures were approximately 24% of GNP, and receipts were approximately 19%, resulting in a deficit equal to more than 5% of GNP. The size of the deficit fluctuated quite a bit over this 37-year period for various reasons that we will discuss later. However, the ratio of total expenditures to GNP showed a consistent, clear upward trend over this entire period. The average rate of increase varies depending on the time period one chooses to use in calculating it. There is no ten-year period one can choose, however, in which total expenditures as a percentage of GNP did not show a significant increase. Taking the numbers for each decade and the first four years of the 1980s from Table 12.1 we have Table 12.2.

From 1950 to 1960 the ratio of expenditures to GNP rose by over four percentage points, and by something over two percentage points in each of the next decades. Receipts also rose more rapidly than GNP and, hence,

TABLE 12.1 Fiscal Policy as Measured by the National Income Accounts Budget, 1947–1983

Year	Expenditures		Receipts		Surplus or Deficit(−)	
	Dollars in Billions	Percent of GNP	Dollars in Billions	Percent of GNP	Dollars in Billions	Percent of GNP
1947	$29.8	12.8%	$43.2	18.6%	$13.4	5.8%
1948	34.9	13.5	43.0	16.6	8.3	3.2
1949	41.3	16.0	38.7	15.0	− 2.6	− 1.0
1950	40.8	14.3	50.0	17.5%	9.2	3.2
1951	57.8	17.5	64.3	19.5	6.5	2.0
1952	71.1	20.5	67.3	19.4	− 3.7	− 1.1
1953	77.1	21.1	70.0	19.1	− 7.1	− 1.9
1954	69.8	20.0	63.7	17.4	− 6.0	− 1.6
1955	68.1	17.1	72.6	18.2	4.4	1.1
1956	71.9	17.1	78.0	18.5	6.1	1.4
1957	79.6	18.0	81.9	18.5	2.3	0.5
1958	88.9	19.8	78.7	17.5	− 10.3	− 2.3
1959	91.0	18.7	89.8	18.5	− 1.1	− 0.2
1960	93.1	18.4	96.1	19.0	3.0	0.6
1961	101.9	19.5	98.1	18.7	− 3.9	− 0.7
1962	110.4	19.6	106.2	18.8	− 4.2	− 0.7
1963	114.2	19.2	114.4	19.2	0.3	0.1
1964	118.2	18.6	114.9	18.1	− 3.3	− 0.5
1965	123.8	18.0	124.3	18.1	0.5	0.1
1966	143.6	20.9	141.8	20.6	− 1.8	− 0.3
1967	163.7	20.6	150.5	18.9	− 13.2	− 1.7
1968	180.5	20.7	174.4	20.0	− 6.0	− 0.7
1969	188.4	20.0	196.9	20.9	8.4	0.9
1970	204.3	20.6	191.9	19.3	− 12.4	− 1.2
1971	220.6	20.5	198.6	18.4	− 22.0	− 2.0
1972	244.3	20.6	227.5	19.2	− 16.8	− 1.4
1973	264.2	19.9	258.6	19.5	− 5.6	− 0.4
1974	299.3	20.9	287.8	20.1	− 11.5	− 0.8
1975	356.6	23.0	287.3	18.5	− 69.3	− 4.5
1976	384.8	22.4	331.8	19.3	− 53.1	− 3.1
1977	421.1	22.0	375.2	19.6	− 45.9	− 2.4
1978	461.0	21.3	431.6	19.9	− 29.5	− 1.4
1979	509.7	21.1	493.6	20.4	− 16.1	− 0.7
1980	602.1	22.9	540.9	20.6	− 61.2	− 2.3
1981	689.2	23.3	627.0	21.2	− 62.2	− 2.1
1982	764.4	24.9	617.4	20.1	− 147.1	− 4.8
1983	826.2	25.0	643.3	19.4	− 182.9	− 5.5

Source: *Economic Report of the President*, February 1984, Table B-1, page 220, and Table B-75, page 308.

TABLE 12.2   Percent of GNP

	Expenditures		Receipts		Surplus (+) or Deficit (−)	
1950	14.3%		17.5%		3.2%	
1960	18.4		19.0		0.6	
Change 1950–1960		+4.1		+1.5		−2.6
1970	20.6		19.3		−1.2	
Change 1960–1970		+2.2		+0.3		−1.8
1980	22.9		20.5		−2.4	
Change 1970–1980		+2.3		+1.2		−1.2
1983	25.0		19.4		−5.5	
Change 1980–1983		+2.1		−1.1		−3.1

the receipts ratio also rose. However, the rate of increase in receipts was not as rapid as expenditures, only 1.5%, 0.3%, and 1.2% for the three decades. The federal government's deficit as a percent of GNP had its greatest increase from 1950 to 1960, and from 1980 to 1983. In these last three years the jump in expenditures as a percent of GNP has been dramatic. Receipts, however, have shown the first decline as a percent of GNP since the recession of 1975. The deficit has risen accordingly. The move of −2.6% in the 1950s as the budget went from a large to a small surplus position is misleading and we will consider the size of the deficit in a moment. The significant point here is that the portion of economic activity directly influenced by the federal government has shown a steady rise during the last three decades. For purposes of business cycle analysis this has had two effects. First is the inflationary pressure that results, all other things being equal, from even a balanced budget increase in the size of the government sector. Second is the stabilizing effect of expenditures that are immune to the usual forces causing cyclical movements. Federal government expenditures are politically, not economically, determined. They are presumably immune to such things as increasing profit margins, euphoric business optimism, and the other factors that propel a boom upward. Similarly, as we have noted, they are not frequently cut back. As a cyclical decline sets in, government expenditures can go merrily on their way since they are not dependent on expected rates of return or anyone's level of income, present or prospective. Indeed, with the right to run deficits, government expenditures are not even dependent on the level of the government's income. Recall J. R. Hicks's theory of the trade cycle discussed in Chapter 6. Certain "autonomous expenditures," including those of the government, determined the floor below which the level of economic activity will not fall. The multiplier times the level of autonomous expenditures gives the minimum equilibrium level of aggregate demand. With 25% of GNP from the federal government, a 50% fall in total expenditures would appear next to impossible. In summary, it is generally accepted that the substantially increased role of the federal government in the national economy has, as a long-term trend over the last thirty years, contributed to increasing inflationary pressures and substantially reduced cyclical vulnerability.

Let us return now to consideration of the size of the surplus or deficit. We indicated above that just considering that the budget moved further towards deficit from 1950 to 1960 than it did from 1960 to 1970 and from 1970 to 1980 was misleading. Although the shift in the surplus position as a percentage of GNP was -2.6% from 1950 to 1960 and only -1.8% and -1.2% for the next two decades, the accumulated deficits were much larger in the last two decades. The largest accumulation of deficits occurred from 1970 through 1983. Figure 12.1 is a graphic presentation of the ratios of expenditures and receipts to GNP given in Table 12.1. The shaded areas indicate the magnitude and duration of government deficits as a percentage of GNP. Accumulating the expenditures, receipts, deficits, and GNP by decade gives us the totals and ratios shown in Table 12.3. By accumulating the deficits we get a better measure of the impact of fiscal policy on the economy. In the 1950s the budget was effectively balanced, although its increased size relative to GNP undoubtedly had an inflationary impact. For the years 1960 through 1969 the total deficits of $20.2 billion were equal to only 0.3% of total GNP. The truly massive deficits occurred in the 1970s and 1980s. The $280.9 billion excess of expenditures over receipts for the last decade was equal to 1.8% of total GNP over the period, and we have started the 1980s with deficits of more than twice that percentage of GNP.

In discussing fiscal policy thus far, we have implied a deliberate policy determining expenditures and receipts. Of course, we have mentioned previously that both receipts and expenditures are sensitive to the level of economic activity. We have another example of two-way causation. Government spending and taxing influence the level of economic activity, and the level of economic activity influences the flow of taxes to the government and its level of expenditures. Fortunately the variation in government expenditures and taxes resulting from cyclical fluctuations in the economy are stabilizing. As the economy booms, corporate profits and other taxable income rise disproportionately and government tax receipts rise faster than GNP. At the same time, many of the federal government's expenditures slow their rate of growth. The cyclically sensitive expenditures are mostly in the category of transfer payments. Agricultural subsidies fall as farm prices rise. The decline in unemployment in a boom reduces the amount of federal support necessary for state unemployment compensation programs. The number of people choosing to begin receiving retirement benefits under social security actually falls in a strong labor market. Conversely, in a recession tax revenues decline precipitously and those expenditure categories just mentioned rise. As a result, the federal government's budget moves

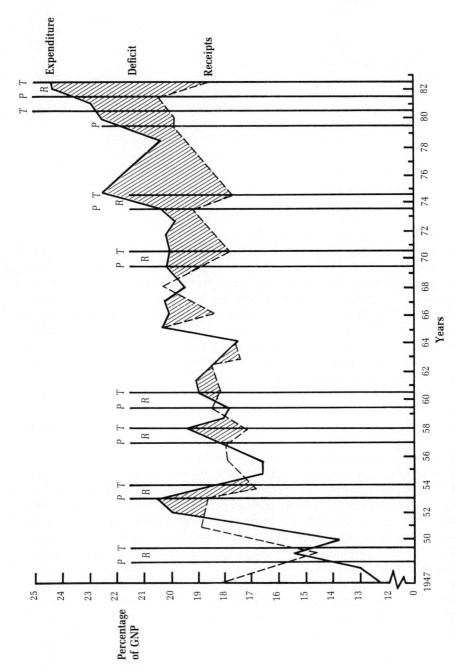

FIGURE 12.1 Federal Government Expenditures and Receipts as a Percentage of GNP.

TABLE 12.3   Fiscal Policy and GNP, 1950–1983

	Expenditures	Receipts	Surplus or Deficits (−)	GNP
1950–1959	$716.1	$716.3	$0.2	$3,894.2
% of GNP	18.4%	18.4%	0.0%	
1960–1969	$1,337.8	$1,317.6	− $20.2	$5,942.8
% of GNP	22.5%	22.2%	− 0.3%	
1970–1979	$3,365.9	$3,083.9	− $282.0	$15,784.0
% of GNP	21.3%	19.5%	− 1.8%	
1980–1983	$2,881.9	$2,428.6	− $453.3	$11,968.3
% of GNP	24.1%	20.3%	− 3.8%	

automatically toward a surplus in boom times and toward a deficit in recessions.

The magnitude of this countercyclical tendency of the federal government's surplus or deficit is evidenced by the fact that a simple correlation between the year-to-year change in the unemployment rate and the surplus or deficit as a percentage of GNP gives a correlation coefficient of − .52. This would indicate superficially that 27% of the variation in the deficit could be "explained" by changes in the average annual unemployment rate. We must say that this conclusion is superficial because, of course, the actual budget is a combination of deliberate fiscal policy moves and cyclically induced variation. However, the increases and decreases in the size of the deficit do seem to be dominated by the business cycle. Observing the expansion and contraction of the shaded areas representing deficits in Fig. 12.1, we can almost track the business cycle history for this period by changes in the size of the deficit. Across the top of Fig. 12.1 are indicators of the points in time at which a peak (P) or trough (T) occurred in the reference business cycle as determined by the NBER. The economy was in recession, R, from (P) to (T) as indicated. The recessions of 1948–1949, 1953–1954, 1957–1958, and 1960–1961 each have their corresponding deficit, either coincident with or slightly lagging the recession. During the economic slowdown in 1967 (sometimes referred to as a mini-recession), real output stopped growing for the first quarter of the year. The NBER did not classify this as a recession but its impact on the deficit is clear. For the year 1967 real GNP grew by only 2.7% compared to 6.6% in 1966 and 4.6% in 1968. The relative drop in receipts from 20.6% of GNP to 18.9% is clearly observable on the graph as being responsible for the $13 billion deficit in 1967. The recessions of 1970–1971 and 1974–1975 along with their resulting deficits are also clearly evident on the graph.

The mild recession of 1980 is only evidenced by a slowdown in the rate of growth in government revenues. The more severe downturn of 1982 shows a substantial drop in government receipts as a percentage of GNP, although some of that drop was the result of deliberate fiscal policy in the form of substantial tax reductions.

The movement of the federal government's budget in a countercyclical fashion makes it the most potent of a number of *automatic stabilizers* in the economy. Although there are other automatic stabilizers that we will discuss later, the budget is probably the most important. The stabilizing function of the federal government's budget is so potent that economists often speak of "automatic fiscal policy" as opposed to "discretionary fiscal policy." Some economists even question, for reasons we will discuss at the end of this chapter, whether there should be any discretionary fiscal policy, such as a deliberate tax cut, to fight a recession or a tax increase to slow an inflationary boom.

A major problem in evaluating fiscal policy is agreeing on some measure of whether current policies are stimulative or restrictive. Given the cyclical variations described above, any policymaker can claim to be following stabilizing policies. The deficit will grow as we go into a recession and constrict as we move toward prosperity. In an attempt to measure discretionary fiscal policy independently of cyclically induced changes in receipts, expenditures, and deficits there is what is referred to as the *high employment budget*. The high employment budget was originally called the full employment budget but no one was comfortable referring to any particular level of the unemployment rate as "full" employment, hence the high employment budget. The high employment budget is the national income accounts budget adjusted for the current level of the unemployment rate. The unemployment rate is used in this context as the reference cycle. It is used to attempt to remove changes in federal government expenditures and receipts brought about by cyclical fluctuations. Specifically, a particular level of the unemployment rate, say 5%, is chosen as "high employment" and the attempt is made statistically to estimate what the federal government's expenditures and receipts would have been under current tax laws and expenditure programs if, in fact, the unemployment rate were 5%. If the unemployment rate is actually 7% the expenditures will be adjusted downward, receipts will be adjusted upward, and the high employment budget deficit will be substantially smaller than the actual budget deficit. On the other hand, on those rare occasions when the actual unemployment rate is lower than the rate chosen as the high employment rate, the adjusted deficit will be larger than the actual deficit.

One procedure for constructing the high employment budget is to run a series of simple regressions with a component of the national income accounts budget as the dependent variable and the unemployment rate as the independent variable in each case. For example, a regression equation would give an estimate of the magnitude of the decline in corporate tax revenues associated with a 1% rise in the unemployment rate. Then to generate the high employment budget, if the current unemployment rate is 6%, we would raise the corporate tax revenues component of receipts by the amount necessary to give us an estimate of what these revenues would have been at an unemployment rate of 5%.

The high employment budget concept has many problems, not the least of which is the choice of what unemployment rate to use as "high" employment. The rate is supposed to be the rate consistent with the economy producing at *potential GNP*. Potential GNP is a measure of the real, price deflated, GNP that the economy could produce at "high" employment. The difference between potential GNP and actual real GNP is referred to as the *GNP gap*. If this appears to be a lot of technical language covering a substantial amount of confusion, you are not deceived by appearance. One has a "which comes first, the chicken or the egg" problem here. Do you estimate potential GNP first and then derive the corresponding unemployment rate? Or do you pick an appropriately low unemployment rate and derive the level of real GNP that seems to go with it? Most analysts seem to do the latter.

Another major problem with the high employment budget is statistical in nature. In the estimating process we are assuming the unemployment rate to be the independent variable and, say, corporate taxes to be the dependent variable. However, the purpose of developing this measure of fiscal policy is to get a measure of the impact of the budget on the economy; that is, we know that changes in corporate taxes influence the level of the unemployment rate. Indeed, we want to use fiscal policy to pursue our goal of noninflationary full employment. This confusion of dependent and independent variables creates a whole host of statistical problems. In nontechnical terms, it is difficult to say precisely what it is one is trying to adjust for. Suppose the policymakers are so wise that they cut taxes and increase expenditures in each recession, while also raising taxes and cutting expenditures as inflation breaks out at the height of the boom. We will then observe movements toward a deficit in a recession and toward a surplus in a boom. Do we want to adjust for this in obtaining a measure of fiscal policy? No, we would like to leave in the deliberate policy actions and take out only the automatic responses—a difficult, if not impossible, task.

These problems notwithstanding, various analysts of the business scene continue to generate estimates of high employment expenditures, receipts, and deficits. One's time would probably be as well spent examining the actual budget figures in the context of the cyclical state of the economy, in conjunction with specific policy actions such as changes in the tax laws and Congressional appropriations. At the time of this writing the only up-to-date estimates of a high employment budget are those prepared by the staff of the Council of Economic Advisors and contained in the January 1981, *Economic Report of the President*. Table 12.4 gives both the actual

TABLE 12.4 The Actual and High Employment Budgets Compared (in Billions)

Year	Expenditures			Receipts			Surplus or Deficit			Percent Un.
	Actual	H.E.	Adj.	Actual	H.E.	Adj.	Actual	H.E.	Adj.	
1973	$264.2	$264.0	−$0.2	$258.6	$252.7	−$5.9	−$5.6	−$11.3	−$5.7	4.9%
1974	299.3	297.6	−1.7	287.8	296.9	+9.1	−11.5	−0.7	+10.8	5.6
1975	356.6	344.5	−12.1	287.3	315.8	+28.5	−69.3	−29.1	+40.2	8.5
1976	384.8	374.8	−10.0	331.8	354.7	+22.9	−53.1	−20.1	+33.0	7.8
1977	421.5	413.8	−7.7	375.1	390.7	+15.6	−46.4	−23.1	+23.3	7.0
1978	460.7	456.8	−3.9	431.5	441.1	+9.6	−29.2	−15.7	+13.5	6.0
1979	509.2	506.5	−2.7	494.4	504.2	+9.8	−14.8	−2.2	+12.6	5.8
1980	601.2	591.6	−9.6	538.9	573.2	+34.3	−62.3	−18.3	+44.0	7.2

Source: *Economic Report of the President*, January 1981, Table 23, page 157.

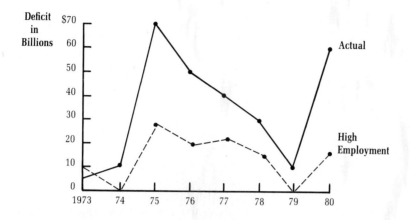

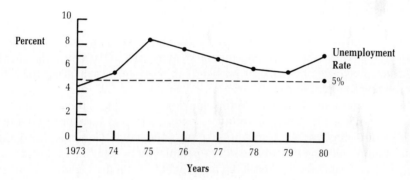

FIGURE 12.2   Budget Deficits and the Unemployment Rate.

national income accounts budget figures and the estimates of a high employment budget. The average annual unemployment rate is also given in
the last column on the right.

Note in Table 12.4 that the deficit is lowered as the adjustments are
made to obtain the high employment budget for each year except 1973.
Note also that the average annual unemployment rate is in excess of 5%
for each year except 1973. The adjusted figures are an estimate of what
expenditures, receipts, and the deficit would have been if the economy had
been operating at a 5% unemployment level and producing at a level equal
to "potential GNP."*

Figure 12.2 shows the actual budget deficits, high employment budget
deficits, and the average annual unemployment rate. From the graph it is

_____

*The exact "benchmark unemployment rates" used were 4.9% in 1973, 5.0% in 1974, and
5.1% thereafter. See: *Economic Report of the President*, January 1980, p. 90.

obvious that the actual deficit rises and falls with the level of unemployment. (The simple correlation between the two is .96.) Although the high employment budget does differ from the actual by an amount that varies with the unemployment rate, it still appears to have a considerable amount of induced variation. The high employment budget deficit seems to vary a great deal in sympathy with the unemployment rate. (The simple correlation coefficient between the two is .81.) If one takes the high employment budget deficit to be the measure of discretionary fiscal policy, our policymakers made a substantial contribution to economic stability over this time period. With the exceptions of 1974 and 1977, every change in the unemployment rate was met with a change in the deficit in the same direction. For five out of the seven year-to-year changes, when unemployment rose the deficit also rose to stimulate the economy; when the unemployment rate fell, the deficit moved toward a surplus to restrain the economy.

One suspects that rather than the policymakers acting in such a stabilizing fashion, it is possible that the decline in the deficit from 1975 through 1979 was *caused* by the increasing rate of economic activity over this period, as evidenced by the declining unemployment rate. One can only suspect and not prove this because of problems in accurately measuring the effect of the level of economic activity on government expenditures and receipts. This problem can be dramatized by looking at the association between the unemployment rate and expenditures and receipts as measured by simple correlation coefficients over the last three decades. Consider the simple correlation coefficients between the unemployment rate, expenditures, and receipts in Table 12.5. These figures should certainly administer a large dose of humility to anyone attempting to isolate the magnitude and direction of causation between the unemployment rate and the government's expenditures and receipts.

Increases in expenditures were clearly associated with *decreases* in the rate of unemployment (and vice versa) in the 1950s and the 1960s. The rise and fall of expenditures in conjunction with the Korean and Vietnam Wars resulted in the flow of causation to be primarily from the government

TABLE 12.5 Correlation of the Unemployment Rate with Government Expenditures and Receipts

Year	Expenditures as a Percent of GNP	Receipts as a Percent of GNP
1950–1959	−0.36%	−0.87%
1960–1969	−0.55	−0.60
1970–1979	+0.96	−0.37

expenditures to the unemployment rate. The level of unemployment rising and falling inversely with government expenditures illustrates the impact of the expenditures on the level of unemployment and gives a negative correlation coefficient. For the decade of the 1970s there is a high positive correlation, .96, between the ratio of government expenditures to GNP and the unemployment rate. There were no wars and there were two recessions, 1970–1971 and 1974–1975. Increases in unemployment were associated with increases in expenditures and vice versa. Apparently the policymakers acted in a very stabilizing fashion or the flow of causation was primarily from the level of economic activity to government expenditures. (The 1950s had two recessions also, but as we will see later, the 1953–1954 recession was clearly the result of an abrupt end to the Korean War expenditures.)

Let us now turn to the apparent relationship between the government's receipts, primarily taxes, and the unemployment rate. Here we at least get a consistent minus sign. Apparently the direction of causation flows primarily from the level of economic activity to revenues, not vice versa. Increases in unemployment are associated with decreases in receipts; decreases in unemployment with increases in receipts. Clearly in the absence of changes in tax laws, there will be a strong contemporaneous association between the unemployment rate and government revenues. The evidence here (and in later chapters) indicates that in this country we have not had an active discretionary countercyclical fiscal policy.

The student should recognize that our computation of ratios of expenditures and receipts to GNP and their correlations with the unemployment rate are not even the beginnings of a model that would measure the structural relationships among these variables. To do that we would, for example, need to consider many possible leads and lags, since the effects of the government expenditures multiplier take time to do their work on the unemployment rate. Our purpose here has been merely to illustrate that the state of fiscal policy at a particular point in time cannot be embodied in a single number. All empirical estimates of the high employment surplus and similar concepts must be taken with at least a grain of salt, if not a whole truckload. Fiscal policy must be evaluated by looking at the actual expenditures and receipts in the context of action by both the Congress and the executive branch of government. No single number is a very good answer to the question of whether fiscal policy is expansive or restrictive.

The Making of Fiscal Policy

Fiscal policy is not the product of a single mind seeking steadily after noninflationary full employment. Fiscal policy, like all other policies of the federal government, is the result of political compromise, historical accident, and very occasional doses of economic logic. To an individual member of

Congress the question of taxes and expenditures in his or her particular geographical area is likely to be more important than the size of total federal government expenditures or revenues and the resulting surplus or deficit. We cannot even say that this viewpoint is erroneous. Any segment of the population *will* be better off if it receives an economic windfall from the federal government, even if it is financed with printing press money. For example, it is questionable whether anyone in the economy would be better off if the government gave *everyone* a $50,000 bonus (regardless of whether it was paid for by taxes, debt, or an expansion of the monetary base). However, there is no question that a $50,000 bonus paid only to college professors would leave that group better off, even if they had to pay their share of a tax increase to support this stimulus to higher education.

Historically what has happened is a great deal of "log rolling" in the area of fiscal policy. One political pressure group seeking tax relief will trade support with another group seeking a particular expenditure program. Each will lobby for the other's program. Even with the inflation that might result from the deficit, one cannot say that, at least in the short run, both groups are not better off. Undoubtedly this sort of political dynamics has been partly responsible for the increased size of the federal government's deficit during the last twenty years.

In an effort to slow, if not reverse, this mutual milking of the public treasury, Congress completely overhauled its budgeting process with the Congressional Budget and Impoundment Control Act of 1974 (Public Law 93-344). The principal change was the requirement that both houses of Congress must vote on a spending ceiling *first,* and then decide on the individual programs. Previously, the total expenditures were simply the sum of all the expenditure programs voted by Congress. The hope was that by establishing the total level of expenditures first, the political dynamics would be reversed. Instead of my agreeing that I will support your spending program if you will support mine, now I seek to have your program defeated so that mine can get in under the limit on total expenditures. The same procedure is mandated for tax policy: first the total, then the details of changes.

The timetable Congress set for itself is to begin work on the next fiscal year's budget as soon as one fiscal year begins. As we mentioned before, the fiscal year begins October 1st. In fact, since elections are held in November and there are many holidays in December, nothing really gets underway until January. Early in the calendar year various committees of both houses of Congress begin hearings to determine totals for various components of the budget to be recommended to the budget committees of both the House and Senate. At this point the recommendations are in the form of so many dollars of expenditures for broad areas such as national defense, agriculture, veterans benefits, and so on. The Senate Finance

Committee and the House Ways and Means Committee make similar recommendations on taxes.

The budget committees of both houses are then supposed to take an overall view of fiscal policy and report to their respective houses by May 15th. A "First Budget Resolution" is supposed to be passed by that date. (It frequently is not.) Of course, if the House and Senate pass resolutions with different totals, they must get together and work out the inconsistencies via a conference committee.

The really detailed line by line, item by item, budget decisions are worked out in the summer and fall. The Senate Finance Committee and House Ways and Means Committee must agree on tax legislation and the two appropriations committees must agree on expenditures. Both the tax revenues and expenditures are supposed to be within the totals agreed to in the first budget resolution passed earlier. However, the totals may be changed by a majority vote of both Houses, and frequently are.

By September 25th the Second Budget Resolution is supposed to be passed, reconciled between the two Houses, and sent to the president with the accompanying tax and appropriations bills. If the president vetoes any of the bills they must, of course, be sent back for amendment or a possible override of the veto. Hopefully the president signs the bills in September, so that the budget can go into effect for the fiscal year beginning October 1st. At that point the whole process begins again.

The office of the president is, of course, involved in the process throughout, not just when the tax and spending bills arrive at the president's desk to be signed or vetoed. As a matter of fact, historically most of the initiatives as well as the ongoing details of the budget have come from the executive branch, specifically from what is now the Office of Management and Budget. The president has a budget director with primary responsibility for submitting the administration's program to the appropriate House and Senate committees. Until 1974, the president's office with what was known as the "Budget Bureau" had almost all the initiative and practically all the expertise. The Budget Bureau prepared all the estimates of expected tax revenues, expected costs of new expenditure programs, and so on. It was difficult for Congress to argue effectively or participate competently in the budgeting process. In passing the Budget Act in 1974 Congress established the Congressional Budget Office, or CBO. The CBO, with a staff of 200, employs economists, statisticians, and other analysts competent to respond to requests from Congress for analysis of various proposals.

Another area where the CBO has helped to put Congress on a more nearly equal footing with the executive branch is the area of economic forecasting. As you know from the first part of this chapter, expected tax revenues and expenditures for the coming fiscal year will depend on the cyclical behavior of the economy. Recessions mean falling revenues and rising expenditures while booms mean just the opposite. The president has had the Council of Economic Advisors since 1946. The council issues what is, in effect, the official economic forecast each year in the *Economic Report of the President* published in January. The Congressional Budget Office now can, and does, update and disagree with the economic forecast of the president's Council of Economic Advisors.

So how is fiscal policy made? Tortuously and endlessly. The process really begins with the president's program drawn up by the Office of Management and Budget and presented to the congressional committees by the budget director. The Office of Management and Budget has continual input as the bills go through Congress with members of the Council of Economic Advisors called on frequently to testify before the committees as to the present and prospective state of the economy. There is, as you would expect from the first part of this chapter, a continuing debate on the effect of the economy on the budget, and the effect of each budgetary item on the economy. The Congressional Budget Office joins in by request and occasionally on its own initiative. One cannot say precisely how the budget is made, one can only say that the budget is that collection of tax and spending legislation that Congress can agree on and the president will sign.

The budget is, however, not the sum total of fiscal policy. The executive branch still has some discretion as to the rate of expenditures. Prior to 1974 presidents would, on occasion, simply not spend money that had been appropriated, a process known as "impoundment." But in the Budget Act of 1974 Congress also included legislation prohibiting this practice. However, there are still innumerable regulatory and administrative decisions to be made by the executive branch that can speed up or slow down both expenditures and revenues.

An important fact regarding fiscal policy is that the vast majority of government expenditures are undertaken for purposes other than that of economic stabilization. The impact of government expenditures on the general level of economic activity is usually a side effect, and frequently an unwelcome side effect at that. Also, although we might say that the government collects taxes primarily for purposes of economic stabilization, most economies use the tax system for a multiplicity of goals. It is true that the reason we have taxes is because printing all the money for government expenditures would create intolerable inflation. But, in addition, we use the tax system in this country to promote home ownership, redistribute income from the rich to the poor, insure people against natural disasters, help with unusually high medical expenditures, encourage education expenditures, promote private philanthropy, and on and on and on. So although defining fiscal policy as government expenditures and revenues is clear enough, and obtaining fairly reliable figures after the fact is possible, the essentially political process by which fiscal policy is made is impossible to describe rigorously and is probably somewhat different each time it happens.

● Questions for Discussion

1. Why do we include all federal government expenditures in our measure of fiscal policy and not just the purchase of goods and services used in the calculation of GNP?
2. Do you think fiscal policy has generally been a stabilizing or destabilizing force in the economy over the last thirty years?
3. Why do you think the unemployment rate is probably the best single predictor of the federal government's surplus or deficit?
4. Who is responsible for the budget, Congress or the president?
5. What changes would you propose to improve fiscal policy?

● Selected Additional Readings

Blinder, Alan S., and Robert M. Solow. Lags and uncertainties in fiscal policy: General considerations, and the 1968–1970 experience. *The Economics of Public Finance*. Washington, D.C.: The Brookings Institution, 1974.

————. Measuring fiscal influence. *The Economics of Public Finance*. Washington, D.C.: The Brookings Institution, 1974.

Carlson, Keith M. Estimates of the high-employment budget: 1947–1967. *Review of the Federal Reserve Bank of St. Louis*, June 1967. Reprint series number 23.

Dornbusch, Rudiger, and Stanley Fischer. *Macroeconomics*. (2d ed.) New York: McGraw-Hill, 1981. Chapter 14.

Gordon, Robert J. *Macroeconomics*. (2d ed.) Boston: Little, Brown, 1981. Chapter 17.

Humpage, Owen F. The high employment budget: Recent changes and persistent shortcomings. *Economic Review* of the Federal Reserve Bank of Cleveland, Spring 1981.

Peckman, Joseph A. Fiscal policies in a troubled economy. *Eastern Economic Journal*, Vol. 6, No. 3–4, August–October 1980.

President's Council of Economic Advisors. Measuring and realizing the economy's potential. In Ronald L. Teigen, ed. *Readings in Money, National Income and Stabilization Policy*. Homewood, Ill.: Richard D. Irwin, 1978.

Scheck, Allen. *Five Years of Congressional Budgeting*. Washington, D.C.: American Enterprise Institute, 1979.

Waterfield, Meynard H. *The Congressional Budget Process at the Crossroads*. Washington, D.C.: The Tax Foundation, 1981.

Tools of Monetary Policy

13

In Chapter 3 we related monetary to fiscal policy with the equation

$$G - T = \Delta D + \Delta MB,$$

where

G = government expenditures,
T = government receipts,
ΔD = change in the government's publicly held debt,
ΔMB = the change in the monetary base.

We defined fiscal policy as the left-hand side of the equation, $G - T$, the size of the government's deficit. We defined monetary policy as the right-hand side of the equation, $\Delta D + \Delta MB$ — how much of the deficit is financed by borrowing and how much by expanding the monetary base. In Chapter 5 we expanded our consideration of these relationships and noted that a pure monetary policy could only be the expansion or contraction of the monetary base by the purchase or sale of government securities by the government itself. With some minor exceptions, any other change in the monetary base or publicly held government debt would involve a fiscal policy surplus or deficit.

The United States has a fairly wide separation of powers between fiscal and monetary policy. Fiscal policy results from the convoluted process we described in the previous chapter and generates a particular surplus or deficit (a deficit during most of the last 30 years). The institutional arrangements in the United States are that the Treasury will issue additional government securities equal to the full amount of the deficit. If the central bank, the Federal Reserve System, chooses not to purchase any of these securities, the full amount of the deficit will be financed by the government borrowing from the public. If the Federal Reserve buys $1 billion of Treasury securities, the monetary base will be expanded by $1 billion and that much of the government deficit will have been financed by "printing press" money.

There are actually three major tools of monetary policy. The most important is *open market operations,* which is the purchase and sale of government securities for purposes of expanding or contracting the monetary base we have been discussing. The government also expands the monetary base by direct loans to the banks. Such loans by regional Federal Reserve Banks are said to be made through the *discount window* and the interest rate charged is called the *discount rate*. The third major tool of monetary policy is the setting of *reserve requirements*. From our study of the monetary mechanism in Chapter 4 it should be obvious that the ability of the banking system to monetize private debt depends on the required reserve ratio. The setting of reserve requirements determines the maximum potential bank lending and deposit creation that can be supported by a given level of bank reserves. If financial institutions must keep an amount equal to 20% of deposits in the form of vault cash and reserve deposits with the Federal Reserve Banks, there will potentially be a much lower level of deposits than if the reserve requirement is only 10%.

Let us take a closer look at each of these major tools of monetary policy.

Open Market Operations

The purchase and sale of government securities by the Federal Reserve System is the primary tool of monetary policy. In order to understand it we need to take a close look at the Federal Reserve System, hereafter referred to as the *Fed*. The Fed consists of twelve regional Federal Reserve Banks and the Board of Governors headquartered in Washington, D.C. (We must note at the outset that most of the power is concentrated in this Board of Governors.) Although each regional Federal Reserve Bank has a local Board of Directors, most actions of any substance must be approved by the Board in Washington. In addition, the Board must approve the appointment of the top two officers of each Federal Reserve Bank (the president and the executive vice-president). Also, the Board has the right to fire those top two officers. The Board has seven members, each of whom is appointed for a fourteen-year term by the president who happens to be in office when a vacancy occurs. The president also gets to appoint one member of the Board as chairman for a four-year term, but the term is not coterminous with that of the president. The president makes these appointments with the advice and consent of the Senate and may not fire the chairman or any of these board members even if he or she appointed them. Most recent presidents have eventually appointed their own chairman, but it has frequently been well into the president's term in office.

Returning to open market operations, the actual purchase and sale of securities for the Fed is done through the regional Federal Reserve Bank in New York City. Technically, the sales or purchase may be for the account of any of the twelve regional banks, each of which keeps a rather pointless set of books that we will consider later. There is a vice-president in charge of open market operations at the New York Federal Reserve Bank who takes instructions from a directive from the *Federal Open Market Committee,* the FOMC. The FOMC consists of twelve voting members. Seven of the twelve votes (a majority) belong to the members of the Board of Governors. The other five belong to presidents of regional Federal Reserve Banks, one to the president of the New York Bank, and the other four rotate among the eleven remaining regions. The meetings are held at the Board of Governors headquarters in Washington every two or three weeks.

All the presidents of the regional Federal Reserve Banks attend the meetings whether they are voting members or not. The procedure is for each bank president and each member of the Board of Governors to state their views of the economy and some generalities of what they feel appropriate monetary policy should be. The Chairman sums up the wording of a directive to the vice-president in charge of open market operations. This is proposed and a vote is taken. We will consider the substance of the directives and some of the controversy surrounding open market operations in more detail later.

Mechanically, open market operations expand or contract the monetary base by increasing or decreasing the public's holding of U.S. government securities. The purchase of securities ($- \Delta D$ in an equation) results in a rise in the monetary base ($+ \Delta MB$). Recall that the monetary base is defined as bank reserves plus currency in the hands of the public. The New York Federal Reserve pays for securities it buys by writing a check drawn on itself. The recipient of the check has only two choices, cashing the check in exchange for currency or depositing it in the banking system. In either case the check enters the banking system and eventually some bank presents it to the Fed for payment. The Fed pays the check by adding that amount to the reserve account of the bank presenting it for payment. This will increase total bank reserves if no currency is drawn out of the banking system. Bank reserves are, by definition, vault cash plus reserve deposits with the Fed. If the public chose to take payment in the form of currency, bank reserves would not be increased. The increase in reserve deposits with the Fed would be offset by a decrease in the holdings of currency in the banks' vaults, vault cash. Whatever happens, a purchase of U.S. government securities by the government itself, in this case the Federal Reserve System, must result in an increase in the monetary base. The proceeds from the sale must remain in the system in the form of currency in circulation or bank reserves.

In the case of open market operations designed to restrict the availability of bank credit, exactly the reverse sequence of events takes place. The New York Federal Reserve sells government securities to the public ($+ \Delta D$), and thereby reduces the monetary base ($- \Delta MB$). Payment to the Federal Reserve is made in the form of a check drawn on a commercial bank. That bank's reserve account at the Fed is debited by the amount of the purchase. That bank loses reserves, no other bank gains them, so there is a net loss in total bank reserves, and thereby in the monetary base. (You *could* pay the Fed in currency, and thereby shrink the currency in circulation part of the monetary base, but that would be highly unusual — and the Internal Revenue Service would probably suspect you of illegal and untaxed sources of income.)

The Discount Window and Rate

The second most important tool of monetary policy is the discount window. Each regional Federal Reserve Bank can make reserves available to banks in its region by lending reserves directly to them. The source of these loans is called the discount window because the loans must be secured with some asset, such as a government security or a commercial loan held by the borrowing institution. The borrowing bank actually physically turns the paper representing this asset, a government security or a note signed by some business, over to the regional Federal Reserve Bank as collateral for the loan. The term was originally "rediscount window" in that loans were originally made only to member banks and were collateralized by notes from farmers and businesspeople. The note had already been "discounted" by the bank at the original borrowing (borrow $95 and pay back $100), and would have to be "rediscounted" by the member bank to the Federal Reserve Bank. In fact, in recent history, direct loans through the discount window have only been made to member banks, although under legislation passed in 1980 all institutions offering checking accounts, and thereby being subject to reserve requirements, have the same rights at the discount window as member banks. Of course, as we will see, no one is too sure what rights, if any, the member banks have at the discount window.

To understand the current state of affairs with respect to the discount window we must briefly review a bit of history. The Federal Reserve came into being early this century as a result of a *money panic* in 1907. A panic occurs when everybody wants cash and no one wants to hold securities. Everyone tries to sell securities at the same time, bond prices move toward zero, and interest rates move toward infinity. Panics periodically occurred in the 1800s in the United States, usually in the fall when farmers borrowed money for planting next year's crop.

After the panic of 1907, Congress held extended hearings on the cause and the numerous suggested cures. The cure decided on was to have an "elastic" money supply. The idea of an elastic money supply was that the reserve base should expand automatically with the "needs of trade." If farmers and merchants needed more credit, they would borrow from their local commercial bank, the commercial bank would take their notes to the regional Federal Reserve Bank and "rediscount" them in exchange for additional bank reserves, thereby expanding the monetary base in accordance with the needs of trade. The bookkeeping for a $100,000 advance at the discount window would be as shown in Table 13.1. As you can see, an addition to the monetary base has been created out of thin air. This is just as much "printing press money" as is the monetization of Treasury deficits.

The Federal Reserve Act was passed in 1912 and the system began operation in 1913. The automatic part of the elastic money supply system did not turn out to be all that automatic. The availability of reserves had to involve some discretionary monetary policy, in that a choice had to be made with respect to the interest rate to be charged on loans of reserves through the discount window. It was quickly discovered that a discount rate of 2% when the rate on bank loans to their customers was 10% would cause an expansion of the monetary base in excess of the "needs of trade." On the other hand, if the discount rate were 6% when the commercial loan rate was 5%, there would be no expansion of the monetary base via the discount rate regardless of the needs of trade. Recall here our discussion of Wicksell's "natural" and "bank" rates of interest in Chapter 6.

The Federal Reserve Act required all banks chartered by the federal government to be members of the Federal Reserve System and allowed state chartered banks to be members if they chose. Being a member had the advantages of a direct tie-in to the Fed's national check-clearing mechanism and some preference at the discount window, but it meant keeping the required reserves on deposit with the Fed and being subject to numerous other regulatory requirements. Historically, member banks held 80% to 90% of total deposits in the nation. The decline to less than 70% by 1980 was undoubtedly a factor in the passage of legislation that substantially reduces the distinction between members and nonmembers.

The discount rate was the primary tool of monetary policy from 1913 through the late 1920s. When the policy was to restrain the economy the rate was raised; when monetary policy was supposed to be stimulative the rate was lowered. For reasons we will explore in the next chapter, the discount window was little used in the 1930s and the 1940s. In 1955 the

TABLE 13.1 Balance Sheets Showing Discount and Window Loans

Commercial Bank		Federal Reserve Bank	
Assets	Liabilities	Assets	Liabilities
+ $100,000 to Reserves	+ $100,000 to Borrowings from the Federal Reserve	+ $100,000 Loan to Member Bank	+ $100,000 Member Bank Reserves

Federal Reserve revised Regulation "A," which covers discount window operations, to state that such borrowings were a "privilege" and not a "right." Since that time the Fed has made the rather inane contention that borrowings are supposed to be for "need," not "profit." In practice the Federal Reserve has insisted on some sort of sad story from supplicants at the discount window before borrowing is approved. The Fed's idea of "need" seems to be some unexpected large withdrawal or other unpredictable occurrence.

During the last 25 years the Fed has controlled both the quantity and the rate. Since borrowing has not been a right, the discount rate could be, and frequently has been, below the rate for alternative sources of funds for any individual bank. (Why else would they borrow?) Discount window loans are, in effect, a subsidy to the borrowing bank. In fact, in the 1970s the Federal Reserve used this subsidy deliberately as an inducement to keep smaller banks from dropping their membership in the Federal Reserve System. The Fed simply made such loans readily available to these banks.

We really need not spend a great deal of time on recent history and the current state of discount window policy, since the policy is currently being intensively studied for possible changes by the officials of the Federal Reserve System. Some substantial changes will undoubtedly be forthcoming in the near future. At this time, however, the most popular policy recommendation seems to be to make borrowing at the discount window freely available to all eligible financial institutions at a penalty rate, say 2% above the rate on 90-day Treasury securities. (This is not a forecast that that particular proposal will, in fact, be adopted.)

The discount window has another function that is most important, but little discussed. As a result of substantial revisions of the law in the 1930s, the Federal Reserve System has been, since 1934, truly the "lender of last resort" to any and all economic units in the nation. The Fed could have legally bailed out Penn-Central, the Chrysler Corporation, New York City, and your corner service station that just filed for bankruptcy. The Fed could have lent money to all these organizations, but fortunately did not. Clearly, the intent of the laws giving this power to the Federal Reserve System is to provide for a liquidity crisis, something akin to the old money panics. Historically, monetary systems have collapsed because everyone wanted the ultimate liquid asset, usually gold. Of course, in a fractional reserve system there was not enough gold to go around, banks broke their promise to redeem their banknotes and deposits in gold, and the system collapsed. There is no excuse for such an occurrence in a system based on "paper gold." As Lord Keynes phrased it in the *General Theory:*

> Unemployment develops, that is to say, because people want the moon; — men cannot be employed when the object of desire (i.e., money) is something which cannot be produced and the demand

for which cannot be readily choked off. There is no remedy but to persuade the public that green cheese is practically the same thing and to have a green cheese factory (i.e., a central bank) under public control.[1]

Although they have authority to lend to anyone and everyone, in practice the Federal Reserve has preferred not to lend to any but member commercial banks. This is part of their policy of keeping a "low profile" in such matters. One suspects that this low profile is desirable because they do not want to be besieged by loan requests from every business, small and large, and every municipality facing financial difficulty. The way the Fed has dealt with what it has regarded as truly temporary liquidity crises, which it deemed in the public interest for the Fed to alleviate, is to have a member bank accommodate the party in distress and then the Fed accommodates the member bank at the discount window. The Fed arranges loans behind the scenes that otherwise would not be obtainable.

Since the rate charged on loans at the discount window need not at the present time bear any particular relationship to market rates, what do changes in the discount rate mean? An increase in the discount rate certainly is not any significant direct increase in the cost of funds to the banking system. Only the smallest fraction (something less than 0.5%) of the banking system's total funds come from the discount window. However, over the 1950s and 1960s, and to a lesser extent in the 1970s, the discount rate did come to have what is called an *announcement effect*. The announcement effect comes about because the officials at the Fed, the bankers, and other money-market watchers all agreed that an increase in the discount rate means that the Federal Reserve is pursuing what it regards as a tight-money policy and intends to continue to do so for the foreseeable future. A reduction in the discount rate means that the Federal Reserve is following what it regards as an easy-money policy and intends to continue to do so for the foreseeable future.

Sometimes a discount rate change can, via the announcement effect, contain a great deal of information if it signals an unexpected reversal of policy, as it did at the beginning and end of the 1957–1958 recession. Sometimes it is a totally expected confirmation of what everybody has already known. In the 1970s it fell more into the latter category as the Fed tended to have discount rate movements follow other rates up or down.

We have been speaking of *the* discount rate as if there were only one. Technically there are twelve, one at each of the regional Federal Reserve Banks. Also, technically, the rate is set by the local Board of Directors at each bank. However, any change in a discount rate must be approved by the Board of Governors in Washington and we have already noted their rather substantial powers over the local bank. It is not too much of an oversimplification to say that with respect to the discount rate, as with most other policy questions, the power resides in Washington with the Board of Governors. Certainly the Board can veto any proposed change that it does not want. Given its other powers it can probably get any rate change it desires initiated by one or more of the regional banks. In general, all the banks change their discount rates simultaneously or within a few days of each other. On occasion one will hold out for a while to evidence some disagreement with the implied policy.

Changes in Reserve Requirements

As we noted at the beginning of this chapter, the potential monetization of private debt through the expansion of bank credit will be much larger with a reserve requirement of 10% rather than 20%. The purpose of a legal reserve requirement is, of course, to limit the expansion of bank credit. In a period of tight money, boom, and high loan demand, reserves tend to be fully used. The amount of excess reserves in the system is small. The reserve requirement at that point is a meaningful constraint on the monetization of private debt. In times of recession and depression, with easy money conditions and low loan demand, there is generally a large amount of excess reserves in the system. The presence of a large amount of unused reserves indicates that the reserve requirements are really not restraining the extension of bank credit much below what it otherwise would have been.

Originally, reserve requirements were written into the law and applied only to banks that were members of the Federal Reserve System. Since 1934 the Board of Governors has had the authority to vary reserve requirements for various categories of deposits within the ranges set by law. The reserves held as deposits in a regional Federal Reserve Bank earn no interest. Most nonmember, state-chartered banks also had reserve requirements set by state law, but such requirements could be met by holdings of government securities and deposits with other banks. Since nonmember banks were able to earn an explicit or implicit rate of return on their reserves, member banks paid a penalty in the form of the reserve percentage of their deposits earning a zero rate of return. As a result, for the last ten years banks have been dropping out of the system until, as mentioned above, Federal Reserve Member Banks held something less than 70% of demand deposits.

In 1980 Congress passed and the president signed into law the Depository Deregulation and Monetary Control Act of 1980. We will take up some other parts of this rather comprehensive piece of legislation at the end of this chapter. For present purposes the most important provision was the granting of the power to all depository type institutions to offer checking accounts on which interest may be paid. These are not "demand deposits" legally, but practically they certainly are since one may write checks on them. The legislation actually did three interrelated things:

1. Allowed payment of interest on checking accounts that had previously been prohibited.
2. Allowed all depository-type institutions (savings and loan associations, mutual savings banks, and credit unions) to offer checking accounts.
3. Required all financial institutions, banks and nonbanks, state or federally chartered, member or nonmember, to hold the same reserves against checking accounts as those required of banks that are members of the Federal Reserve System.

This certainly makes reserve requirements potentially a very effective tool of monetary policy. We have to say "potentially" because historically the Fed has not used reserve requirements as an active countercyclical tool of monetary policy. Many money and banking textbooks and not a few Fed people will contend that the reason reserve requirements are not so used is because changes in reserve requirements are more like a "meat-axe" than the "scalpel" of open market operations. It is true that a one percentage point change in reserve requirements does have a massive effect on the availability of reserves in the banking system. But nothing in law or logic says reserve requirements must be changed by a full percentage point. The Fed could set reserve requirements to four decimal places, say at 14.1234%, and change the last decimal place on the right in an announcement every other Monday morning. Reserve requirements *could* be an active tool of monetary policy, but, in fact, have never been and the Fed shows no propensity to move in that direction.

What changes in reserve requirements have been used for is to attempt to influence the structure of liabilities in the banking system. The Fed has historically used the level of reserve requirements to encourage banks to be more conservative, to take less risk in their borrowing and lending policies. Conservative finance dictates that one should borrow for as long a time period as possible; there is less risk of not being able to pay it back when due. Banks, of course, borrow money by taking deposits. They borrow money repayable on demand when they issue liabilities subject to having checks written on them. Savings accounts not subject to check can be thought of as having a slightly longer maturity — the time and inconvenience it takes depositors to come in for their money. As a result, reserve requirements have historically been higher on demand deposits than on savings accounts: 12% versus 3% currently. More relevant to our discussion here, however, are the fixed maturity liabilities called certificates of deposit, or CDs. These deposits customarily run from a few days to two years in maturity with the heaviest concentration of maturities being at three months and six months. In an effort to encourage banks to engage in more long-term and less short-term borrowing, the Fed has historically imposed higher reserve requirements on CDs maturing in less than six months (see Table 13.2). Currently "nonpersonal time deposits" have a zero reserve requirement

TABLE 13.2 Reserve Requirements of Depository Institutions (Percent of Deposits)

Member Bank Requirements before Implementation of the Monetary Control Act

Type of Deposit, and Deposit Interval	Percent	Effective Date
Net Demand		
$0 million–$2 million	7	12/30/76
$2 million–$10 million	9 1/2	12/30/76
$10 million–$100 million	11 1/4	12/30/76
$100 million–$400 million	12 1/4	12/30/76
Over $400 million	16 1/4	12/30/76
Time and Savings		
Savings	3	3/16/67
Time		
$0 million–$5 million, by maturity	3	3/16/67
30–179 days	2 1/2	3/16/67
180 days to 4 years	1	1/8/76
4 years or more		10/30/75
Over $5 million, by maturity	6	
30–179 days	2 1/2	12/12/74
180 days to 4 years	1	1/8/76
4 years or more		10/30/76

Depository Institution Requirements after Implementation of the Monetary Control Act

Type of Deposit, and Deposit Interval	Percent	Effective Date
Net transaction accounts		
$0–$26.3 million	3	12/30/82
Over $26.3 million	12	12/30/82
Nonpersonal Time Deposits		
By original maturity		
Less than 1 1/2 years	3	10/6/83
1 1/2 years or more	0	10/6/83
Eurocurrency liabilities		
All types	3	11/13/80

Source: *Federal Reserve Bulletin*, December 1983.

if their original maturity is over 1.5 years and the 3% reserve requirement if of shorter term. The higher reserve requirement on the shorter maturity CDs and the demand deposits raises the cost of these funds to a bank since, as we mentioned above, reserves are nonearning assets.

To understand what the Fed is concerned about we must take a closer look at how banks meet their reserve requirements. First, the requirement is in terms of an average level of reserves over a two-week period for checking accounts and over a one-week period for time deposits. If an individual bank sees the end of the reserve accounting period coming on it and estimates that it may be short, it has three short-run alternatives. It can go into the certificate of deposit market with a high rate of interest and seek deposits, and thereby reserves from other banks. It can borrow reserves from another bank by what is called a "federal funds" transaction. And lastly, it can go to the discount window for a direct loan of reserves from its regional Federal Reserve Bank. Not meeting its reserve requirement is not an alternative. It simply is not done.

Let us consider more closely the second alternative, borrowing in the Fed funds market. The mechanics of this transaction are simple enough since both member banks have reserve accounts with the Fed. If the transaction is to be for $10 million for one day, the Fed merely reduces the reserve account of the lending bank by $10 million for one day and increases the reserve account of the borrowing bank by $10 million. The banks then exchange checks dated one day apart with the borrowing bank's check being larger by an amount equal to one day's interest on $10 million (which is not insignificant; at 20%, one day's interest on $10 million is $5,556).

Occasional transactions between a bank with excess reserves and another that is going to be short, is how the Fed funds market began in the 1950s. However, it has grown to the point where most major money center banks now borrow billions of dollars overnight from smaller banks. The loans are one-day liabilities and they are used by the large banks to support regular commercial lending. Combine the Fed funds borrowing with short-term certificates of deposit and there is a potential problem. Many large, money center banks have up to 60% of their total liabilities coming due in large multimillion dollar blocks within three to six months. Just the maturity is not the problem. The Fed funds money and the large, short-term CDs are placed in the bank, not by a multitude of small depositors who are unlikely to all want their money at the same time, but by other banks and corporate treasurers who *are* all likely to want their money at the same time. The small depositor has federal government insurance (FDIC) up to $100,000 even if the bank goes broke. However, Fed funds are not deposits, and hence, not insured. A corporate treasurer holding a $1 million CD is really not interested in explaining to her Board of Directors how she collected FDIC insurance of 10¢ on the dollar ($100,000 on $1 million). Hence, the Fed funds and the large certificate of deposit money is likely to stop flowing to a particular bank all at once.

Here we have the modern-day equivalent of the old time "run" on a bank. All it takes is for fact or rumor to establish a suspicion in the financial community that a particular large bank has some small probability of going under. The belief need have no basis in fact. The belief alone is sufficient. There is no major money center bank in the United States today that could stay in business three months without massive assistance from the Fed if no other bank would lend it Fed funds and no corporation would buy its certificate of deposit. As soon as the word hits the financial press, either the bank is closed or the Fed steps in. The Fed can, of course, extend the massive aid necessary through the discount window. It has done so in the case of three large banks, one of which was kept open and the others merged out of existence.

At any rate, the Fed worries about this particular problem enough to attempt to use reserve requirements and other regulations to encourage banks to lengthen the average maturity of their liabilities. Current (1983) reserve requirements in effect reflect this concern. A page out of the *Federal Reserve Bulletin* (December 1983) is reproduced in Table 13.2, giving "Member Bank Reserve Requirements" before implementation of the Monetary Control Act and "Depository Institution Requirements" after implementation of the Monetary Control Act. The old set of reserve requirements has reserves on time deposits in excess of $5 million falling from 6% to 1% as the maturity is extended to over four years. The second set simply has a 3% requirement on time deposits of less than 1.50 years and no reserves on time deposits in excess of 1.50 years.

The transition from one set of reserve requirements to the other takes place in equal annual increments over four years for member banks and over eight years for all other depository institutions. As indicated on the table, the marginal reserve requirement on checking accounts was lowered from 16.25% to 12% from 1980 through 1983 for member banks, and goes from 1.5% to 12% for nonmember institutions from 1980 through 1987.

By way of summary, what can we say about reserve requirements as a tool of monetary policy? They are not used as an active tool of monetary policy although they have the potential to be so used. They are a factor in influencing the structure of financial institutions' liabilities by changing the cost of particular liabilities to the institution. The outlook is for no great changes in this policy. This is not to say that the Fed would not actively use changes in reserve requirements in extreme cases. If the Fed faced a deep depression in the economy, massive cuts in reserve requirements would certainly be likely, and in a hyperinflation a substantial rise in reserve requirements might well be forthcoming.

● Questions for Discussion

1. What type of monetary policy would result from open market operations designed to maximize bond trading profits for the Fed?

2. Discuss the impact of open market operations in terms of the general equilibrium equation, $(S - I) + (B - L) + (\Delta M - H) = 0$.

3. What is meant by the statement that the discount window enables the Fed to be the "lender of last resort" without limit?

4. Choose one provision of the "Depository Deregulation and Monetary Control Act of 1980" and discuss its implications, if any, for monetary policy.

● Source Notes

[1]John Maynard Keynes. *The General Theory of Employment, Interest, and Money*. New York: Harcourt, Brace, 1936, p. 235.

● Selected Additional Readings

Gordon, Robert J. *Macroeconomics*. (2nd ed.) Boston: Little, Brown, 1981. Chapter 15.

Hester, Donald D. Innovations and monetary control. *Brookings Papers on Economic Activity*, No. 1, 1981. Washington, D.C.: The Brookings Institution, 1981.

Measuring Monetary Policy

14

The candidates for an indicator of monetary policy come in two broad categories. The first category is the various measures of bank reserves and the money supply, referred to as *monetary aggregates*. The second category is the interest rate measures. The most popular interest rate measure of monetary policy is the Fed funds rate, although the 90-day U.S. Treasury bill rate and the commercial bank prime lending rate are also candidates. Almost no one suggests the Federal Reserve discount rate, since as we have discussed, it is not a market rate. The decision about which category of indicators to prefer can almost be reduced to answering the question: What do you want as your measure, the price or quantity of credit?

First, we must try to state clearly what it is we are trying to measure. We are trying to measure policy. Here again, the issue is confused by the problem of two-way causation. The level of interest rates influences the level of business activity and the level of business activity certainly influences the level of interest rates. We believe the rate of increase in the money supply influences the level of economic activity or we would not be concerned with monetary policy. But we also know that the level of economic activity influences the money supply. Money is created when private debt is monetized, and that depends on loan demand.

As we mentioned in Chapter 4 in our discussion of monetary theory, the real essence of money is liquidity. We defined the liquidity of any asset as the ability to exchange it for other assets at a reasonably certain rate of exchange. We noted that all assets with economic value, from currency to real estate, have various degrees of liquidity. We also noted that each and every credit transaction creates some liquidity. Monetary policy attempts to influence the level of economic activity in the economy by influencing the level of total liquidity through an impact on the extension of credit of various types. How should it be measured? Interest rates are the price of credit. The swap rate between a dollar today and a dollar next year is one plus the interest rate. If you can get $1.10 one year from now by giving up $1.00 now, the interest rate is said to be 10%. We have discussed this previously in terms of the reciprocal of this ratio, the price of financial assets. In this case the price of a one-year financial asset is said to be 91, since $1.00 divided by $1.10 is $0.91. To get $100 a year from now you would have to invest $91 today.

Recall our discussion of the general equilibrium equation in Chapter 3.

$$(S - I) + (B - L) + (\Delta M - H) = 0,$$

where

$$(S - I) = \text{net supply in the goods market},$$
$$(B - L) = \text{net supply in the financial assets markets},$$
$$(\Delta M - H) = \text{net supply of cash balances}.$$

Open market operations operate directly on the supply and demand for financial assets and cash balances. If the goal is to stimulate the economy via open market operations the Fed buys government securities, creating a net demand for financial assets, $(L > B)$, and a net supply of cash balances, $(\Delta M > H)$. This should drive up the value of financial assets in terms of money, bond prices. Of course, an increase in bond prices, say from 91 to 95, is a drop in the interest rate from 10% to approximately 5% (100/91 = 1.10, 100/95 = 1.05). The Fed has demanded bonds by supplying cash.

The question is, do we measure this activity by the quantity of cash supplied, ΔM, or the change in interest rates? If we decide that question, we then have to decide what definition of the money supply and which interest rate we want to use.

Monetary Aggregates as Measures of Monetary Policy

The most direct quantitative measure of monetary policy is the monetary base. The Fed controls the monetary base directly via open market operations and the discount window. If the Fed buys $1 million of government securities, the public's holding of government securities falls by $1 million and the monetary base is increased by $1 million. Similarly, if the Fed lends the banking system $1 million through discount window operations, the monetary base will expand by $1 million.

The Fed can control the monetary base fairly tightly via open market operations. However, as illustrated in Fig. 14.1, it is a long way from the monetary base to the unemployment and inflation rates. The goal of both monetary and fiscal policy is, of course, to make some contribution toward noninflationary full employment. The schematic diagram in Fig. 14.1 shows the minimum number of linkages in monetary policy. The first linkage is that between the monetary base and bank reserves or currency in circulation. The public has the choice of holding an increase in the monetary base in the form of currency in circulation or depositing it in the banking system. The amount deposited in the banking system will be an increase in bank

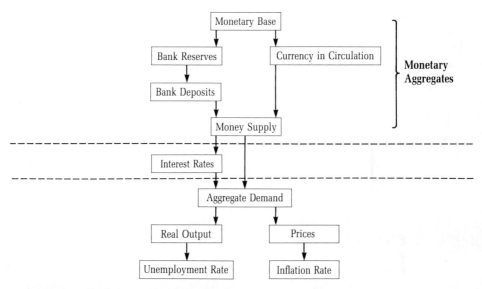

FIGURE 14.1 Linkages in Monetary Policy.

reserves. This increase in bank reserves *may* cause an increase in bank lending and a further increase in the money supply. We will look at various definitions of the money supply shortly, but the most common definitions include currency in circulation and various combinations of demand and time deposits.

The effect of changes in the money supply on aggregate demand is subject to the controversy we discussed in Chapter 4 when we considered classical and Keynesian monetary theory. The Keynesian approach is depicted in Fig. 14.1 by the flow of causation from the money supply through interest rates to aggregate demand. As we discussed in Chapter 3, the Keynesian assumption is that the excess money balances will be used to buy financial assets, thereby driving up their price and lowering interest rates. The lower interest rates will encourage investment that via the multiplier will increase aggregate demand. On the other hand, the classical assumption that excess money balances will create an excess demand for goods directly is shown by the arrow straight from the money supply to aggregate demand.

The most frequently used quantitative measures of monetary policy are as follows: the monetary base, total reserves, and various definitions of the money supply. There is occasional support for *unborrowed reserves,* total reserves minus Fed loans to banks via the discount window. *Free reserves* (or *net free reserves*) is a measure that has been used historically, but has been substantially discredited by now. Free reserves are defined as excess reserves minus bank borrowings at the discount window. This entire collection of measures is referred to as the monetary aggregates.

The most popular definitions of the money supply are referred to as
*M*1 and *M*2. *M*1 includes the currency in the hands of the public plus *all*
the deposits subject to check in all financial situations. Until the 1970s,
demand deposits held by commercial banks represented almost all the deposits
subject to check in the economy. As we have already noted, legislation
effective in 1981 gave the right to offer checking accounts to credit unions,
savings banks, and savings and loan associations nationwide.

The other popular definition, *M*2, includes *M*1 plus a large collection
of other highly liquid assets held by households. Specifically, *M*2 includes
in addition to the *M*1 components: personal savings and time deposits,
overnight "repurchase agreements," and "money market fund" shares.
The last two components we have not previously defined. A *repurchase
agreement* is actually a loan to a bank collaterized by a government security.
This device was popularized before interest could legally be paid on checking
accounts and it is also a way for banks to avoid reserve requirements. The
game is played as follows. An individual has a fairly large deposit with a
bank. The bank sells a government security to the depositor before the
close of business each day, reducing the deposit to zero. The next morning
the bank buys the security back at a price just enough higher than the
selling price to pay the depositor one day's interest on the deposit. The
bank has no deposit at the close of business each day on which it must
hold reserves, and the depositor is receiving interest on the deposit. The
bank promises in advance to repurchase the security, hence, the name
repurchase agreement. Repurchase agreements are frequently referred to
as *repos* for short. Banks also do large denomination repurchase agreements
for corporate customers and other financial institutions. The measure of
money supply *M*2 seeks to count only those done with individuals. A similar
caveat refers to time and savings deposits of all types, especially certificates
of deposit. The attempt is made to exclude nonhousehold deposits. The
most common approach is to assume that the very large ones (over $1
million) are corporate and the smaller ones are household. The next broader
measure of the money supply, *M*3, includes all sizes of certificates of deposit
and repurchase agreements.

Money market funds are mutual funds invested in short-term securities.
The manager of such a fund, usually a brokerage house, takes the "deposits"
of a large number of individuals and invests them in short-term government
and corporate securities such as Treasury bills, commercial bank certificates
of deposit, commercial paper, and so on. Money market funds came into
being when the government had a regulation saying that a certificate of
deposit of less than $100,000 could receive a rate no higher than, say 6%,
but amounts in excess of that could receive whatever the market dictated.
In a high-interest rate period, when small CDs were paying 6% and the
large ones were getting 16%, it did not take a genius to find ten people,
each with $10,000, and put together the first money market fund. Those

regulations have been phased out, but these financial intermediaries continue to survive because there are great economies of scale in the required transactions. Multimillion dollar transactions can be undertaken for a fraction of the percentage of the investment required of an individual investing a few thousand dollars. The individual receives an attractive rate of return, especially in tight money periods when short-term rates are higher than long-term rates. The fund stands ready to buy out any individual wanting his money back. As with any successful process of financial intermediation, this arrangement apparently provides a combination of liquidity and yield to these individuals that is superior to what they could receive by investing directly on their own or through some other financial intermediary.

So what is a good quantitative measure of monetary policy? If there were a stable, known relationship encompassing each of the linkages shown in Fig. 14.1, it would not make any difference which of the monetary aggregates we chose. If a certain percentage change in the monetary base always gave rise to a certain percentage change in bank reserves and currency, and the change in bank reserves always gave a predictable impact on bank lending and deposits, we could derive a known relationship between the monetary base and the money supply.

Let us consider how stable the linkages from the monetary base to the money supply have been in recent years. Table 14.1 gives the three relevant ratios for the sixteen-year period 1965 through 1980. The first ratio, total reserves to the monetary base, shows what proportion of the outstanding monetary base has been deposited in the banking system. For example, in 1965 the average values for total reserves and the monetary base were such that 36¢ out of every dollar in the monetary base was held in the form of bank reserves. This means, of course, that 64¢ out of each dollar of the monetary base was held in the form of currency in circulation. The proportion held as reserves has shown a definite downward trend over this sixteen-year period. By 1980 only 29¢ out of every dollar of monetary base was in the form of bank reserves, and 71¢ was held as cash balances.

TABLE 14.1 Ratios of Reserves, $M1$, and $M2$ to the Monetary Base, 1965–1980

Year	Res./MB	M1/MB	M2/MB	Year	Res./MB	M1/MB	M2/MB
1965	.36	2.98	8.00	1973	.34	2.85	9.22
1966	.35	2.96	8.08	1974	.34	2.76	9.04
1967	.36	2.92	8.22	1975	.33	2.68	9.20
1968	.36	2.93	8.35	1976	.31	2.64	9.68
1969	.35	2.95	8.41	1977	.31	2.62	10.11
1970	.34	2.91	8.32	1978	.30	2.59	10.08
1971	.34	2.88	8.65	1979	.29	2.58	10.13
1972	.35	2.88	9.06	1980	.29	2.54	10.23

The next two ratios in Table 14.1 are commonly called *money multipliers.*
The ratio of the money supply to the monetary base shows the combined
effects of the use of bank reserves and the public's demand for cash balances.
To the extent that there is strong load demand and little in the way of idle
reserves in the system, the money multipliers will be large. However, to
the extent that the public desires to hold the monetary base in the form of
cash balances, the money multipliers will be reduced in size. A dollar of
monetary base held in the form of cash balances outside the banking system
can only be one dollar of the money supply under any definition. However,
a dollar of the monetary base that is deposited in the banking system has
two effects. The deposit, either in a checking or time account, may be
counted as part of the money supply depending on the definition. Second,
the banking system receives reserves that it can use to monetize private
debt, further increasing the money supply. In other words, a dollar of
monetary base held as currency can only be one dollar of the money supply,
but a dollar of the monetary base deposited in the banking system can
potentially expand the money supply by some multiple of the base.

The trend of the money multipliers tells us something of the changing
structure of liquid assets over the last fifteen years. (We are using sixteen
data points, so we have fifteen years of change.) We know from the first
ratio that the proportion of the monetary base actually available to the
banking system as reserves has fallen from 35¢ on the dollar to 29¢. With
some cyclical variation to which we will return later, the $M1$ multiplier has
fallen over this time period while the $M2$ multiplier has risen. We obtain
a better picture of exactly what went on over this fifteen-year period if we
put in all the dollar values for 1965 and 1980 and take them as ratios to
the monetary base. The figures are shown in Table 14.2.

The last column on the right in Table 14.2 is probably the most informative.
As we observed, during this fifteen-year period the division of the monetary
base between reserves and currency in circulation has shifted by 7¢ on the
dollar from bank reserves to currency. Due to numerous institutional developments, not the least of which is the credit card, the public's need for
checking accounts has declined substantially in proportion to the monetary
base. The 51¢ decline in checking accounts from $2.34 to $1.83 per dollar
of monetary base, when combined with the 7¢ rise in currency held, results
in a decline in the size of the $M1$ multiplier of 44¢.

The public has learned to economize on checking accounts, but it has
learned to love the other interest-earning assets that are included in the
definition of $M2$. These other assets grew from $5.02 to $7.69 per dollar
of monetary base. This increase of $2.67 was enough to more than offset
the decline in the $M1$ multiplier, so the $M2$ multiplier had a net increase
of $2.23.

From our examination of the trends in the monetary mechanism over
this fifteen-year period, it is clear that the proportion of aggregate liquidity

TABLE 14.2   Change in Monetary Aggregates between 1965 and 1980

	Billions of Dollars		
	1965	1980	Change
(1) Monetary Base = (2) + (3)	$55.1	$156.6	$101.5
(2) Total Reserves	19.8	44.8	25.0
(3) Currency	35.3	111.8	76.5
(4) Checking Accounts	129.2	286.5	157.3
(5) M1 = (3) + (4)	164.5	398.3	233.8
(6) Other Liquid Assets in M2	276.1	1,204.1	928.0
(7) M2 = (5) + (6)	440.6	1,602.4	1,161.8

	Per Dollar of Monetary Base		
	1965	1980	Change
(1) Monetary Base = (2) + (3)	$1.00	$1.00	-0-
(2) Total Reserves	0.36	0.29	− 0.07
(3) Currency	0.64	0.71	+ 0.07
(4) Checking Accounts	2.34	1.83	− 0.51
(5) M1 = (3) + (4)	2.98	2.54	− 0.44
(6) Other Liquid Assets in M2	5.02	7.69	+ 2.67
(7) M2 = (5) + (6)	8.00	10.23	+ 2.23

held in the form of currency has risen and the proportion in the form of checking accounts has fallen. The latter effect has been the larger of the two so the $M1$ multiplier has fallen. In addition to an increased demand for currency holdings, we found that the public has very substantially increased its holdings of time and savings deposits and holdings of money market mutual fund shares. The growth of these interest-bearing liquid assets has been so great as to give a large positive trend value to the $M2$ multiplier.

Having examined the implications of the trends in these ratios, let us remove the trend and look at the cyclical variation. As we indicated in Chapter 7, a trend is an association with the passage of time. To establish the existence and magnitude of a trend we need only run a simple regression between each ratio as a dependent variable and time as the independent variable. The statistical results of such regressions are as follows:

Dependent Variable	Correlation Coefficient	Regression Coefficient
Res./MB	− .93	− .005
$M1/MB$	− .96	− .032
$M2/MB$	+ .98	+ .163

The values of the correlation coefficients are all statistically significant, indicating what we already know. There is a meaningful trend to be removed. We want to remove the trend to observe the cyclical variation of the time series. (With annual data there is, of course, no possibility of seasonal variation.) To detrend these time series we must remove the increase associated with the passage of time. Table 14.3 gives the detrended values for these three time series. We derived the numbers in the table by leaving the 1965 figure for each at its original value and subtracting the value of the regression coefficient for each year past 1965. For example, in the case of the ratio of reserves to the monetary base, Res./*MB*, the regression equation indicates a time trend of $-.005$ per year. To subtract that effect from the unadjusted data we *add* .005 per year beginning with 1966. When we add the .005 to the unadjusted value of .35 we get .355, which we round to .36 as shown. To the 1967 figure of .36 we add two times .005 (or .01) to get a detrended figure of .37, and so on, for each year. By 1980 the negative trend value to be removed is fifteen times .005 (or .075), which when added to .29 gives the rounded value of .37.

From the adjusted data in Table 14.3 it appears that the ratio of reserves to the monetary base, Res./*MB*, has no particular cyclical movement. The shift from reserves to currency in circulation seems to have been primarily a long-term trend movement with no particular cyclical fluctuations. The ratio is at .36 in 1965, rises to .39 around the middle of the period, and then falls back to .37 by 1980. There is no apparent relationship to the recessions of 1970–1971 and 1974–1975.

The money multipliers, on the other hand, do appear to have a pronounced cyclical variation of the expected type. The values of the detrended money multipliers are shown in Fig. 14.2. (The peaks and troughs of the NBER reference cycle are again indicated as *P* and *T* with the *R* for recession periods.) The removal of the trend does make the cyclical movement quite clear. For both time series, a recession means a decline with a rise immediately thereafter. However, the two indicators do behave quite differently.

TABLE 14.3 Detrended Ratios of Reserves, *M*1, and *M*2 to the Monetary Base, 1965–1980

Year	Res./MB	M1B/MB	M2/MB	Year	Res./MB	M1B/MB	M2/MB
1965	.36	2.98	8.00	1973	.38	3.11	7.92
1966	.36	2.99	7.92	1974	.39	3.05	7.57
1967	.37	2.98	7.89	1975	.38	3.00	7.57
1968	.38	3.03	7.86	1976	.37	2.99	7.89
1969	.37	3.08	7.76	1977	.37	3.00	8.15
1970	.37	3.07	7.51	1978	.37	3.01	7.96
1971	.37	3.07	7.67	1979	.36	3.03	7.85
1972	.39	3.10	7.92	1980	.37	3.02	7.79

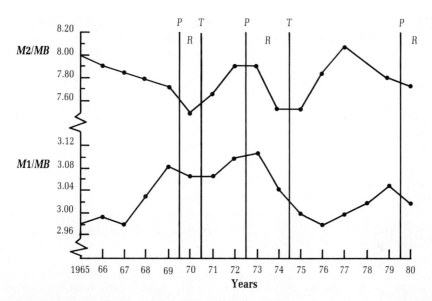

FIGURE 14.2   Trend-Adjusted Money Multipliers.

What does this tell us about whether $M1$ or $M2$ is the "better" monetary indicator? The primary difference in the behavior of the two money multipliers is that the $M2$ multiplier has a more pronounced and reliable cyclical movement. The $M2$ multiplier falls decisively in both recessions to approximately its previous low point. The $M1$ multiplier falls only very slightly in the 1970–1971 recession. Quantitatively, if we use the change in the unemployment rate as our reference cycle we find dramatic statistical differences in cyclical association. The simple correlation coefficient between the $M2$ multiplier and the year-to-year change in the unemployment rate is a $-.82$. This indicates a fairly reliable negative association between the two. In a boom, when the unemployment rate is falling the $M2$ money multiplier is rising. As we would expect, a dollar of monetary base is used to generate more dollars of money. In a recession, when the unemployment rate is rising the $M2$ money multiplier is falling. There is less money created per dollar of monetary base.

The statistical relationship between the $M1$ multiplier and the change in unemployment is very near zero and has the wrong sign. With a value of $+.09$ for the correlation coefficient we have to infer that the movements of the $M1$ multiplier during this time period were close to being independent of the level of unemployment. This is especially obvious for the 1970–1971 recession as can be seen in Fig. 14.2.

Let us now take the next step in the monetary linkage by looking at the velocities of $M1$ and $M2$, that is, their relationship to GNP. Table 14.4

TABLE 14.4 Velocity of M1 and M2, 1965–1980

	GNP/M1		GNP/M2		GNP/M1		GNP/M2
	Unadj.	Detrended			Unadj.	Detrended	
1965	4.20	4.20	1.57	1973	5.14	3.88	1.59
1966	4.40	4.24	1.61	1974	5.30	3.88	1.62
1967	4.47	4.15	1.59	1975	5.48	3.90	1.60
1968	4.57	4.10	1.60	1976	5.75	4.01	1.57
1969	4.66	4.03	1.63	1977	5.97	4.08	1.55
1970	4.72	3.93	1.65	1978	6.21	4.16	1.60
1971	4.80	3.85	1.60	1979	6.45	4.24	1.64
1972	4.93	3.82	1.56	1980	6.59	4.22	1.64

presents $M1$ and $M2$ velocities for the same period we have been using, 1965–1980. There seems to be a rather pronounced positive trend in the velocity of $M1$ and no particular trend in $M2$. This is confirmed by a simple correlation with time. For $M1$ the computed correlation coefficient is .98 and the regression coefficient is .16. For $M2$ the computed correlation coefficient is an insignificant .12 and the regression coefficient is a near zero .0008. The insignificance of the indicated trend value for $M2$ is clear when we note that if we were to adjust for trend, the largest adjustment we would make would only be .01, since $15 \times .0008 = .012$.

The strong positive trend in $M1$ velocity is consistent with the strong negative trend in the $M1$ money multiplier. We noted while discussing the multiplier that over this time period people learned how to get along with relatively smaller amounts in their checking accounts. Since $M1$ is currency in circulation plus checking accounts, a positive trend in its velocity, GNP/$M1$, merely means GNP went up at a faster rate than these two components of this definition of the money supply.

Turning to the cyclical behavior of the velocities, Fig. 14.3 shows the $M2$ velocity, unadjusted, and the detrended values for $M1$ velocity. The $M1$ velocity exhibits no particular cyclical variation. This is not to say that it shows no variation at all. A neoclassical economist seeking a constant velocity would find little comfort in either time series. And, of course, the $M1$ velocity was even less of a constant before it was detrended.

On the other hand, the behavior of the velocity of $M2$ shows a pronounced cyclical variation that might give some comfort to a Keynesian seeking a positive relationship between velocity and the level of interest rates. Looked at as a coincident indicator, $M2$ velocity would seem to be negatively related to the general level of economic activity. In fact, the correlation between changes in the unemployment rate and the $M2$ velocity is $+.45$, indicating

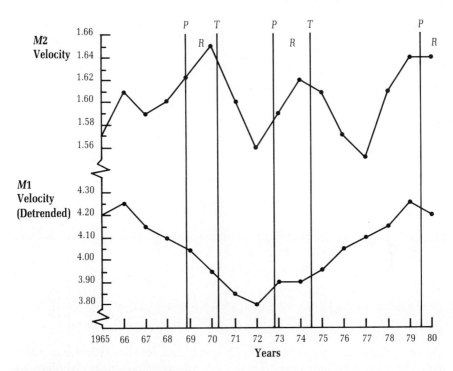

FIGURE 14.3   Velocity of *M*1 and *M*2.

a countercyclical movement. However, let us recall the expected linkages. Keynesian monetary theory contends that velocity will increase as interest rates rise. We noted in Chapter 9 that interest rates are usually a lagging economic indicator. Suppose high rates do cause an increase in velocity by causing people to economize on the use of money. We would expect a positive association between velocity and interest rates. If interest rates lag the general business cycle (which they do) we would expect a negative relationship between interest rates and the general level of economic activity.

We mentioned earlier three interest rates that are popular as monetary indicators: the Fed funds rate, the 90-day Treasury bill rate, and the commercial bank prime lending rate. We will consider the behavior of all three rates in the next section of this chapter when we consider them as monetary indicators *per se,* but here let us merely relate *M*2 velocity to the Fed funds rate. For reasons we will discuss in some detail later all interest rates have had a rising trend over the last fifteen years and the Fed funds rate is no exception. It increased an average of .37% per year over the years 1965–1980. In its unadjusted state its correlation coefficient with *M*2 velocity is .69 and if the trend is removed the coefficient rises to .79. (*M*1 velocity detrended is only .24; if neither is detrended their common trend gives them a significant .65 correlation coefficient.) In any case, as expected, high velocity seems to be associated with high interest rates.

Let us return to the consideration of monetary aggregates as a measure of the influence of monetary policy on aggregate demand. A straightforward approach would be simply to consider the association between percentage rates of change. We know that if velocity were constant, the percentage change in the money supply would be equal to the percentage change in GNP. Let us refer to the velocity of $M1$ as V_1 and the velocity of $M2$ as V_2. Recalling our basic macroeconomic relationships from Chapters 3 and 9, we can state the following identity:

$$(M1)\,(V_1) = (M2)(V_2) = \text{GNP} = (P)(Q).$$

(Recall that P is the GNP price index and Q is real, price deflated GNP.) From the identity above we can say that the sum of the percentage changes of each of the terms separated by an equal sign are approximately equal, $(\approx)$

$$(\%\Delta M1) + (\%\Delta V_1) \approx (\%\Delta M2) + (\%\Delta V2) \approx \%\Delta\text{GNP}$$
$$\approx (\%\Delta P) + (\%\Delta Q).$$

Table 14.5 presents the data for this last equation for the fifteen-year period 1966–1980. At the bottom of Table 14.5 are the fifteen-year averages for each time series.

TABLE 14.5 Percentage Changes in Money, Velocity, and GNP, 1966–1980

	M1	V_1	M2	V_2	GNP	P	Q
1966	4.6	4.8	6.6	2.5	9.4	3.2	6.0
1967	3.9	1.6	7.0	−1.2	5.8	3.0	2.7
1968	7.1	2.2	8.4	0.6	9.2	4.4	4.6
1969	6.0	2.0	6.2	1.9	8.1	5.1	2.8
1970	3.7	1.3	3.9	1.2	5.2	5.4	−0.2
1971	6.7	1.7	12.1	−3.0	8.6	5.0	3.4
1972	7.1	2.7	12.5	−2.5	10.1	4.2	5.7
1973	7.3	4.3	10.0	1.9	11.8	5.7	5.8
1974	4.9	3.1	6.2	1.9	8.1	8.7	−0.6
1975	4.6	3.4	9.5	−1.2	8.0	9.3	−1.1
1976	5.5	4.9	13.2	−1.9	10.9	5.2	5.4
1977	7.5	3.8	12.9	−1.3	11.6	5.8	5.5
1978	8.2	4.0	8.9	3.2	12.4	7.3	4.8
1979	7.8	3.9	8.9	2.5	12.0	8.5	3.2
1980	6.4	2.2	9.1	-0-	8.8	9.0	−0.2
Average	6.1	3.1	9.0	0.3	9.3	6.0	3.2

A summary statement of what happened to these variables over this time period can be read from the average values. The last three columns on the right indicate that nominal GNP went up by about 9% per year as a result of 3% real growth and 6% inflation. In terms to $M1$, the 9% increase in nominal GNP resulted from a 6% increase in the money supply and a 3% increase in its velocity. In terms of the broader definition of the money supply, $M2$, the 9% increase in GNP was almost totally the result of an average annual increase in the money supply with no significant change in its velocity during the period.

The near zero change in V_2 during the period as a whole might be taken as an indication that $M2$ would be the better indicator of monetary policy. However, when we examine the cyclical changes in V_2, we come to the opposite conclusion. The behavior of the rate of growth in $M2$ and, thereby, in its velocity would give more support to Keynesian than monetarist or neoclassical monetary theory. V_2 varies in response to interest rates in such a way as to reduce the impact of changes in the money supply on GNP. The percentage change in the money supply is negatively correlated with the percentage change in its velocity. (The correlation coefficient is $-.65$.) When the money supply increases at a high rate such as the 12% and 13% rates in 1971, 1972, 1976, and 1977, velocity declines. On the other hand, in the tight money years of 1966, 1969, and 1974, the velocity of $M2$ went up at the rather substantial rates of 2.5%, 1.9%, and 1.9%, respectively. In both cases the impact of the changes in the money supply was reduced by offsetting changes in velocity.

The sequence seems to be that in a boom, as demand for loan funds rises, a slowdown in the rate of monetary growth designed to restrain the economy causes interest rates to rise. The higher rates make it worthwhile to economize on cash balances and the lack of growth in the money supply is partly offset by an increase in its velocity. This enables GNP to continue to grow. For example, from 1977 to 1978 the rate of growth in $M2$ was reduced from 12.9% to 8.9%. If velocity had continued to fall by the more than 1% a year as it had during the previous two years, GNP in 1978 would have grown by less than 8%. Instead, velocity increased by more than 3%, and GNP grew by more than 12%. The change in the rate of growth in velocity substantially offset the restrictive effect of monetary policy.

The countercyclical variations in the velocity of $M2$ are a substantial detriment to its use as a measure of monetary policy. As we discussed in conjunction with Figure 14.1, "Linkages in Monetary Policy," what we want is a measure of the effect of policy on aggregate demand. The linkage between $M2$ and GNP slips a good bit as indicated by changes in its velocity. The standard deviation of the percentage change in V_2 is 2.00 while the standard deviation of the change in V_1 is only 1.2. Another way to say the same thing is that a simple correlation between $M1$ and GNP is .84 while the correlation between $M2$ and GNP is only .62. Therefore, we must conclude (along with other more comprehensive studies of this question)[1] that the rate of growth in $M1$ is the better measure of monetary policy.

Interest Rate Measures of Monetary Policy

In the search for an interest rate measure of monetary policy we run into the same sort of problems we had with the money supply measures: causation flows both ways. The level of interest rates impacts on the level of economic activity, and the level of economic activity impacts on the level of interest rates. Interest rates are, as we noted earlier, the inverse of the price of financial assets. When, on an ex ante basis, the supply of such assets is greater than the demand for them, their price will tend to fall and interest rates to rise. In terms of our general equilibrium model, when borrowing is greater than lending, interest rates will rise. Conversely, a shortage of financial assets, or a surplus of money and goods, will tend to drive rates down.

The Federal Reserve can influence the demand for financial assets both directly and indirectly. As we observed above, when the Fed engages in open market operations it demands or supplies financial assets in exchange for money. The money it injects or removes from the system is an increase or decrease in the monetary base, and thereby a change in the availability of bank reserves. The availability of reserves influences the ability and willingness of banks and other financial institutions to make loans (that is, to demand financial assets). So the Fed has a direct impact on the demand for financial assets as it buys and sells government securities. It has an indirect impact by changing the availability of bank reserves.

Of course, the Federal Reserve is not the only purchaser (lender) and seller (borrower) of financial assets. The underlying stimulant to credit transactions comes from savers seeking to acquire paper assets as an income-producing store of value and investors seeking to finance expenditures in excess of their own cash flow. There is a definite, predictable pattern to the demand for financial assets during the business cycle. On the upswing of the business cycle the supply of financial assets (borrowing) will, on an ex ante basis, exceed the demand for financial assets (lending). An excessive demand for funds causes rates to rise. When the recession comes, rates begin to fall with the lags we discussed earlier. The demand for financial assets exceeds the supply, their price rises, and interest rates fall.

So how can one measure monetary policy by the use of interest rates? Well, of course, one can certainly say that restrictive open market operations (selling securities) will at that time make interest rates higher *than they otherwise would have been*. This does not mean, however, that rising interest rates are a clearcut sign of restrictive monetary policy because of the effect of the rate of economic activity on the level of interest rates.

A problem of macroeconomics in general and interest rate theory in particular is the assumed independence of supply and demand curves. In the standard classroom example of supply and demand (e.g., a microeconomic market similar to the one discussed in Chapter 2), we assume that a shift in the supply curve will *not cause* a shift in the demand curve. Both curves might coincidentally happen to shift at the same time, but there is no direct connection between the movement of one and the movement of the other. The usual treatment is as shown in Fig. 14.4. The shift in the supply curve from S_1 to S_2 causes the quantity sold to rise from Q_1 to Q_2, while the price falls from P_1 to P_2. Although the usual assumption of "all other things being equal" is never completely true, it is a reasonable approximation of many real world situations. In the case of interest rates and the supply and demand for loanable funds (or the demand and supply of financial assets), the assumed stability of the demand curve as the supply curve shifts is not even a good approximation. Consider a reduction in interest rates resulting from aggressive open market operations by the Federal Reserve. The Fed runs up the price of government securities and the interest rate on them down. The lower interest rates spread throughout the money and capital markets and encourage investment and other income generating activities. As the Fed succeeds in its goal of stimulating the economy, the *demand* for credit rises as a result of an increase in the *supply* of credit. Figure 14.5 is a graphic presentation of this sequence. Initially the supply of credit is increased by the Fed's open market operations. The supply curve of credit related to the level of interest rates shifts from S_1 to S_2. Interest rates decline from r_1 to r_2 as the amount of borrowing and lending increases from Q_1 to Q_2. Under the usual assumptions of an ordinary microeconomic market, that would be the end of the story. In the case of the credit markets, however, the increased lending at lower interest rates stimulates the economy and demand for credit shifts upward, from D_1 to D_2. The shift in demand

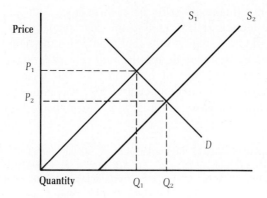

FIGURE 14.4 Independent Supply Increases and Price Falls.

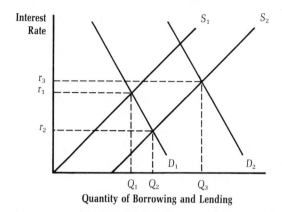

FIGURE 14.5 Supply Increase Causes Demand Increase and Interest Rate Rises.

causes interest rates to rise again. In Fig. 14.5 we have rates rising to r_3, which is above their original level, r_1. Although this may be the case, it is certainly theoretically possible that the shift in the demand curve could be sufficiently small that interest rates are permanently lowered by an increase in the supply of credit. We know that the induced shift in the demand for funds will cause interest rates to rise, but whether it will cause them to more than offset the shift in the supply depends on many things, one of the most important being what happens to the expected rate of inflation as a result of the increased supply of funds.

Let us take a closer look at the connection between interest rates and expected rates of inflation. Recall our general equilibrium model in which we have classified the entire economy into three markets: the market for goods, the market for financial assets, and the market for cash balances. Demand for each will be influenced by what people expect to happen to their relative values. If I expect rapid inflation in the price of goods, I want to hold goods, not financial assets or cash balances. In fact, I would like to borrow some money at 10% (sell a one-year security for a price of 90), if I thought I could buy some goods that would rise in value by 15% during the coming year. Economists define the *real rate of interest* as the market rate minus the expected rate of inflation.* In this case the real rate of interest would be approximately a negative 5%, 10% minus the 15% inflation rate. Of course, in this case, if the lender also expected 15% inflation he

---

*This is based on the definition of the market rate, r_m, as the sum of the expected inflation rate, $\%\Delta P$, and the real rate, r_r; $r_m = r_r + \%\Delta P$, so $r_r = r_m - \%\Delta P$. Technically, this is only an approximation since percentage gains from inflation should really be compounded. The exact formulation is: $(1 + r) = (1 + r_r)(1 + \%\Delta P)$, so $r_r = (r_m - \%\Delta P)/(1 + \%\Delta P)$. With a 10% market rate and a 5% inflation rate the approximation would give a 5% real rate, while the exact calculation would give 4.8%.

would not lend to me at 10%. He would either buy goods himself or more likely find someone who would pay him more than 15% so that he was earning a positive real rate of interest.

We have then the paradoxical situation in which an increase in the availability of credit via expansionary monetary policy can cause interest rates to rise via increased inflationary expectations. Conversely, a highly restrictive monetary policy would eventually give us low interest rates. If the Fed sold enough government securities to reduce $M1$ to about one-half its initial size, undoubtedly sufficient chaos would be created in the money and capital markets (a "panic"?) to collapse the economy into depression or at least into a very deep recession. As we have discussed previously, in a recession the demand for credit falls so much that interest rates decline. In this case the low interest rates would have resulted from an initial reduction in the availability of credit. In the words of Milton Friedman:

> As an empirical matter, low interest rates are a sign that monetary policy *has been* tight — in the sense that the quantity of money has grown slowly; high interest rates are a sign that monetary policy *has been* easy — in the sense that the quantity of money has grown rapidly.[2]

As a result, Professor Friedman concludes that

> These considerations not only explain why monetary policy cannot peg interest rates, they also explain why interest rates are such a misleading indicator of whether monetary policy is "tight" or "easy." For that, it is far better to look at the rate of change of the quantity of money.[3]

Friedman's position that monetary policy *cannot* peg, or fix, interest rates is, of course, not literally true. An interest rate is the price of a security. The Federal Reserve has, for all practical purposes, an infinite supply of government securities. They can keep the price of this security from rising above any given target by simply offering to sell at that price. On the other side of the market the Fed can create an infinite demand for government securities via open market operations. The Fed can keep the price of government securities from falling by simply offering to buy without limit at a given price. When you can influence both the supply and demand for something without limit one can most certainly fix its price. The Federal Reserve most certainly *can* set the yield on U.S. government securities by standing ready to buy or sell at prices just below and just above the price required to give the target rate of return.

What Friedman means is that a one-shot increase in the money supply will not permanently lower interest rates, and further, as inflationary expectations increase, it may take ever larger increases in the money supply to keep rates down. In Fig. 14.5 the rate of interest could be driven back down to r_1 or r_2 from r_3 by an additional increase in the supply of credit. For example, if the rate of growth in $M1$ were increased from 6% per year to 9% by increased availability of bank reserves, this might cause the rate on bank loans to fall from say 10% to 7%. However, it is possible that the expected rate of inflation would go from 8% to 11%. At an 8% inflation rate, the real rate of interest is 2% when loans are made at 10%. With 11% inflation, a loan rate of 13% is required for a 2% real rate of return. This is exactly what a "monetarist" economist would say would eventually happen. A lender who demanded 10% at the outset would eventually demand, and get, 13%. The government could only avoid this by increasing the money supply at an ever-increasing rate.

Note the similarity between the interest rate mechanism just discussed and the discussion in Chapter 11 of the Phillips curve, where we noted that an increase in the rate of inflation that comes as a surprise would temporarily reduce the unemployment rate and increase the level of output in the economy. However, this would not last and the level of unemployment would begin to rise (and output fall) as the *expected* rate of inflation began to rise. Similarly, in this section we have noted the monetarists' contention that an increase in the money supply will only temporarily lower market and real rates of interest. As the *expected* rate of inflation rises the market rates will rise enough to put the real rate of interest back where it was. This is truly a neoclassical position in that it contains the dual contention that there is a "natural" rate of unemployment and a "natural" or long-term equilibrium real interest rate toward which the system always moves. (There appears to be somewhat more acceptance of this position among the economics profession with respect to the unemployment rate than to interest rates.)

Another way to formulate this view of the economy is in terms of the elasticities discussed in Chapter 3. Recall the following relationships:

$$Y = (P)(Q) = (M)(V),$$

where

Y = nominal GNP,
P = the GNP price index,
Q = real GNP,
M = the money supply,
V = the velocity of the money supply.

From the above we obtain

$$\% \, \Delta Y = \% \, \Delta P + \% \, \Delta Q = \% \, \Delta M = \% \, \Delta V,$$
$$1.00 = (\% \, \Delta P)/(\% \, \Delta Y) + (\% \, \Delta Q)/(\% \, \Delta Y),$$
$$= (\% \, \Delta M)/(\% \, \Delta Y) + (\% \, \Delta V)/(\% \, \Delta Y),$$
$$1.00 = E_{p/y} + E_{q/y} = E_{m/y} + E_{v/y},$$

where

$E_p/_y$ = the elasticity of prices with respect to changes in aggregate demand,

$E_q/_y$ = the elasticity of real output with respect to changes in aggregate demand,

$E_m/_y$ = the elasticity of the money supply with respect to changes in aggregate demand, and

$E_v/_y$ = the elasticity of the velocity of the money supply with respect to changes in aggregate demand.

The classical position, as we stated in Chapter 3, is that $E_{q/y} = E_{v/y} = 0$. Real output and velocity are constants. Changing the money supply will only change nominal GNP via changes in prices, not through changes in employment and real GNP. As we noted in Chapter 4, in its extreme form the classical monetary theory implies an adjustment process in which all excess money balances are used to buy goods (none for buying financial assets) and, thereby, we obtain changes only in the price level (not in interest rates). We also noted the implication of this is a constant velocity of the money supply and the "quantity theory of money." A 10% increase in the money supply increases GNP by 10% and prices by 10% as velocity, output, employment, and real interest rates hold constant.

Today no one accepts literally, completely, and naively the classical model. Everyone agrees that "in the short run" monetary policy does affect real interest rates. It is also recognized that investors' opinion of the expected inflation rate can bounce around quite a bit. The questions are: How long is the short run? What determines inflationary expectations?

Although we never receive an accurate measure of inflationary expectations and are not sure what determines them, frequently they are simply ignored. There is a great deal of confusion in the popular discussion of the gains and losses between borrowers and lenders because expectations are ignored. For example, one frequently hears that the lender lost to the extent that inflation rates are anything other than zero. Nonsense! The contention that bankers lost and borrowers gained the 9% inflation rate of 1980 (as measured by the GNP price index) implies that both the bankers and the borrowers entered into a one-year loan agreement at the beginning of 1980 expecting a zero rate of inflation. In fact, the prime bank loan rate in 1980 averaged 15.3%. If both bankers and borrowers had expected a zero rate of inflation, do you think it would have been that high? The reason we had a historically high rate on bank loans was, in fact, *because* of the 9% inflation rate, or, more precisely, because both bankers and borrowers expected an inflation rate substantially higher than zero. Of course, as in the other markets we have discussed, expectations are a factor whether they are accurate forecasts or not.

The equity argument about who gains and who loses can take some interesting turns with inaccurate expectations. An example will illustrate that the question of what is a gain or loss due to inflation is as much a psychological question as a mathematical one. Suppose bankers expected 10% inflation while borrowers expected 8%. A one-year loan agreement written at 15% would leave the bankers expecting a real rate of return of 5%, 15% minus the 10% inflation rate; and the borrowers would expect to pay a real cost of 7%, 15% minus their expected inflation rate of 8%. Let us say the actual rate of inflation turns out to be 9%. The bankers are happy because they were expecting a real rate of return of only 5% but received, ex post, 6%, or 15% minus 9%. The borrowers expected a real cost of 7% but ended up having to pay only 6% ex post. They both won!

Let us now consider our experience with real rates of interest during the fifteen-year period 1966 through 1980. Table 14.6 presents the average level of the prime rate of commercial bank loans, the Fed funds rate, and the rate on new issues of the government's 90-day Treasury bills. The table shows each of these as "nominal" and "real." The nominal rate is the average rate for the year of actual recorded transactions. The real rate is

TABLE 14.6 Interest Rates before and after Adjustment for Inflation, 1966–1980

	Nominal Rates				Real* Rates		
	Prime Rate	Fed Funds	Treas. Bills	% ΔP*	Prime Rate	Fed Funds	Treas. Bills
1966	5.6%	5.1%	4.9%	3.2%	2.4%	1.9%	1.7%
1967	5.6	4.2	4.3	3.0	2.6	1.2	1.3
1968	6.3	5.7	5.3	4.4	1.9	1.3	0.9
1969	8.0	8.2	6.7	5.1	2.9	3.1	1.6
1970	8.0	7.2	6.5	5.4	2.5	1.8	1.1
1971	5.7	4.7	4.4	5.0	0.7	−0.3	−0.6
1972	5.3	4.4	4.1	4.2	1.1	0.2	−0.1
1973	8.0	8.7	7.0	5.7	1.3	3.0	1.3
1974	10.8	10.5	7.9	8.7	2.1	1.8	−0.8
1975	7.9	5.8	5.8	9.3	−1.4	−3.5	−3.5
1976	6.8	5.1	5.0	5.2	1.6	−0.1	−0.2
1977	6.8	5.5	5.3	5.8	1.0	−0.3	−0.5
1978	9.1	7.9	7.2	7.3	1.8	0.6	−0.1
1979	12.7	11.2	10.0	8.5	4.2	2.7	1.5
1980	15.3	13.4	11.5	9.0	6.3	4.4	2.5
Average	8.1	7.2	6.4	6.0	2.1	1.2	0.4
Standard Deviation	2.8	2.7	2.0	2.0	1.6	1.8	1.4

*The % ΔP is the year-to-year change in the GNP price index. Real rates in this table are nominal rates minus the % ΔP.

estimated here by simply subtracting the percentage rate of change in the GNP price index from the nominal rate. The inflation rate as measured by that index is shown in the middle column as $\%\Delta P$. Other studies sometimes use other indexes, and it is common to use a moving average of past inflation rates in the computation of an estimate of the real rate. Various statistical methods can be used to try to obtain a measure of expected inflation rates. You should recognize that we are discussing an ex ante concept with ex post data in Table 14.6.

We indicated at the beginning of this chapter that the three interest rates given in the table are the three most commonly used as a measure of monetary policy. The prime lending rate is a candidate for a measure of monetary policy since it reflects the cost of funds to businesspeople who are, in fact, providing the supply of financial assets to be monetized by the banking system. The Fed funds rate is a candidate since it is what the Fed more or less directly controls via open market operations, the discount window, and reserve requirements. Since the vast majority of the Fed's open market operations are conducted in 90-day Treasury bills, that market is also more or less directly controlled by monetary policy.

For the neoclassical equilibrium to prevail, the expected rate of inflation has to equal the actual rate of inflation; that is, the inflation rate must be fully anticipated. From the data in Table 14.6 one would have to conclude that unanticipated changes in the rate of inflation apparently cause realized real rates to vary considerably from year to year. For example, in 1975 nominal rates dropped dramatically from their 1974 levels. The Fed, at least, allowed this to happen, but apparently the magnitude of the inflation of 1975 (greater than 1974) came as something of a surprise since all three markets show significant negative real rates. Without pursuing this further we will conclude that monetary policy can, and probably has, influenced the level of both nominal and real rates of return for periods as long as a year.

Figure 14.6 shows the nominal rates on a monthly (rather than annual) basis. The cyclical behavior is more clearly observable. Furthermore, we can also note the government's classification of these rates as leading, lagging, or coincident indicators on this excerpt from *Business Conditions Digest*. The notation (*Lg, Lg, Lg*) on the prime rate indicates that it has been judged to lag at peaks, troughs, and overall. The Federal funds rates is judged to lead, (*L*), at peaks and lag at troughs and overall, (*Lg, Lg*). The Treasury bill rate is classified as being coincident, (*C*), at peaks, and to lag at troughs and overall. Looking at the annual data on the table and the monthly data on the graph one might wonder what the argument is all about. These indicators do not seem to give conflicting signals. Since they are all readily available, why not use them all? As a good business cycle analyst that is exactly what you should do.

Certainly from Table 14.6 and Figure 14.6 it is obvious that in some

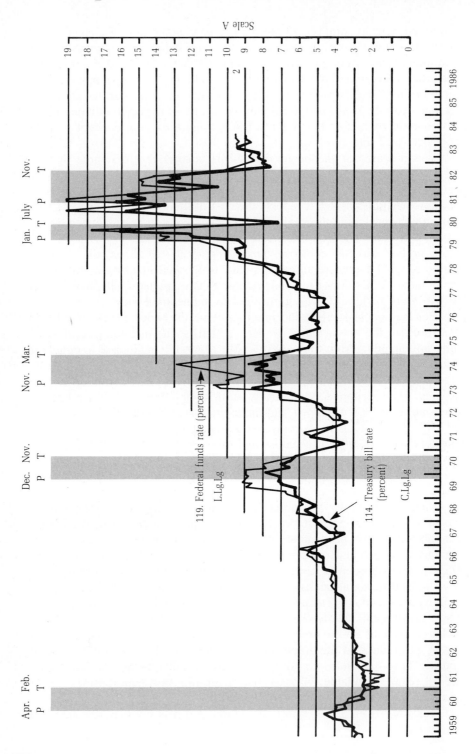

Scale A

119. Federal funds rate (percent)
L.Lg.Lg

114. Treasury bill rate (percent)
C.Lg.Lg

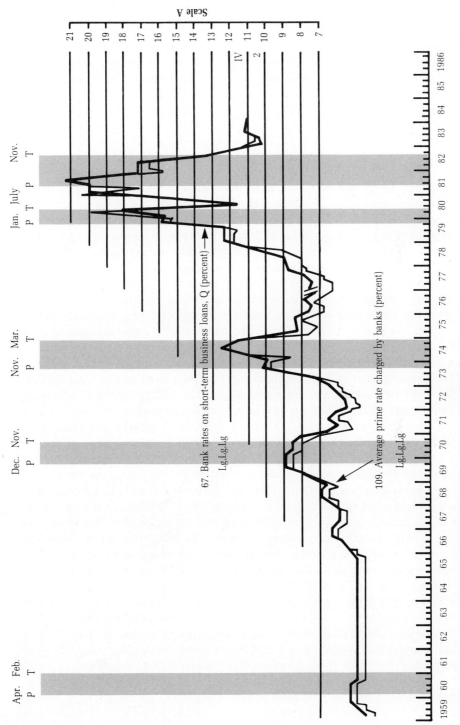

FIGURE 14.6 Interest Rates, 1956–1983. (*Business Conditions Digest,* March 1981.)

sense the "tight" money years were 1966, 1969, 1974, and 1980. Distinguishing the degree of tightness is a complicated business and the answer can vary depending on the market about which one is speaking. In any case one should probably look to the appropriate real rate as a guide to the degree of credit restraint in a particular market. If real estate prices are rising at a 22% annual rate and mortgage money is available at 12%, you may have historically high mortgage interest rates but you do not have tight money in the mortgage market.

Monetary Aggregates versus Interest Rates

Although as a business cycle analyst we have no problem using both the monetary aggregates *and* any and all interest rate measures in assessing whether monetary policy is stimulating or restraining the economy, we must note some practical advantages of interest rates over the monetary aggregates. Nominal interest rates have a clearcut definition, are available quickly, and are generally subject to revision only if someone made a clerical error. The monetary aggregates on the other hand are subject to changing definitions as well as being estimated early and frequently revised later. For example, what are bank reserves? That depends on law and regulations. Both are subject to change. All monetary aggregates are an attempt to measure what is happening to aggregate liquidity in the economy. As we have discussed, what constitutes a change in aggregate liquidity depends on technology, bank regulations, and the attitudes and habits of the public. In contrast, the Fed funds rate and the Treasury bill rate have quite precise and unchanging definitions. Members of the business community frequently observe that the level of interest rates is a direct, daily factor in individual transactions, while the monetary aggregates are macroeconomic abstractions.

The controversy regarding whether the monetary aggregates or interest rates are the better measure of monetary policy becomes confused with the related question of what constitutes an optimum monetary policy. The problem of what monetary policy would be "best" for the economy involves a multitude of considerations, which we will not examine in this book. We can briefly sketch the argument, however, by returning to our statement made at the beginning of the chapter that monetary aggregates measure the quantity of credit (liquidity) made available while interest rates measure the cost of it. The monetarists or neoclassical economists believe that the economy would best be served by stabilizing the rate of growth in some monetary aggregate — a measure of quantity. So-called Keynesians, and to a large extent the business community, appear to believe that the best monetary policy would be one that either stabilizes interest rates (the cost of credit) or causes them to move in a countercyclical fashion.

The question of what monetary policy would make the greatest contribution to achieving our goal of noninflationary full employment would be fairly simple if we understood completely all the lags and linkages in the monetary system *and* knew the source of the cyclical instability in the system. If the source of all the instability were from shifts in the supply and demand for goods $(I - S)$, then stabilizing some measure of the money supply would be optimum. On the other hand, if the source of instability in the economy is shocks from disturbances in the money and capital markets, $(L - B)$ and $(H - M)$, then stabilizing the price of securities by stabilizing interest rates is best. Let us see why this is so by considering the appropriate policy response to a sudden surge in the demand for credit and a resulting tendency for interest rates to rise. Suppose the demand for credit and upward pressure on interest rates resulted from businesspeople and consumers suddenly wanting to increase their spending for goods, $(B > L)$, because $(I > S)$. In this case, the economy is about to have an inflationary problem. The increase in interest rates is serving a stabilizing function in restraining investment and other expenditures. Any increase in the money supply to bring down interest rates would be destabilizing. It would just make the inflationary pressure worse. In this case the goal of stabilizing the money supply would help stabilize the economy even if it drove interest rates higher.

On the other hand, suppose that the initial destabilizing shock came from an increase in the demand for liquidity, not goods: $(B > L)$ because $(H > \Delta M)$. The demand for cash balances suddenly increases. The rise in interest rates will discourage investment and the economy may go into a recession, $(S > I)$. In this case it is obvious that the interest rate should be stabilized. If people want liquidity, give them liquidity. Otherwise demand for money will result in an excess supply of goods, output will fall, and unemployment will rise.

As we said at the outset, since the monetarists believe the demand for money (liquidity) is very stable and economic instability originates in fluctuating demand for goods, they argue for stabilization of the monetary aggregates. On the other hand, the Keynesians, or those who think economic instability emanates from changes in the demand for liquidity, recommend stabilizing interest rates. Certainly each group can point to historical incidents confirming its position. Since each business cycle is unique, an eclectic approach to the problem is undoubtedly best. Why ignore any indicator? Watch them all and try to determine the source of the cyclical instability while trying to remedy or cope with it.

● Questions for Discussion

1. Discuss the change in the composition of the public's holdings of the most liquid types of assets during the last fifteen years. How much was this due to changing public preferences, changing institutional structure, government regulation, and rising interest rates?

2. Discuss the cyclical behavior of the $M2$ money multiplier (ratio of $M2$ to the monetary base) in terms of the Keynesian monetary theory discussed in Chapter 4.

3. Explain the statement that "The strong positive trend in $M1$ velocity is consistent with the strong negative trend in the $M1$ money multiplier."

4. Why does the text conclude that $M1$ is a better measure of monetary policy than is $M2$?

5. Why does Milton Friedman conclude that "Interest rates are . . . a misleading indicator of whether monetary policy is 'tight' or 'easy' "?

6. What is the "real rate of interest," ex ante and ex post? Why do you think most ex post real interest rates were negative in 1975?

7. Comment on the following lament:

   It is too bad that the U.S. government is faced with the two unhappy alternatives of either borrowing the money and running up interest rates, or printing the money and creating inflation.

8. Discuss what connection, if any, you think there is between the rate of growth in the money supply and the rate of inflation.

● Exercise

1. If GNP increases by 9½% for a year in which prices and $M1$ increase by 6% while $M2$ increases by 9%, what are the approximate rates of change in real GNP, and the velocities of $M1$ and $M2$?

● Source Notes

[1]For example, see: "Selecting a Monetary Indicator: A Test of the New Monetary Aggregates" in the Federal Reserve Bank of *St. Louis Review*, February 1981. Footnote 19 in that study reports the results of a more complex regression analysis and concludes, "This evidence further supports the choice of $M1B$ as the most likely monetary indicator from the aggregates examined."

[2]The role of monetary policy. *American Economic Review*, Vol. 58, March 1968, p. 4.

[3]*Ibid.*

● Selected Additional Readings

Davis, Richard G. Monetary objectives and monetary policy. *Quarterly Review* of the Federal Reserve Bank of New York (Spring 1977).

Friedman, Milton. The role of monetary policy. *American Economic Review*, Vol. 58, No. 1 (March 1968).

Gilbert, R. Alton. Will the removal of regulation Q raise mortgage rates? *Review* of the Federal Reserve Bank of St. Louis, Vol. 63, No. 10 (December 1981).

Gordon, Robert J. *Macroeconomics.* (2nd ed.) Boston: Little, Brown, 1981. Chapter 16.

Gramley, Lyle E. Guidelines for monetary policy — The case against simple rules. In Ronald L. Teigen, ed. *Readings in Money, National Income and Stabilization Policy,* Homewood, Ill.: Richard D. Irwin, 1978.

Hamburger, Michael J. The lag in the effect of monetary policy: A survey of recent literature. *Monetary Aggregates and Monetary Policy.* Washington, D.C.: Federal Reserve Bank of New York, 1974.

Kareken, John H. The Federal Reserve's Modus Operandi. *Controlling Monetary Aggregates.* Boston: Federal Reserve Bank of Boston, 1969.

Mayer, Thomas. Some reflections on the current state of the monetarist debate. In Ronald L. Teigen, ed. *Readings in Money, National Income, and Stabilization Policy.* Homewood, Ill.: Richard D. Irwin, 1978.

Poole, William. Rules-of-thumb for guiding monetary policy. *Open Market Policies and Operating Procedures — Staff Studies.* Washington, D.C.: Board of Governors of the Federal Reserve System, 1971.

—————. Interpreting the Fed's monetary targets. *Brookings Papers on Economic Activity,* No. 1, 1976. Washington, D.C.: Brookings Institution, 1976.

Teigen, Ronald L. A critical look at monetarist economics. *Review* of the Federal Reserve Bank of St. Louis (January 1972).

Economic Fluctuations in the United States, 1918–1948

15

In this chapter we trace the course of the business cycle in the U.S. economy from immediately after World War I to immediately after World War II. The degree of numerical detail in this chapter will be considerably less than in the next chapter in which we look at the more recent cycles. This is partly because much of the relevant data were simply not recorded prior to World War II and we must work with somewhat soft estimates. In addition, the structure of the U.S. economy has changed so much in the last fifty years as to severely limit the relevance of much of this historical experience. Certainly we have already observed that the magnitudes and character of monetary and fiscal policy have changed dramatically in the last thirty years. As a result we will reserve our detailed, year-by-year examination of the business cycle for the next chapter in which we examine the post–World War II period, 1948–1983.

The 1920s — Schumpeterian Fluctuations and Prosperity

The boom that accompanied World War I lasted three years and eight months. The NBER reference cycle shows a trough in December 1914, and a peak in August 1918. Although the United States did not formally enter the war until April 1917, the impact on the economy was felt long before because we sold goods to our allies. We also provided the necessary financing for this export boom. As is common to all major international conflicts, the world commodity markets were a bit disorganized but experienced substantial inflation of prices. Wholesale prices in the United States went up at an average annual rate of 20% during the period. Farmers and speculators prospered.

When the war ended in November 1918, the economy was already in a mild recession that had begun in August as the economy began converting from wartime to peacetime activities. According to NBER dating the following were the cyclical fluctuations over the eleven-year period from August 1918 to August 1929:

A 7-month *recession* ending March 1919.

A 10-month *expansion* ending January 1920.

An 18-month *recession* ending July 1921.

A 22-month *expansion* ending May 1923.

A 14-month *recession* ending July 1924.

A 27-month *expansion* ending October 1926.

A 13-month *recession* ending November 1927.

A 21-month *expansion* ending August 1929.

The four recessions during this time period averaged 13 months each, while the four expansions averaged 20 months each. In other words, during this eleven-year period the economy was in recession about 40% of the time and in recovery and boom about 60% of the time. Although by today's standards this record would be regarded as highly cyclical, in historical context "good times" outweighing "hard times" by 1.5 to 1.0 was regarded as close to perpetual prosperity.

The 7-month recession in 1919 was no more than a pause, but the recovery was also short, only 10 months. The recession of 1920–1921 was the longest and severest of this time period. In some ways it was the *real* post–World War I recession. The wartime export boom really ended, the federal government stopped running deficits and even ran a surplus. The Federal Reserve increased the discount rate. Although national income accounts as we know them today were not compiled at that time, the magnitude of the recession is indicated by the fact that industrial production is estimated to have declined by 25%, while wholesale prices are estimated to have dropped by 64% in the last four months of 1920.[1]

Although the recession was officially over in July 1921, the economy really did not get moving again until 1922 and then generated almost pure prosperity until mid-1929. There were the two short recessions of 1923–1924 and 1926–1927, but from July 1921 to August 1929, the economy experienced 70 months of recovery and boom and only 27 months of recession — a 2.6 to 1.0 ratio. The two questions of acute interest to the business cycle analyst are (1) what made the "roaring twenties" roar? and (2) what brought them to an end?

A large part of the driving force in the U.S. economy in the 1920s was apparently long-term investment arising from a whole series of Schumpeterian innovations: the automobile and all its support industries; the telephone, developing from an oddity to a necessity; the radio, another new necessity; urban and rural electrification that opened a whole host of new economic opportunities. All these were true Schumpeterian innovations in the sense that entrepreneurs earned large profits, largely reinvested in the business, from products that were spectacularly successful in the marketplace. The innovations of the 1920s were not restricted to new products. Innovations in manufacturing, such as the introduction of the assembly line, were enough to cause an almost continuous rise in labor productivity. Wages rose less than productivity so the labor cost per unit of output declined throughout this time period. This, of course, worked wonders on corporate profits.

The prosperity from 1921 to 1929 was solidly based on rising real output. The rise in corporate profits was genuine and thus a rise in the level of stock market prices was justified. There was a steady expansion of bank credit but, until the very last, credit expansion was not so great as to fuel a speculative boom. There was no great amount of real estate or commodity speculation on a national scale. (Florida real estate did have its own credit bubble and collapse in the mid-twenties.) World commodity markets collapsed in 1925, and domestic commodity prices were so stable thereafter that one could say that this country's agricultural sector really did not share in the boom of the latter 1920s.

Of course, all this came to an end in 1929. Why? Given that the prosperity of the 1920s was based on solid gains in real output, not on some sort of speculative bubble, why did it all collapse so dramatically in 1929? In particular, why the famous stock market crash of 1929? Although there is much we do not know about the beginning of the depression of the 1930s and a great deal we do not understand about what we do know, the stock market collapse was the result of a speculative binge that had to end dramatically. We noted above that the stock market's rise from 1922 onward could be justified by gains in real corporate profits. That was true until about June 1928, at which point pure speculation set in. From June 1928, to September 1929, a period of just 15 months, the market went up by more than it had in the previous four years! People simply caught the speculative fever and banks and stockbrokers enabled them to indulge it. The banks provided the monetary fuel to keep the speculative machine running. They made loans to stockbrokers and the brokers made loans to their customers. Federal Reserve statistics indicate the member bank loans to brokers went from $3.2 billion at the end of March 1927 to $8.5 billion by the end of September 1929 — an increase of 66%, or an annual growth rate of 48%. If you wanted to "play the market" you placed your 5¢ on the dollar and borrowed 95¢ from the broker. If the stock went up by 1%, you made 20% on your money. A 5% rise doubled your money. With the rate at which the banks were making loans to brokers there was plenty of purchasing power for me to buy a stock at $10, for you to buy it from me at $15, for me to buy it back from you at $20 to sell to you at $25, and so on. We are both delighted with the money we are making on the basis of this self-fulfilling prophecy. It is great fun as long as the process continues, but, of course, at some point I may decide I want to take my winnings and walk away. I do not want to play anymore. This leaves you with something of a problem. Keynes appropriately compared the purely speculative era of the U.S. stock market to a game of musical chairs (make sure *you* don't get caught when the music stops).

The Federal Reserve officials quite properly took a very dim view of the rampant speculation in the stock market in 1928–1929. They set out to stop it and succeeded with a vengeance. Although the discount rate had not been above 4% since mid-1924, beginning in January 1928, the New York Federal Reserve Bank rate went up in a quick series of increases from 3.5% to 6% by August 1929. Although open market operations was not the formalized tool of monetary policy it is today, the Federal Reserve had discovered its impact and moved from being a substantial net buyer of government securities in 1927 to a substantial net seller in 1928. In short, the Fed went for progressively stronger tight money in 1928–1929.

The tight money of 1928–1929 did eventually collapse the stock market as we will discuss below, but it also had other effects as well. Apparently, the economy had begun to slow down in 1928 anyway, and the tight money turned slow decline into a precipitous collapse. As usual, residential construction peaked first (early 1928), new orders for durable goods began falling in early 1929, and industrial production peaked in August 1929. As we indicated above, according to NBER dating, the recession began in August, 1929 — but the stock market roared on until late October.[2]

The 1930s — Massive Disequilibrium, Underemployment

The Great Depression of the 1930s made such an indelible impression on the players in the economic game that one cannot begin to understand their later behavior in any other context. A whole generation of businesspeople, economists, and politicians with active memories of this event had, in effect, a "depression psychosis" that guided their behavior throughout the 1940s, 1950s, and even to some extent into the 1960s.

The magnitude of the depression eventually exceeded anything experienced before or since. The lowest level of unemployment in the eight-year period 1931 to 1939 was 14.3% in the relative boom of 1937. In 1933 unemployment reached 25% of the labor force, up from 3.2% in the prosperity of early 1929. Consider a world in which what is perceived to be a brief decline, as in the 1920s, continues with increasing ferocity for three years and seven months. The country had experienced four recessions since World War I, the shortest of which was 7 months and the longest of which was 18 months. But this turned out to be a 43-month decline. Ten years after the depression had begun the unemployment rate was still close to 17%. The depression was not only deep, it was long.

It is estimated that there was a 45% decline in current dollar GNP and a 30% decline in real GNP from peak to trough. Farm prices were not high to start with and they then fell 50%. Wholesale prices fell by 32%. Retail prices even fell by 20%. The value of anything denominated in money rose as prices declined but, conversely, debt became that much heavier. The value of real assets and paper assets secured by real assets declined precipitously. If you had an $80,000 loan at the bank on your factory worth $100,000 in 1929, when the value dropped to $50,000 in 1932 the bank did not really care to renew the loan, especially since your sales had dropped by 50%. Of course, from your point of view you should just as well let them have the factory. It was worth less than the debt. The rising value of money resulting from the generalized decline in prices created chaos in the financial markets.

As mentioned above, the general belief when the downturn started in 1929 was that it would be over quickly as the recessions of the 1920s had been. Wages rates and retail sales held up throughout most of 1930 in anticipation of a quick turnaround. But instead the economy did not even hit bottom (much less begin to recover) until March 1933. Why? What made the Great Depression "Great"? It is to some extent generally agreed that the more significant, identifiable, contributing factors were simply bad luck, a financial structure vulnerable to collapse under strain, and unwise monetary and fiscal policies.

The bad luck classification covers the juxtaposition of a couple of more or less independent cycles with the general business cycle — agriculture and construction. As we indicated above, agriculture really did not recover from the 1923–1924 recession and at that time more than 20% of the population was still on the land. Wholesale prices peaked in 1926 and declined thereafter. Then, thoughtful Providence gave us an extended drought, which resulted in the dustbowl of the 1930s. There is no necessary connection between the stock market crash and a series of lean agricultural years, but they came together to depress a lot of people in the United States in the 1930s.

The construction cycle is perhaps somewhat less exogenous to the rest of the economy than is agriculture, but we seem to have mild recessions when construction spending holds up and severe recessions when it falters. For example, in constant dollar terms construction spending did fall in the rather severe recession of 1920–1921 but on an annual basis it fell not at all in the relatively mild recession of 1923–1924. However, construction peaked in 1926 after a five-year boom and was apparently already in a long-term decline before 1930. Why? Perhaps the Schumpeterian innovations requiring construction investment simply ran out?

The financial structure subject to collapse has already been alluded to in reference to the speculative boom in the stock market. Although the collapse of the stock market generated many financial tragedies for individuals and corporations, it is generally not felt to have been the cause of the magnitude and duration of the depression. The collapse of the banking system seems to have been a more important contributing factor.

The collapse of the monetary system must be discussed in the context of monetary policy. We have already mentioned the tight money of 1928–1929. After the collapse of the stock market, the Federal Reserve did move fairly vigorously toward easy money. The New York Federal Reserve Bank's discount rate fell from 6% in 1929 to 1.5% by May of 1931. The Fed did purchase government securities, but a more significant source of bank reserves in the 1930–1931 period was a heavy gold inflow. The depression was worldwide and as the banking systems of Europe collapsed there was a run into the dollar. People converted foreign currencies to gold and then sold the gold to the U.S. government for dollars. The gold purchases of the government expanded the monetary base from 1930 to 1931 after it had shrunk from 1929 to 1930.

In late 1931 all this changed. A gold outflow hit the United States. At that time currency (Federal Reserve notes) had to be backed by gold holdings of the Fed. (This was changed in 1932.) This put the Fed in the position of trying to raise domestic interest rates so that foreigners would want to hold dollar time deposits rather than gold. The Fed needed the gold because it was just at this time that U.S. citizens began not to trust the banks to be able to redeem deposits in currency. The outflow of currency from the banking system also reduced the availability of bank reserves.

A critical element in the collapse of the U.S. banking system was that at this time there was no federal insurance of bank deposits. When a bank closed because it could not meet the demands of its depositors for cash, it just left the depositors as general creditors. In other words, as a depositor in a bank that closed, you just lost your money! Our banking system had built into it the old problem of the gold standard. Depositors did not ordinarily all want cash at the same time. However, any chance that a bank could not meet demands for cash withdrawals set off an immediate demand by all depositors for their money — a "run" on the bank. And, of course, no bank could meet the demands by *all* depositors for cash, at least not without massive help from the Federal Reserve System. Such help was simply not provided, for reasons we will not detail here. Obviously, what should have been done was massive lending to the banking system via the discount window with the banks given the proceeds of such loans in cash to meet depositors' requests for currency. The Bureau of Printing and Engraving might have had to run the printing presses overtime, but as we know from the old gold standard, as soon as people became convinced that they could get currency for their bank deposits anytime they wanted it, they would no longer want it.

Early in 1932 the Fed did finally shift from what had been essentially a tight money policy resulting from the gold outflow to a fairly aggressive easy money policy. The discount rate for the New York Federal Reserve Bank went to 2.5% while most of the others went to 3.5%. The Federal Reserve Banks collectively bought enough U.S. government securities to create substantial excess reserves in the system. But it was too late to avoid disaster.

By 1932 most banks technically had no net worth. With price declines of 30 to 50%, their loan losses (whether taken or hidden in the books) were large enough to wipe them out. In such circumstances depositors wanted their money for more than purely technical liquidity reasons. The bank runs started in Detroit, spread throughout the Midwest, and eventually throughout the entire nation. In fact, there is no doubt that every financial institution in the country (commercial bank, savings bank, or savings and loan) would have had to close its doors in default if it had not been for arbitrary "bank holidays," first imposed by individual state governments. By March 4, 1933, every state in the Union had declared a bank holiday and, upon inauguration as president on March 6, Franklin Roosevelt made it a nationwide federal banking holiday.

After the federal banking holiday was declared in March 1933, the Federal Reserve was primarily out of the picture in the process of the rehabilitation of the banking system. A consortium of various agencies in the executive branch conducted an examination of each bank and reopened them one at a time with the seal of approval of the U.S. government. The approval carried with it the weight of the Federal Deposit Insurance Corporation, the FDIC. If the bank ever closed again, an agency of the federal government stood ready to give the depositors their money. The FDIC was one of the many depression-born federal government agencies. Another was the Reconstruction Finance Corporation, which made direct low-interest loans to banks requiring assistance. Some banks never reopened, but most did and, of course, as confidence was restored by early 1934 the currency was pouring back into the banking system.

The runs on the banks and the problems created thereby indicate that part of the cyclical instability of the U.S. banking system was the inability or unwillingness of the Fed to make unlimited amounts of currency available to the banks and the risk of total loss to depositors if a bank closed. With the creation of the Federal Deposit Insurance Corporation, that particular problem was fairly well solved.

Another weakness inherent in the U.S. monetary system remains with us to this day. The economy is dependent on the monetization of private debt. In the depression, as nominal GNP shrank, bank credit and the money supply shrank commensurately. Between 1929 and 1932 loans by commercial banks declined by approximately 40%. Every loan paid off or defaulted on decreased the money supply accordingly. One can see why the monetarists think that monetary policy should be guided by rates of growth in the monetary aggregates and not the level of interest rates. Interest rates did decline. For example, the commercial bank prime loan rate fell from 6% in 1929 to 1.5% in 1934. On that basis the Federal Reserve authorities of that day could say that monetary policy was stimulative throughout the time period. The decline in interest rates notwithstanding, the vast majority of economists today believe the performance of the Federal Reserve Board of Governors for the period 1928–1933 was abysmal.

In seeking something for which to commend the Federal Reserve, one can say that in terms of the historical reason for the creation of the Fed, avoidance of a money panic, they were successful. We managed to collapse the entire banking system and have the economy slide into deep depression without a good old-fashioned money panic. Throughout this time period, except for the bank holiday, if you had good collateral you could always borrow money — and at ever lower rates.

After 1933 monetary policy was pretty much irrelevant until after World War II. The federal government ran very large deficits that increased the monetary base to such an extent that the banking system was loaded with excess reserves from 1933 on. The monetary base more than doubled from 1933 to 1939. The money supply did not increase proportionately but did rise substantially with $M1$ estimated to have risen by 73%. Aggregate spending as measured by GNP rose by only 63%. Velocity went into a long-term decline beginning in 1933. The experience of this time period is the basis for many people's rejection of monetary policy as a stabilization tool because "you can't push on a string."

Fiscal policy does not come off much better than monetary policy over this time period and gets even worse marks later, in 1936–1937. The collapse of the economy in 1930–1933 generated involuntary federal government deficits, which were regarded as part of the problem. Prosperity could only be restored by getting rid of them. Franklin Roosevelt was elected on a Democratic platform that vowed to balance the federal government's budget. That plank was in every party platform, Democratic and Republican, throughout the 1930s. Roosevelt was not successful in balancing the budget but it is worth noting that in 1937 when the economy had come back to the point where GNP was within 13% of its 1929 level, the federal government's tax collections were 84% above the 1929 level!

Of course the political pressures for relief were sufficiently strong that the federal government's expenditures rose even more rapidly than its tax collections and the deficit rose accordingly. But, as with monetary policy, there really was not significant fiscal policy stimulus until after 1933. Economists still argue about whether the deficits were too little but most agree they were too late. The net deficit including the new Social Security program more than doubled from 1933 to 1934 from $1.3 billion to $2.9 billion. The deficit fell slightly in 1935 to $2.5 billion, and rose quite substantially in 1936 to $3.5 billion.

The NBER reference dates show a trough in March 1933 and a peak in May 1937. It was a long (4 years and 2 months) but weak recovery. As noted previously, GNP in 1937 was still slightly below the 1929 level but with the growth in the labor force over eight years there was still substantial unemployment. Real consumption in 1937 was about 5% above 1929 while gross investment was still about 10% below. Construction was a mere 47% of its 1929 level! The economy was essentially providing for the current consumption needs of the people. No one would have characterized the economic recovery from 1933 to 1937 as a boom. It appeared more like bouncing along the "floor" in Hicks's *Trade Cycle* — minimum autonomous expenditures times the multiplier with no accelerator operative.

However, the prosperity of 1937, such as it was, collapsed abruptly. It collapsed with a substantial downturn in the economy. Industrial production fell by 30% in the eight months from September 1937, to May 1938. Did some of the autonomous expenditures supporting the floor in a Hicksian model stop? Apparently so. The precipitating cause of the 1937 downturn appears to have been fiscal policy with perhaps a little help from monetary policy. The federal deficit in 1936 was $3.5 billion. In 1937 it fell to a mere $0.2 billion. What happened was that a large World War I veterans' bonus was paid in 1936 and, of course, not repeated in 1937. Also, the excess of collections over payments in the Social Security System jumped from $0.3 billion to $1.4 billion.

The Federal Reserve also did a couple of things that ordinarily would be interpreted as being very restrictive. In August 1936, reserve requirements were increased by 50% and in March through May 1937 raised by another 33.33%, thereby doubling reserve requirements during this time period. As we have noted before, the banking system had such a supply of excess reserves at this point in time that the change was pretty much irrelevant. Also, in December 1936, the Fed began to offset gold purchases with the sale of government securities in order that such purchases not increase the monetary base. Nevertheless the monetary base increased by 10% from 1936 to 1937.

Although the decline of 1937 was sharp, it was at least short. NBER reference dating puts the peak at May 1937 and the trough at June 1938, a 13-month decline. In 1938–1939 fiscal policy really became expansionary in anticipation of World War II. The deficit rose to $2 billion in 1938 and to $2.2 billion in 1939. The monetary base rose by 10% in 1938 and by 21% in 1939. The stage was set for the long expansionary period encompassing World War II. There would not be another recession for six years and eight months.

World War II — Massive Disequilibrium, Excess Demand

The central economic problem of a wartime economy is excess demand. If one thinks of our original circular flow diagram in Chapter 3, the problem is readily apparent. The government spends massive amounts of money for the production of war material. Government expenditures in the United

States were, by 1944, larger than GNP was in 1939. The production of war goods creates a commensurate amount of personal income, but it makes no consumer goods available. The goods are shipped overseas and blown up. Aggregate demand is increased spectacularly, while the aggregate supply of civilian goods is severely restricted. Hence, excess demand is *the* problem of a wartime economy.

However, if one must go into a wartime economy, coming out of deep depression is probably as good a time to do it as any. There are both real economic and psychological opportunities to be exploited. The first virtue of a depression for conversion to a wartime economy is the tremendous amount of unemployed resources, primarily labor. They do not have to be shifted from civilian to military production. They merely have to be removed from the ranks of the unemployed, a much less inflationary shift. As a result, the elasticity of real output with respect to aggregate demand, $\%\Delta Q/\%\Delta Y$, is quite high. When government expenditures put the previously unemployed to work, demand does indeed create its own supply. The elasticity of real output with respect to aggregate demand surprised everyone in World War II. On average, real output increased by 9.8% compounded annually from 1939 to 1944 for a total increase of 60%! The country was able to overwhelm its enemies with a massive outpouring of military goods with no net reduction in consumer goods. In fact, depending on definition, one can make a strong case that the aggregate availability of consumption goods rose during World War II. The vast majority of the population was better off economically in World War II than they were during the depression. Such measures as per capita meat consumption rose significantly. Many a farm boy was better housed, fed, and clothed in the army during the war than he had been on the farm during the depression.

The other dimension in which the wartime economy benefited from the depression was in consumers' attitudes and their resulting behavior. Having just been through a long deflationary period, the last thing consumers feared was inflation. Recall our discussion of the location of the Phillips curve in terms of inflationary expectations. In 1939 the opportunity was wide open for a substantial increase in output and employment with a relatively small amount of inflation.

The experience of World War II pulling the U.S. economy forcefully out of the Great Depression convinced millions of citizens and no small number of economists that government expenditures were a good thing. Such expenditures created a demand for goods that otherwise would not have been produced. That is true if you have 17% unemployment and a population recently conditioned by a depression in which prices *fell* year after year. In a near full employment economy with strong inflationary expectations, an increase in aggregate demand resulting from an increase in government expenditures will generate little additional real output and employment. Unless an increase in government expenditures is matched by a decrease in private demand, more inflation is likely to be the result. Of course, a reduction in private demand calls for increased taxes and/or higher interest rates. At the beginning of World War II the choices were attractive in the sense that more government expenditures could create more goods and little inflation.

Although things were about as favorable as they could be for an expansion of aggregate demand via fiscal policy, the massive growth of government expenditures did eventually generate strong inflationary effects. The magnitude of the fiscal policy impact can be seen from the fact that demand for output from the economy by all levels of government rose from $13.3 billion in 1939 to $98.6 billion in 1945 — over a sevenfold increase. The multiplier effect of the increase in government expenditures then created a strong consumer demand for everything from housing to nylon stockings.

The degree of inflation was, of course, partly a function of how the government financed the wartime deficits. Taking federal government expenditures from mid-1939 to June 1946 as our time period, we find the expenditures were financed about 45% by taxes, 28% by borrowing from the public, and 27% via money creation. In other words taxes paid 45¢ on the dollar of government expenditures so that a deficit of 55¢ resulted. About 12¢ on the dollar was financed by the sale of securities to the Fed and other government agencies, 15¢ per dollar of deficit was covered by the sale of securities to commercial banks, and 28¢ represented borrowing from the nonbank public. Given the massive excess reserves available to the commercial banks, their purchase of federal government debt meant that it was monetized.

To run a disequilibrium system of this type, national policy was as follows: (1) raise taxes to the point that they start having severe disincentive effects (people stop showing up for work); (2) convince the public to save and buy government debt so as not to increase the demand for consumer goods (War Bond drives); and (3) finance whatever additional expenditures are required with the printing press. The printing press, of course, is just ordering the Federal Reserve and commercial banks to buy all the Treasury securities that the public will not buy.

Although in general the financing of World War II is considered to have been an impressive performance, there is one debatable issue. The government refused to use high interest rates as a tool to fight inflationary pressures. Interest rates were simply not allowed to rise. They were pegged at their depression level. Treasury Bills were pegged at 0.38% and long-term government bonds at 2.5%. The Federal Reserve was committed to buying without limit U.S. Treasury securities at prices high enough to keep yields down to the agreed on levels. The commercial bank prime rate naturally stayed at the 1.5% level where it had been since 1934. The rationale for the pegging of interest rates was the desire to attain the twin goals of ensuring that no one suffered a capital loss on Treasury securities and that the budget cost of the national debt was kept low.

Given the public's recent experience with extended deflation (rising value of money) in the depression, they were generally happy to accumulate dollar denominated liquid assets. For many people, to see a dollar of "cash money" in the depression was a unique event; to have $2,000 in war bonds or in a savings account was a comfort indeed. As a result, consumption expenditures *in relation to income* were abnormally low during the war years.

There were, of course, direct wage and price controls with the concomitant requirement for rationing. Although there were illegal "black-market" transactions, the system held up quite well on a mostly voluntary basis. After all, the survival of Western civilization was at stake and your neighbor and you had just sent your sons off, perhaps to die. Patriotism can influence consumer behavior. In purely economic terms it was widely believed that the dollars not spent for rationed goods during the war would become more valuable after the war when the depression returned.

In summary, World War II took this country out of the depression. We surprised ourselves and the rest of the world with the vast productive capacity of the economy. We gained the (perhaps sinful) knowledge that massive federal government intervention in economic affairs does not bring collapse and could even be beneficial.

1945–1948, Reconversion and — "Surprise! No Depression"

Reconversion was a contemporary word of the 1940s referring to switching production from military goods back to civilian goods. It was widely thought to pose some intractable economic problems. The consensus forecast at the time was that a severe cutback in government expenditures would create a substantial recession and very possibly a renewal of the depression. There was indeed a substantial cutback in the government component of aggregate demand. Total government purchases of goods and services reached a peak in the first quarter of 1945 and dropped like a rock over the next year and a half. By the fourth quarter of 1946 government demand for goods and services had declined by 70%, from an annual rate of about $100 billion to $30 billion.

However, instead of a prolonged recession or depression resulting from the massive cutback in government expenditures there was a sharp, but short, recession in 1945. The NBER reference dates put the decline at eight months — from February to October 1945. As we noted above, the severe cutback in government expenditures ran through the fourth quarter of 1946, but, after a sharp 10% drop in GNP in 1945, aggregate demand and all its nongovernment components turned around and started rising early in 1946. Consumer expenditures largely replaced the decreased government demand. Most economists underestimated the influence of all those liquid assets the consumers had built up during the war. The consumers were willing and able to spend. In the eighteen-month period referred to above during which government demand for goods and services dropped by $70 billion, consumer expenditures increased at an annual rate of 20% for an increase of $37 billion. Business investment was also strong. Reconversion of plants from wartime to peacetime production required expenditures on new tooling and construction. Gross private domestic investment rose from under an annual rate of $8 billion in the first quarter of 1945 to over $30 billion in the fourth quarter of 1946.

Other factors besides consumers' eagerness and money helped to mitigate the immediate postwar recession. The end of the war was well anticipated, with substantial time between the German and Japanese surrenders. Business had time to plan reconversion activities. In addition, the employment scene was helped by a voluntary and welcome reduction in the work week. Eventually the labor force participation rate dropped as females and very old and very young males dropped out.

After the trough of the recession in October 1945, there was a three-year boom running until November 1948. Over this period there was substantial inflation. Wage and price controls had been ended promptly at the end of the war. Wholesale prices rose by about 60%, and retail prices rose by 35% from the beginning of 1946 to mid-1948. In general, the 1946–1948 period was a broadly based boom propelled by well-financed consumer demand. Private investment in both business fixed equipment and residential construction rose rapidly in response to that demand.

Although there was dissatisfaction with double-digit rates of inflation, and some sense of indignation at the windfall profits accruing to speculators when the price controls were removed abruptly, the period was generally met with a tremendous sigh of relief that the depression had not returned. There were still many vivid memories of the depression and many people felt it would inevitably return before long. They planned their lives and businesses accordingly and demanded that the government go on record with a commitment to intervene. Hence, Congress enacted the Employment Act of 1946, Section 2 of which contains the commitment that "It is the continuing policy and responsibility of the Federal Government to use all practicable means . . . to promote maximum employment, production and purchasing power." Although the legislation really does not *require* the federal government to take any specific action it does embody the intellectual legacy of the depression and World War II that the federal government can and should work actively to stabilize the economy at a high level of employment.

● Questions for Discussion

1. Choose some Schumpeterian innovation of the 1920s (the automobile, electric power, radio, and the telephone are all candidates) and discuss its impact on other industries.

2. Choose a Schumpeterian innovation of the 1970s or 1980s and discuss its implications for the diffusion of its economic growth. Did investors overshoot the mark and create excess capacity in this industry?

3. Comment on the contention that the depression of the 1930s was a direct result of the excesses of the 1920s.

4. Consider the contention that World War II was a cure for the Great Depression, and that having had the depression helped the U.S. economy to cope with the war.

5. Make a case for forecasting a return of the depression at the end of World War II. Why didn't it happen?

6. The average propensity to consume was, historically speaking, unusually low during World War II and unusually high immediately afterwards. Was this behavior by consumers stabilizing or destabilizing? Why do you think it happened?

● Source Notes

[1]The time series data referred to in this chapter are from various sources referenced at the end of the chapter. Given the frequency of revision and differences in definition, different sources will give slightly different figures for the time series mentioned. (About the only firm time series are interest rates.) However, none of the conclusions given here is altered by differences in data sources or subsequent revisions.

[2]There are so many excellent studies of the stock market crash, both scientific and journalistic, that we will skip the details here. It is a fascinating story in both human and economic terms. (See especially the *Galbraith* and *Allen* references given at the end of the chapter.) Also the relevance of more detail than given here for contemporary business cycle analysis would seem to be small.

● Selected Additional Readings

Allen, Frederick Lewis. *Only Yesterday*. New York: Harper & Brothers, 1931.

Bowsher, Norman N. Interest rates, 1914–1965. *Review* of the Federal Reserve Bank of St. Louis (October 1965). Reprint series number 15.

Brunner, Karl, ed. *The Great Depression Revisited*. Boston: Martinus Nijhoff Publishing, 1981.

Galbraith, John K. *The Great Crash of 1929*. Boston: Houghton Mifflin, 1961.

Gordon, Robert A. *Business Fluctuations.* (2d ed.) New York: Harper and Row, 1961. Chapter 14.

1930–1980, A phenomenal half-century. *Fortune* (February 11, 1980).

The past, how the crash and the depression changed the structure of business and the economy. *Businessweek* (September 3, 1979).

Temin, Peter. *Did Monetary Forces Cause the Great Depression.* New York: W. W. Norton, 1976.

Economic Fluctuations in the United States, 1948–1983

16

The 1950s — Three Recessions and Another War Boom

According to NBER reference cycle dates, the 1950s experienced:

An 11-month *recession* ending October 1949.

A 45-month *expansion* ending July 1953.

A 10-month *recession* ending May 1954.

A 39-month *expansion* ending August 1957.

An 8-month *recession* ending April 1958.

A 24-month *expansion* ending April 1960.

Only 29 months of recession out of a total of 137 months is not a bad record. The economy was expanding 79% of the time and in recession only 21% of the time. A ratio of 3.7 to 1.0 certainly beats the prewar experience, even including the 1920s. Of course, we did have those three recessions but for the period as a whole real output grew at an average annual rate of 3.5%. Inflation was no great problem with the consumer price index up at an average annual rate of only 1.8% for the period. Consumers were obviously improving their standard of living with real growth in the rate of consumption expenditures at an average rate of 3.2% per year to finish the period 44% higher than at the beginning.

Still, the economy of the 1950s was far from smooth sailing. Table 16.1 documents the cyclical fluctuations for this time period. At this point we switch to quarterly dating for our analysis because beginning with 1948 we have a fairly consistent set of national income accounts with which to work. All the numerical analyses in this chapter are based on historical updatings of each of the time series as published in various issues of *Business Conditions Digest*.

The recession of 1948–1949 was the longest of the three recessions in the 1950s by NBER dating, but the mildest by many measures as can be seen from Table 16.1. For example, real output declined by only 1.4% as compared to 2.6% and 2.7% for the other two recessions. Part of the reason

TABLE 16.1 Changes in U.S. Economic Time Series Between NBER Reference Dates, IV48–II60*

	(−) IV48–IV49 (4 Qtrs.)	(+) IV49–III53 (15 Qtrs.)		(−) III53–II54 (3 Qtrs.)		(+) II54–III57 (13 Qtrs.)		(−) III57–II58 (3 Qtrs.)		(+) II58–II60 (8 Qtrs.)	
	Total Change	Tot. Chg.	Ann. Rate	Tot. Chg.	Ann. Rate	Tot. Chg.	Ann. Rate	Tot. Chg.	Ann. Rate	Tot. Chg.	Ann. Rate
GNP, %Δ											
Current $	−3.4	+43.5	10.1	−1.7	−2.2	+24.0	6.9	−1.9	−2.6	+14.9	7.2
Price Deflated	−1.4	+27.2	6.6	−2.6	−3.5	+13.2	3.9	−2.7	−3.6	+10.2	5.0
CPI, %Δ	−2.2	+13.5	3.4	−0.1	−0.2	+5.3	1.6	+2.1	2.8	+2.3	1.1
$ Unemployment	+3.2	−4.3	−1.1	+3.1	4.1	−1.6	−0.5	+3.2	4.3	−2.2	−1.1
Consumption											
Total, %Δ											
Current $	+1.3	+28.0	6.8	+1.7	2.2	+20.7	6.0	+1.4	1.9	+13.6	6.6
Price Deflated	+2.3	+12.7	3.2	+0.7	1.0	+13.4	3.9	−0.1	−0.2	+9.5	4.6
Durable Goods, % Δ											
Current $	+15.0	+21.3	5.3	−2.2	−2.9	+23.0	6.6	−7.9	−10.9	+21.9	10.4
Price Deflated	+14.9	+10.9	2.8	−1.0	−1.3	15.9	4.7	−7.3	−9.6	+17.5	8.4
Investment											
Total Fixed, %Δ											
Current $	−7.7	+38.6	9.1	−0.8	−1.0	+29.4	8.2	−10.3	−13.6	+19.5	9.3
Price Deflated	−7.3	+19.5	4.9	−0.4	−0.5	+14.7	4.3	−9.5	−12.4	+17.0	8.2
Change in Inventories ($ in billions)	−$3.1	−$18.6	$5.0	−$2.4	−$3.2	+$12.6	$3.9	−$3.2	−$4.3	+$10.1	$5.0
Fed. Govt. Exp., %Δ	+6.2	85.0	17.8	−9.1	−12.0	+14.7	4.3	+10.0	13.6	+5.1	2.5
Deficit (−), % of GNP	−1.0%	+0.6%		−2.7%		+0.8%		−1.6%		−0.4%	
Money Supply, M1, % Δ	−0.7	+15.8	4.0	+0.6	0.8	+5.9	1.8	+0.4	0.6	+3.8	1.9
Treasury Bill Rate, Δ%	−0.07%	+0.95%		−1.21%		+2.57%		−2.36%		+2.07%	

*Recessions shown as minus (−): expansions as plus (+).

for the mildness of the 1948–1949 recession was, of course, the strong consumer demand. On both a current and price deflated basis consumption expenditures for durable goods continued to grow at the spectacular rate of approximately 15% during the recession. Unemployment did rise from 3.8% to 7%. This recession was the post-World War II recession that had been deferred when hostilities actually ceased in 1946. The immediate price increases resulting from postwar price decontrol had overshot their mark. As wartime shortages had disappeared inventory piled up and had to be liquidated. Note that the consumer price index actually fell by 2.2%.

Table 16.1 shows that the *level* of inventories was $3.1 billion lower in the fourth quarter of 1949 (IV49) than in the fourth quarter of 1948 (IV48), but what is not shown is that inventories were being accumulated at an annual *rate* of $4.3 billion in IV48 and liquidated at an annual rate of $5.3 billion in IV49 for a swing of $9.6 billion. Although the change in the rate of inventory accumulation was $9.6 billion, the fall in GNP was only a little over $8 billion. It was truly an inventory recession, but the liquidation was over quickly since consumer demand continued strong. Although the NBER dates the cycle at 11 months or 4 quarters, real GNP only declined for two quarters, the first and second quarters of 1949.

Probably more by accident than design, fiscal policy turned out to be stabilizing in the 1948–1949 recession. Congress reduced taxes in the spring of 1948 and authorized increased defense and foreign aid expenditures at the same time. Given that prices were falling, the 6% annual growth rate in federal government expenditures was significant, as was the deficit equal to 1% of GNP.

Discretionary monetary policy did not really exist at this time as the Fed was still committed to holding the price of Treasury securities at par. Actually interest rates fell slightly and the price of Treasury securities rose above par briefly. The money supply actually contracted slightly as a result of the decline in the demand for bank credit as inventories were liquidated. All things considered, the recession of 1948–1949 is probably the closest thing to a "textbook recession" of the period.

By mid-1950 the recovery from the recession was well underway when one of those clearly exogenous events occurred, the Korean War. Unlike the Vietnam War of the 1960s, the Korean War began with one discrete event. On June 24, 1950, a Russian client-state, North Korea, launched a full-scale invasion across the border of a U.S. client-state, South Korea. President Truman as Commander in Chief of the U.S. Armed Forces initially responded with limited intervention in the form of air support based in Japan. However, the United States quickly became committed to a major war effort on land, sea, and air through a series of events, the details of which are not relevant here.

We have to remember the psychological condition of the public at this time. When it was announced in June 1950 that the United States was, in fact, in a war, memories of World War II were only four years old. Wage and price controls with their necessary accompanying shortages and rationing were anticipated immediately. Consumers and business went on a six-month spending spree that drove the inflation rates to 15% for a short time period. Initially the inflationary impact came from the private sector in anticipation of federal government expenditures, but by 1951 defense expenditures were increasing dramatically and continued to do so until mid-1953.

The expansion of the early 1950s began as a typical recovery from the inventory recession of 1949 and then was propelled by a war-time boom. Note on Table 16.1 that while current dollar GNP increased by 43.5%, federal government expenditures were up by 85%. While GNP increased at an average annual rate of 10%, federal goverment expenditures rose at an average annual rate of close to 18%. The federal budget actually showed a slight surplus over the period as a result of an across-the-board tax increase in September 1950 and the impact of inflation on revenues. Although there was an initial burst of inflation, with controls much less pervasive than those of World War II the reported inflation rate was kept to 3.4% for the CPI and approximately 3% for the GNP price index.*

Of course, again as with World War II, wartime demand hit the economy at a time when it had some slack in it. By driving the unemployment rate from 7% to 2.7%, the increase in aggregate demand increased real output at an annual rate of 6.6% for a total increase of over 27%. A sustained growth rate that high has never been experienced since. As a result, the U.S. economy was able to provide men and material for the Korean War and simultaneously increase the supply of civilian goods to an even greater extent than in World War II. Price deflated expenditures for consumer goods rose at an annual rate of 3.2%.

---

*Regarding the rates of change in prices both given and implied by Tables 16.1, 16.2, and 16.5, we must remember all the technicalities we discussed in Chapter 9 regarding the index number problem in general and its relevance to the CPI in particular. These tables are designed to transmit the maximum amount of information with the fewest possible numbers. There is no built-in redundancy. The rate of change in the GNP price index can be computed from the rates of change in the current dollar and price deflated GNP; e.g., we know that during the first recession the GNP price index fell by approximately 2% because current $ GNP fell by 3.4% while price deflated GNP fell by only 1.4%. Similarly, a consumption goods price index (Paasche) can be computed from current dollar and price deflated consumption. For the first recession it fell by approximately 1% at an annual rate since current dollar consumption expenditures rose by 1.3% while price deflated consumption expenditures rose by 2.3%. The CPI (Laspeyres) is estimated to have fallen by 2.2%; a strange variation between the two perhaps but the market basket of goods purchased by consumers was changing very rapidly immediately after World War II. The relative position of the indexes is more in line with expectations for the recession of 1980 (Table 16.5). From that table we can read an annual rate of increase in the CPI of 11.4% and calculate implied inflation in the price of consumer goods and GNP at 9.6% and 9.8%, respectively.

In addition to the restrictive fiscal policy in the form of the tax increases mentioned above, the Korean War marked the return of discretionary monetary policy for the first time since the 1930s. In March 1951, the Federal Reserve and the Treasury reached an agreement, the "Accord." Under this agreement the Fed was required only to ensure that the market for Treasury securities had "depth, breadth, and resiliency," but was not required to support the price of these securities at par.

Prior to the Accord, as the demand for bank credit expanded, the banks merely sold some of the large amounts of Treasury securities acquired during World War II at par, effectively obtaining loanable funds at the cost of the low yields on Treasury securities. The Fed was obligated to buy all the securities the banks wanted to sell. After the Accord, the Fed was under no obligation to buy the securities at par, their prices could fall, interest rates could rise, and credit could become more expensive. During the Korean War the yield on 90-day Treasury Bills almost doubled from approximately 1% to just over 2%. Allowing an increase in $M1$ of only 4% per year, while current \$GNP increased at an annual rate of over 10%, was indeed the first meaningful use of tight money as a stabilization tool since 1929.

Just as the Korean War boom was an obvious wartime expansion, the timing of its termination was an equally clearcut example of a recession resulting from a rapid drop in government expenditures. As with its beginning, the end of the Korean War came as something of a surprise. Eisenhower had been elected president on a platform to end the war and that he did. When the war did end, the Eisenhower Administration cut defense expenditures drastically in mid-1953. From the second quarter of 1953 to the second quarter of 1954 expenditures by the federal government for goods and services actually fell by more than 20%. Of course, the decline in orders to defense contractors from the government came in the latter part of 1953 and began to slow the economy immediately.

The recession of 1953–1954 was sharp but brief by the historical standards of the time, 10 months by NBER dating. On a quarterly basis real GNP declined 3.2% from the second quarter of 1953 to the second quarter of 1954 while, as indicated on Table 16.1, it declined by 2.6% over the period of the reference cycle. The unemployment rate rose by over 3 percentage points, from 2.7% to 5.8%. The CPI went down fractionally while the GNP price index slowed its rise to around 1%. Inventories built up during the war had to be liquidated, but other investment expenditures hardly fell at all.

In the policy area, the money supply was virtually unchanged, at 0.6%, for the period. With nominal GNP falling at an annual rate of 2.2%, the Fed considered this to be aggressive easy money as evidenced by the rapid drop in interest rates to levels below where they had been when the Korean War boom had begun. Fiscal policy was largely involuntary and a tremendous surprise to the Eisenhower Administration. Through the effects of the level of economic activity on government revenues, a deficit of truly horrendous magnitude developed. As indicated on Table 16.1, the deficit was equal to 2.7% of GNP, a relative size not achieved for any recession again until 1980: The first Republican administration since Hoover's with an all-time record deficit for peacetime!

Voluntary or involuntary, fiscal policy undoubtedly did make a contribution to keeping the recession short. The wartime taxes came off in January 1954, just as the cutback in government expenditures had ended. Consumers then returned to buying durable goods in general and automobiles in particular. As Table 16.1 shows, while total consumption expenditures had continued to rise throughout the recession, durable goods expenditures had fallen off at an annual rate of about 3% in current dollar terms. This is apparently the point at which the post-World War II demand for consumer durable goods had finally been at least temporarily satisfied.

The recovery that began in the second quarter of 1954 went on to be a genuine private sector boom. Table 16.1 shows that, while total consumption expenditures rose at an annual rate of 3.9% in price deflated terms, durable goods expenditures rose by 4.7% per year. Fixed investment, both in housing and business plant and equipment, was also strong, rising more rapidly than GNP over this period — 8.2% versus 6.9% per year. Government expenditures rose less rapidly than GNP — 4.3% versus 6.9%. The unique feature of this boom was that it was propelled by autonomous private sector demand. The previous two expansions had been based on pent-up demand from World War II and the Korean War.

Both monetary and fiscal policy can be considered as restrictive in the 1954–1957 expansion, especially monetary policy. Through the automatic impact of the cycle on the budget, the federal government actually showed a slight surplus during this time period. The money supply increased considerably less rapidly than total expenditures as indicated by GNP — 1.8% per year versus 6.9%. Interest rates reached the highest levels since the 1920s with the Treasury Bill rate going over 3% briefly. The Federal Reserve discount rate was raised above 3%, and the Board of Governors revised the regulation covering the discount window to state explicitly that member bank borrowing was a "privilege, not a right."

During the 1954–1957 expansion a number of policy debates began, which are still going on. The first of these involved the possibility of a conflict between full employment and inflation, which we considered in some detail in Chapter 11. During this boom the unemployment rate never went below 4%, whereas in the 1953–1954 boom it had gone below 3%. During this time period, 4% unemployment had somehow become enshrined as "full employment." Inflation rates of the CPI and GNP index at 2 to 3% were considered high by historical standards.

This was also the time during which other debates involving monetary and fiscal policy began. Regarding fiscal policy, the term "fiscal drag" was coined during this period. With the federal budget actually recording a surplus equal to 0.8% of GNP over the 13 quarters of this expansion, it was felt to be a "drag" on continued prosperity and lower unemployment rates. The contention was that the structure of the tax mechanism was such that every time the economy moved toward the 4% "full employment" level, the federal government's budget moved toward such a large and deflationary surplus as to throw the economy into another recession. Of course, in this particular time period part of the reason for the federal government's surplus was the Federal Aid Highway Act of 1956. Effective in June 1956, a federal excise tax was levied on motor fuel, trucks, and tires sufficient to generate $2.5 billion per year for the purpose of building the interstate highway system.

The issues regarding monetary policy were in regard to both its effectiveness and its timing. It was demonstrated in late 1957 that high interest rates were at least effective in slowing down investment in residential construction. Their effectiveness in influencing other forms of investment seemed to be quite small, at least in the short run.

The problem with the timing of monetary policy that became apparent was with lags of two types: *outside* or *recognition lag,* and *inside* or *transmission lag.* The recognition lag is the time between when the economy reaches a turning point, say enters a recession, and the monetary authorities recognize what has happened and realize that a stimulative policy would be countercyclical. The transmission lag is the problem we discussed in Chapter 14 under the heading of "Lags and Linkages." Monetary policy actions taken today apparently do not have an impact on aggregate demand until some months or quarters later.

The problem of the recognition lag in monetary policy was particularly obvious (after the fact) both at the beginning and end of the 1957–1958 recession. According to the NBER reference cycle, the economy reached a peak in August 1957, but the shift to a monetary policy of ease instead of restraint did not come until November. Of course, meaningful statistics take that long to become available. One must forecast if one is going to follow a stabilizing policy. If you wait for reliable statistical confirmation of a turning point you will be late with the policy shift.

In the 1957–1958 recession when the Fed did shift to a stimulative policy, it did so very aggressively if you use the criterion of interest rate levels. The Treasury Bill rate fell from above 3% to 1% in a matter of a few months. However, by the criterion of the rate of growth in the money supply, $M1$, one can question the degree of stimulus. The money supply grew during the recession at an annual rate of less than half its rate of growth in the preceding boom, 0.6% versus 1.8%.

The recession of 1957–1958 was briefer on a monthly basis as measured by the NBER than the 1953–1954 recession, eight months versus ten months;

but by most measures the 1957–1958 recession was slightly more severe. Real GNP fell by 2.7% versus 2.6% in 1953–1954, the unemployment rate rose by 3.2% versus 3.1%, total consumption fell slightly in real terms in 1957–1958, whereas it rose slightly in 1953–1954. A major difference between the two recessions was in consumption expenditures for durable goods, off by 7.3% in real terms in 1957–1958 but down by a mere 1% in 1953–1954. In addition, whereas the peak unemployment rate in 1954 had been less than 6%, in 1958 it reached 7.5%. Also notable in 1958 was the first big cutback in investment in ten years including both inventories and business fixed investment. In the 1953–1954 recession inventories had been liquidated but fixed investment had hardly declined at all. In 1958 a number of people felt sure that this was finally the return of the Great Depression that had only been postponed.

Of course it did not turn out to be the return of the Great Depression. When interest rates came down during the recession, residential construction quickly bounced back and the recovery officially began shortly thereafter. The two-year expansion of 1958–1960 was, in retrospect, a healthy one. Real output grew at an average annual rate of 5%, while prices rose by only 1% and 2% per year as measured by the CPI and GNP price index, respectively. The expansion was not heavily dependent on federal government expenditures, which grew only at an average annual rate of 2.5%. Interest rates rose, but not by as much as they had come down in the previous recession. With the current $ GNP going up by 7.2% per year, a growth rate in the money supply of 1.9% annually certainly does not appear to be irresponsibly easy.

When older people of today refer to the "good old days" this expansion is the type of thing they have in mind. When GNP can rise by over 7% per year and only 2% of it is inflation, that is a nice ratio. The business community regarded 1960 (the end of eight years with a Republican president in the White House) with some foreboding; but Eisenhower's vice-president, young Richard Nixon, seemed competent enough to take over. However, the Democratic opposition focused on "fiscal drag" and the recurrence of recessions in 1953–1954 and 1957–1958. Also, as indicated by a reference cycle peak in April 1960, the economy began to slow down in the second quarter just in time for the presidential campaign of 1960.

The 1960s — One Short Recession and the Longest Expansion in History

The Democratic candidates for president and vice-president in 1960, John Kennedy and Lyndon Johnson, ran on a campaign slogan of "Let's get this country moving again!" The slogan was appropriate since the recession that began in April was evidenced by a rise in the unemployment rate from 4.8% in February to 6.1% in October.

The economic issue of the election (and there were certainly noneconomic issues as well) was the proposal to restructure the tax system to prevent these recurring recessions. This was to be done with a combination across-the-board tax cut and tax incentives to encourage business investment. The concern with recessions apparently had some appeal, especially to the traditional Democratic constituency of unionized labor. In the latter 1950s inflation had been of no great concern to the labor unions with the CPI increasing at less than 2% per year, but the recessions of 1953–1954, 1957–1958, and now 1960 resulted in substantial layoffs of labor in the heavily unionized auto and steel industries. Periodic unemployment was an issue of sufficient importance for the unions to negotiate for, and receive, "Supplementary Unemployment Benefits," or "SUB" payments. With a contract providing for SUB payments, the employer was required to deposit some amount in a fund in proportion to the total payroll. The idea was that in boom times with high employment the fund would build up so that in the event of a recession and unemployment of union members, the unemployed worker received, in addition to state unemployment compensation, a supplementary unemployment benefit.

Since the presidential election of 1960 was a very close election, one may arguably maintain that any one factor was *the* deciding factor. However, the loser, Richard Nixon, has indicated in later writings a firm belief that the business cycle did him in. He was also impressed with an economic advisor to President Eisenhower, Arthur Burns — who had told him in advance of the coming recession and its likely impact on the election. (Nixon later appointed Arthur Burns Chairman of the Federal Reserve Board of Governors after his later successful attempt to become president.)

The recession of 1960–1961 lasted 10 months by NBER dating, from April 1960 to February 1961. It was essentially a zero-growth situation with the decline in the private sector being to some extent offset by increased federal government expenditures. (See Table 16.2.) The unemployment rate rose well into 1961 when it exceeded 7%. The inflation rate slowed significantly to about 1% for consumer goods and to less than 0.5% per year for the GNP price index.

Monetary policy during the recession was not all that stimulative. If one looks at the level of interest rates, we find that the Fed did cut the discount rate twice, but not below 3%. In the previous recession it had been below 2%. Treasury Bill yields fell but not nearly to their levels of previous recessions. It is interesting to note that the average annual growth in the money supply at 1.9% was exactly the same during this recession as in the two-year expansion that preceded it. Of course, during the expansion the current dollar value of GNP rose at an annual rate of 7.2%, but by only 0.5% during the recession. Obviously there was a substantial cyclical decline in velocity.

The end of the 1960–1961 recession in February 1961 marked the

TABLE 16.2 Changes in U.S. Economic Time Series Between NBER Reference Dates, II60–IV69*

	(−)		(+)	
	II60–I61 (3 Qtrs.)		I61–IV69 (35 Qtrs.)	
	Total Change	Annual Rate	Total Change	Annual Rate
GNP, %Δ				
Current $	+0.4	0.5	+89.3	7.6
Price Deflated	−0.1	−0.1	+47.2	4.5
CPI, %Δ	+0.8	1.1	+25.6	2.6
% Unemployment	+1.6	2.1	−3.2	−0.4
Consumption				
Total, %Δ				
Current $	+0.8	1.1	+82.0	7.1
Price Deflated	−0.0	−0.0	+46.2	4.4
Durable Goods, $Δ				
Current $	−9.6	−12.6	+116.6	9.2
Price Deflated	−8.8	−11.6	+91.4	7.7
Investment				
Total Fixed, %Δ				
Current $	−4.6	−6.1	+99.7	8.2
Price Deflated	−3.6	−4.8	+61.0	5.6
Change in Inventories ($ in billions)	−$4.8	−$6.4	+$73.0	$8.3
Fed. Govt. Exp., %Δ	+7.2	9.6	+95.1	7.9
Deficit (−), % of GNP	−0.3		−0.4	
Money Supply, M1, %Δ	+1.4	1.9	+44.1	4.3
Treasury Bill Rate, Δ%	−0.71%		+4.94%	

*Recessions shown as minus (−); expansions as plus (+).

beginning of an expansion that was to set an all time historical record for its duration. Table 16.2 indicates 35 quarters, by NBER dating on a monthly basis; the expansion lasted 106 months from the trough in February 1961 to the peak in December 1969. A boom lasting 8 3/4 years has never been recorded in the annals of U.S. business cycle history before or since. The boom associated with World War II only lasted 6 2/3 years. Obviously, this was a unique time period in American economic history. Table 16.3 gives some relevant data for the period on an annual basis. At various

TABLE 16.3 Annual Data on the U.S. Economy, 1959–1969

| | Annual Percentage Rate of Growth in: | | | | | | Average Level of: | | |
Year	Real GNP	GNP Price Index	CPI	Fed. Govt. Expd.	Mont. Base	M1	Unempt. Rate (%)	T-Bill Rate (%)	Fed. Govt. Def.*
1959	6.0	2.4	0.8	2.4	1.6	3.9	5.5	3.41	−$1.1
1960	2.2	1.6	1.6	2.3	0.2	0.0	5.5	2.95	+3.0
1961	2.6	0.9	1.0	9.5	2.5	2.0	6.7	2.38	−3.9
1962	5.8	1.8	1.1	8.3	3.5	2.5	5.5	2.78	−4.2
1963	4.0	1.5	1.2	3.4	4.7	3.0	5.7	3.16	+0.3
1964	5.3	1.5	1.3	3.5	5.5	3.9	5.2	3.55	−3.3
1965	6.0	2.2	1.7	4.7	5.6	4.3	4.5	3.95	+0.5
1966	6.0	3.2	2.9	16.0	5.9	4.6	3.8	4.88	−1.8
1967	2.7	3.0	2.9	14.0	5.2	3.9	3.8	4.33	−13.2
1968	4.6	4.4	4.2	10.3	6.8	7.1	3.6	5.34	−6.0
1969	2.8	5.1	5.4	4.4	5.4	6.0	3.5	6.69	+8.4

*Dollars in billions. Deficit shown as minus (−); surplus as plus (+).

points in this section we will even want to look carefully at the quarter-to-quarter changes.

We have already considered some of the unique features of the labor market during the 1960s. Recall that in Chapter 11 we commented on the fact that the 18–24-year-old age group grew three times as fast as the general population during this time period. We also noted in Chapter 11 the increase in the female labor participation rate from 37% to 51% of the female population between the ages of 16 and 65. Despite this mass of new entrants to the labor force, the economic expansion was sufficiently strong that the unemployment rate declined throughout this period. As shown on Table 16.3, the average annual unemployment rate peaked at 6.7% in 1961, fell to around 5.5% for the early 1960s, and declined steadily for the rest of the decade. In 1966 it fell below 4% and stayed there for over four years!

The dimensions of the expansion between the cyclical dates can be seen from the data in Table 16.2. Superficially, the growth of the economy looks healthy enough when this time period is taken as a whole. Real GNP grew at an average annual rate of 4.5% while the unemployment rate was reduced by over 3 percentage points. The public and private sectors both provided an impetus to expansion. The growth in federal government expenditures was slightly faster than GNP at 7.9% per year versus 7.6%, but total consumption expenditures grew by just over 7% with the durable goods component up by over 9% per year. Except for the inflation rates, which were a little high by historical standards at 2.6% for the CPI and 3% for the GNP index, one could look at the record in Table 16.2 and conclude that we must have done almost everything right to have had 8 3/4 years of such prosperity. However, while the economic growth of the 1960s was genuine and the net results were positive in many dimensions, a closer look at this period will reveal a number of problems and some serious policy mistakes.

The year-by-year picture of the economy in Table 16.3 gives a clearer picture of the 1960s. As the Democrats came into office, they were faced with an economy in which real output was growing at only 2% to 3% per year, unemployment was 5% to 7%, but inflation rates were only 1% to 2%. Note that federal government expenditures had grown by only 2.4% and 2.3%, respectively, in 1959 and 1960. In addition, the Treasury had shown a net budget surplus of $2 billion during those two years. Interest rates were down in 1960, but so was the growth of the money supply — to zero.

We can now trace the details of this boom. It started with tax cuts and increases in nondefense federal government expenditures. Then in 1966, 1967, and 1968 a wartime boom was imposed on the economy, posing the classic "guns or butter" dilemma. As a result, by 1969 when the Republicans recaptured the White House, unemployment was down dramatically, to 3.5%, but the inflation rates were in excess of 5% and interest rates were at levels not seen since the 1920s.

The change in presidential administrations to one with a desire to "get this country moving again" is most obvious in the annual percentage rate of growth in federal government expenditures: 2.4% and 2.3% in 1959 and 1960, rising to 9.5% and 8.3% in 1961 and 1962. Rates of growth in the monetary base and the money supply (M1) also increased significantly. Early in the decade under stimulative monetary and fiscal policy all the good things that were supposed to happen did begin to happen. Real GNP began to grow at 4% to 5%; the unemployment rate fell; and, best of both worlds, inflation remained below 2%. The first significant legislation directly affecting macroeconomic policy was, surprisingly for a Democratic administration, a tax break designed to stimulate investment. The Revenue Act of 1962 provided a tax credit to business equal to 7% of the cost of new investment with a useful life of more than eight years. Buildings were excluded from the tax credit, but depreciation guidelines on building were liberalized.

President Kennedy was assassinated in 1963 and Lyndon Johnson was elected president by a landslide in 1964. President Johnson and his advisors proposed, and Congress enacted, a major overhaul of the tax system in 1964 designed to remove "fiscal drag" and fight unemployment, which remained stubbornly above the 5% rate. The Revenue Act of 1964 not only cut personal taxes by more than 20%, but also lowered the marginal tax rates permanently from a range of 20% to 91% to a range of 14% to 70%. The corporate income tax was allowed to fall from 52% to 48%. Although some of the provisions were postponed until 1965, most of the personal tax benefits went into effect for 1964 and withholding rates were reduced as early as March 1964. Additional legislation passed in 1965 removed federal excise (sales) taxes from everything from television sets to jewelry and lowered the level of such taxes on automobiles and long distance telephone calls.

Of course, the immediate effect of that large tax cut in 1964 was a Treasury deficit of something in excess of $3 billion. We should note also the fairly steady increase in the rate of growth in the monetary base, from 2.5% in 1961 to a growth rate of 5.5% in 1964. Similarly, the growth rate in the money supply had risen steadily from 2% in 1961 to 3.9% in 1964. The federal government deficits were obviously being funded to a significant extent by money creation despite the rise in the Treasury Bill rate from an average of 2.4% in 1961 to 3.6% in 1964.

In retrospect most analysts conclude that the tax cut of 1964 was wise policy in the context of the times. (Who knew the Vietnam War was coming?) The economy did grow by 6% in real terms in 1965, unemployment fell, the deficit disappeared, and inflation rates did not go up in the first half of 1965.

Of course, what was not foreseen was a massive increase in federal government expenditures for the Vietnam War. On Table 16.3, note that while federal government expenditures were up by only 3.5% in 1964 and

4.7% in 1965, suddenly for the three years beginning in 1966 this stimulus to aggregate demand rose by 16%, 14%, and 10%! Compounded, that is a 46% increase in three years during which total GNP went up by only 26%. This level of expenditure generated large federal government budget deficits, $13.2 billion in 1967. The funding of these deficits raised both interest rates and the monetary base. The monetary base increased by 6.8% in 1968, an all-time record for modern times. Correspondingly, the rate of growth in the money supply at more than 7% was also at a record high.

The rapid growth in the monetary base and the money supply in 1968 did not come about without the Federal Reserve having put up a fight. When it became apparent late in 1965 that Defense Department expenditures were rising spectacularly, there was widespread agreement that the inflationary impact of this, coming on top of the tax cut of 1964, was excessive economic stimulus. In fact, President Johnson's advisors unanimously recommended increased taxes. The prospect of going to Congress and the people to request an increase in personal taxes to help pay for an increasingly unpopular war was not something for which President Johnson had much enthusiasm. All that was passed in the way of fiscal restraint in 1966 was restoration of some of the previously removed excise taxes and a temporary suspension of the investment tax credit.

The chairman of the Federal Reserve Board of Governors, William McChesney Martin, did not suffer from the reticence of the politicians in taking action to fight excessive aggregate demand. The term "credit crunch" was first applied to the money and capital markets in 1966. The commercial bank prime lending rate rose from 4.5% in December 1965 to 6.25% by November 1966. As indicated in Table 16.3, the Treasury Bill rate averaged about a full percentage point higher in 1966 than in 1965, 4.88% versus 3.95%. The Treasury Bill rate actually peaked at around 5.5% late in 1966.

Although these interest rates of the tight money period of 1966 seem quite low by the standards of the 1980s, we must put them in the context of the times. No one had seen rates that high since the 1920s. Despite the fact that the money supply grew slightly faster in 1966 than in 1965, 4.6% versus 4.3%, monetary restraint was effective. Current dollar GNP went up by 8.3% and 9.4% in 1965 and 1966, respectively. The credit crunch of 1966 had a tremendous psychological impact on the business community. In addition to the predictable effect on residential construction, the unprecedented level of interest rates scared businesspeople (and increased their cost sufficiently) so that they went from accumulating inventories at an annual rate in excess of $20 billion in the fourth quarter of 1966 to below $10 billion in the first quarter of 1967. The quarterly data for annual rates of increase in federal government expenditures and real GNP are shown in Table 16.4. The quarter-to-quarter data show that the rate of growth in real GNP peaked in the fourth quarter of 1965 at an annual rate of 10% and declined each quarter thereafter through the first quarter of 1967 to an annual rate of growth of only 0.5%.

TABLE 16.4 Quarterly Annual Percentage Rates of Growth in Federal Government Expenditures and Real GNP, 1965–1967

	1965		1966		1967	
	Govt. Exp.	Real GNP	Govt. Exp.	Real GNP	Govt. Exp.	Real GNP
I	0.7	9.3	17.3	8.0	23.1	0.5
II	7.7	5.8	13.0	1.6	2.5	2.6
III	20.3	6.4	21.2	3.6	10.9	4.9
IV	14.7	10.1	14.0	3.6	9.5	4.4
Year	4.7	6.0	16.0	6.0	14.0	2.7

Late in 1966 many economists forecast a recession for 1967. The forecast was made on the erroneous assumption that federal government expenditures, after rising at double-digit rates throughout 1966, would stabilize at this new higher level in 1967. On an annual basis, we thought the 16% year-to-year increase in 1966 was the build-up for the war, and would now hold at that level with perhaps a 4% to 5% increase in 1967. The 14% increase in federal government expenditures in 1967 did, of course, help avoid a recession in that year, although the rate of growth in real GNP did slow dramatically for the year to a mere 2.7% versus 6% for the two previous years.

Avoiding a recession in 1967 was also helped by a shift in monetary policy. An active policy of ease was followed by the Fed throughout 1967 and most of 1968. Interest rates dropped initially as a result of the economic slowdown in 1967 and both the monetary base and money supply recorded slower rates of growth. Both were deliberately increased in early 1968.

The inflationary problem began to become apparent to the general public by the middle of 1968. By the second quarter of 1968 the CPI was rising at an annual rate of more than 5%. This was regarded as a national disaster in the light of the 1, 2, and 3% rates of inflation experienced over the previous ten years. The degree of concern by the body politic is evidenced by the fact that in 1968, an election year, Congress passed and the president signed into law a personal and corporate income tax *increase!* The Revenue Expenditure Control Act of 1968 enacted in June 1968 levied a 10% surtax on personal income taxes retroactive to April 1 and on corporate taxes retroactive to January 1, 1968. The public knew the source of the inflation, government deficits and printing press money, and was perfectly prepared to accept what was required to fight it.

The public was also prepared to vote for someone (Richard Nixon) who campaigned on a platform of fiscal restraint — and a commitment to end the war in Vietnam. Insofar as economic policy was an issue, the Republicans of 1968 sounded a great deal like the Republicans would sound in 1980. They promised to get control of the bureaucracy, cut spending, eliminate the deficit, and generally fight inflation. With the unemployment rate at 3.5%, that was not a major concern.

Nixon was elected president and immediately imposed a restrictive fiscal policy. The 10% tax surcharge was scheduled to expire on June 30, 1969. It was extended to December 31, 1969. In December it was extended at a 5% rate to June 30, 1970. On the expenditure side, one can observe that while federal government expenditures had increased by 16%, 14%, and 10% in the three years prior to Nixon's taking office, in 1969 the increase was a mere 4.4%. With inflation running in excess of 5%, this was a decrease in real terms. As a result, the Treasury budget on a calendar year basis moved from a deficit of $6 billion in 1968 to a surplus of $8.4 billion in 1969.

Also in 1969, the Federal Reserve imposed a tight money policy that some regarded as more severe than the credit crunch of 1966. The rate of increase in the monetary base dropped from 6.8% in 1968 to 5.4% in 1969, while the rate of increase in the money supply dropped from 7% to 6%. Interest rates again set new records. Instead of saying, as they had in 1966, that we were experiencing the highest rates since the 1920s, the press now observed that many interest rates were the highest they had been since the Civil War. The commercial bank prime rate went from 6% in November 1968 to 8% by November 1969. The Treasury Bill rate covered about the same range over the same time period.

The decade ended with the conclusion of an expansion that had run almost nine years. The economy was deliberately slowed by a policy of restraint consisting of the following: (1) tax surcharges, (2) reduced federal government expenditures in real terms, and (3) restrictive monetary policy. This slowed the rate of growth in real GNP from 4.6% in 1968 to 2.8% in 1969 and economists again began to forecast a recession. This time they were right. As the saying goes: "Make the same forecast long enough and eventually you will be right."

The 1970s — Exogenous Shocks and Bad Policy Take Us to Double-Digit Inflation

As indicated on Table 16.5, the 1970s opened with the first recession in a very long time, followed by two expansions each of which ended with a recession. The business cycle was back. Specifically, according to NBER dating, during the 1970s we experienced:

An 11-month *recession* ending in November 1970.

A 36-month *expansion* ending in November 1973.

A 16-month *recession* ending in October 1975.

A 58-month *expansion* ending in January 1980.

A 6-month *recession* ending in July 1980.

TABLE 16.5 Changes in U.S. Economic Time Series Between NBER Reference Dates, IV69–III80*

	IV69–IV70 (4 Qtrs.) (−)	IV70–IV73 (12 Qtrs.) (+)		IV73–I75 (5 Qtrs.) (−)		I75–I80 (20 Qtrs.) (+)		I80–III80 (2 Qtrs.) (−)	
	Total Change	Tot. Chg.	Ann. Rate	Tot. Chg.	Ann. Rate	Tot. Chg.	Ann. Rate	Tot. Chg.	Ann. Rate
GNP, %Δ									
Current Dollars	+4.9	+36.4	10.9	+7.5	5.9	+73.8	11.7	+2.6	5.2
Price Deflated	−0.1	+16.8	5.3	−4.8	−3.9	+24.5	4.5	−2.0	−4.0
CPI, %Δ	+5.7	+16.0	5.1	+14.1	11.1	+50.6	8.5	+5.5	11.4
% Unemployment	+2.3	−1.1	−0.3	+3.4	2.7	−2.0	−0.4	+1.3	2.6
Consumption									
Total, %Δ									
Current Dollars	+6.1	+31.6	9.6	+12.1	9.6	+74.3	11.7	+3.2	6.5
Price Deflated	+1.5	+13.9	4.4	−0.4	−0.4	+22.6	4.2	−1.5	−3.0
Durable Goods, %Δ									
Current Dollars	−4.2	+42.7	12.6	+4.1	3.3	+79.9	12.5	−5.0	−9.7
Price Deflated	−7.1	+38.2	11.4	−9.1	−7.4	+36.5	6.4	−8.1	−15.6
Investment									
Total Fixed, %Δ									
Current Dollars	+2.1	+49.3	14.3	−3.8	−3.0	+86.2	13.2	−5.0	−9.7
Price Deflated	−2.0	+28.0	8.6	−19.2	−15.7	+26.7	4.9	−12.0	−22.6
Change in Inventories (Dollars in billions)	+$3.2	+$36.4	$12.1	−$0.2	−$0.2	+$69.8	$14.0	−$2.2	−$4.4
Fed. Govt. Exp., %Δ	+9.0	+29.0	8.8	+23.0	18.0	+69.3	11.1	+8.9	18.6
Deficit (−), % of GNP	−1.2	−1.2		−1.3		−2.1		−2.7	
Money Supply, M1, %Δ	+5.0	+22.5	7.0	+5.5	4.4	+41.7	7.2	+2.7	5.4
Treasury Bill Rate, Δ%	−1.96%	+2.10%		−1.59%		+7.59%		−4.22%	

*Recessions shown as minus (−); expansion as plus (+).

Although the NBER reference cycle places the 1969–1970 recession at 11 months, or 4 quarters, real GNP fell for only two quarters. Real GNP reached a peak in III69 and fell by a total of 1% during the next two quarters. While GNP hit bottom in the first quarter of 1970, other indicators such as the unemployment rate continued to deteriorate throughout most of 1970; hence, the NBER terminal date of November.

We must reemphasize that this was the first recession the business community had experienced in almost nine years. Most of us operate on a naive forecasting system that assumes that the world will continue to function as it has over the last six months, or at least as it has during the last six years. It is difficult to believe today, but many people in the business community and no small number of economists had come to believe that the "business cycle is dead" — that we would *never* have another recession of any severity. Growth might be fast or slow, but a meaningful decline in real GNP? Not likely. We would just have to talk about "growth recessions" or "rolling readjustments." The late Arthur M. Okun was certainly a competent economist, but even he held the opinion in April 1969 that:

> Today few research economists regard the business cycle as a particularly useful organizing framework for the overall analysis of current economic activity, and few teachers see "business cycles" as an appropriate title for a course to be offered to their students.
> . . .
> In 1965 President Johnson was making a controversial statement when he said: "I do not believe recessions are inevitable." That statement is no longer controversial.[1]

Since the business community had not seen a recession for about nine years, it is not surprising that it was more than a bit nervous and upset. Although they were pleased with the drop in interest rates that began in January 1970, they were appalled that inflation not only did not abate, but seemed to be accelerating. For calendar year 1970 the CPI was up by 5.9%, compared to 5.4% in 1969. The GNP price index was up by 5.4%, compared to 5.1% in 1969. The bad news of inflation was accompanied by the additional bad news of a steady rise in the unemployment rate from 3.5% in December 1969 to 6.1% in December 1970. Generally speaking, the nation was disappointed, upset, and confused by the recession of 1970.

The dissatisfaction of the people, and the political pressure on the federal government, became even greater in 1971 after economists said the recession was over, and things showed no immediate improvement. In fact, to many people things appeared to be getting worse as 1971 wore on. The "recovery" year of 1971 started with the unemployment rate holding at 5.9% and rising slightly from there. Real GNP rose at an annual rate of 10.3% in the first quarter, but fell back to a 2% rate of increase in the second quarter. The CPI was up at an annual rate of only 3% in the first quarter, but jumped to a rate of approximately 4.5% in the second quarter. All this generated irresistible pressure for the federal government to do something.

Of course, if the inherent inertia in the economic system had been recognized, the behavior of the economy in 1971 would have come as no great surprise. Consider what it took to slow the economy down: the 1968 tax surcharge, the 1969 credit crunch, and a reduction in federal government expenditures in real terms. It should have come as no surprise that once slowed down, the economy would not likely bounce back immediately. The tendency of the economy to keep doing what it has been doing in the recent past is why it is hard to improve on a naive forecast. However, despite the fact that the behavior of the economy after the 1970 recession was not extraordinarily sluggish for that stage of the cycle, President Nixon applied some extraordinary policy measures. We must note that 1972 was a presidential election year and Nixon felt he had lost the election of 1960 because of the economy. The extraordinary measures consisted of going on television the evening of August 15, 1971, and, under power previously passed by Congress, declaring a complete wage and price freeze for the next 90 days. That is one way to halt inflation in its tracks!

The immediate short-run effect was psychologically and politically very favorable. The stock market began to rise. President Nixon's ratings in the public opinion polls went up. Business confidence surged. It is not difficult to understand why. The typical businessperson was faced with a heavy burden of uncertainty. He or she had just been through a recession, something not seen in about nine years; the market in which he or she was trying to sell remained weak and unreceptive to price increases while suppliers, labor in particular, continued to push up costs. He or she was faced with a whole array of tough managerial decisions until the president said: "No changes in wages or prices allowed by anybody!" A business could not increase prices, but then neither could suppliers, and labor could get no wage increases. No managerial decisions were left to be made. The businessperson could just as well play golf. All the uncertainty had been removed.

Of course, as the 90-day wage-price freeze wore on, the complete certainty of fixed wages and prices came to be replaced with the uncertainty of how do we "unfreeze" things. This worry was reflected in a falling stock market and declining presidential popularity. What the president did was appoint a Wage Board and a Price Board to approve wage and price increases selectively. These boards established rules on appropriate increases in average wage rates, cost pass-through to prices, and a whole host of other criteria for granting wage and price increases. When the boards went into action, it was called "Phase II" of the wage-price freeze. We will not here go into phases III, III 1/2, and so on, of the progressive decontrol on the grounds that this is not an experience we are likely to repeat in the foreseeable future.* We will merely note that throughout 1972 wages and prices were being slowly decontrolled.

The 1972 expansion was also helped along by a substantial tax cut in 1971. Personal exemptions were increased, auto excise taxes were repealed, and the investment tax credit of 7%, which had been repealed in 1969, was reinstated. As a result, in 1972 the federal government continued stimulative fiscal policy with a third successive year of a large deficit while increasing expenditures by 10.7%. Not surprisingly, if we ignore suppressed inflationary pressures, 1972 was something of a vintage year. As can be seen from the annual data in Table 16.6, growth in real GNP jumped to 5.7% from 3.4% in 1971. The inflation rate on the GNP index fell from 5% in 1971 to 4.2%, while the rise in the CPI fell from 4.3% to 3.3%. Interest rates were low and the unemployment rate fell from 6% in December 1971 to 5.6% by election time 1972. Richard Nixon easily won reelection to the White House. The pent-up inflationary pressure would be fully released in 1973.

The year 1973 was a year in which the economy paid the price for a number of bad policy decisions made earlier and at the same time was subject to a number of exogenous shocks. All this culminated in what the NBER dates as a business cycle peak in November 1973. As we will discuss below, there is room for debate regarding when the recession of 1974–1975 began, or at least we should note two distinct phases of that decline.

But before examining the recession of 1974–1975, we should take a closer look at the 1970–1973 expansion. The expansion was a healthy one in all but one important aspect. The negative factor on the economic scene during this period was the accelerating rate of inflation as wages and prices were decontrolled. Of course, there is no question that the average annual rate of growth in real GNP would not have been the 5.3% shown in Table 16.5 if wages and price controls had not been relaxed. For the period as a whole federal government expenditures were up by less than GNP. The consumer came on strong, especially in the demand for durable goods. In real terms total consumption expenditures rose at an average annual rate of 4.4%, while the durable goods part of consumption was up at an annual rate of 11.4%. Investment was strong, particularly residential construction. Total fixed investment, price deflated, rose at an average annual rate of 8.6% from IV70 to IV73.

---

*This is not to say a president would not invoke such powers, but rather that Congress could not agree on the details of what powers to give him if they thought in fact they would immediately be used. Nixon's power to impose a wage-price freeze (since expired) was given to him by a Democratic Congress that was firmly convinced that such a right-wing Republican would never interfere with the free market so massively. Congress did, however, want to be able to tell their constituents that they had given the man in the White House the power to stop inflation in its tracks, but he simply refused to do it. He surprised them.

TABLE 16.6 Annual Data on the U.S. Economy, 1970–1980

| | Annual Percentage Rate of Growth in: | | | | | | Average Level of: | | |
Year	Real GNP	GNP Price Index	CPI	Fed. Govt. Expd.	Mont. Base	M1	Unemp. Rate (%)	T-Bill Rate (%)	Fed. Govt. Def.*
1970	−0.2	5.4	5.9	8.4	5.6	3.7	4.9	6.44	−$12.4
1971	3.4	5.0	4.3	8.0	7.9	6.7	5.9	4.34	−22.0
1972	5.7	4.2	3.3	10.7	7.3	7.1	5.6	4.07	−16.8
1973	5.8	5.7	6.2	8.1	8.7	7.3	4.9	7.03	−5.6
1974	−0.6	8.7	11.0	13.3	8.5	4.9	5.6	7.87	−11.5
1975	−1.1	9.3	9.1	19.1	7.9	4.6	8.5	5.82	−69.3
1976	5.4	5.2	5.8	7.9	8.4	5.5	7.8	5.00	−53.1
1977	5.5	5.8	6.5	9.5	8.4	7.5	7.0	5.26	−46.4
1978	4.8	7.3	7.6	9.3	9.4	8.2	6.0	7.22	−29.2
1979	3.2	8.5	11.4	10.5	8.5	7.8	5.8	10.04	−14.8
1980	−0.1	9.0	13.4	18.1	8.0	6.4	7.2	11.63	−62.3

*Dollars in billions. Deficit shown as minus (−); surplus as plus (+).

The bad news in this expansion was the unprecedented rate of inflation. The quarterly changes at annual rates in real GNP, the GNP price index, and the CPI are shown in Table 16.7. Note the fairly steady increase in the inflation rates as the rate of growth in real GNP declined. The reference cycle peak is in IV73 by which time the GNP price index was rising at an annual rate of 8.6%, the CPI at 9.9%, and real growth had fallen to a rate of 3.3%. But worse was yet to come. As the rate of growth in real GNP went negative in 1974, the rate of inflation continued to accelerate — a truly unprecedented state of affairs.

Of course, this unprecedented state of economic affairs in 1974 was matched by an unprecedented political situation. It was in August 1974 that President Nixon announced his resignation in the face of impeachment and likely conviction for illegal activities. The president and Congress were a bit distracted from the problems of the economy by the "Watergate" investigation in the months preceding the president's resignation.

During 1973, as the business expansion came to a close, the economy was subjected to a number of exogenous economic shocks. First, consumers went on a durable goods spending binge in the first quarter of the year with an increase of 30% at an annual rate. Note the 11% rate of growth in real GNP for I73 in Table 16.7. The consumers slowed their rate of purchases for the rest of the year and the economy received its first "OPEC" shock in the fourth quarter. Petroleum, in general, and gasoline in particular, took a spectacular jump in price. As a result of Nixon's having cut the dollar completely free from gold at the time of his August 1971 wage-price freeze, its value on international markets was dropping rapidly in 1973. This made all imports more expensive in the United States. Furthermore, in 1973 the world's three main centers of economic activity (the United States, Western Europe, and Japan) suffered from close synchronization of their business cycles. The 1974 boom was worldwide and it put tremendous demand

TABLE 16.7 Quarterly Annual Percentage Rates of Growth in Real GNP and Prices, 1972–1975

		Real GNP	GNP Prices	CPI			Real GNP	GNP Prices	CPI
1972	I	7.9%	5.6%	3.3%	1974	I	− 3.8%	7.3%	11.5%
	II	7.6	2.9	3.3		II	0.5	10.3	11.8
	III	5.0	3.4	3.6		III	− 2.4	10.7	13.0
	IV	7.5	5.2	3.5		IV	− 5.1	12.0	12.0
1973	I	11.1	5.6	5.8	1975	I	− 8.2	10.7	7.5
	II	0.6	7.1	9.0		II	5.0	5.1	6.5
	III	2.5	6.9	9.1		III	9.3	7.3	8.8
	IV	3.3	8.6	9.9		IV	3.7	7.5	6.5

pressures on the world's supply of raw materials. There were dramatic price increases in the commodity markets.

Domestically, as a result of government allocation of petroleum products, shortages of all sorts began to occur. The shortages were of sufficient frequency and magnitude to be a major factor restraining the growth of real GNP in the first three quarters of 1974. This is the problem with the dating of the 1974–1975 recession. The NBER reference peak of November 1973 most certainly did not usher in a standard post-World War II recession. As you know by now, in the typical recession in this country businesspeople find themselves with sales below expectations, inventories build up, production is cut back, and unemployment rises. In this recession unemployment did hit a low of less than 6% in November 1973, and then rose steadily throughout 1974, reaching 8% by December. However, for at least the first three quarters of 1974, business was suffering no disappointment in the demand for products. Quite the contrary, many industrial goods were being rationed by suppliers. Machinery was manufactured but could not be shipped for want of some small part made of a plastic petroleum derivative being allocated by the federal government. The economy was slowed, not by insufficient demand, but by supply constraints imposed by government allocation of petroleum products. The impact of these shortages was magnified by the previous experience with full wage-price controls and the shortages that accompanied those regulations. In fact, many businesspeople expected a reimposition of direct wage-price controls at any moment throughout 1974. As a result there was a great reluctance to cut prices of industrial materials when shortages later turned to gluts for fear of being caught in a low price situation when the controls were imposed.

During the first half of 1974 the business community took on a "shortage mentality." Some businesspeople even came to believe the position espoused by some modern-day Malthusians that the world was soon to run out of petroleum, bauxite, copper, and any and all the other nonrenewable resources. Hoarding commodities was the order of the day. As a result, the economy experienced declining real output and *increased* inflationary pressures at the same time, the worst of both worlds. Compare 1974 to 1973. Real GNP rose by 5.8% in 1973 but fell by 0.6% in 1974. The GNP price index was up by 5.7% in 1973, and by 8.7% in 1974. The CPI jumped from an inflation rate of 6.2% in 1973 to 11% in 1974.

Of course, as government controls were relaxed and the speculative fever died down in the fourth quarter of 1974, we had a good old-fashioned inventory liquidation recession in the first quarter of 1975. The unemployment rate went rapidly from 8% to 9%, but the inflationary pressures quickly diminished. As can be seen from Table 16.7, the inflation rate as measured by the GNP price index went from an annual rate of 12% in IV74 to 5.1% in II75. The CPI went from 12% to 6.5% inflation over the same time period.

The much-revised inventory accumulation figures available today give a clear picture of what happened. (The figures published at the time did not give such a picture.) Business happily accumulated inventories for the first three quarters of 1974 at annual rates in excess of $10 billion. In the fourth quarter they suddenly saw all the shortages disappear, order backlogs evaporate, and additional involuntary inventory accumulation. In response to this, inventories were liquidated at annual rates approaching $15 billion in the first two quarters of 1975. The cuts were massive but over by midyear.

While keeping in mind the two distinct phases of the 1974–1975 recession, some comments are appropriate to the decline in its entirety. It was the most severe recession in the post-World War II period. As can be seen from Table 16.5, real GNP fell by 4.8% during five quarters. While, as usual, consumer durables were down by more than GNP at 9% in real terms, the decline in fixed investment was unusually large at over 19% in real terms. Both business-fixed investment and residential construction experienced dramatic declines over this period. A significant factor in the decline in investment was the active monetary restraint pursued throughout most of 1974. Interest rates did not peak until August 1974. For the recession period as a whole (IV73–I75) the money supply increased at an annual rate of only 4.4%, compared to 7% in the preceding expansion (IV70–IV73).

Discretionary fiscal policy in this recession was late but substantial. The Tax Reduction Act of 1975 increased the investment tax credit from 7% to 10%, lowered corporate income taxes, increased the standard deduction for individuals, and provided a 10% tax rebate of 1974 taxes to all individuals up to a maximum of $200. Its revenue effect is estimated to have been a reduction in taxes of approximately $23 billion. The deficit of $69 billion in 1975 was the largest of the last 30 years both in absolute and relative terms. At 4.5% of GNP, this deficit would have by itself created something of a problem in financing it. However, the next two years compounded the problem. The years 1975, 1976, and 1977 turned out to be the three largest deficits as a percent of GNP we have had since World War II. They were 4.5%, 3.1%, and 2.4%, respectively. But the recession was over early in 1975. Why the continuing deficits in 1976 and 1977? To answer that question we must now turn to the economic and political situation during the 1975–1980 expansion.

As mentioned above, Nixon took early retirement from the presidency in August 1974, as the recession was underway. Gerald Ford presided over the tax cuts enumerated above and sought to be elected president in the election of 1976. His business cycle forecasters did not help his cause much in that, given the lags in the reporting of statistics and our perceptions, when he took office in 1974 the primary economic problem facing the economy seemed to be the accelerating rate of inflation. He is most remembered for a "summit conference" of top economists, businesspeople, and labor leaders called to determine how to "*Whip Inflation Now.*" Lapel buttons bore the acronym WIN. Of course, no sooner had the meeting adjourned than it was discovered that we were in the deepest recession since the depression of the 1930s as the unemployment rate moved first to 8% and then to 9%.

In 1976, after the 1975 tax cuts described above, the economic environment was good with inflation, unemployment, and interest rates all declining. One might have thought that the incumbent, President Ford, would have an easy time being elected on a vote of confidence in the election of 1976. However, it appears that the economy and economic policies were not the issue in the 1976 election. The dishonesty and/or criminality of President Nixon apparently was. Republicans, in general, and President Ford, in particular, bore a stigma for it. President Ford had given Nixon a presidential pardon for any and all crimes he might have committed while President. Jimmy Carter was elected on the distinctly noneconomic slogan "I will never lie to you!"

The years of the Carter presidential administration were, by a combination of bad policy and bad luck, the worst in the last 30 years in a number of dimensions of economic stability. In particular, inflation rates increased each of the four years 1977–1980 and we still managed to end the period with the recession of 1980. The GNP price index went steadily from a rate of increase of 5.2% in 1976 to 9% in 1980, while the CPI went from 5.8% to 13.4% during the same period. Interest rates fluctuated widely but rose steadily under erratic monetary policy. The Treasury Bill rate averaged 5.26% in 1977 and 11.63% in the recession year of 1980.

We mentioned previously the large Treasury deficits of 1975, 1976, and 1977. Under President Carter the Treasury continued running deficits, although smaller, in 1978 and 1979. The combination of election-year spending and a recession in 1980 ran the deficit up to the 2.4% of GNP it had been in 1977. There was enough printing press financing of these deficits for the years 1977–1980 to generate historically high rates of increase in the monetary base and the money supply. Federal government expenditures did decline as a percentage of GNP for the first three years of the Carter Administration, but then took a jump from 21.1% of GNP to 22.9% in the election year of 1980. The increase in expenditures that year was more than 18%, while current $ GNP rose by less than 9%.

The period of the entire cyclical expansion running from I75 to I80 (see Table 16.5) was fairly well balanced in terms of the components of real growth. Real GNP increased at an average annual rate of 4.5%, while total consumption rose at 4.2% and fixed investment grew by 4.9% per year. What made the period unique was a number of interrelated macroeconomic variables beginning with the federal government's deficits and ending with double-digit inflation rates.

The federal government's deficits as a percentage of GNP set an all-time record in the 1975–1980 expansion in comparison to previous expansions. The first two post-World War II expansions each actually resulted in a small surplus for the Treasury. In the next two expansions we experienced a deficit equal to 0.4% of the GNP over those years. The 1970–1973 expansion set a new record with a deficit equal to 1.2% of GNP. However, that record was broken in the 1975–1980 expansion with accumulated deficits equal to 2.1% of GNP during the period.

Of course, government deficits must be financed. The only two options are an expansion of the monetary base (and, thereby, the money supply) or borrowing from the public. Expanding the money supply is inflationary and borrowing from the public is likely to raise interest rates. U.S. policy did enough of each to generate the worst of both worlds. We experienced accelerating inflation *and* sharply rising interest rates. We have already quantified the inflation problem above. The increase in interest rates was equally without previous precedent in recent history. Treasury Bill rates were below 5% in late 1977 but were well above 15% by early 1980. Both the inflation problem and the high interest rates were, of course, to a large extent the result of the financing of the deficits. Recall from previous chapters that even avoiding borrowing by monetizing the deficit only holds rates down temporarily until the inflation premium gets built into interest rates on the basis of expectations. Note on Table 16.5 that in this expansion the money supply grew at an average annual rate of 7.2% — substantially faster than in either recession preceding or following this expansion. The growth of the money supply was also rapid in comparison to previous expansions. The first four expansions after World War II all had rates of growth in the money supply of less than 6%. The expansion of 1970–1973 with a rate of growth in the money supply of 7% per year was a new high but was exceeded by the 1975–1980 expansion. Each of those last two expansions made its own contribution to later inflation and high interest rates.

Table 16.8 presents annual data for 1976–1980 on the most important macroeconomic indicators and quarterly data for the four years 1977–1980. Looking first at the annual rates of growth in real GNP, we get a fairly steady progression downward from 1977 through 1980: 5.5%, 4.8%, 3.2%, and −0.1%. However, if one looks at the quarterly data the cyclical sequence is far from smooth. In observing quarterly data one must keep in mind that in estimating such data there are acute problems of price deflation combined with seasonal adjustment. As a result much of the data probably come out more erratic than we believe the real world to be.

The monetary and interest rate data are probably more firmly based in reality than most of the other indicators, and they depict a regrettable monetary policy. The rate of growth in the money supply was highly erratic on a quarterly basis, but did grow at accelerating rates for the first three years of the expansion: 5.5% in 1976, 7.5% in 1977, and 8.2% in 1978.

TABLE 16.8 Annual and Quarterly Data on the U.S. Economy, 1977–1980

Year	Qtr.	Annual Percentage Rate of Growth in:						Average Level of:		
		Real GNP	GNP Price Index	CPI	Fed. Govt. Expd.	Mont. Base	M1	Unemp. Rate (%)	T-Bill Rate (%)	Fed. Govt. Def.*
1976	Yr.	5.4	5.2	5.8	7.9	8.4	5.5	7.8	5.00	−53.1
1977	I	9.6	5.7	7.3	3.2	7.8	10.0	7.5	4.62	−38.1
	II	5.3	6.8	8.9	10.2	8.0	7.4	7.1	4.83	−42.7
	III	6.7	5.4	5.9	16.1	9.6	7.1	6.9	5.47	−52.2
	IV	1.7	6.3	4.4	12.6	9.0	9.0	6.6	6.14	−52.5
	Yr.	5.5	5.8	6.5	9.5	9.8	7.5	7.0	5.26	−46.4
1978	I	3.1	5.8	7.2	5.5	9.8	7.6	6.3	6.41	−48.8
	II	9.0	10.6	10.7	3.3	9.6	9.7	6.0	6.48	−27.4
	III	3.9	7.7	9.6	11.6	8.7	8.4	5.9	7.32	−22.8
	IV	5.4	9.8	8.3	15.4	8.5	7.2	5.8	8.68	−17.9
	Yr.	4.8	7.3	7.6	9.3	9.4	8.2	6.0	7.22	−29.2
1979	I	3.9	8.4	10.5	6.7	7.4	5.5	5.8	9.36	−11.5
	II	−1.7	7.8	14.4	4.7	7.9	10.3	5.7	9.37	−8.1
	III	4.1	7.8	13.7	18.9	8.9	9.4	5.8	9.63	−15.2
	IV	0.6	8.1	12.3	18.9	8.5	4.5	5.9	11.80	−24.5
	Yr.	3.2	8.5	11.4	10.5	8.5	7.8	5.8	10.04	−14.8
1980	I	3.1	9.3	16.6	20.8	7.1	6.9	6.2	13.46	−36.3
	II	−9.9	9.8	15.2	17.0	6.5	−3.1	7.3	10.05	−66.5
	III	2.4	9.2	7.7	20.2	9.9	14.5	7.5	9.24	−74.2
	IV	3.8	10.7	11.0	18.1	10.0	11.2	7.5	13.71	−67.9
	Yr.	−0.1	9.0	13.4	18.1	8.0	6.4	7.1	11.63	−62.3

*Dollars in billions. Deficit shown as minus (−); surplus as plus (+).

Interest rates also rose at an accelerating rate: up by 0.26% in 1977 and by 2% in 1978.

In 1979 we saw the rate of growth slow appreciably, going briefly negative for the second quarter. Some economists argue that the reference cycle peak should be designated to have occurred sometime in 1979; however, the behavior of the unemployment rate and other indicators do seem to justify the NBER's judgment in dating the peak of the cycle as January 1980. The unemployment rate averaged 5.8% for 1979, which was lower than the 6.0% average for 1978.

The recession of 1980 was unique in a number of dimensions, primarily in its brevity. At six months, this recession is the shortest ever recorded for as far back as the records go, to 1854. The immediate post-World War I recession in 1919–1920 is close at seven months.

One surprising turn in this short recession was the behavior of interest rates. As we discussed earlier, interest rates are, in general, coincident or lagging economic indicators, generally lagging at the trough. Certainly in the previous two recessions interest rates did not start back up until some time after the beginning of the recovery of the general level of economic activity. In the 1969–1970 recession interest rates peaked in December 1969 at the same time as the reference cycle but did not hit bottom and start to rise again until January 1972, fourteen months after the trough in the reference cycle. Interest rates fell for two years and one month. In the 1974–1975 recession, rates fell from August 1974 to December 1976, a period of two years and four months. So when interest rates peaked in March 1980, the presumption (and the consensus forecast of economists) was for a decline lasting for something between one and two years. What happened was the shortest interest rate cycle on record. Rates fell for only three months until June 1980, and then began an abrupt rise to new record levels by December 1980. Further increases followed until late 1981. The decline in interest rates (3 months) being shorter than the decline in the reference cycle (6 months) combined with the recession being the shortest on record made for a unique period in the money and capital markets. It also made for a high degree of uncertainty among the participants in the markets given that the interest rate forecasts based on historically typical behavior had been so far off the mark.

When interest rates did reach another peak in 1981, the economy went into another recession after a recovery lasting less than one year. The 1980–1981 expansion is the shortest since the ten-month recovery from March 1919 to January 1920. Note the parallel. The shortest previous recession of seven months in 1918–1919 preceded the shortest previous expansion of ten months in 1919–1920, just as the six-month recession of 1980 was followed by an expansion of less than one year. Incidentally, the short expansion in 1920 was followed by an eighteen-month recession lasting until July 1921.

The 1980s Open with a Recession That Does the Job on Inflation — with Ten Percent Unemployment

According to NBER dating we began the 1980s with the relatively short 12-month expansion that began in July 1980 and ended in July 1981, and then had a 16-month recession that officially ended in November of 1982.

As can be seen from Tables 16.8 and 16.9, the unemployment rate rose steadily from the first quarter average of 6.2% in 1980 to average more than 10% for the last half of 1982 and the first half of 1983. Looking at inflation rates as measured by the CPI on an annual basis, we find the steady decline for the years 1980 through 1983 of: 13.4%, 10.4%, 6.2%, and 3.2%. If the capitalistic system is cursed with unemployment in order to be blessed with some degree of price stability, the system seemed to be working.

Looking at the numbers grouped on the basis of business cycle dates, Table 16.10, we can note that although the recession in and of itself was not of record-setting severity, with a 3% decline in real GNP spread over five quarters, the record setting unemployment rates resulted from the fact that it followed the very weak 12-month recovery of 1980–1981. We can contrast the one-year recovery III80–III81 with the first year of the next recovery, IV82–IV83. In the earlier recovery real GNP grew by only 4.2%, but by 6.1% in 1982–1983. Consumer durable goods expenditures in real terms grew by only 6.1% in the earlier recovery, but by 16.9% in the more recent one.

What made the 1981–1982 recession so severe was its proximity to the recession of 1980 and the weak recovery thereafter. The economy essentially stagnated in terms of real economic growth for the four-year period 1979–1982. Real GNP in 1982 was only 3.25% higher than in 1978 for an annual average rate of growth of a mere 0.8%.

We discussed earlier the new records being set in the federal government's deficit in this period. We can note here that when the data are grouped by cyclical timing the outstanding anomaly is the deficit as a percentage of GNP actually *rising* in a period of strong economic expansion. Although the deficit rose to 2.7% of GNP in the recession of 1980, it fell back to 1.8% in even the weak recovery of 1980–1981. In contrast the deficit rose spectacularly to 4.5% of GNP in the recession of 1981–1982, but then rose further to 5.5% in the first year of the recovery. This is clearly the result of active fiscal policy. As noted earlier, the difference is not in the federal government's level of expenditures but is the result of declining revenues relative to GNP from the 1981 tax cuts. Although expenditures increased at an annual rate of 13.5% in the recovery of 1980–1981, they rose at a rate of only 3.2% in the first year of the most recent recovery.

TABLE 16.9 Annual and Quarterly Data on the U.S. Economy, 1981–1983

Year	Qtr.	Annual Percentage Rate of Growth in:						Average Level of:		
		Real GNP	GNP Price Index	CPI	Fed. Govt. Expd.	Mont. Base	M1	Unemp. Rate (%)	T-Bill Rate (%)	Fed. Govt. Def.*
1981	I	9.0	10.6	11.0	13.7	4.0	5.0	7.4	14.37	−43.4
	II	0.7	5.9	9.6	5.6	6.8	9.2	7.6	14.83	−47.3
	III	3.6	9.4	12.0	20.0	3.7	3.1	7.4	15.09	−62.4
	IV	−4.9	9.0	5.4	14.3	2.9	3.3	8.3	12.02	−95.8
	Yr.	2.6	9.4	10.4	14.5	6.4	7.1	7.6	14.08	−62.2
1982	I	−5.5	4.3	3.3	1.7	9.6	11.0	8.8	12.90	−108.5
	II	1.0	5.6	6.2	4.1	8.6	3.3	9.4	12.36	−113.5
	III	−1.0	3.7	7.9	22.4	6.0	6.3	10.0	9.71	−158.3
	IV	−1.3	3.8	0.8	26.9	7.6	13.7	10.6	7.94	−208.2
	Yr.	−1.8	6.0	6.2	10.9	6.6	6.5	9.7	10.73	−147.1
1983	I	2.6	5.5	−0.3	−6.8	12.4	14.9	10.4	8.08	−183.3
	II	9.7	3.3	5.1	6.1	11.6	12.7	10.1	8.42	−166.1
	III	7.6	3.6	4.9	6.9	5.7	9.2	9.4	9.19	−187.3
	IV	4.0	4.5	3.5	7.2	7.4	2.1	8.5	8.79	−194.9
	Yr.	3.3	4.2	3.2	8.1	9.1	10.9	9.6	8.62	−182.9

*Dollars in billions. Deficit shown as minus (−); surplus as plus (+).

Comparison of Reference Cycles and Specific Cycles of Real GNP, 1949–1980

By way of summarizing the cyclical fluctuations in the post-World War II period, let us compare the changes in real GNP over the reference cycle and the specific cycle of that time series. First, let us make sure we understand the difference between a turning point in a reference cycle and a specific cycle. We discussed the NBER's definition and dating of peaks and troughs in some detail in Chapter 9. We noted in that chapter that the reference cycle is manifested in no single economic indicator but rather is a judgment of what constitutes a turning point in the "general level of economic activity." In Tables 16.1, 16.2, 16.5, and 16.10, we presented the change in various economic indicators during the time period of the reference cycle. Each indicator had its own peaks and troughs, which most likely did not coincide with the peaks and troughs of the reference cycle. The peaks and troughs of each individual time series mark the beginning and ending of the specific cycle for that particular indicator.

In the press and in public discussion of the economy, the general level of economic activity is frequently characterized by what happens to real GNP, so let us compare the change in that particular economic indicator over the reference cycle and over its own specific cycle. Tables 16.11 and 16.12 present the dates of turning points, the length of each cycle, and the total and annual rate of change in real GNP both on the basis of reference cycle dates and the specific peaks and troughs of real GNP.

Looking first at Table 16.11, which presents the data on the expansions, we find there is not that much difference in the reference and the specific cycles. In terms of dates, the peaks and troughs vary by more than one quarter in only two cases, the 1970 and 1949 troughs, and coincide in a large number of cases. In the case of the 1970 trough, real GNP, after falling for two quarters, hit bottom in the first quarter of 1970, rose for two quarters, then fell for one quarter, and then continued its rise. Hence, we date the trough of the specific cycle in the first quarter of 1970 for a total increase of 17.2% before the peak in IV73. The reference cycle trough comes three quarters later and shows a total rise of only 16.8% until the peak in IV73. Of course, the reference cycle period shows a faster rate of increase at 5.3% per year than the specific cycle at 4.3% per year. A similar circumstance occurred in 1949 with the reference cycle expansion showing a rate of growth of 6.6% over 3 3/4 years, while the specific cycle shows 6.4% per year for 4 years.

In general, as evidenced by the averages at the bottom of Table 16.11, the specific cycle of real GNP is not all that different from the reference cycle. One can say that the average of the six expansions since World War II lasted about 4 1/2 years, with real GNP up at an annual rate of just under 5% for a total increase of something over 23%. Of course, the variation among the cycles themselves was quite significant over this period as indicated

TABLE 16.10   Changes in U.S. Economic Time Series Between NBER Reference Dates, III80–IV83*

	(+) III80–III81 (4 Qtrs.) Total Change	(−) III81–IV82 (5 Qtrs.) Tot. Chg.	 Ann. Rate	(+) IV82–IV83 (4 Qtrs.) Total Change
GNP, %Δ				
Current Dollars	+ 13.9	+ 3.5%	2.8%	+ 10.4
Price Deflated	+ 4.2	− 3.0	− 2.4	+ 6.1
CPI, %Δ	+ 10.9	+ 6.0	4.8	+ 3.3
% Unemployment	− 0.1	+ 3.2	2.6	− 2.1
Consumption				
Total, %Δ				
Current Dollars	+ 12.0	+ 8.5	6.8	+ 9.1
Price Deflated	+ 3.6	+ 1.7	1.4	+ 5.4
Durable Goods, %Δ				
Current Dollars	+ 13.9	+ 3.5	2.8	+ 17.1
Price Deflated	+ 6.1	− 0.5	− 0.4	+ 14.2
Investment				
Total Fixed, %Δ				
Current Dollars	+ 14.2	− 6.5	− 5.3	+ 18.0
Price Deflated	+ 6.1	− 9.3	− 7.5	+ 16.9
Change in Inventories (Dollars in billions)	+ $11.1	− $20.9	− $16.7	− 6.9
Fed. Govt. Exp., %Δ	+ 13.5	17.1	13.4	+ 3.2
Deficit (−), % or GNP	− 1.8	− 4.5		− 5.5
Money Supply, M1, %Δ	+ 6.8	7.4	5.9	+.9.6
Treasury Bill Rate, Δ%	+ 5.85%	− 7.15%		+ 0.85%

*Recessions shown as minus (−); expansions as plus (+).

by the standard deviations at the bottom of the table. The length of the expansions ranges from 2 years to 8 3/4 years. Excluding the very long expansion associated with the Vietnam War, the range of 2 to 5 years does cover the experience of this period.

The recessions described by the data presented in Table 16.12 are much more heterogeneous than the expansions. In the first place it makes a great deal of difference whether you date the decline of real GNP by the reference cycle or its own specific cycle. The dates coincide only for one recession, IV73–I75, out of seven and in two instances are different by more than

TABLE 16.11 Expansions, Reference, and Specific Cycles for Real GNP, 1949–1980

	NBER Reference Cycle Dates			%Δ Real GNP			Real GNP Specific Cycle Dates			%Δ Real GNP	
Trough	Peak	Length (Years)	Total	Annual Rate		Trough	Peak	Length (Years)	Total	Annual Rate	
IV49	III53	3 3/4	27.2%	6.6%		I49	I53	4	28.1	6.4	
I54	III57	3 1/4	13.2	3.9		I54	III57	3 1/4	13.2	3.9	
I58	I60	2	10.2	5.0		I58	I60	2	11.3	5.5	
I61	IV69	8 3/4	47.2	4.5		IV60	III69	8 3/4	49.2	4.7	
IV70	IV73	3	16.8	5.3		I70	IV73	3 3/4	17.2	4.3	
I75	I80	5	24.5	4.5		I75	I80	5	24.5	4.5	
Average		4.29	23.18%	4.97				4.45	23.92%	4.88	
Standard Deviation		2.19	12.27%	0.85%				2.08	12.76%	0.83	

TABLE 16.12 Recessions, References, and Specific Cycles for Real GNP, 1949–1980

| | NBER Reference Cycle Dates | | | | | Real GNP Specific Cycle Dates | | | | |
| | | | | %Δ Real GNP | | | | | %Δ Real GNP | |
Peak	Trough	Length (Years)		Total	Annual Rate	Peak	Trough	Length (Years)	Total	Annual Rate
IV48	IV49	1		−1.4%	−1.4%	IV48	I49	1/2	−1.5%	−3.0%
III53	II54	3/4		−2.6	−3.5	I53	II54	1	−3.2	−3.2
III57	II58	3/4		−2.7	−3.6	III57	I58	1/2	−3.3	−6.6
I60	I61	3/4		−0.1	−0.1	I60	IV60	3/4	−1.2	−1.6
IV69	IV70	1		−0.1	−0.1	III69	I70	1/2	−1.0	−2.0
IV73	I75	1 1/4		−4.8	−3.9	IV73	I75	1 1/4	−4.8	−3.9
I80	III80	1/2		−2.0	−4.0	I80	II80	1/4	−2.6	−10.0
Average		0.86		−1.96%	−2.37%			0.68	−2.51%	−4.33
Standard Deviation		0.23		1.53%	1.65%			0.32	1.27%	2.08

one quarter. Of course, given the shorter average length of the recessions as compared to the expansions, even one quarter is a substantial quantitative difference.

The average length of a recession calculated on the basis of reference cycle dates is a little over 10 months (.86 of a year) and around 8 months (.68) if the average is based on the specific cycle of GNP. Although only two months is not much in absolute terms, over those time periods the average decline in real GNP was 1.96% for the reference cycle and 2.51% for the specific cycle. The difference in the average rate of fall is even greater, a 2.37% rate for the reference cycles versus a 4.32% for the specific cycles. In general, the reference cycle usually extends beyond the end of the decline in real GNP and some of the lost ground has been regained by the time a reference cycle trough is designated to have occurred.

We can perhaps try to generalize about recessions during the last thirty years and not distinguish between the reference and specific real GNP cycle by saying that recessions last, on average, eight to ten months. However, as we noted above, with regard to the "typical" decline in real GNP, we have to give 1.96%, as the average, if we use the reference cycle and 2.51% if we use the specific cycle. Of course, more importantly, none of the averages given in Table 16.12 is very representative given the range of experience covered by the individual recessions. We have had a one quarter decline in real GNP characterized as a recession, 1980; and we have seen a decline lasting five quarters, 1973–1975. The total percentage declines have ranged from 1% to 4.8%; the rate of fall has ranged from 1.6% to 10%. As we noted in Chapter 1, each business cycle is unique. What we can say additionally at this point is that expansions seem to have slightly more in common with each other than do recessions, most of which are unique indeed.

As this book goes to press the expansion is strong into 1984. If it is to run the average of 4.29 years shown in the table, it has a long way to go. If one excludes the Vietnam War expansion but includes the short 1980–1981 expansion, the average is exactly three years on NBER dating. If one uses that to forecast the beginning of the next recession, one would expect it to begin in the fourth quarter of 1985. However, given the diversity of our experience, a wide range of dates before and after that date can certainly be considered as almost equally probable. Chapter 17 is concerned with trying to do a more complete job of macroeconomic forecasting, rather than merely showing the simple use of unadjusted historical averages.

● **Questions for Discussion**

1. Consider the contention that World War II made Keynesians of us all, while the Korean and Vietnam wars reestablished the relevance of classical economics.

2. Why was the difference between nominal and real rates of interest suddenly emphasized much more in the 1970s than in the 1950s and 1960s?

3. Make the case that the 1970s were, except for the rate of inflation, more like the 1950s than the 1960s in terms of business cycle history.

4. Is there any basis in history for the popular idea that the Democrats follow stimulative macroeconomic policies creating low unemployment and increased rates of inflation while the Republicans do the opposite?

● Source Notes

[1]Okun, Arthur M. *The Political Economy of Prosperity.* New York: W.W. Norton, 1970, p. 33. The quotation of President Johnson is from the *Economic Report of the President,* January 1965, p. 10.

● Selected Additional Readings

Bronfenbrenner, Martin, ed. *Is the Business Cycle Obsolete?* New York: Wiley-Interscience, 1969.

Dornbusch, Rudiger, and Stanley Fischer. *Macroeconomics.* (2d ed.) New York: McGraw-Hill, 1981. Chapters 10 and 16.

Fama, Eugene F. Inflation, output and money. *The Journal of Business,* Vol. 55, No. 2 (April 1982).

Gordon, Robert A. *Business Fluctuations.* (2d ed.) New York: Harper and Row, 1961. Chapters 15 and 16.

Klein, Philip A. *Business Cycles in the Postwar World.* Washington, D.C.: American Enterprise Institute, 1976.

Maloney, Kevin J., and Michael L. Smirlock. Business cycles and the political process. *Southern Economic Journal,* Vol. 48, No. 2 (October 1981).

McNees, Stephen K. The forecasting record for the 1970s. *New England Economic Review* of the Federal Reserve Bank of Boston (September/October, 1979).

Okun, Arthur M. *The Political Economy of Prosperity.* New York: W. W. Norton, 1970.

Resler, David H. The formation of inflation expectations. *Review* of the Federal Reserve Bank of St. Louis, Vol. 62, No. 4 (April 1980).

Schultze, Charles L. Some macro foundations for micro theory. *Brookings Papers on Economic Activity,* No. 2, 1981. Washington, D.C.: The Brookings Institution, 1981.

Stein, Herbert. The 1930s and the 1980s. *The AEI Economist (November 1979).*

Tatom, John A. Potential output and the recent productivity decline. *Review* of the Federal Reserve Bank of St. Louis, Vol. 64, No. 1 (January 1982).

Yohe, William P., and Denis S. Karnosky. Interest rates and price level changes, 1952–69. *Review* of the Federal Reserve Bank of St. Louis (December 1969). Reprint series number 49.

Macroeconomic Forecasting

17

Although this chapter is concerned with the making of a macroeconomic forecast, or evaluating those made by others, we should emphasize that all the preceding chapters are relevant to the task. What we are doing here is placing what we discussed earlier in the context of this specific application. In this chapter we will look at some of the mechanics of making a forecast and attempt to highlight the economic analysis most relevant to macroeconomic forecasting. We will also examine various approaches to forecasting with a comment on the availability and use of the econometric forecasting services.

At this point, however, I would urge the student of business cycles and forecasting to read a short essay reproduced in full at the end of this chapter. "Economic Forecasting and Science," by Paul A. Samuelson, is an entertaining but insightful presentation. Professor Samuelson puts modern macroeconomic forecasting into proper perspective. He does conclude that, with all the weaknesses in orthodox economics, "There is no efficacious substitute for economic analysis in business forecasting." He emphasizes that ex post the best point estimate of some economic variable frequently turns out to be someone's random guess, but that is because there are random guesses covering the full range of possible outcomes (and even a lot of impossible outcomes). One of them is bound to be right. Of course, our ability to duplicate the accuracy of a lucky one-shot hit is nonexistent. As Samuelson indicates, any serious forecaster would be delighted to come in second consistently year after year in the macroeconomic forecasting derby.

Evaluating an Economic Forecast, Ex Ante

The objective criteria by which one can evaluate a forecast, ex ante, as opposed to the ex post criterion of simple accuracy, are mainly the requirements imposed by consistency, both historically and prospectively.

By historical consistency we mean that a reasonable forecast will contain values for economic time series that fit, at least broadly, within the range of our historical experience. For example, we have never experienced a doubling of real GNP from one year to the next. Such a forecast would be regarded as nonsensical on the simple basis of historical experience. More realistically, we would regard a forecast of an annual increase in real GNP of anything in excess of 5% as requiring substantial justification in the form of evidence about unemployed resources, increasing demand, and so on.

The mention of unemployed resources leads us into the second type of consistency we referred to above, the prospective internal consistency of a forecast. Some consistency involves only identities and there can be no argument that any forecast must, if it is to be taken seriously, conform to definitional identities; that is, we have previously discussed the relationship among the change in nominal GNP; real GNP, (Q); the GNP price index, (P); the money supply, (M); and its velocity;

$$\% \Delta GNP = \%\Delta P + \%\Delta Q + (\%\Delta P)(\%\Delta Q),$$
$$= \%\Delta M + \%\Delta V + (\%\Delta M)(\%\Delta V),$$

which we derived from the definitional identities

$$GNP = (P)(Q) = (M)(V).$$

Few forecasters are going to be guilty of the mistake of not conforming to the above equations since it amounts essentially to a mistake in arithmetic.

More meaningful and subtle problems of consistency arise from the generally accepted theory of the functioning of the economy along with our range of historical experience. Every behavioral pattern we have examined in all the preceding chapters has the potential of imposing a consistency requirement. For example, we noted the cyclical sensitivity of the federal government's budget surplus or deficit. In the absence of significant changes in tax or expenditure programs, a forecast of deep recession accompanied by a movement toward an increased budget surplus would be regarded as an internally inconsistent forecast. Just as with historical consistency, there is room for disagreement regarding what is "reasonably consistent" for purposes of internal comparison.

In previous chapters we have considered the historically typical behavior of many economic time series and their usual relationship to each other over the cycle. However, we have not considered one relationship that is very important in compiling an internally consistent macroeconomic forecast. It is the relationship between the growth of the economy and unemployment. The fairly consistent relationship between the percentage change in real GNP and the change in the unemployment rate has come to be known as "Okun's Law" after the late Arthur Okun.[1]

"Okun's Law," the Relationship between Economic Growth and Unemployment

There is, of course, a rather complete theoretical structure underlying any specific hypothesized relationship between output and the unemployment rate. Some of the relevant macroeconomic theory has already been covered. We have discussed the growth of the labor force, fluctuations in the labor force participation rate, and other factors relevant to the relationship between the unemployment rate and the rate of growth in real output. However, up to this point we have not been explicit about that relationship; and we are still going to skip a lot of theory having to do with "potential GNP" and the "GNP gap." These concepts were much in vogue in the 1960s when we thought we could be a lot more precise about these matters than it turns out we can be. Economists' infatuation with precision in these matters, both theoretical and empirical, rose and fell with the rise and fall of faith in the Phillips curve. (See Chapter 11.)

Our failure to discover stable, reliable relationships among output, employment, and inflation notwithstanding, we can look at the historical bounds of association between, say, changes in the unemployment rate and the rate of growth in real GNP and declare certain combinations to be extremely unlikely. Figure 17.1 shows the experience of the U.S. economy for the years 1950 through 1980. Note that the relationship is between the rate of growth in real GNP, $\%\Delta Q$, and the *change* in the percentage unemployment rate, $\Delta \%Un$. Again we find the usefulness of naive forecasting. The *level* of the unemployment rate next year is to a large extent a function of its level this year. We can only find a relationship between growth in real GNP and the change in the unemployment rate from one year to the next.

Figure 17.1 does indicate that the range of experience for the U.S. economy is wide but not totally random. In general, a higher growth rate for real GNP is associated with a fall in the unemployment rate while low rates of growth result in increases in the unemployment rate. We have never had both these variables go negative in the same year. A least-squares line treating the change in the unemployment rate as the dependent variable fitted to the data for 1950–1979 gives an R^2 of .75 and an estimating equation of: $\Delta \%Un = 1.45 - .38 \%\Delta Q$. Note that on average over this time period when $\Delta \%Un = 0$, $\%\Delta Q = 3.77$; that is, on average real GNP had to grow at an annual rate of 3.77% just for unemployment not to rise. Conversely, if $\%\Delta Q = 0$, $\Delta \%Un = 1.45$; if the economy did not grow at all, the unemployment rate went up by about 1.5 percentage points each year as a result of the growth in the labor force. For each percentage point reduction in the unemployment rate during this time period, it took about 2.6% more in the growth rate of real GNP. The greater than one-for-one trade-off is not purely a result of population growth or declining productivity of labor.

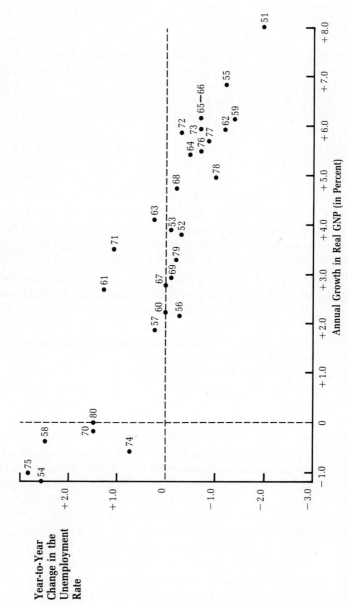

FIGURE 17.1 "Okun's Law" Illustrated Empirically, 1950–1980

As we discussed earlier, the labor force expands and contracts in a procyclical fashion and also there has been an upward trend in the national labor force participation rate over this time period.

We can dramatize the lack of stability in this relationship if we calculate a different estimating equation for each of the three decades. The results for each decade separately and for all three together are given in Table 17.1. The correlation coefficient and the parameters of the estimating equation all fall from the 1950s to the 1960s and then rise again in the 1970s but none reach the old level of the 1950s. However, the rate of growth in real GNP required to hold the unemployment rate constant, $\Delta\%Un = 0$, fell from 3.85% in the 1950s to 3.56% in the 1960s, but jumped to 4.02% in the 1970s. This is obviously another manifestation of the rising trend in the unemployment rate over the last thirty years we discussed in Chapter 11.

Although we would expect generally that shifting from annual to quarterly data reduces the accuracy of forecasts, we should especially note that this particular relationship becomes much less reliable on a quarterly basis than on an annual basis. There are even some quarters when both the variables are negative. A decline in real GNP is accompanied by a *drop* in the unemployment rate. (One suspects that this is an example of particularly bad effects from seasonal adjustment.)

A Forecasting Sequence

The mechanics of forecasting consist of filling in the blanks in a table showing values for economic data for coming time periods. For example, for a minimum detail general economic forecast one could simply make an estimate for next year from the figures shown in Table 17.2 (Table 10.1,

TABLE 17.1 Okun's Law Done Empirically, 1950–1979

$$\Delta\% \ Un \ = \ a \ + \ b \ \% \ \Delta Q$$

	Least-Squares Line Fitted to Data for:			
	1950–1979	1950–1959	1960–1969	1970–1979
R^2	.75	.78	.58	.69
a	1.45	1.52	1.14	1.45
b	−.38	−.39	−.32	−.36
$\%\Delta Q$ when $\Delta\%Un = 0$	3.77	3.85	3.56	4.02
$\Delta\%Un$ when $\%\Delta Q = 0$	1.45	1.52	1.14	1.45
Means:				
$\%\Delta Q$	3.78	3.95	4.19	3.19
$\Delta\%Un$	−.003	−.04	−.20	.30

TABLE 17.2 Recent Data on the U.S. Economy* (Dollars in Billions)

	1975			1976			1977		
	Level	Change		Level	Change		Level	Change	
		Amount	Percent		Amount	Percent		Amount	Percent
Consumption									
Durable Goods	132.2	10.7	8.8	156.8	24.6	18.6	178.8	22.0	14.0
Other**	844.2	77.6	10.1	927.5	83.3	9.9	1026.7	99.2	10.7
Total	976.4	88.3	9.9	1084.3	107.9	11.1	1205.5	121.2	11.2
Investment									
Business Fixed	157.7	1.1	0.7	174.1	16.4	10.4	205.5	31.4	18.0
Res. Const.	55.3	−2.6	−4.5	72.0	16.7	30.2	95.8	23.8	33.1
Inventory Change	−6.9	−21.0	—	+11.8	+18.7	—	+21.0	+9.2	—
Total	206.1	−22.6	−9.9	257.9	51.8	25.1	322.3	64.4	25.0
Government									
Federal Defense	83.0	6.0	7.8	86.0	3.0	3.6	93.3	7.3	8.5
Other Federal	39.7	5.8	17.1	43.2	3.5	8.8	50.6	7.4	17.1
Total Federal	122.7	11.7	10.5	129.2	6.5	5.3	143.9	14.7	11.4
State and Local	217.2	24.1	12.5	232.9	15.7	7.2	250.6	17.7	7.6
Total Government	339.9	35.8	11.8	362.1	22.2	6.5	394.5	32.4	8.9
Net Exports	+26.8	+13.4	—	+13.8	−13.0	—	−4.2	−18.0	—
Total GNP	1549.2	115.0	8.0	1718.0	168.8	10.9	1918.0	200.0	11.6
"Real" GNP (1972 $)	1233.9	−14.1	−1.1	1300.4	66.5	5.4	1371.7	71.3	5.5
GNP Price Index	125.56	10.64	9.3	132.11	6.55	5.2	139.83	7.72	5.8
Unemployment Rate	8.5%	2.9%	—	7.8%	−0.7%	—	7.0%	−0.8%	—
Consumer Price Index	161.2	13.5	9.1	170.5	9.3	5.8	181.5	11.0	6.5
T-Bill Rate, Average	5.82	−2.05	−26.0	5.00	−0.82	−14.1	5.26	+0.26	+4.9

*This is what the Department of Commerce thinks happened as of February 1984; they will change their minds and there will be revisions.

**This figure is obtained by subtracting durable goods expenditures from total consumption expenditures as reported for GNP accounting.

338

TABLE 17.2 (continued)

	1978 Level	1978 Change Amount	1978 Change Percent	1979 Level	1979 Change Amount	1979 Change Percent	1980 Level	1980 Change Amount	1980 Change Percent
Consumption									
Durable Goods	200.2	22.0	12.3	213.4	13.2	6.6	214.7	1.3	0.6
Other**	1146.3	120.1	11.7	1293.8	147.5	12.9	1453.4	159.6	12.3
Total	1346.5	142.1	11.8	1507.2	160.7	11.9	1668.1	160.9	10.7
Investment									
Business Fixed	248.9	43.7	21.3	290.2	41.3	16.6	308.8	18.6	6.4
Res. Const.	111.2	15.4	16.1	118.6	7.4	6.7	102.9	−15.7	−13.2
Inventory Change	+26.5	+3.5	—	+14.3	−12.2	—	−9.8	−24.1	—
Total	386.6	62.5	19.3	423.0	36.4	9.4	401.9	−21.1	−5.0
Government									
Federal Defense	100.3	7.5	8.1	111.8	11.5	11.5	131.2	19.4	17.4
Other Federal	53.3	2.7	5.3	56.5	3.2	6.0	65.9	9.4	16.6
Total Federal	153.6	10.2	7.1	168.3	14.7	9.6	197.0	28.7	17.1
State and Local	278.3	27.9	11.1	306.0	27.7	10.0	340.8	34.8	11.4
Total Government	431.9	38.1	9.7	474.4	42.5	9.8	537.8	63.4	13.4
Net Exports	−1.1	+2.9	—	+13.2	+14.3	—	+23.9	+10.7	—
Total GNP	2163.9	245.6	12.8	2417.8	253.9	11.7	2631.7	213.9	8.8
"Real" GNP (1972 $)	1438.6	68.9	5.0	1479.4	40.8	2.8	1475.0	−4.4	−0.3
GNP Price Index	150.42	10.37	7.4	163.42	13.00	8.6	178.42	15.0	9.2
Unemployment Rate	6.0%	−1.0%	—	5.8%	−0.2%	—	7.1%	+1.3%	—
Consumer Price Index	195.3	13.8	7.6	217.6	22.3	11.4	246.8	29.2	13.4
T-Bill Rate, Average	7.22	+1.96	+37.3	10.04	+2.82	+39.1	11.51	1.47	14.6

*This is what the Department of Commerce thinks happened as of February 1984; they will change their minds and there will be revisions.

**This figure is obtained by subtracting durable goods expenditures from total consumption expenditures as reported for GNP accounting.

TABLE 17.2 (continued)

	1981			1982			1983		
	Level	Change		Level	Change		Level	Change	
		Amount	Percent		Amount	Percent		Amount	Percent
Consumption									
Durable Goods	236.1	21.4	10.0	244.5	8.4	3.6	278.6	34.1	13.9
Other**	1621.1	167.7	11.5	1747.4	126.3	7.8	1880.0	132.6	7.6
Total	1857.2	189.1	11.3	1991.9	134.7	7.3	2158.6	166.7	8.4
Investment									
Business Fixed	352.2	43.4	14.1	348.3	−3.9	−1.1	347.7	−0.6	−0.2
Res. Const.	104.3	1.4	1.4	90.8	−13.5	−12.9	130.5	39.7	43.7
Inventory Change	+18.5	+28.3	—	−24.5	−43.0	—	−6.9	+17.6	—
Total	474.9	73.0	18.2	414.5	−60.4	−12.7	471.3	56.8	13.7
Government									
Federal Defense	154.0	22.8	17.4	179.4	25.4	16.5	200.3	20.9	11.6
Other Federal	75.2	9.3	14.1	79.3	4.1	5.5	74.9	−4.4	−5.5
Total Federal	229.2	32.2	16.3	258.7	29.5	12.9	275.2	16.5	6.4
State and Local	366.5	25.7	7.5	390.5	24.0	6.5	415.0	24.5	6.3
Total Government	595.7	57.9	10.8	649.2	53.5	9.0	690.2	41.0	6.3
Net Exports	+26.3	+2.4	—	17.4	−8.9	—	−10.6	−28.0	—
Total GNP	2954.1	322.4	12.3	3073.0	118.9	4.0	3309.5	236.5	7.7
"Real" GNP (1972 $)	1513.8	38.8	2.6	1485.4	−28.4	−1.9	1534.8	49.4	3.3
GNP Price Index	195.14	16.72	9.4	206.88	11.74	6.0	215.63	8.75	4.2
Unemployment Rate	7.6%	+0.5%	—	9.7%	+2.1%	—	9.6%	−0.1%	—
Consumer Price Index	272.4	25.6	10.4	289.1	16.7	6.1	298.4	9.3	3.2
T-Bill Rate, Average	14.08	2.57	22.3	10.69	−3.39	−24.0	8.62	−2.07	−19.4

*This is what the Department of Commerce thinks happened as of February 1984; they will change their minds and there will be revisions.

**This figure is obtained by subtracting durable goods expenditures from total consumption expenditures as reported for GNP accounting.

which is reproduced again here). This table gives the major components of GNP plus the CPI, the unemployment rate, and the average for the Treasury Bill rate. If you were to come up with estimates for each of those for the coming year any competent businessperson or economist would certainly have a fairly clear idea of what you expect the macroeconomic environment to be in the coming year. Even without a description of your procedures (which would most certainly be required if you were doing the forecast for pay or course credit) the interrelationships of the variables would even give some evidence of why you expect a particular outcome, say a rate of growth in real GNP of only 1%.

A workable method of generating a reasonable macroeconomic forecast is as follows:

1. Generate a "first-cut" forecast for each major component of nominal GNP. Each component can be estimated separately and the estimating procedure can be as crude or elaborate as the balance between time, money, and the component's importance seems to indicate. In many cases one might forecast the percentage change from the previous year and solve for the dollar amount. For example, suppose for whatever reasons you expect expenditures for consumer durables in real terms not to grow at all over the forecast period. Your estimate of the rate of price change will then be your estimate of the percentage change in that component of nominal GNP. For some components of GNP, such as consumer expenditures for nondurables and services, some form of naive forecasting technique might be adequate. For other more cyclical components such as the rate of change in inventories or capital equipment expenditures, more complex analysis using a great deal of external information may be required.

2. Total up the GNP components in dollar terms and calculate the implied percentage change in total nominal GNP from the previous time period. Is it reasonable? (Probably not, the first time around.) You undoubtedly started the process with some idea of where in the business cycle the economy stood and there are some rates of change in nominal GNP that you simply will not feel to be reasonable. For example, a 2% increase in nominal GNP in an economy running an 8% inflation rate implies a percentage change in real GNP (approximately -6%) that might be more of a depression than you want to forecast. If so, it is back for another estimation of the components of GNP. You continue such iterations until you are satisfied, at least for the moment, with the implied total.

3. Divide the percentage change in nominal GNP into the percentage change in real GNP and the GNP price deflator. This can be accomplished by independently forecasting *one* of the following four economic indicators:

a. The level of real GNP for the forecast period, Q.

b. The percentage change in real GNP from the current period to the forecast period, $\%\Delta Q$.

c. The level of the GNP price index for the forecast period, P.

d. The percentage change in the GNP price index from the current period to the forecast period, $\%\Delta P$.

Any one of these four, along with last period's values and the forecast for total nominal GNP, will give you enough information to fill in all the values in the following two equations:

$$\text{GNP} = (P)(Q),$$
$$\%\Delta\text{GNP} = (\%\Delta P) + (\%\Delta Q) + (\%\Delta P)(\%\Delta Q).$$

Again, this may be the point at which you have to go back for another iteration. If there is no reasonable combination of real economic growth, $\%\Delta Q$, and the inflation rate, $\%\Delta P$, that is consistent with your forecast of growth in nominal GNP, $\%\Delta\text{GNP}$, you may decide to take another look at the components from which you built the total.

4. Apply whatever variant of Okun's Law seems appropriate to obtain a reasonable forecast of the average unemployment rate over the forecast period. In step three you settled on the rate of real economic growth, $\%\Delta Q$; you can now use that to get at least a first approximation of the unemployment rate. For example, history as embodied in Okun's Law indicates that something in excess of 3% real growth is required just to keep the unemployment rate from rising. If your estimate of $\%\Delta Q$ is only 2% for the coming year, a fall in the unemployment rate would seem to be an unreasonable forecast. The exact amount of the rise in unemployment you want to forecast would depend on a number of factors, many of which we have considered in previous chapters.

5. Relate the economic environment indicated by your forecast of $\%\Delta P$, $\%\Delta Q$, and the level of unemployment rate to the money and capital markets and produce your interest rate forecast in whatever degree of detail you require. Given the experience of recent years, what is reasonable covers quite a large range. These are still broad parameters on interest rate behavior, however. Of course, regarding the term structure, both history and theory tell us that as all interest rates rise, short-term rates will rise faster and further than long-term rates; and, as rates fall, short-term rates will also fall faster and further.

6. Examine your forecast in its entirety. Does it fit together as a package? Does each component fit with its own history? This sixth step is really an instruction to go back and do the other five over and over again until you feel like you have at least satisfied the requirements of consistency and reasonableness (consistency both among the separate com-

ponents and with historical experience). You cannot forecast the large exogenous shocks to the economy. If you are serious you will not try. You will assume that the world does not take large, discrete jumps although, in fact, it sometimes does. Accurate forecasts of war, assassinations, and gold discoveries are the result of luck, not scholarly work. Recall the introductory lecture by Samuelson.

Although each business cycle is unique, the variables are consistent enough that changing any component of a macroeconomic forecast has implications for most all the other components. An economic forecast is like a large matrix in which a shift in any one element requires shifts in all others. Much of this book has been devoted to examining these relationships. By way of a very condensed review we can, without too much oversimplification, depict the major economic variables as rows and column headings on a matrix to show the direction of their interrelationship. We will use a plus sign $(+)$ to indicate variables that move in the same direction and a minus $(-)$ to indicate movements in opposite directions. The matrix is shown in Table 17.3.

The connections implied by the pluses and minuses in the matrix are descriptive of typical business cycle behavior, *not* an analytically accurate picture of flows of causation. For example, we show a negative relationship between net exports and %ΔGNP, when we know from the circular flow of income that, ceterus paribus, if net exports rise, so does GNP. However,

TABLE 17.3 Movement in an Economic Forecast: Together $(+)$ or in Opposite Directions $(-)$

	Net Exports	Federal Budget Surplus	% ΔGNP	% ΔP	% ΔQ	% Unemp.	Interest Rates
Most Cyclically Sensitive Components of GNP	$(-)$	$(+)$	$(+)$	$(+)$	$(+)$	$(-)$	$(+)$
Net Exports		$(-)$	$(-)$	$(-)$	$(-)$	$(+)$	$(-)$
Federal Budget Surplus			$(+)$	$(+)$	$(+)$	$(-)$	$(+)$
% ΔGNP				$(+)$	$(+)$	$(-)$	$(+)$
% ΔP					$(+)$	$(-)$	$(+)$
% ΔQ						$(-)$	$(+)$
% Unemp.							$(-)$

in the typical business cycle, a jump in %ΔGNP is usually associated with a decline in net exports and vice versa. If you forecast rising net exports in a boom, you should have some particular reason for expecting this departure from the typical cyclical pattern.

Econometric Macroeconomic Models

Here we are discussing mathematical models of the economy containing many equations and identities, sometimes up to several hundred. The procedure is to estimate mathematically the relationship between a dependent variable, say consumer expenditures on automobiles, and all the relevant independent variables such as disposable personal income, the level of interest rates, and so on. Of course, these "independent" variables are, in turn, dependent on other variables such as the rate of growth in the money supply and fiscal policy variables. This leads to the construction of a large system of simultaneous equations, the parameters of which are estimated on the basis of historical experience.

Large econometric forecasting models have come to prominence in the last twenty years. Most of the underlying theory has been around much longer, but the necessary data and the computational capacity did not exist. Many studies have assessed the forecasting accuracy of econometric macroeconomic models, the most recent of which are referenced at the end of this chapter. In general, they conclude that one cannot show an improvement in forecasting due solely to the use of these models.

One must note, however, that in investigating the relative forecasting accuracy of econometric models, there is a problem with obtaining a measure of exactly what you are trying to determine. The first problem is that one cannot separate the utility of an econometric model from the competence of the people who operate it. The equations of econometric models are primarily linear. For example $\hat{Y}_t = a + bX_t$ where $\hat{Y}_t$ is the economic time series variable to be forecast and X_t is the input variable to be used in the forecast. (Of course, X_t may be Y_{t-1}.) The economists making the forecast do not just blindly feed the numbers into the computer and then accept whatever forecast spews forth. The operators of the models quite properly exercise considerable professional judgment. If the computer spews forth nonsense, they rework it until they have a forecast that meets the tests of reasonableness and consistency we discussed above. For example, at one large econometric forecasting service they spend a great deal of time in what are referred to as "intercept adjustment meetings" in the preparation of each quarterly forecast. What is an "intercept adjustment meeting?" The intercept in the equation $\hat{Y}_t = a + bX_t$ is obviously a. When a judgmental adjustment in the forecast $\hat{Y}_t$ is desired, the easiest thing to do is simply to add or subtract an amount from the constant term, a. For example, if a militant union is facing a basic industry, say steel, and a strike is a real possibility, steel users are most likely stockpiling steel in anticipation of a strike. The estimating equation's parameters, a and b, were based on typical cyclical behavior and could well consistently miss the forecast in a prestrike period. The operators of the model must be careful, of course, that they make the adjustment only once. In the example we are using, if the quantity demanded by steel users were adjusted, one would not want to adjust separately the intercept in the equation forecasting the demand for iron ore, or for coal, or for any number of other things that would, in fact, be increased due to the increased demand for steel. The one adjustment in the steel equation would do; any additional adjustments would be double counting.

The example above of adjusting the demand for steel by users in anticipation of an impending strike is but one example of the exercise of professional judgment by the operators of large econometric forecasting models. As a result, evaluating the contribution of the mathematical models, per se, is difficult if not impossible. The end result, the published forecast, contains a large component of the skill and judgment of the professional economists using the model.

Another problem in attempting to measure the independent contribution of econometric models to forecasting is that today it is impossible to obtain a forecast by any professional economist in government, industry, or an educational institution that you can say has not been influenced by the output of the econometric forecasting services. The latest computer runs of Wharton Econometrics, Chase Econometrics, Data Resources, Inc., and others are widely reported in the financial and popular press. Although we all have our personal opinions of the reliability and biases of each of these, certainly no forecaster is oblivious to their output. Hence, a strict comparison of econometric and noneconometric forecasts based on published forecasts is impossible.

Although a truly independent econometric or noneconometric forecast probably does not exist, there is one capability of the large econometric models that distinguishes them from their less mathematical competitors in the forecasting business. This distinguishing advantage is the ease with which they can generate multiple forecasts based on different sets of assumptions.

Most individual economic forecasters in government, business, and educational institutions choose what they think will be the most likely exogenous occurrences and base their forecasts on the resulting environment. That is, one explicitly assumes there will be a tax cut or there will not, that the Federal Reserve will continue its present monetary policy or it will change, that consumers will change their buying patterns regarding durable goods or they will not. One might present one or two alternative possibilities as part of the discussion of the necessary uncertainty of any forecast.

However, suppose your clientele requested a whole series of forecasts: (1) assume taxes are cut while monetary policy and consumer behavior remain the same; (2) assume taxes are not cut while monetary policy and consumer behavior remain the same; (3) assume monetary policy is changed but taxes are not cut and consumers suddenly start buying cars like crazy . . . and on through (6), (7), and (8) to include all possible combinations. The number of possibilities goes up geometrically as the number of required assumptions rises. Specifically, if the assumed variable can only have two values, there are 2^n possible forecasts if there are n independent assumptions required.

A request to an economics professor or bank economist for eight or more separate forecasts embodying all possible outcomes is not likely to be favorably received. However, the analysts with the macroeconomic model on the computer merely type one different input number and push the "run" button. The computer then prints out all the details of an alternate economic forecast.

The major econometric forecasting services typically publish three or four alternative forecasts on a regular basis. One is referred to as the "control" forecast. This is the one reflecting the most likely set of assumptions or a naive forecast of the areas of concern (no new fiscal policy initiatives, a continuation of current monetary policy, etc.). The other alternatives published on a regular basis would reflect the estimated impact of currently proposed tax changes and other exogenous factors given a high probability of occurring. The paid subscribers to the consulting services have the option of custom designing their own forecast under their own set of assumptions.

An additional major benefit to those who subscribe to the econometric forecasting services is the availability of a large, perpetually updated data base. Most services have from 1,500 to 2,000 time series available to subscribers electronically. Subscribers can then correlate any national economic time series with their own internal company data. This means that, in addition to obtaining the forecast for expenditures by consumers on durable goods, subscribers can also determine what, if any, relationship there has been historically between their sales and the national data.

The Monetarist, St. Louis Forecasting Model

We used the expression "*large* econometric model" in our discussion above. There is, however, one *small* (five equations) econometric model that has gained some prominence. This model is associated with the Research Department of the Federal Reserve Bank of St. Louis. The number of equations in the model is not only small, but the equations are, to a large extent, independent of each other; the model is not a set of highly interdependent simultaneous equations. In fact, sometimes when reference is made to the "St. Louis model," what is meant is only *one* equation.

The single equation at the heart of the St. Louis macroeconomic model is one that forecasts the quarterly percentage change in nominal GNP as a function of monetary policy and fiscal policy. Monetary policy is measured by the percentage change in the money supply, $M1$, over the most recent five quarters including the quarter to be forecast. Fiscal policy is measured by the percentage change in the "high employment" level of government expenditures over the same five quarters. The high employment level of government expenditures, is, as we discussed in Chapter 12, federal government expenditures adjusted to what they would have been at some fixed rate of unemployment. In other words, an attempt is made to remove cyclical changes in expenditures using the unemployment rate as the cyclical indicator.

Algebraically, the "St. Louis equation," as it is called, can be stated as follows:

$$\%\Delta\text{GNP}_t = a + \sum_{i=0}^{4} b_i\%\Delta M_{t-i} + \sum_{i=0}^{4} c_i\%\Delta G_{t-i},$$

where $\%\Delta M$ = change in $M1$, and $\%\Delta G$ = change in the high employment level of government expenditures. Estimates of the parameters derived from quarterly data from 1960 through 1980 are as follows:[2]

a =	2.46		c_0 =	.06
b_0 =	.40		c_1 =	.02
b_1 =	.39		c_2 =	+.02
b_2 =	.23		c_3 =	$-.02$
b_3 =	.06		c_4 =	.01
b_4 =	$-.01$		$\Sigma c's$ =	.06
$\Sigma b's$ =	1.07		SEE =	3.49
R^2 =	.35			

There are several interesting implications to these parameters. The result most emphasized by the monetarists is, of course, that the sum of the regression coefficients for changes in the money supply is very close to 1.00 and the sum of the regression coefficients for fiscal policy is very close to zero. In other words a $\%\Delta M$ is reflected in a $\%\Delta\text{GNP}$ one-for-one in less than four quarters. Note that the last coefficient on the money supply is an insignificant $-.01$. On the other hand, a $\%\Delta G$ has no effect after a year and a very small effect in the interim. The largest coefficient, the .06 in the same quarter as the change in GNP, is only about one and a half times its standard error. Even if the point estimates of the fiscal policy regression coefficients were taken as significantly different from zero in the statistical sense, as a practical matter the regression coefficients for the first two quarters, .06 and .02, would imply that a 10% jump in government expenditures would result only in an increase in the rate of growth in GNP of less than 1%, specifically 0.8%. This would happen in the first six months and then reverse itself with no permanent impact.

The monetarists take this as empirical proof that monetary policy is potent and fiscal policy is impotent. More precisely, it shows that changes in this particular measure of fiscal policy are apparently not associated with changes in the rate of growth in GNP. Using an alternative, but similar, measure of fiscal policy, the "high employment surplus," gives almost identical results.[3]

In Chapter 12 we discussed the rather substantial empirical and theoretical problems with adjusting these fiscal policy measures for changes in the unemployment rate. Thus, although it is apparent that merely changing the magnitude of one of the measures of fiscal policy will not have a predictable effect on GNP, most economists are not ready to conclude that discretionary changes in taxes and government expenditures are irrelevant to changes in the level of GNP.

On the positive side, the St. Louis model certainly has the best single equation estimator for nominal GNP. Let us look at estimates and errors for the 1970s. These estimates were generated using an equation whose parameters were based on data from 1960 through the year preceding the year to be estimated. The exercise was performed with and without the fiscal policy variable and the results are as given in Table 17.4.

TABLE 17.4 St. Louis Equation Forecast of Percentage Change in GNP, 1970–1979

		Forecast % ΔGNP and Error			
		% ΔM only		% ΔM and % ΔG	
Year	Actual % ΔGNP	y_t	e_t	y_t	e_t
1970	5.2	5.0	.2	5.0	.2
1971	8.6	6.5	2.1	7.0	1.6
1972	10.1	8.7	1.4	8.0	2.1
1973	11.8	13.0	− 1.2	13.6	− 1.8
1974	8.1	5.8	2.3	6.1	2.0
1975	8.0	7.6	.4	7.3	.7
1976	10.9	9.7	1.2	9.8	1.1
1977	11.6	9.0	2.6	8.8	2.8
1978	12.4	14.2	− 1.8	14.3	− 1.9
1979	12.0	12.1	− .1	12.6	− .6
Average Error			.7		.6
Average Absolute Error			1.3		1.4
Standard Deviation of the Error			1.4		1.5

Source: Hafer, R. W. "The Role of Fiscal Policy in the St. Louis Equation." *Review* of the Federal Reserve Bank of St. Louis, January, 1982, Vol. 64, No. 1, Table 4, p. 27.

An average absolute error of less than 1.5% is not all that bad. The fact that the average error is positive indicates a bias of slightly more than .5%. The bias is reduced somewhat with the addition of the fiscal policy variable but the mean absolute deviation as well as the dispersion of the error terms are both somewhat larger with the fiscal policy variable included. It appears that if you want a single equation forecasting model for nominal GNP, the %ΔM by itself is the best you can do until we develop a better measure of fiscal policy.

The remainder of the St. Louis model is composed of four additional behavioral equations and a number of identities. The other four equations are:

1. *Changes in the GNP price deflator* as a function of the current inflation rate and the "slack" in the economy. The slack in the economy is defined as the gap between potential and actual real GNP based on a potential GNP measure developed at the St. Louis Federal Reserve Bank.

2. *The long-term bond rate* as a function of the rate of change in the money supply, the rate of change in real GNP, the unemployment rate, and the inflation rate.

3. *The short-term interest rate* (four- to six-month commercial paper rate) as a function of the rate of change in the money supply, the rate of change in real GNP, the inflation rate, and unemployment.

4. *The unemployment rate* as a function of the gap between potential and actual real GNP.

In summary, what the St. Louis model does is nicely quantify and refine what many forecasters do intuitively and less rigorously. One virtue of the model is that it is small enough for one to be able to observe the interactions among the variables. The model uses the current rate of output and unemployment to generate a forecast of the next period's unemployment. It then takes the implied slack in the economy and uses a quasi-Phillips curve approach to estimate whether the inflation rate will rise or fall. Using the rate of growth in the money supply to generate the rate of growth in nominal GNP, the rate of growth in real GNP can be calculated by adjusting for the forecast inflation rate.

We must note that the error terms are smallest for nominal GNP, larger for real GNP and the inflation rate, and largest of all for forecasts of interest rates, which only goes to show that forecasting with the St. Louis model is very similar to forecasting with any other approach.

An Exercise in Constructing and Using a Small Econometric Model

Although we have discussed econometric models in some detail, it would still be useful to go step-by-step through the estimation and use of such a model. We will construct a trivially small model (three equations) so you can see exactly what is going on. Let us say that we wish to construct a model that will give us at least a first-cut estimate of the coming year's percentage rate of growth in real GNP ($\%\Delta Q$), the GNP price index ($\%\Delta P$), and the unemployment rate ($\%Un$). With these three we would at least have the broad outlines of the economic environment for the coming year.

We certainly do not want to use equations that do not improve on a naive forecast that the level of the variables will be the same as last year, so let us simply attempt to forecast their change from one year to the next. Having just examined the St. Louis model, we can start by assuming a relationship between the money supply and nominal GNP. Specifically, our first equation will be

$$(\%\Delta\text{GNP})_t = (\%\Delta\text{GNP})_{t-1} + \alpha_1 + \beta_1\,(\%\Delta M)_t, \tag{1}$$

or

$$(\%\Delta\text{GNP})_t - (\%\Delta\text{GNP})_{t-1} = \alpha_1 + \beta_1\,(\%\Delta M)_t.$$

Recalling our earlier discussion of the so-called "noninflationary unemployment rate," we next could hypothesize a relationship between the rate of inflation as measured by the GNP price index and the level of the unemployment rate:

$$(\%\Delta P)_t = (\%\Delta P)_{t-1} + \alpha_2 + \beta_2\,(\%Un)_t, \tag{2}$$

or

$$(\%\Delta P)_t - (\%\Delta P)_{t-1} = \alpha_2 + \beta_2\,(\%Un)_t.$$

For the forecast of the level of unemployment, we can use some variant of Okun's Law. In this case let us use

$$(\%Un)_t = (\%Un)_{t-1} + \alpha_3 + \beta_3\,(\%\Delta Q)_t, \tag{3}$$

or

$$(\%Un)_t - (\%Un)_{t-1} = \alpha_3 + \beta_3\,(\%\Delta Q)_t.$$

To close the system we now need only the identity stating that the percentage change in GNP is a function of the percentage change in the GNP price index and the percentage change in real GNP. For our purposes the approximation that states that ($\%\Delta\text{GNP}$) is the sum of ($\%\Delta P$) and ($\%\Delta Q$) is good enough. So, our fourth equation (for which we need not estimate any parameters) is

$$(\%\Delta\text{GNP})_t = (\%\Delta P)_t + (\%\Delta Q)_t. \tag{4}$$

The three equations we now want to estimate empirically are:

$$(\%\Delta\text{GNP})_t - (\%\Delta\text{GNP})_{t-1} = \alpha_1 + \beta_1\,(\%\Delta M)_t, \tag{1}$$

$$(\%\Delta P)_t - (\%\Delta P)_{t-1} = \alpha_2 + \beta_2\,(\%Un)_t, \tag{2}$$

$$(\%\Delta Un)_t - (\%Un)_{t-1} = \alpha_3 + \beta_3\,(\%\Delta Q)_t. \tag{3}$$

As indicated at the end of the chapter, an excellent exercise for the student is to estimate the α's and β's by simple regression analysis or some more complex procedure. Of course, you must decide on the historical time period on which to base your estimates and which definition of the money supply is appropriate. For purposes of continuing this exposition we have used the fifteen years of data (1966 through 1980) with $M1$ as the definition of the money supply. Ordinary least–squares estimates of parameters and multiple correlation coefficients on three equations for that time period give us Table 17.5.

The regression coefficients are all of the proper sign and statistically significant. However, that is not to say that there are not a whole host of statistical and econometric problems that could be considered to improve even this simplistic model. Let us insert these estimates into the equations to see what our estimated model looks like.

$$(\%\Delta GNP)_t = (\%\Delta GNP)_{t-1} - 5.62 + .92\,(\%\Delta M)_t, \tag{1}$$

$$(\%\Delta P)_t = (\%\Delta P)_{t-1} + 2.41 - .35\,(\%Un)_t, \tag{2}$$

$$(\%Un)_t = (\%Un)_{t-1} + 1.37 - .37\,(\%\Delta Q)_t, \tag{3}$$

$$(\%\Delta GNP)_t = (\%\Delta P)_t + (\%\Delta Q)_t. \tag{4}$$

Equation (1) indicates that, based on our experience over this period, if the rate of growth in the money supply went to zero, the rate of growth in GNP would drop by about 5.6% from one year to the next. If $(\%\Delta M)$ is not zero, 92% of it is reflected in current dollar GNP, perhaps close enough to 100% to satisfy the monetarists. Equation (2) indicates that the "noninflationary unemployment rate" (where $\%\Delta P_t = \%\Delta P_{t-1}$) was approximately equal to 6.9% during this period. Not an unreasonable number. Equation (3) is, of course, an Okun's Law relationship that we both estimated and discussed early in this chapter.

TABLE 17.5 Least-Squares Estimates

	Equations		
	(1)	(2)	(3)
α	−5.62	2.41	1.37
β	.92	−.35	−.37
R	.54	−.35	−.87
R^2	.29	.12	.76

Let us now use these equations to generate a forecast. We have estimated the parameters using actual annual data for 1966 through 1980. We will now generate a forecast for 1981. The one exogenous variable needed for the model is the percentage rate of change in the money supply ($\%\Delta M$). In reality one would have to forecast this policy variable independently, but we can cheat and use the actual growth of $M1$ for 1981, 7%.

The other outside information is, of course, the lagged values of the variables we are trying to forecast. So we must start with the following necessary information:

$$(\%\Delta M)_t = 7.0 \qquad (\%\Delta P)_{t-1} = 9.0,$$
$$(\%\Delta GNP)_{t-1} = 8.9 \qquad (\%Un)_{t-1} = 7.2.$$

For ease in solving these equations it is convenient to combine equations (1) and (4) and rearrange the terms so that all the unknowns are on the left-hand side as follows:

(1) and (4) $\qquad (\%\Delta P)_t + (\%\Delta Q)_t = \alpha_1 + \beta_1 (\%\Delta M)_t + (\%\Delta GNP)_{t-1},$

(2) $\qquad\qquad (\%\Delta P)_t - \beta_2(\%Un)_t = \alpha_2 + (\%\Delta P)_{t-1},$

(3) $\qquad\qquad - \beta_3 (\%\Delta Q)_t + (\%Un)_t = \alpha_3 + (\%Un)_{t-1}.$

If we fill in the parameters and the lagged terms and combine the terms on the right we have as follows:

$$(\%\Delta P)_t + (\%\Delta Q) = 9.71,$$
$$(\%\Delta P)_t + .35 (\%Un)_t = 11.41,$$
$$.37(\%\Delta Q) + (\%Un)_t = 8.57.$$

The three simultaneous equations just above can be solved either by substitution or matrix manipulation.* The solutions are as follows:

$$(\%\Delta P)_t = 8.56,$$
$$(\%\Delta Q)_t = 1.15,$$
$$(Un)_t = 8.14.$$

Comparing this forecast for 1981 with what actually happened, we obtain the data on Table 17.6.

This simple model forecasts a decline in the inflation rate of 0.4% and instead the rate rose by 0.2%. We got a forecast of growth in real GNP of 1.2% and instead real GNP rose by a full 2%. The unemployment rate was forecast to rise by 1%, but went up by only 0.5%. We should note that

---

$$* \begin{vmatrix} 1 & 1 & 0 \\ 1 & 0 & .35 \\ 0 & .37 & 1 \end{vmatrix} = \begin{vmatrix} 9.71 \\ 11.41 \\ 8.57. \end{vmatrix}.$$

TABLE 17.6 Error Terms for Absolute and First Difference Forecasts, 1981

		1981			Year-to-Year Change		
	1980	Actual	Forecast	Error	Actual	Forecast	Error
%ΔP	9.0	9.2	8.6	.6	.2	−.4	.6
%ΔQ	−.1	2.0	1.2	.8	2.1	1.3	.8
%Un	7.1	7.6	8.1	−.5	.5	1.0	−.5

with the help of knowing in advance the actual growth in the money supply this model did not generate an outrageously bad forecast. Many professional forecasters did much worse that year since, as we have previously noted, the duration of the 1980 recession (only six months) is without precedent in business cycle history. The model generated an internally consistent forecast of lower growth with declining inflation and a larger increase in the unemployment rate than in fact occurred.

Again, we must emphasize that we are using this model to illustrate the details involved in the two quite separate and distinct activities of estimating the parameters of a model and then utilizing such a model to generate a forecast. Different professional skills and knowledge are brought to bear on the job of estimating the parameters of econometric models and in the separate job of using the model to generate the best possible forecast for the users of that forecast.

As an exercise the student can estimate the parameters for this model for different time periods. You can try it as a quarterly model. And, of course, you can use more complex estimating procedures than the simple ordinary least-squares applied to first differences. You can then combine the results with your judgment for some coming time period. Whatever method you use to estimate the parameters, they will only reflect the average behavior of the economy over the time period covered. You may have good reason to believe the time period of your forecast is not going to be typical, in which case you will want your forecast to differ from the mechanically generated forecast.

A Concluding Word on the Accuracy of Macroeconomic Forecasts

The numerous studies attempting to evaluate forecasting accuracy have concluded in general that the "measures do not show any of the forecasters to be consistently and generally superior to others."[4] Table 17.7, reproduced from the *New England Economic Review*, published by the Boston Federal Reserve Bank, gives some information on thirteen regularly published macroeconomic forecasts. The studies of these forecasts result in conclusions

TABLE 17.7 Summary Information on Forecasting Organizations Studied*

Forecasting Organization (Abbreviated Title) contact for further information	Number of Macroeconomic Variables Forecasted	Typical Forecast Horizon, Quarters	Frequency of Release, Per Year	Date Forecast First Issued Regularly	Forecasting Technique(s) (Approximate Weights)
1) American Statistical Association and National Bureau of Economic Research Survey of regular forecasts, median, (ASA), Greg Tang, National Bureau of Economic Research	8	45	4	1968	Most participants rely primarily on an "informal" GNP model; the majority also consider econometric model results.
2) Bureau of Economic Analysis, U.S. Commerce Department, (BEA), Al Hirsch	about 800	7	8	1967	Econometric model (65%), judgment (25%), current data analysis (5%), interaction with others (5%)
3) Charles R. Nelson Associates, Inc., Benmark forecast, (BMARK), Charles R. Nelson	3	4	4	1976	Time-series methods (100%)
4) Chase Econometric Associates, Inc., (CHASE), Lawrence Chimerine	about 700	10 to 12	12	1970	Econometric model (70%), judgment (20%), time-series methods (5%), current data analysis (5%)
5) Data Resources, Inc., (DRI), Robert Gough	about 1,000	8 to 12	12	1969	Econometric model (55%), judgment (30%), time-series methods (10%), current data analysis (5%)
6) Economic Research and Forecasting Operation, General Electric Co., (GE), Frank Murphy	360	8	4	1962	Econometric model (50%), judgment (50%)
7) Economic Forecasting Project, Georgia State University, (GSU), Donald Ratajczak	215	8	12	1973	Econometric model (60%), judgment (30%), current data analysis (10%)
8) Kent Economic and Development Institute, (KEDI), Vladimir Simunek	1,699	10	12	1974	Econometric model (60%), judgment (20%), time-series methods (10%), interaction with others (10%)
9) Manufacturers Hanover Trust, (MHT), Irwin Kellner	37	4 to 5	4	1970	Econometric model (50%), judgment (50%)
10) Research Seminar on Quantitative Economics, University of Michigan, (RSQE), Saul Hymans	about 100	8	3	1969	Econometric model (80%), judgment (20%)

11) Townsend-Greenspan & Co., Inc., (TG), Alan Greenspan	about 800	6 to 10	4	1965	Econometric model (45%), judgment (45%), current data analysis (10%)
12) UCLA Business Forecasting Project, Graduate School of Management, University of California, Los Angeles, (UCLA), Robert M. Williams	about 1000	8 to 12	4	1968	Econometric model (70%), judgment (20%), interaction with others (10%)
13) Wharton Econometric Forecasting Associates, Inc., (WEFA), Lawrence R. Klein	10,000	−2	12	1963	Econometric model (60%), judgment (30%), current data analysis (10%)

*McNees, Stephen S. "The Forecasting Record for the 1970s." *New England Economic Review*, September/October 1979, Federal Reserve Bank of Boston, pp. 46–47.

TABLE 17.8 Theil Coefficients Based on Relative Forecast Errors in the 1970s

	GNP		Real GNP		Treasury Bill Rate	
	Level	Change	Level	Change	Level	Change
Chase Econometrics	.223	.364	.465	.680	1.027	1.090
Data Resources, Inc.	.191	.321	.533	.701	.794	.881
Wharton Econometrics	.182	.323	.448	.670	.869	.960

that should not surprise us. The mean absolute deviations and Theil coefficients (discussed in Chapter 7) rise indicating a decline in absolute and relative accuracy:

1. As the forecast goes further into the future.
2. As the forecast goes from forecasting the level to forecasting the change in absolute or percentage terms.
3. As one moves from current dollar to real variables.
4. As one goes from aggregates such as GNP to volatile components such as inventory change and consumption expenditures.
5. As one tries to predict interest rates.

Some representative Theil coefficients for the three most prominent econometric forecasting services' record in forecasting the coming four quarters in the 1970s are shown in Table 17.8.[5] Of course, a coefficient greater than 1.00 means that a smaller sum of squared error terms would have resulted from the use of a naive model. (It is chance selection that the only Theil coefficients greater than the one shown here are for interest rate forecasts by a forecasting firm named after a bank.)

Regarding the distance into the future that one is looking, a competently done macroeconomic forecast has substantial information content only out to about 12 to 18 months. Beyond that the accuracy decays rapidly. There is just too much that can happen between now and then. As a recent study of the state-of-the-art in macroeconomic forecasting puts it, "At the present time the predictive value of detailed forecasts reaching out further than a few quarters ahead must be rather heavily discounted."[6]

- ## Questions for Discussion

1. Would you contend that a forecast of a 15% unemployment rate next year was unreasonable? On what grounds?
2. Evaluate a naive (no change in rate) forecast for annual inflation and unemployment rates over the last ten years. In what years are the errors largest? Why?

3. Comment on the policy advice of Professor Samuelson when he recommended that "Although the chance of a recession next year is only one-third, for policy purposes we should treat it as if it were two-thirds."

4. Grade school children today run computer programs. If given the model could they generate a competent econometric forecast?

5. Discuss the estimated St. Louis equation given in the text as empirical proof that fiscal policy is impotent.

6. Consider the rise in the level of real growth required to keep unemployment from rising (as shown in Table 17.1) from 3.85% in the 1950s to 4.02% in the 1970s. Relate this to the increase in the "noninflationary unemployment rate" discussed in Chapter 11.

7. Make a case for your company subscribing (or not subscribing) to the services of one of the large econometric forecasting firms.

● Source Notes

[1]*The Political Economy of Prosperity*. New York: Norton, 1970, p. 135.

[2]R. W. Hafer. The role of fiscal policy in the St. Louis equation. Federal Reserve Bank of St. Louis *Review*, Vol. 64, No. 1, January 1982, Table 1, p. 19. For the same equation fitted to data from 1955 through 1980 see: Meyer, Laurence H., and Chris Varvares. A comparison of the St. Louis model and two variations: Predictive performance and policy implications. Federal Reserve Bank of St. Louis *Review*, Vol. 63, No. 10, December 1981, p. 13.

[3]Hafer, *op. cit.*

[4]Victor Zarnowitz. An analysis of annual and multiperiod quarterly forecasts of aggregate income, output and the price level. *Journal of Business*, Vol. 52, No. 1, January 1979, p. 23.

[5]Steven S. McNees. The forecasting record of the 1970s. *New England Economic Review*, September/October 1979, Federal Reserve Bank of Boston, Table 3, pp. 46 and 47.

[6]Zarnowitz, *op cit.*, p. 31.

● Selected Additional Readings

Andersen, Leonal, and Keith M. Carlson. A monetarist model for economic stabilization. *Review* of the Federal Reserve Bank of St. Louis (April 1970). Reprint series number 55.

Armstrong, J. Scott. Forecasting with econometric methods: Folklore versus fact. *The Journal of Business*, Vol. 51, No. 4 (October 1978).

Blinder, Alan S., and Robert M. Solow. Lags and uncertainties in fiscal policy: General considerations, and the 1968–1970 experience. *The Economics of Public Finance*. Washington, D.C.: The Brookings Institution, 1974.

Carlson, Keith M. Money, inflation, and economic growth: Some updated reduced form results and their implications. *Review* of the Federal Reserve Bank of St. Louis, Vol. 62, No. 4 (April 1980).

Fama, Eugene F. Inflation, output and money. *The Journal of Business*, Vol. 55, No. 2 (April 1982).

Hafer, R. W. The role of fiscal policy in the St. Louis equation. *Review* of the Federal Reserve Bank of St. Louis, Vol. 64, No. 1 (January 1982).

Hamburger, Michael J. The lag in the effect of monetary policy: A survey of recent literature. *Monetary Aggregates and Monetary Policy*. Washington, D.C.: Federal Reserve Bank of New York, 1974.

Keen, Howard Jr. "Who forecasts best? Some evidence from the Livingston Survey." *Business Economics*, Vol. 16, No. 4 (September 1981).

Keynes, John Maynard. *The General Theory of Employment Interest and Money*. New York: Harcourt Brace, 1936. Chapter 12.

Lackman, Conway L. Short range macroeconomic forecasting methods. *Business Economics*, Vol. 17, No. 3 (May 1982).

McNees, Stephen K. The forecasting record for the 1970s. *New England Economic Review* of the Federal Reserve Bank of Boston (September/October, 1979).

————. The recent record of thirteen forecasters. *New England Economic Review* of the Federal Reserve Bank of Boston (September/October 1981).

Madansky, Albert, ed. Symposium on forecasting with econometric methods. *The Journal of Business*, Vol. 51, No. 4 (October 1978).

Meyer, Laurence H., and Chris Varvares. A comparison of the St. Louis model and two variations: Predictive performance and policy implications. *Review* of the Federal Reserve Bank of St. Louis Vol. 63, No. 10 (December 1981).

Okun, Arthur M. *The Political Economy of Prosperity*. New York: W. W. Norton, 1970. Appendix "Potential GNP: Its Measurement and Significance."

President's Council of Economic Advisors. Measuring and realizing the economy's potential. In Ronald L. Teigen, ed. *Readings in Money, National Income and Stabilization Policy*. Homewood, Ill.: Richard D. Irwin, 1978.

Spivey, W. Allen, and William J. Wrobleski. *Econometric Model Performance in Forecasting and Policy Assessment*. Washington, D.C.: American Enterprise Institute, 1979.

Tatom, John A. Potential output and the recent productivity decline. *Review* of the Federal Reserve Bank of St. Louis Vol. 64, No. 1 (January 1982).

Wojnilower, Albert M. The central role of credit crunches in recent financial history. *Brookings Papers on Economic Activity*, No. 2, 1980. Washington, D.C.: The Brookings Institution, 1980.

Zarnowitz, Victor. An analysis of annual and multiperiod quarterly forecasts of aggregate income, output, and the price level. *The Journal of Business*, Vol. 52, No. 1 (January 1979).

———— and Geoffrey H. Moore. Sequential signals of recession and recovery, *The Journal of Business*, Vol. 55, No. 1 (January 1982).

APPENDIX: <u>Economic Forecasting and Science, A Guest Lecture by</u>
<u>Paul A. Samuelson</u>*

If prediction is the ultimate aim of all science, then we forecasters ought to award ourselves the palm for accomplishment, bravery, or rashness. We are the end-product of Darwinian evolution and the payoff for all scientific study of economics. Around the country, students are grinding out doctoral theses by the use of history, statistics, and theory — merely to enable us to reduce the error in our next year's forecast of GNP from $10 billion down to $9 billion.

Just as ancient kings had their soothsayers and astrologers, modern tycoons and prime ministers have their economic forecasters. Eastern sorcerers wore that peaked hat which in modern times we regard as a dunce's cap; and I suppose if the head fits, we can put it in.

Actually, though, I am not sure that the ultimate end of science is prediction — at least in the sense of unconditional prediction about what is likely to happen at a specified future date. Students are always asking of professors. "If you are so smart, how come you ain't rich?" Some of our best economic scientists seem to be fairly poor forecasters of the future. One of our very best economists, in fact, couldn't even correctly foresee the results of the last election. Is it legitimate to ask of a scholar: "If you are so scientific and learned, how come you are so stupid at predicting next year's GNP?"

I think not, and for several different reasons. In the first place, a man might be a brilliant mathematician in devising methods for the use of physicists and still be a very poor physicist. Or he might be a genius in devising statistical methods while still being rather poor at conducting statistical investigations. Let us grant then at the beginning, that a person might be poor himself at any predictions within a field, and still be a useful citizen. Only we would then call him a mathematician — rather than simply a physicist, statistician, or economist.

The late Sir Ronald Fisher, for instance, was a genius, as we all gladly acknowledge. And perhaps he did good empirical work in the field of agronomy and applied fertilizer. But I must say that his work on genetics — in which he blithely infers the decline of Roman and of all civilizations from the dastardly habit infertile heiresses have of snatching off the ablest young men for mates, thereby making them infertile — seems awfully casual statistical inference to me. And I can't think Fisher covered himself with immortal glory at the end of his life when he doubted that cigarette smoking and inhaling has anything to do with reducing longevity.

Yet even a good economist or physicist may be a bad predictor — if we want simply an ability to forecast the future. My old teacher, Joseph Schumpeter, was by anyone's admission a pretty good economist. But I would certainly not have trusted him to predict next year's income or tomorrow's stock market. His vision was focussed to a different distance. He could tell you what was going to happen to capitalism in the next fifty years, even though he often had to ask his wife twice for the time of day. Of course, the inability to predict well does not thereby make

*Paul A. Samuelson is Institute Professor at Massachusetts Institute of Technology. This paper appeared in the *Michigan Quarterly Review* in 1965. Reprinted by permission.

a man a better economist. Schumpeter would not have been soiled if he had been able to make shrewd guesses about the near future.

A good scientist should be good at some kind of prediction. But it need not be flat prediction about future events. Thus, a physicist may be bad at telling you what the radioactivity count in the air will be next year, but be very good at predicting for you what will be the likely effects on air pollution of a given controlled experiment involving fissionable materials. If he is a master scientist, his hunches about experiments never yet performed may be very good ones.

Similarly, a good economist has good judgment about economic reality. To have good judgment means you are able to make good judgments — good predictions about what will happen under certain specified conditions. This is different from having a model that is pretty good at doing mechanical extrapolation of this year's trends of GNP to arrive at respectable guesses of next year's GNP. Time and again your naive model may win bets from me in office pools on next year's outcome. But neither of us would ever dream of using such a naive model to answer the question, "What will happen to GNP, compared to what it would otherwise have been, when the Kennedy-Johnson massive tax cut is put into effect?" The mechanical, naive model does not have in it, explicitly, the parameter tax rates. And if we insist upon differentiating the result with respect to such a parameter, we will end up with a zero partial derivative and with the dubious conclusion that massive tax cuts cannot have any effect on GNP. The model that I use, which is perhaps very nonmechanical and perhaps even non-naive, may be bad at predicting unconditionally next year's GNP, and still be very good at answering the other-things-equal question of the effect of a change in tax rates or in some other structural parameter of the system.

What I have been saying here can be put in technical language: to make good year-to-year predictions, you need not necessarily have accomplished good "identification" of the various structural relations of a model. And conversely, to be a scientist skilled in making predictions about various hypothetical structural changes in a system, you do need to have what Haavelmo, Koopmans, and others call "identification," of the type that is by no means necessarily contained in models that perform well in ordinary predictions.

Is it possible to have everything good? — to be able to make good annual predictions as well as good predictions of identified structural relationships? The best economists I have known, in the best years of their lives, were pretty good at making just such predictions. And that is what I call good judgment in economics.

Obviously, they have to be men of much experience. In the last analysis, empirical predictions can be made only on the basis of empirical evidence. But it is an equal empirical truth that the facts do not tell their own story to scientists or historical observers, and that the men who develop top-notch judgment have an analytical framework within which they try to fit the facts. I should say that such men are constantly using the evidence of economic time series; the evidence of cross-sectional data; the evidence of case studies and anecdotes, but with some kind of judgment concerning the frequency and importance of the cases and instances. And they are even using conjectures of the form, "What if I were no smarter than these businessmen and unionists? What would I be likely to do?"

We all know the great statistical problems involved in the small samples economic statisticians must work with. We have few years of data relevant to the problem at hand. Maybe the data can be found by months or by quarters; but since there is much serial correlation between adjacent monthly data, we can by no means blithely assume that we have increased our degrees of freedom twelvefold or more þy using monthly data. Nature has simply not performed the controlled experiments that enable us to predict as we should wish.

This means that the master economist must piece together, from all the experience he has ever had, hunches relevant to the question at hand.

If science becomes a private art, it loses its characteristic of reproducibility. Here is an example. Sumner Slichter, from 1930 to his death in the late 1950s, was a good forecaster. Dr. Robert Adams of Standard Oil (New Jersey), comparing different methods of forecasting, found that "being Sumner Slichter" was then about the best. But how did Slichter do it? I could never make this out. And neither, I believe, could he. One year he talked about Federal Reserve policy, another year about technical innovation. Somehow the whole came out better than the sum of its parts. Now what I should like to emphasize is that the private art of Sumner Slichter died with him. No less-gifted research assistant could have had transferred to him even a fraction of the Master's skill. And thus one of the principal aims of science was not achieved — namely, reproducibility by any patient person of modest ability of the empirical regularities disconcerned by luck or by the transcendental efforts of eminent scholars.

The models of Klein, Goldberger, Tinbergen, and Suits have at least this property. Take away Frankenstein and you still have a mechanical monster that will function for awhile. But unlike the solar system, which had to be wound up by Divine Providence only once, any economic model will soon run down if the breath of intelligent life is not pumped into it. When you see a 7094 perform well in a good year, never forget that it is only a Charlie McCarthy; without an Edgar Bergen in the background it is only a thing of paint and wood, of inert transistors and obsolescing matrices.

How well can economists forecast? The question is an indefinite one, and reminds us of the man who was asked what he thought about his wife, and had to reply, "Compared to what?"

When I say that as an economist I am not very good at making economic forecasts, that sounds like modesty. But actually, it represents the height of arrogance. For I know that bad as we economists are, we are better than anything else in heaven and earth at forecasting aggregate business trends — better than gypsy tea-leaf readers, Wall Street soothsayers and chartist technicians, hunch-playing heads of mail order chains, or all-powerful heads of state. This is a statement based on empirical experience. Over the years I have tried to keep track of various methods of forecasting, writing down in my little black book what people seemed to be saying before the event, and then comparing their prediction with what happened. The result has been a vindication of the hypothesis that there is no efficacious substitute for economic analysis in business forecasting. Some maverick may hit a home run on occasion; but over the long season, batting averages tend to settle down to a sorry level when the more esoteric methods of soothsaying are relied upon.

What constitutes a good batting average? That depends on the contest. In baseball these days, .300, or 300-out-of-1,000 is very good. In economic forecasting of the direction of change, we ought to be able to do at least .500 just by tossing a coin. And taking advantage of the undoubted upward trend in all modern economies, we can bat .750 or better just by parrotlike repeating, "Up, Up." The difference between the men and the boys, then, comes between an .850 performance and an .800 performance. Put in other terms, the good forecaster, who must in November make a point-estimate of GNP for the calendar year ahead, will, over a decade, have an average error of perhaps one percent. And a rather poor forecaster may, over the same period, average an error of 1-1/2 percent. When we average the yearly results for a decade, it may be found that in the worst year the error was over 2 percent, compensated by rather small errors in many of the years not expected to represent turning points.

In a sense this is a modest claim. But again I must insist on the arrogance underlying these appraisals. For I doubt that it is possible, on the basis of the evidence now knowable a year in advance, to do much better than this. It is as if Nature does not even begin to toss the dice upon which next year's fate will depend by November of this year. There is then nothing that the clever analyst can peek at to improve his batting average beyond some critical level.

I do not mean to imply that this critical level is fixed for all time. Once our profession got new surveys of businessmen's intentions to invest, of their decisions as to capital appropriations, and of consumers' responses to random polling, the critical level of imprecision was reduced. In all likelihood, the critical level of uncertainty is a secularly declining one. But is its asymptote (for forecasting a year ahead, remember) literally zero? I do not know how to answer this question. Although it may seem pessimistic to give a negative answer. I am tempted to do so. For remember, you cannot find what is in a person's mind by interrogation, before there is anything in his mind. That is why preliminary surveys of the McGraw-Hill type, taken in October before many corporations have made their capital-budgeting decisions, are necessarily of limited accuracy — which does not deny that they are of some value to us.

The imprecision inherent in forecasting raises some questions about the propriety of making simple point-estimates. If you twist my arm, you can make me give a single number as a guess about next year's GNP. But you will have to twist hard. My scientific conscience would feel more comfortable giving you my subjective probability distribution for all the values of GNP. Actually, it is a pain in the neck to have to work out the whole probability distribution rather than to give a single point-estimate. But satisfying one's scientific conscience is never a very easy task. And there is some payoff for the extra work involved.

For one thing, just what does a point-estimate purport to mean? That is often not clear even to the man issuing it. Do I give the number at which I should just be indifferent to make a bet *on either side,* if forced to risk a large sum of money on a bet whose side can be determined by an opponent or by a referee using chance devices? If that is what I mean in issuing a point-estimate, I am really revealing the *median* of my subjective probability distribution. Other times estimators have in the back of their minds that over the years they will be judged by their mean-square-error, and hence it is best for them to reveal the arithmetic mean of their subjective distribution.

I have known still others who aimed, consciously or unconsciously, at the mode of their distribution — sometimes perhaps using the modal value of forecasts among all their friends and acquaintances as the way of arriving at their own mode.

Warning: the distribution of all point-estimates issued from a hundred different banks, insurance companies, corporations, government agencies, and academic experts is usually more bunched than the defensible *ex ante* subjective probability distribution any one of them should use in November. This is illustrated by a story I heard Roy Blough once tell at a Treasury meeting. He said: "Economic forecasters are like six eskimos in one bed; the only thing you can be sure of is that they are all going to turn over together." Blough is right. In a few weeks time one often sees all the forecasts revised together upward or downward.

The difference between median, mean, and mode is not very significant if our expected distributions are reasonably symmetrical. But often they are not: often it will be easier to be off by $15 billion through being too pessimistic rather than too optimistic. Making your soothsayer provide you with a probability range may seem to be asking him to be more pretentiously accurate than he can be. But that is not my interpretation: using the language of arithmetical probability is my way of introducing and emphasizing the degree of uncertainty in the procedure, not its degree of finicky accuracy. There is a further advantage of using probability spreads rather than single point-estimates. One of the whizziest of the Whiz Kids in the Pentagon told me that they get better point estimates from Generals and Admirals if they make them always give high and low estimates. Before, you could never be sure whether some conservative bias or discount was not already being applied to data. Henri Theil of Rotterdam has studied how well forecasters perform and has found a similar tendency toward conservative bias in economic forecasters.

Suppose we think that GNP is likely to rise, say by $30 billion. If we issue the forecast of a rise of $20 billion, we shall certainly have been in the right direction. And we shall be in the ball park with respect to general magnitude. Why be hoggish and try for better? Particularly since GNP might go down, and then you would be standing all alone out there in right field, more than $30 billion off the mark. "Better be wrong in good company, than run the risk of being wrong all alone" is a slogan that every Trustee knows to represent wisdom for his actions.

But here I am talking about science, not about gamesmanship for the forecaster. Gamesmanship introduces a whole new set of considerations. Many forecasters, particularly amateurs, don't really care whether they turn out to be wrong or by how much they turn out to be wrong. They want to tell a good story. To amateurs it usually does not matter by how much you are wrong. The only prize is to be at the top. In science and in real economic life, it is terribly important not to be wrong by much. To be second-best year after year in a stock-portfolio competition would be marvelous for a mutual fund manager, and especially where the first-place winners are a shifting group or crapshooters who stake all on one whim or another.

As an economic scientist, I take economic forecasting with deadly seriousness. I hate to be far wrong. Every residual is a wound on my body. And I'd rather make two small errors, than be right once at the cost of being wrong a second time by the sum of the two errors. The reason is not vanity — because forecasting serves a purpose: each dollar of error costs something in terms of corporate or national policy: and if the "loss function" or "social welfare function" is a smooth one in the neighborhood of its optimum, it will be the square of the error of forecast that gives a rough measure of local error.

If we use mean-square-error as our criterion of fit, I think it will be found that forecasters have another persistent bias, namely a tendency to be too pessimistic.

This is different from the conservatism that makes forecasters shade both their upward and downward forecasts below the true magnitude. Why is there this downward bias? First, because it is never easy to know where next year's dollar is going to come from, and many forecasters try to build up their total by adding up the elements that they can see. There is a second, perhaps more defensible, reason for erring on the downward or pessimistic side in making a forecast. The social consequences of unemployment and underproduction may be deemed more serious than those of over-full-employment and (mild) demand inflation. I once shocked the late John Maurice Clark at a meeting in Washington by saying, ''Although the chance of a recession next year is only one-third, for policy purposes we should treat it as if it were two-thirds.'' He thought that a contradiction in terms. But in terms of his colleague Wald's loss-function concept, I could make sense of my statement by postulating that each dollar of deflationary gap had social consequences more serious than each dollar of inflationary gap.

Often a forecaster is forced to give a single point-estimate because his boss or consumers cannot handle a more complicated concept. Then he must figure out for himself which point-estimate will do them the most good, or the least harm. Years ago one of the publishing companies used to have every staff member make a prediction of the sales each textbook would enjoy. If people try to play safe and guess low figures, the President of the company would penalize them for having too little faith in the company's sales staff and authors. (Incidentally, the sales manager used to come up with the least inaccurate predictions, odd as that may sound.)

A good speech should tell the audience something that it already knows to be true. Then having gained their good approval for soundness, it should tell them something they didn't previously know to be true. I don't know whether I have been able to complete the second part of this recipe, but I want to add a third requirement for a good speech. It should call attention to some problem whose true answer is not yet known. Let me conclude, therefore, by raising an unanswered question.

Naive models based upon persistence, momentum, or positive serial correlation do rather well in economics as judged by least-square-error of predictions. An extreme case is one which merely projects the current level or the current direction of change. Yet such models do badly in ''calling turning points.'' Indeed, as described above, such naive models are like the Dow System of predicting stockmarket prices, which never even tries to call a turning point in advance and is content to learn, not too long after the fact, that one has actually taken place.

Forecasters regard models which merely say, ''Up and up,'' or ''more of the same,'' as rather dull affairs. When I once explained to editors of a financial magazine that one disregarded this continuity only at one's risk, they said: ''Professor, that may be good economic science, but it's darn dull journalism.'' But are we forecasters here to have a good time? Dullness may be part of the price we must pay for good performance. More than that? Are we here to cater to our own vanity? One hates to be wrong; but if one's average error could be reduced at the cost of being more often wrong in direction, is that not a fair bargain?

I don't pretend to know the answer to these questions. But they do have a bearing on the following issue. Often an economist presents a model which he admits does worse than some more naive model, but which he justifies for its better fit at the turning points. Is this emphasis legitimate? That question I leave open.

Is policy action most important at the turning points? Is policy action most potent at the turning points? Is a correct guess about turning points likely to lead to correct guesses for the next several quarters? And if so, why doesn't this importance of accuracy of the turning points already get duly registered in the minimum-squared-error criterion? The whole notion of a turning point would be changed in its timing if we shifted, as many dynamic economies in Europe have to do, to changes in direction of trend-deviations rather than changes in absolute direction as insisted on by the National Bureau. Does this lack of invariance cast doubt on the significance of turning points?

Finally, is it possible that public preoccupation with economics is greatest at the turning point and that we are essentially catering to our own vanity and desire for publicity when we stress accuracy at such times?

I promised to end up with a question, and I find by count that I have ended up with seven. I guess that is what practical men must expect when they invite an academic theorist to give a lecture.

But for all that, to the scientific forecaster I say, "Always study your residuals." Charles Darwin, who lived before the age of Freud, made it a habit to write down immediately any arguments *against* his theory of evolution, for he found that he invariably tended to forget those arguments. When I have steeled myself to look back over my past economic forecasts in the London *Financial Times*, they have appeared to be a little less prescient than I had remembered them to be. Janus-like, we must look at the past to learn how to look into the future.

After I had made some innocent remarks like this in my 1961 Stamp Memorial Lecture at the University of London, I ran into Professor Frank Paish, himself one of England's best economic forecasters.

"Great mistake ever to look back," he quipped, "you'll lose your nerve."

This is almost precisely what the great Satchel Paige of baseball said. "Never look backward. Somebody may be gaining on you."

Like Sir Winston, I bring you blood, sweat, and tears. The way of the scientific forecaster is hard. Let Lot's wife, who did look back, be your mascot and guide. What Satchel Paige didn't mention is that "they may be gaining on you anyway." Know the truth — and while it may not make you free — it will help rid you of your amateur standing.

International Aspects of the Business Cycle

18

The obvious economic connection among the economies of the world is the exchange of goods and services in the form of imports and exports. In this chapter we will first consider the impact of foreign trade on the demand and supply of goods in the context of the circular flow of goods and income we considered in Chapter 3. We will then digress a bit to pick up the vocabulary of international financial bookkeeping, the balance of payments accounts, in order to trace the transmission of fluctuations from one economy to another via the supply and demand for the various national currencies, the foreign exchange markets. We then consider the impact of monetary and fiscal policy depending on whether a government has or has not undertaken a commitment to hold the exchange rate constant. We conclude with a caution and an admission of how little we know about forecasting exchange rates.

The Transmission of Fluctuations via Foreign Trade

Recalling the output-income identity from Chapter 3:

$$\text{output} = \text{income},$$
$$C + I + G = C + S + T.$$

This identity simply made explicit the ex post equality of the supply and demand for goods and services. The output of the economy was all to be classified as consumer goods, investment goods, or output claimed by the government. The production of these goods would, of course, generate an exactly equal amount of income that, as the equation above indicates, could be either spent for consumption goods, saved, or paid to the government in taxes.

This ex post bookkeeping allowed us to define equilibrium in the goods market as the state of affairs in which the ex ante values for investment plus government were equal to savings plus taxes. Equilibrium is when the household's voluntary savings and involuntary tax payments exactly match investment and government claims on the output of the economy.

Now we want to give more detailed consideration to the possibility that our citizens might spend some of their income on goods produced in other countries, imports (*Im*); and the possibility that producers in this country might earn some income by selling goods and services to foreigners, exports (*Ex*). Our ex post identity and ex ante equilibrium condition now becomes:

$$C + I + G + Ex = C + S + T + Im,$$
$$\text{or} \quad I + G + Ex = S + T + Im.$$

Some of the output of the economy might be shipped out, and some of the income of citizens of this economy might be spent on foreign goods. Recall that on an ex ante basis if the left-hand side of the equation is larger than the right-hand side ($I + G + Ex > S + T + Im$), the demand for goods exceeds their supply and the economy will be subject to inflationary pressures. For example, if the economy were in equilibrium and foreigners suddenly developed a mad desire (and an effective economic demand) for our goods, our economy would experience an increase in aggregate demand. Increased exports are inflationary for the same reason as investment and government expenditures — consumers received income for the production and sale of the goods but the goods are not available for domestic consumers to buy.

Conversely, if the economy were in equilibrium and our citizens decided they were really wild about foreign goods, the economy would receive a deflationary impact — a decline in aggregate demand. Imports are deflationary for the same reason as savings and taxes; someone earned money by producing goods in this economy and then did not spend it on those or equivalent goods produced in this country. Like savings and taxes, import expenditures take purchasing power out of this economy. Imports make goods available in the domestic U.S. market without any U.S. economic unit receiving the income from the sale. One economic unit has an expenditure without another one having income.

We have discussed imports and exports before in Chapter 10 when we considered the behavior of the "net export" component of GNP, net exports being exports minus imports. In discussing the cyclical behavior of net exports, recall that we observed a rise in net exports as the economy goes into a recession and a fall in boom times. This countercyclical movement in net exports develops primarily because of changes in imports. As the economy booms the demand for imported goods rises, causing net exports to fall. As the economy goes into a recession, imports fall and net exports rise. Although the demand for imports is sensitive to our cyclical fluctuations, the demand for exports depends, among other things, on the cyclical fluctuations in the economies of our trading partners.

Let us consider the impact of our cyclical fluctuations on the economies of our trading partners. Our imports are, of course, their exports. As we go into a boom and our demand for imports rises, the foreign countries from whom we import will by definition see their exports rising. Since imports are like savings and exports are like investment, the effect of this on aggregate demand here and over there is to transmit our boom to the economies of our trading partners. In other words, the "leakage" of purchasing power from our economy is an injection of aggregate demand into their economy.

Recall that in Chapter 3 under the discussion of the determination of aggregate demand we discussed the concept of the investment multiplier. In a simple macroeconomic model we found the multiplier to be the reciprocal of the marginal propensity to save. An injection of income via increased investment would circulate through the economy until it had been drained off in savings; investment increases total expenditures enough to generate an equal amount of savings since equilibrium in the goods market requires savings equal investment. Now we must consider the possibilities when investment-like injections can come from exports, and imports can withdraw spending power in the same way as savings.

We find that the multiplier in an "open" economy, one in which we include a foreign trade sector, is equal to the reciprocal of the sum of the marginal propensity to save plus the marginal propensity to import. We also find that there is a "foreign trade multiplier" exactly analogous to the investment multiplier. An increase in exports can have an effect on aggregate demand that is some multiple of itself in the same way as an increase in investment does. A simple algebraic model of income determination including autonomous exports, Ex, and Imports, Im, that depend on the level of total income, Y, is as follows:

$$Y = C + I + G + Ex - Im,$$
$$C = aY,$$
$$Im = bY,$$
$$Ye = aYe + I + G + Ex - bYe,$$
$$Ye\,(1 - a + b) = I + G + Ex,$$
$$Ye = (I + G + Ex)/(1 - a + b).$$

The marginal propensity to consume domestic goods is a so the marginal propensity to save is $(1-a)$. The marginal propensity to import is b. In this simple model all of the multipliers will be equal to the reciprocal of the sum of the marginal propensity to save plus the marginal propensity to import; in essence,

$$\Delta Ye/\,\Delta I = \Delta Ye/\,\Delta G = \Delta Ye/\,\Delta Ex = 1/\,(1 - a + b).$$

This indicates that, all other things being equal, a high marginal propensity to import, a large value for b, would help make an economy more stable by lowering the size of the multipliers. This is true. If the citizens of a country will spend most of an increment in income on imported goods, the inflationary impact of an increase in demand by government or investors will be severely reduced as it will be transferred to the exporting country. Conversely, if income drops in a country with a high marginal propensity to import, the impact will be mitigated to a great extent because as consumers stop buying imported goods the deflationary impact and accompanying unemployment, if any, will occur in the exporting country.

Although the foregoing is analytically correct, we should not let it lead us to believe that economies heavily involved in foreign trade are inherently stable. Indeed, the exact opposite is more nearly the case because our "all other things being equal" assumption is not met in the real world. Countries with a very high *marginal* propensity to import typically also have high *average* propensities to import and must necessarily sell a large part of their output as exports. (How else are they going to pay for all those imports? More on the financial aspects later in this chapter.) This means that their economies are not only subject to the multiplier impact of changes in government expenditures and domestic investment demand but also fluctuations in demand for their exports resulting from cyclical fluctuations in the level of economic activity in other countries.

Furthermore, we must also note that the usual formulation of the multiplier in terms of absolute change instead of percentage change is a bit oversimplified. Instead of $\Delta Y/\Delta I$ or $\Delta Y/\Delta Ex$ we might be more interested in the elasticity or ratio of percentage changes, $\%\Delta Y/\%\Delta I$ and $\%\Delta Y/\%\Delta I$. These elasticities are also *reduced* by an increase in the size of the *marginal* propensity to import and save but they are *increased* by an increase in the *average* propensity to import and save. In fact, the elasticity is equal to the ratio of the average to the marginal propensity to save and import.*

Consider two countries. Let us designate country A as one which must import most of its food and other basic necessities and so has an average propensity to import of .80, but a marginal propensity to import of only .10. We will assume country A's saving rate both marginal and average to be .10 also. Our other country, B, imports very little. Let us say it has marginal and average propensities to import of 10%. To dramatize the impact of the differing average propensity to import, we will give country B an average and marginal propensity to save equal to that of country A, or .10. The size of the multipliers and elasticities for the two countries would be as shown in Table 18.1. If exports or domestic investment rose by $1 in either one of these economies, the equilibrium level of total expenditures would rise by $5, but if that $1 represented a 10% increase in investment plus exports the $5 would represent only a 10% increase in total

---

*This is most easily demonstrated with the simple multiplier: The elasticity of total expenditures to a change in investment is $\%\Delta Y/\%\Delta I = (\Delta Y/Y)(\Delta I/I) = (I/Y)/(\Delta I/\Delta Y) = (S/Y)/(\Delta S/\Delta Y)$ since $I = S$ is in equilibrium.

TABLE 18.1 Foreign Trade Multipliers of Countries with High vs. Low Average Propensities to Import

	A	B
Average propensity to import (IM/Y)	.80	.10
Marginal propensity to import ($\Delta Im/\Delta Y$)	.10	.10
Marginal and average propensities to save ($S/Y = \Delta S/\Delta Y$)	.10	.10
Multipliers $= 1/.20$ ($\Delta Ye/Ex = \Delta Ye/\Delta I$)	5	5
Elasticity $=$ ($\%\Delta Y)/\%\Delta$ ($I + Ex$)	$.90/.20 = 4.5$	$.20/.20 = 1$

expenditures in country B, but a 45% increase in country A! Simply stated, if a majority of your GNP is exported, a small percentage change in total exports can bring about a large percentage change in aggregate demand.

The mechanism described above is the reason why the raw-materials–producing countries of the world find their business cycle to result almost exclusively from fluctuations in world commodity markets. Such countries typically have a very high marginal propensity to import, which we might naively think would, by reducing the size of the multiplier, give them a very stable economy; but they typically also have a very large average propensity to import. To afford these imports, they must export a very high proportion of their total output. Fluctuations in the demand from the rest of the world for their output generate massive fluctuations in such an economy. The fluctuations in demand for a country's raw material exports can come about either because of fluctuations in the level of economic activity in the buyers' countries (the U.S. does not buy as much bauxite in a recession) or from changes in the output of other suppliers (a frost on the Brazillian coffee crop is great for the demand for African coffee producers).

By way of summary, the business cycle is transmitted from one economy to another via demand for imports. A country experiencing a boom will transmit some of its inflationary pressure to its trading partners via its demand for imports. Conversely, a country in recession or depression reduces its imports (and other's exports) thereby causing aggregate demand to fall in its trading partners' economies. As we will see, such diffusion of inflationary and deflationary pressures applies also to pressures brought about by monetary and fiscal policy, but before getting into that we must get into the bookkeeping of international payments, the balance of payments accounts.

The Balance of Payments Accounts

The balance of payments of a particular country is a bookkeeping record of the payments by that country to other countries (called *debits*), and receipts from other countries (called *credits*) that took place during a particular time period. The term *balance* can be misleading since in bookkeeping terms the balance of payments is more nearly analogous to a profit and loss statement than a balance sheet; it is a statement of flows over a period of time rather than a statement of stocks or balances at a point in time.

For most industrialized countries such accounts are broken down into many detailed subaccounts. For illustrative purposes here, let us consider in Table 18.2 only four major income and expense accounts. Item (1) is self-explanatory. Item (2) is somewhat more complex. It consists not only of such obvious transactions as the sale of stocks or bonds by the citizens or government of one country to the citizens or government of another country (long-term financial assets), but the incurring of a short-term debt such as an accounts receivable (a short-term financial asset). If, for example, the country about which we are speaking imports some goods but has not yet paid for them during the period for which the accounts are applicable, there would be a debit to account (1) and a credit of an equal amount of account (2) as the accrual of the debt to foreigners is classed as the sale of a financial asset.

Here we should note that, strictly speaking, the balance of payments *always* balances. The accounts are defined in such a way that if there were no errors or omissions, debits would exactly equal credits for each and every country. In fact, however, there are errors and omissions and the reported figures include an account so labeled. We shall defer for the moment what is meant by the statement that a country has a "surplus" or "deficit" in its balance of payments, in which case the term "balance of payments" must necessarily be redefined.

The definition of item (3), the sale or purchase of gold or other international reserves, varies with the international financial agreements and other institutional arrangements in effect at a particular point in history. If gold is

TABLE 18.2 Balance of Payments Accounts

Credits (Receipts or Income)	Debits (Payments or Expenditure)
(1) Exports of Goods and Services	(1) Imports of Goods and Services
(2) Sale of Financial Assets	(2) Purchase of Financial Assets
(3) Sale of Gold or Other International Reserves	(3) Purchase of Gold or Other International Reserves
(4) Unilateral Receipts	(4) Unilateral Payments

the only acceptable international currency, then that is all that would be included. However, throughout history most countries have had holdings (or short-term claims on) other countries' currencies and the purchase and sale of these is also included. We will have more to say on this below when we discuss the surplus or deficit in the balance of payments. In any case, this account refers to an outflow (sale) or an inflow (purchase) of whatever is usable as international monetary reserves under the institutional arrangements existing at the time. In the simple case of a country that imports substantially more goods and services than it exports and has no other receipts (borrowings) to pay the difference, the net debit balance on trade would have to be offset by an equal credit balance as it pays the difference in gold or other internationally acceptable reserves.

The "balance of trade" is distinguished from the overall balance of payments in that it refers only to that portion of the balance of payments included in the import and export of goods and services accounts, those accounts numbered (1) above. The actual "balance of trade" for a given time period refers to whether exports exceed imports or vice versa. If exports exceed imports a country is said to have a trade "surplus" or sometimes a "favorable" balance of trade. Conversely, if imports exceed exports a country is said to have a trade "deficit" or an "unfavorable" balance of trade. The quotation marks around "favorable" and "unfavorable" are doubly meaningful as it is impossible to say without further information whether a trade surplus or deficit is the more advantageous to a particular country over a particular time period. The desirability of one over the other will be discussed in greater detail below.

Similarly to the surplus or deficit in the trade account, one may define a surplus or deficit in the "capital account," which is the net of credits and debits in account number (2) above, sale and purchase of financial assets. If a country is a net creditor for the period (purchase of financial assets exceeds the sale of financial assets), it is said to have a "deficit on capital account." If a country is a net debtor for the period (sales of financial assets exceed purchases), the country is said to have a surplus in its capital accounts.

Surplus or Deficit in the Balance of Payments

As indicated above, the balance of payments as a bookkeeping system always balances in that each and every transaction gives rise to equal debits and credits. However, the term *balance of payments* is used in a different sense than as a term to describe the set of books recording payments between countries. The idea of an overall balance of payments surplus or deficit is whether or not a country is losing or accumulating gold or other international reserves. In other words, do debits exceed credits in account number (3) above? If a country's purchases of international reserves exceed its sales in a particular time period, its stock of reserves will grow and it is said to have a balance of payments surplus. If a country's sales of international reserves exceed its purchases, its stock of reserves will fall and it has a balance of payments deficit.

Conceptually the idea of a "favorable" (surplus) or "unfavorable" (deficit) in the balance of payments is simple. In practice the concept is difficult to apply. First, there is no world central bank to define legally what constitutes international reserves. At the present time monetary gold stocks certainly qualify as well as a country's holdings of "strong" currencies of other countries (*not* bookkeeping balances of its own currency). Second, since individuals and governments typically do not hold demand deposits or the actual pieces of paper currency of another country for very long but prefer some sort of short-term claim (which earns interest), there is the problem of what constitutes a "financial asset" and what constitutes an "international reserve."

As a result, there are numerous definitions of a country's stock of international reserves and, thereby, numerous definitions as to the size of the surplus (or deficit) in the balance of payments. Under some definitions, some of the transactions are removed from account (2), "purchase and sale of financial assets," and placed in account (3), "purchase and sale of gold or other international reserves." It is the short-term assets and liabilities that are likely to be considered as additions or subtractions from the stock of international reserves. The long-term financial instruments are clearly not usable international reserves, but the definition of "long-term" and "short-term" is not entirely unambiguous, although one year is the customary point of demarcation.

As a result of these ambiguities, measures of the balance of payments surplus or deficit are not always comparable between countries, and many countries will calculate and publish figures for more than one definition of the balance of payments surplus or deficit.

At this point it should be apparent that the balance of trade (imports and exports) may be positive for a particular country while the overall balance of payments may be negative depending on what goes on with respect to the capital account (purchase and sale of financial assets) and the magnitude and direction of unilateral transfers. For example, it is possible for a country to have a large surplus in its balance of trade accounts (exports much more than it imports) and still have a zero or negative balance of payments flow if foreigners borrow a great deal of money in this country's capital markets (this country "imports" a large amount of financial assets) and this country has large foreign aid commitments (large negative unilateral transfers). This was the position of the United States for a number of years after World War II.

A Truly Fixed Exchange Rate System, the Gold Standard

We start the study of international payments mechanisms with the full recognition that a gold standard never existed in an absolutely pure form. Such a system has great utility, however, in illustrating the inherent characteristics of all so-called "fixed exchange rate" systems. If you understand the workings of a gold standard, you will understand most of the problems countries have in trying to hold a particular exchange rate in a changing world.

Our first assumption is that the countries of the world each have a domestic monetary system based on gold. The money supply in each country will always be equal to its gold stock (or some constant multiple thereof). The gold is the reserve for the nation's currency and the domestic money supply expands or contracts with the inflow or outflow of gold. This happens because the government stands ready to buy and sell gold at a fixed price. New money is issued to the public when someone sells gold to the government, and money is retired from circulation when someone exercises his or her right to have the currency redeemed in gold (buys gold from the government).

A primary function of any international payments mechanism is to set the value of one currency in terms of others — to establish exchange rates. If two countries are both on the gold standard, this ratio of exchange between them is set automatically via the common denominator of gold. Let us say that the U.S. government stood ready to buy and sell gold at \$35 per ounce while the British government stood ready to buy and sell gold at £17.50 per ounce. It then follows that the exchange rate cannot depart too far from \$2 per pound (35/17.50 = 2). Actually the exchange rate can depart only by an amount equal to the cost of moving gold from one country to another. The upper and lower bounds of the exchange rate under a gold standard are called "gold points." Let us see why the gold points are effective.

First, consider the meaning of the two governments' guarantees of their currency in terms of gold to a British trader seeking dollars with which to buy American goods. It assures him that the minimum number of dollars he need ever accept for his pound is the amount to be obtained by selling pounds to his government in exchange for gold at the rate of £17.50 per ounce, shipping the gold to the United States, and selling it to the U.S. government for \$35 per ounce. The trader would net \$2 for each pound invested, less the cost of gold shipment. If the cost of insuring and transporting gold were 1% of its value, then the trader would never take less than \$1.98 for a pound in the foreign exchange market since he could always obtain that much by shipping gold to the United States.

Similarly, a U.S. trader seeking pounds with which to buy British goods would never pay more than \$2.02 per pound. He could always obtain pounds at that price by turning in his dollars for gold, shipping the gold to Great Britain, and selling it for pounds.

In day-to-day operations of the foreign exchange market, various supply and demand forces, to be discussed in detail later, will set the exchange rate somewhere between $1.98 and $2.02. If the demand and supply situation is such as to push the price outside the gold points, gold will move from one country to another. Specifically, in our example, if the rate fell below $1.98, gold would move from Great Britain to the United States. If the rate fell to $1.95 speculators would buy pounds, turn them in for gold, ship the gold to the U.S., turn it in for dollars, and then buy more pounds. They would be netting $1.98 per pound on each trip while obtaining pounds at a cost of $1.95. Conversely, if the rate rose to $2.05, gold would move from the U.S. to Great Britain. Speculators would turn dollars in for gold, ship the gold to Great Britain, turn it in for pounds, and exchange the pounds (at the $2.05 rate) for more dollars to start all over again. When obtaining dollars in the market they would be getting $2.05 per pound, whereas when turning in the dollar to the U.S. government for gold to ship, they would be obtaining one pound sterling for each $2.02 invested. Buying pounds for $2.02 and selling them for $2.05 is nice work if you can get it.

Let us look at the supply and demand forces at work in the short run. In the first case the exchange rate at $1.95 was "below" the gold point. Relative to the gold point the dollar is overvalued and the pound is undervalued. As the speculators turn in pounds for gold, the total supply of pounds outstanding will tend to be reduced. As they turn in gold for dollars, the total supply of dollars will tend to be increased. With an increase in the supply of dollars and a decrease in the supply of pounds, the value of the dollar relative to the pound should fall; the number of dollars to purchase one pound (the exchange rate) should rise from $1.95 toward $1.98.

In the second case the exchange rate at $2.05 was above the gold point. The pound is overvalued and the dollar is undervalued relative to the gold point. Gold will move from the U.S. to Great Britain. As dollars are turned in for gold the supply is reduced. As gold is turned in for pounds the supply of pounds is increased. The relative increase in the supply of pounds will cause the value of the pound to fall from $2.05 toward $2.02.

It should be obvious that so long as both governments have a sufficient supply of gold, the exchange rate can never move very far outside the limit set by the gold points either because of the action of speculators or because exporters and importers on both sides of the Atlantic would prefer to ship gold rather than pay or receive a less favorable price than that obtainable by doing do.

What if the supply and demand forces caused one country to begin to lose all its gold stock? Could it run out of gold and cause a drastic change in the exchange rate? The answer is no. Let us see why. Recall the effect of changes in the government's gold stock on the domestic money supply under the gold standard. Each dollar's worth of gold exported would reduce the domestic money supply by at least $1. A massive gold outflow from one country would result in an equally massive contraction in its money supply. A massive gold inflow into the other country would result in an equally massive increase in its money supply. Eventually (and perhaps painfully), if this situation were allowed to take its course, the country losing gold would undoubtedly fall into recession or depression, and the country receiving the gold would experience a substantial degree of inflation. Through these deflationary and inflationary effects, we shall now illustrate that "balance of payments problems" under a gold standard are self-correcting and no country would ever exhaust its gold supply, that is, have its money supply reduced to zero.

To understand the automatic functioning of a gold standard, let us think of what is happening to the balance of payments of each country. A country losing gold is, by definition, running a balance of payments deficit; a country gaining gold is running a surplus. The deficit country is having its money supply constricted while the surplus country is having its money supply expanded.

Consider the effects on the level of interest rates in each of these countries. The deficit country with its decreasing money supply is forced to have tight money and high interest rates. This will cause its citizens to prefer to borrow overseas and sales of financial assets will rise. Foreigners will consider this country a good one to loan money in, but a bad one to borrow from. Purchasers of its financial assets will fall. The capital account of the deficit country will move toward a surplus as the money supply is constricted. Exactly the opposite will happen in the surplus country as its money supply is expanded. It will automatically have easy money and low interest rates. Its capital account will move toward a deficit position.

Now consider the balance of trade. If the change in the money supply persists long enough, prices of goods and services are going to rise in the surplus country with its increasing money supply, and they are going to fall (or rise less rapidly) in the deficit country with its decreasing money supply. This will make the citizens of the surplus country decide that foreign goods are a bargain and citizens of the deficit country will feel domestic goods are a bargain relative to those expensive foreign goods. Exports of the deficit country will rise while its imports will fall. It will move toward a balance of trade surplus. Conversely, the surplus country with its inflation will see its balance of trade move toward a deficit.

So we see that under the gold standard when balance of payments surpluses and deficits develop, the very movement of the international reserves sets up forces in both the capital and trade accounts to eliminate the surplus or deficit.

It should be obvious why the international gold standard has never been allowed to work unfettered. For a gold outflow to be stopped by increased exports, the country losing the gold has to have a relative price decline. In many cases prices are not flexible downward, and they are not determined solely by the money supply but by the general level of aggregate demand relative to the productive capacity of the economy. Similarly, interest rates in the deficit country must rise relative to the rest of the world. Interest rates also are not solely determined by the money supply. In general, what is required of the gold-losing country to overcome its balance of payments problem is a significant decline in aggregate demand (and probably employment) along with rising interest rates. This is not palatable medicine for most national policymakers. On the other hand, the gold-receiving country is required to encourage inflation by allowing interest rates to fall. Again, this is not an appealing package to policymakers, and the country accumulating gold reserves by running a surplus does not really feel it has a problem.

Although a pure international gold standard has never really been allowed to function, these same basic elements are contained in all alternative fixed exchange rate systems. Hence, the mechanics of the gold standard system must be understood if more complex fixed exchange rate systems are to be comprehended. To reiterate, under the gold standard, if a country runs a balance of payments deficit, it must pay the difference out of its gold stock and reduce its domestic money supply accordingly. Eventually the reduced money supply of the deficit country and the expanding money supply of the surplus country will cause the surplus and deficit to cease *with no change in the exchange rate* beyond that allowed by the gold points. Under the gold standard, currencies are never devalued; economies are only deflated.

Other Fixed Exchange Rate Systems

The essence of any fixed exchange rate system is simply a commitment by the world's central banks to buy and sell their currency at some fixed rate in terms of international reserves. Under the so-called "gold exchange standard," which officially died in August 1971, the U.S. (via International Monetary Fund agreements) supposedly would exchange dollars for gold with governments (not private citizens) at a rate of $35 per ounce. Other countries then merely would set a fixed rate between their currency and gold or the dollar and that would set the exchange rate.

The problem with any fixed exchange rate system is, of course, that unless the rules of the game that apply to the gold standard are followed, exchange rates cannot remain fixed in a changing world. Politically the rules are not all that appealing. A country running a surplus may not want to expand its money supply to create low interest rates and inflation. In addition, the country running the surplus does not really feel that it has a problem. Morally they feel that they are the "good guys" who are giving the world economy more than they are taking out of it. It is the deficit country that is "living beyond its means" and should take its medicine of tight money, high interest rates, and deflation. As a practical matter the surplus country can continue to run surpluses without limit while the deficit country can only run deficits until it runs out of gold or its stock of others' currencies. Hence, from 1946 through 1971 there were many more devaluations of currencies by deficit countries than there were upward revaluations by surplus countries.

One must recognize that even the most ardent supporters of fixed exchange rate systems recognize that exchange rates are never fixed forever. What is sought is to minimize the fluctuations and to have the changes come about in an "orderly" manner. The advocates of fixed exchange rate systems feel that such an arrangement is more conducive to international commerce than fluctuating exchange rates.

The varieties of fixed exchange rate systems are as numerous and varied as the possible agreements among nations on what is to constitute an internationally acceptable reserve currency. A world central bank, in which the nations can have deposits to be traded for international settlements, can create "paper gold" if it can make deposit-creating loans. The "special drawing rights" of the International Monetary Fund are an attempt at this sort of arrangement.

Under a fixed exchange rate system, when the pressures of supply and demand in the foreign exchange market become too great, a nation has a devaluation or (more rarely) an upward revaluation of its currency. How this might help to remove a troublesome deficit or surplus is better understood if we look at a system of fluctuating exchange rates.

A System of Fluctuating Exchange Rates

By a system of fluctuating exchange rates, we mean that the ratio of exchange between two currencies will be determined by the working of supply and demand in the foreign exchange market without governmental interference. Of course, this system also has never existed in the pure state because governments will intervene in something so vital to them as their exchange rate.

First, let us return to the balance of payments accounts. All the credit accounts create a demand for a nation's currency and all the debit accounts create a supply of it in the foreign exchange market. An increase in exports, sale of financial assets, sale of gold or international reserves, or unilateral receipts would create a demand for a nation's currency and, all other things being equal, would cause its value to rise. Conversely, an increase in imports, lending to foreigners, buying gold or other international reserves, or unilateral payments to foreigners would increase the supply of a nation's currency and cause its value to fall.

Of course, if we had a system of freely fluctuating exchange rates (no government intervention) there would be no purchase or sale of international reserves. This account is how governments influence the exchange rate of their currency under a system of fluctuating exchange rates. Under such a system the balance of payments surplus or deficit is merely a measure of the degree of government intervention necessary to have the results that do come about. A country showing a balance of payments surplus (the accumulation of gold and foreign exchange) under a system of fluctuating exchange rates is one whose government did not want the value of its currency vis-à-vis other currencies to rise. It, therefore, increased the supply of its currency by accumulating foreign exchange. A country showing a deficit under a system of fluctuating exchange rates has had to increase the demand for its own currency by selling gold or foreign exchange. We will discuss the economic and political reasons for such exchange rate "management" later.

Exchange rates, just like other prices, serve the economic purpose of allocating goods and services among those willing and able to pay for them and the purpose of reconciling the desires to borrow and lend money. There is pressure for exchange rates to change because desires for credit or goods change and productive capacities change. If suddenly the citizens of the U.S. decided that they want to buy more British goods, the British will have less of their own goods, and they will have either less total goods or more U.S. and other foreign goods. The increased imports by the U.S. and exports by the British will put pressure on the exchange rate so that the value of the dollar falls relative to the pound. This will make U.S. goods cheaper in world markets and British goods more expensive. With the value of the pound up, the British can buy more foreign goods and with the value of the dollar down, the U.S. can export more competitively to pay for the sudden demand for imports.

The only alternative of the Americans to paying for their increased imports with increased exports is to borrow the difference — to obtain the goods on credit. The dollar need not fall in value on foreign exchange markets due to the increased supply of dollars resulting for increased imports if a demand for dollars can be created by the sale of financial assets.

To reiterate, the mechanics of a system of fluctuating exchange rates is quite simple: all the items shown on the left-hand side of the balance of payments accounts shown in Table 18.2 create a demand for a nation's currency and all the items shown on the right-hand side create a supply: demand and supply set the value in terms of other currencies.

Monetary Policy and the Exchange Rate

If a country pursues a restrictive monetary policy (the central bank is selling bonds to the public and reducing the size of the money stock), in the short run interest rates will rise. This will make this particular country an attractive place for foreigners to invest their money and an unattractive place in which to borrow money. The sale of financial assets by citizens to foreigners will rise, the purchase of financial assets from foreigners will fall. As indicated in the balance of payments accounts, this will increase the demand for this country's currency. Under a fixed exchange rate system, the capital account will move toward surplus and under a flexible exchange rate system the value of this nation's currency will tend to increase. As a result, higher interest rates cause the demand for a nation's currency on the foreign exchange markets to rise, while lower interest rates cause the demand to fall.

The accumulation of foreign exchange under a fixed exchange rate will tend automatically to offset the restrictive monetary policy. As the government absorbs foreign exchange and issues its own currency to keep the exchange rate from rising, it is engaged in "reverse open market operations." Its sale of bonds to restrict the domestic money supply will be to some extent offset by its purchase of foreign exchange. If the international money flows are large enough, a government can lose control of its money supply; more precisely, it can either set the exchange rate or domestic interest rates but not both. A departure of interest rates in one country from those of the rest of the world's major money markets may set up currency flows that tend to equalize interest rates by causing surpluses in high-interest-rate countries (and forcing an expansion of the money supply) and deficits in the low-interest-rate countries (and forcing a contraction of the money supply).

Under a system of flexible exchange rates, if a country has relatively high interest rates the tendency of investors to lend there and borrow elsewhere will cause the value of the currency in the high-interest-rate country to rise. This will cause its exports to fall and its imports to rise. It will have a capital account surplus offset by a trade account deficit. Conversely, the country trying to maintain low interest rates in a high-interest-rate world will under a system of flexible exchange rates find the value of its currency declining in the foreign exchange market. It will move toward a trade account surplus offset by a capital account deficit. The high-interest-rate country will be buying more goods than it is selling and going into debt for the difference, while the low–interest–rate country will be selling more goods than it is buying and accepting paper claims for the difference.

The foregoing indicates clearly why it is generally accepted that monetary policy is more effective under a system of fluctuating exchange rates than under a system of fixed exchange rates. Under fixed rates the government is committed, to a greater or lesser extent, to offset pressures on the exchange rate by actions that will affect the monetary base. Under a flexible exchange rate system it is possible for the effects of independent monetary policy to exist for longer periods of time. If the French want to follow a monetary policy that results in low interest rates and an inflation rate of 12%, while the Germans follow a more restrictive monetary policy resulting in higher interest rates and an inflation rate of 6%, this situation is made tenable by the value of the French franc falling relative to the D-mark.

Fiscal Policy and the Exchange Rate

Just as contemporary economic theory contends that monetary policy is more effective under a system of fluctuating exchange rates than under a fixed-rate system, it is said that fiscal policy is more effective under a system of fixed rates. (Note that this implies *nothing* about the effectiveness of fiscal policy vis-à-vis monetary policy under either system.) We noted above that the required intervention under a system of fixed rates could potentially offset monetary policy actions. In the case of fiscal policy the required intervention is supportive of the fiscal policy goals.

For example, suppose a country attempts to stimulate aggregate demand via a tax cut or increased government expenditures. This would cause interest rates to rise if there were no change in monetary policy. If exchange rates were flexible, the country's currency would rise in value. However, under a system of fixed exchange rates, the government is committed to buying foreign exchange with domestic currency to keep the exchange rate from rising. This is, of course, stimulative open market operations being conducted in foreign exchange rather than in government bonds. The monetary base will be increased as long as there is upward pressure on interest rates and the value of the currency. Conversely, a restrictive fiscal policy, say a tax increase, would tend to make interest rates fall and require the purchase of domestic currency and a move toward tight money, which would re-enforce the restrictive fiscal policy.

The foregoing is the standard textbook treatment of fiscal policy under fixed and flexible exchange rates. It must be emphasized, however, that the conclusion that fiscal policy will be more effective under fixed rather than flexible exchange rates is based on the assumption that the interest rate effects will dominate the price effects over the relevant time horizon. By that we mean that we would get the opposite result if stimulative fiscal policy caused such a burst of inflation that the resulting trade deficit put downward pressure on the exchange rate. In that case counterproductive purchasing of the domestic currency would be required to hold a fixed exchange rate in place. Experience does indicate that interest rate effects occur sooner and do dominate price effects on exchange rates over the time horizon of the business cycle. Longer term trends in exchange rates seem to be dominated by relative inflation rates.

Summary of International Aspects of the Business Cycle

An increased rate of economic activity (and inflation) will cause a country's balance of trade to move toward a deficit; a decreased rate of economic activity (and recession) will cause a country's balance of trade to move toward a surplus. The source of the cyclical instability is irrelevant. It is simply a fact that if aggregate demand and prices rise faster in a country than in its trading partners, its demand for imports will rise faster than the demand for its exports. Under a fixed exchange rate system it will be subjected to the discipline of the gold standard. It will lose foreign exchange reserves, its monetary base will be automatically restricted, and it will move toward tight money and high interest rates that may or may not take care of the inflation. Under a system of flexible exchange rates the value of the country's currency will tend to fall; this will automatically lower the real price of its exports from the viewpoint of foreigners and raise the price of imports to its own residents. This may or may not bring the balance of trade into equilibrium depending on the sensitivity to price of internationally traded goods — it will with certainty bring complaints from importers.

Just as no government is willing to subject itself to the automatic discipline of the pure gold standard to hold exchange rates truly fixed, no government has shown a willingness to stand idly by and allow the free play of supply and demand forces to set the value of its currency in the foreign exchange markets. All governments intervene to a greater or lesser extent. In fact, under a system of fluctuating exchange rates the balance of payments surplus or deficit (the gain or loss of foreign exchange reserves) is only a measure of the degree of government intervention. A government that shows a surplus has intervened to keep the value of its currency from rising and a government showing a deficit has intervened to keep the value of its currency from falling.

The limits of governments' intervention in the foreign exchange market are set by the fact that each country has an infinite supply of its own currency and a limited supply of others'. In a strictly mechanical sense, a country can keep the value of its own currency low by merely perpetually buying up others' with newly issued currency. It runs a large balance of payments surplus. It *can* do this, but as noted above it has lost control of its domestic money supply which might well lead to inflation and eventually to the deficit in the balance of trade it was seeking to avoid. As with the gold standard, if the exchange rate is not allowed to adjust, forces will be brought into play that will try to force the domestic economy to make the needed adjustment. On the other side, a country may only keep the value of its currency from falling by buying it up with foreign currencies or other acceptable international reserves. These must be obtained by historical balance of payments surpluses or borrowing from other countries. The net result is that countries usually have a choice as to the timing of an appreciation in the value of their currency, and are forced into a devaluation of their currency as soon as it is generally recognized that they are running out of foreign exchange with which to support it.

What is really going on in economic terms under all the paper shuffling in international finance is that one country is selling its goods and services to the rest of the world, and in exchange obtaining either goods and services during the present time period or claims to goods and services that can be exercised at some future time period.

A country running a surplus in its balance of trade is putting more goods into world trade than it is receiving, but in exchange is accumulating paper claims to future goods. A country running a deficit is taking more goods out of the world economy than it is putting in and, of course, it is doing this on credit. Other countries hold financial claims against it for the difference.

The exchange rate is the pricing mechanism. It establishes, in conjunction with domestic prices, the ratios of exchange between the economic goods — how many bottles of French wine exchange for one Volkswagen, and so on. A fall in the value of a nation's currency via a change in the exchange rate moves the terms of trade against it. By devaluation a country reduces the price of all its goods and services to foreigners. A rise in the value of a nation's currency is an increase in the price of its exports.

If imports and exports are sensitive to price, then a devaluation by lowering prices of exports and increasing prices of imports should cause the balance of trade to move toward a surplus. By definition, its trading partners will find that the real price of their exports to this country has risen while the price of imports from that country have fallen. If, in a fixed exchange rate system, a country insists on keeping the value of its currency so low that it continuously runs a balance of trade surplus, it is simply keeping the relative price of its exports sufficiently low that the foreigners take more goods than they give this country and the country must accumulate paper claims against its trading partners. Whether this is good or bad is a wide-open debate. The exporters in this country will like it; the importers will regard it as a national disaster and plead for an upward revaluation to lower the price of imports.

In understanding contemporary international financial problems an important rule is to pay no attention whatsoever to public statements by national leaders. A politician must necessarily be slightly schizophrenic in the process of reconciling the conflicting interests of the domestic body politic. The nature of international financial problems dictates that there will be no unanimity within a country. The exporters want the value of the nation's currency held down so that they may be more competitive in international markets. The importers of finished goods and raw materials for domestic production will want the value of the currency held up so that foreign goods can be obtained more cheaply in terms of the domestic currency.

The political problem varies tremendously by the extent and form of a country's involvement in international trade. The grocery shopper in the United States is almost totally unconcerned with the value of the dollar on foreign exchange markets; the British shopper has discovered that every time the pound is devalued groceries cost more.

One should look to what central banks and ministers of finance *do* and not to what they *say*. Even looking to the facts and applying basic economics, however, forecasting exchange rate movements is a hazardous occupation in that the duration of untenable foreign exchange arrangements is amazing. Lord Keynes is reported to have said that he almost went broke numerous times in the foreign exchange market because he would forget "how long it can take for the inevitable to happen" — Not a bad thought on which to conclude a book on business cycles and forecasting.

● Questions for Discussion

1. Consider the contention that: Since imports are deflationary and a high marginal propensity to import lowers the size of the multiplier, the ideal situation for noninflationary stability would be a country with a very high average and marginal propensity to import.

2. Given that under an international gold standard there would be international movements of gold as a result of surpluses and deficits in the balance of payments, how can we be sure that no country would ever run out of gold as long as they all played by the "rules of the game"?

3. If fixed exchange rates are better for international trade than fluctuating rates, why don't the world's central banks just agree on a set of exchange rates and hold them there? After all, each central bank has an infinite supply of its own currency.

4. What difference does it make to the economic well-being of a particular country whether it runs a surplus or deficit in its balance of trade?

5. Exporters want the exchange rate to fall while importers want it to rise. Why?

6. Describe the connection between monetary policy and exchange rate stabilization policy, especially with regard to surplus and deficits in the capital account.

7. Is fiscal policy more likely to have a greater impact under a system of fixed or fluctuating exchange rates?

● Exercises

1. Show the debit and credit entries in a set of balance of payments accounts for the U.S. like those shown on page 372 resulting from the following transactions:
   a. The U.S. sells Russia $100 million worth of wheat on credit.
   b. The U.S. imports oil from the Middle East and pays for it with dollars on deposit in New York banks.
   c. The U.S. ships agricultural machinery to an underdeveloped country as part of a foreign aid program.

2. Calculate the size of the simple foreign trade multiplier ($\Delta Y_e/\Delta Ex$) if the marginal propensity to save is .10 and the marginal propensity to import is .30. Ignore income taxes and other automatic stabilizers.

3. Indicate whether each of the following would be more likely to put upward pressure on the value of the U.S. dollar relative to foreign currencies, (+), or tend to devalue the dollar, (−).

( ) Americans are suddenly convinced to "buy American" and stop buying imported goods.

( ) The chairman of the Federal Reserve Board is forced to resign and is replaced with an "easy money" man as chairman.

( ) A recession in the U.S. ends and the economy begins a tremendous economic boom.

( ) The U.S. government sells all the gold in Fort Knox on the open market.

( ) It becomes apparent that Switzerland and Sweden are going Communist and will become Russian satellites.

● Selected Additional Readings

Bowers, David A. Should a managed float use reserve levels or exchange rate goals? An interesting parallel with domestic monetary policy. *Journal of Political Economy* Vol. 83, No. 51 (1975).

Dornbusch, Rudiger. Exchange rate economics: Where do we stand?, *Brookings Papers on Economic Activity*, No. 1, 1980. Washington, D.C.: The Brookings Institution, 1980.

——————, and Stanley Fischer. *Macroeconomics*. (2d ed.) New York: McGraw-Hill, 1981. Chapters 18 and 19.

——————, and Paul Krugman. Flexible exchange rates in the short run. *Brookings Papers on Economic Activity*, No. 3, 1976. Washington, D.C.: The Brookings Institution, 1976.

Ethier, Wilfred, and Arthur I. Bloomfield. Managing the managed float. *Essays in International Finance*, No. 112. Princeton, N.J.: Princeton University, 1975.

Gordon, Robert A. *Business Fluctuations*. (2d. ed.) New York: Harper and Row, 1961. Chapter 22.

Gordon, Robert J. *Macroeconomics*. (2d. ed.) Boston: Little, Brown, 1981. Chapter 19.

Mintz, Isle. *American Exports During Business Cycles, 1879–1958*. New York: National Bureau of Economic Research, 1961.

Sachs, Jeffrey D. The current account and macroeconomic adjustment in the 1970s. *Brookings Papers on Economic Activity*, No. 1, 1981. Washington, D.C.: The Brookings Institution, 1981.

Whitman, Marina V. N. Global monetarism and the monetary approach to the balance of payments. *Brookings Papers on Economic Activity*, No. 3, 1975. Washington, D.C.: The Brookings Institution, 1975.

Index